WISCONSIN PUBLICATIONS IN THE HISTORY OF SCIENCE AND MEDICINE

Number 1

General Editors

WILLIAM COLEMAN

DAVID C. LINDBERG

RONALD L. NUMBERS

René VILLERMÉ, 1782-1863

Membre de l'Académie de Médecine
et de l'Académie des sciences Morales et Politiques.

Death Is
A Social Disease

Public Health
and Political Economy
in Early Industrial France

William Coleman

The University of Wisconsin Press

Published 1982

The University of Wisconsin Press
114 North Murray Street
Madison, Wisconsin 53715

The University of Wisconsin Press, Ltd.
1 Gower Street
London WC1E 6HA, England

First printing

Printed in the United States of America

For LC CIP information see the colophon

ISBN 0–299–08950–9

For Louise

Contents

Illustrations

Tables

Acknowledgments

During the preparation of this study I have received assistance and unfailing hospitality from many persons and institutions, above all at the Institute for Research in the Humanities, University of Wisconsin, and the Institute of the History of Medicine, Johns Hopkins University School of Medicine. I began my work while a visitor in Madison and completed it many years later, once again as a visiting fellow of the Humanities Institute. To the directors of the institute, E. David Cronon and Robert M. Kingdon, and to my associates there I express my appreciation for their support and encouragement. The opportunity for undertaking this study owes much to the generous welcome accorded me over a period of sixteen years by Owsei Temkin and Lloyd G. Stevenson, successive Directors of the Institute of the History of Medicine. To them, to fellow students in Baltimore, and no less to the sustained and friendly interest of my colleagues on the Homewood campus of Johns Hopkins I owe the gradual accretion of nerve, and perhaps also some knowledge, that has permitted me to write this book.

It is well also to mention a scholar whose name will recur frequently in the following pages. Like so many others who study the history of French and Continental medicine I have found unending stimulus in the writings of Erwin H. Ackerknecht. He has dealt often with my theme, which in fact is his theme, and I hasten to acknowledge here in a manner more emphatic than the following documentation permits my great debt to his scholarship.

During the past decade I have received financial assistance for research from the American Council of Learned Societies, the Johns Hopkins University, the American Philosophical Society, the National Endowment for the Humanities, and the Graduate School of the University of Wisconsin. Their assistance has made this book possible, and I record my gratitude for their support.

I have also received much direct assistance in the preparation of this volume. The staff at the library of the Faculté de médecine, the Académie

nationale de médecine, the Bibliothèque nationale, the Archives nationales, all in Paris; the William H. Welch Medical Library, Baltimore; and
the William S. Middleton Medical Library, Madison, have helped me in
innumerable ways. In this regard, I owe a particular debt to Mlle. Mou-
reaux, Archiviste de l'Université, Paris, and to Mrs. Dorothy Hanks, Historical Division, National Library of Medicine, Bethesda. John Neu, Jean
Théodoridès, and Caroline Hannaway have lent their usual and greatly
appreciated aid. Hosam Elkhadem of the Bibliothèque royale de Belgique,
Brussels, kindly made available to me the Villermé-Quetelet correspondence. Not least, to my students in a seminar held at the Université de
Montréal in 1976 and dealing principally with French sociomedical investigation I owe many valuable suggestions. Loretta Freiling and Jean
Zwaska kindly typed the manuscript—and caught many a slip. I am grate-
ful to Lori Grant, Susan Towles and Colleen Wickey for assistance in
preparing the index. The frontispiece is reproduced with permission of the
Académie nationale de médecine, Paris.

    At a much delayed moment a draft of this book came into existence.
Placed in the hands of Keith M. Baker, Abraham M. Lilienfeld, and Camille Limoges, my work was transformed. They will easily recognize in
new dress the suggestions they offered; for other readers I merely indicate
that in both structure and argument my book depends heavily upon their
criticism and advice. Barbara G. Rosenkrantz, too, provided thoughtful
suggestions. But I also offer the usual and necessary caution: my helpful
critics must not be held responsible for what a willful author has chosen
to say. This book is dedicated to my wife, whose patience, like that of my
children, has outlasted my own.

                                                        William Coleman

Madison, Wisconsin
May 1981

Introduction

Some bade them eat cake, but the economist was content if they did not eat at all. Unless, of course, they—the poor and the dispossessed, even the weak and the sickly—developed the initiative and moral strength to find and to keep remunerative employment and thus gain a modest livelihood. The economist, or *économiste*, as the partisan of political economy in France chose to call himself, recognized that unemployment and destitution posed serious threats to the social order. But state intervention and, in particular, public support of the poor or the destitute were not, he knew, the correct response to the challenge. Economic salvation was an individual matter. It was attainable only by those who would assume responsibility for their own well-being. This was held to be the fundamental lesson of science—and none thought themselves more rigorously scientific than the economists. Economists reasoned only from facts, or so they claimed, and they drew strength and confidence from a set of seemingly sure and unvarying first principles. Political economy, these doctrinaires argued, having themselves recently discovered the very springs of human action, had now only to set a course that would embrace the entire social domain. Intrinsic to that domain were the social parameters of man's physical well-being or decrepitude. Thus did the study of public health find an important place in the discourse of political economy.

I examine in this book the emerging scientific approach to problems of public health in early-nineteenth-century France. The temporal and social context of this activity, notably the rapidly changing demographic and economic situation in urban France between 1815 and 1848, also demands attention, as does the social philosophy that defined the major premises of early French sociomedical investigation. The leaders of this movement were committed men, committed not only to their technical inquiries but to the tenets of political economy. My principal concern in the following pages is to delineate the ideology behind their inquiry. By means of extended examination of a representative set of scientific hygienic investigations I seek to show how that ideology was related to the concrete apprehension of social reality. My constant and articulate informant in this task is Louis René Villermé, the foremost hygienic investigator of the period and a dedicated advocate of the principles of political economy. My discourse is not that of social history as currently understood but is rather a study of the intellectual development of the physicians who first sought a reliable empirical basis for rigorous analysis of social phenomena. The products of their analysis continue to provide, of course, varied and useful but also recalcitrant material for contemporary efforts to reconstruct the lived reality of early industrial France. These efforts, however, are different from my own. I seek to provide a portrait of a particular and important social outlook, a sense of the doctrinal purpose or ideology informing that outlook, and analysis of the relation of both to an earlier generation's effort to grasp the essential phenomena of social structure and change.

Public health investigation was a distinctive feature of nineteenth-century European society. Interest in, broadly speaking, the sanitary condition of discrete populations easily crossed national boundaries and created within two generations a recognizable medical speciality. The hygienists were armed with novel conceptual and methodological tools, they soon won academic and other employment, and they were backed by remarkable public interest in their undertakings. Both British and French physicians had given early stimulus to this movement. In the quarter century after the Congress of Vienna, however, leadership passed to France; and it was there, principally in Paris, that *hygiène publique*, or public health, won formal constitution as a science.

Diverse factors encouraged this development. Although lagging far behind Britain and moving more slowly, French manufacture after 1815 advanced steadily towards greater mechanization and organization of the factory system. France, and particularly her industrializing regions, was at this time a developing nation, a nation beginning to abandon traditional economic activities in favor of highly capitalized industrial endeavor. As has been the case in developing nations since 1945, French industrial development was slow and was accompanied by profound social disruption. While it cannot be claimed that France in 1848 had become a truly industrial nation, she had nonetheless committed herself to that objective and already was reaping the social consequences of so fundamental a change in the character and pace of national economic life. Industrialization led to concentration of population, uncertain employment, and a dissolution of traditional social bonds. An unmistakable consequence of these changes was vastly increased destitution, morbidity, and mortality in the populations most at risk. Among such populations, principally the urban poor, French public health investigators discovered not only human suffering on an alarming scale but an inexhaustible subject for scientific scrutiny.

The French medical community was prepared to respond to the opportunity. That community was large and expanding, and more importantly, many of its members had had previous experience with similar public health problems. Military experience, often extending over a decade or more of combat, had accustomed the French surgeon-physician to dealing with large numbers of individuals. The health of the troops and no less that of endlessly uprooted civilian populations was always uncertain and often poor. Disease and wounds were common, yet lack of sanitation, poor shelter and clothing, and above all, inadequate and ill-balanced diet were seen to pose the most serious threat to soldier and civilian alike. Such problems generally were manifest on a mass scale. The military surgeon who returned to civilian life soon encountered these conditions again, now in the crowded and poverty-stricken quarters of Restoration Paris and in the emerging industrial towns and cities of his homeland.

France, moreover, within a period of twenty-five years had witnessed unprecedented political turmoil. Between 1789 and 1815 she had experimented with monarchy, republic, empire, and monarchy again, now hopefully tamed by constitutional provisions. The nation had known and still knew no agreement on what constituted the best form of government and possessed no assured mechanisms for the orderly expression of political will. She was rich, however, in competing social philosophies. Reason was applied not so much to statecraft as to plans for systematic and often dramatic social reconstruction. In this endeavor the economists spoke with loud and resolute voice. Their position was as closely reasoned and fully developed as those put forward by more celebrated contemporaries. Beside Henri de Saint-Simon, Auguste Comte, and Karl Marx stood Jean Baptiste Say and Simonde de Sismondi and their numerous associates. The seeming concreteness of the economists' inquiries, their matter-of-fact treatment of complex social phenomena, and the simplicity and apparent certainty of their principles suggested to hygienists and others that here, and not in the utopian extravagances of the "Prophets of Paris" (Manuel), were to be found principles upon which to erect a truly rigorous science of society. Hygienists were by definition students of the social process, and many among them—not least such leaders as Villermé, Jean Baptiste Parent-Duchâtelet, Hippolyte Royer-Collard, and François Mélier— were advocates of liberal political philosophy and the claims of political economy. There thus arose within the larger French public health community a respected and outspoken corps of investigators whose understanding of the social order reached well beyond the special concerns of the medical profession. We shall observe hereafter how new social problems, medically perceived, and a corps of seasoned and socially aware observers, in association with a sharply defined view of what constitutes the nature of society, joined to create in France in the decades after 1815 that coherent body of method, discovery, and conclusion that constituted the early domain of public health investigation.

It must not be thought that, like a cannon, hygienic inquiry was simply taken from the armory and trained upon a new target. On the contrary, public health investigation as a distinct undertaking virtually created itself in the course of its inquiries into the manifold problems of the new industrial society. In large part, the development of the science of public health represented the rapid response on the part of important elements of the medical profession to widely perceived social malaise. At the same time, reports by hygienists on such problems as poor housing, overcrowding, impure water supplies, inadequate diet, and filth served to identify these conditions as essential parameters in defining the nature of the foremost social problem itself, the condition and prospects of the new working class.

In pursuing their studies of social dysfunction, the hygienists, and not least Villermé, increasingly found themselves torn by competing demands. Their science rendered public a disheartening record of poverty, sickness, and early death. Their eyes beheld the full spectrum of human degradation. Their social convictions, however, told them that economic liberty, the supreme good, demanded of each individual personal accountability for his or her success or failure in the great race of life. Without individual self-sufficiency and unremitting labor there could be no economic success, and biological survival itself might well be put in question. The state could do nothing because it should do nothing.

In extremis, the argument assured the destitute that they deserved their lot. Certain economists preached precisely that dismal message and with an enthusiasm ill-becoming their claim to dispassionate analysis. Hygienists rarely indulged in such luxuries. They knew too well the harsh realities facing the urban proletariat, and many appreciated the critical fact that poverty was not unfailingly or even often the consequence of moral depravity or lack of will. They realized that society itself, as reflected in the distribution and exercise of economic power, exerted a profound and usually irresistible influence upon the fate of those who lacked access to such power. But having traced in striking detail the great differences in mortality and morbidity that divided the rich from the poor and having pointedly assigned that difference to dissimilar economic condition, the hygienists retreated from what seemed to more determined critics an obvious remedy. The hygienist could envisage gradual social reform, focused upon one or another discrete problem, but he dared not contemplate the therapy—

namely, revolutionary social transformation—that the diagnosis might appear to demand. At precisely this point political economy exercised its hegemony over public health. Villermé displayed no false consciousness. He was well aware of his convictions and of their foundation in the liberal ethos systematized and popularized by Say. And he was utterly candid in giving expression to his convictions. His expression, therefore, of the ideology of sociomedical investigation—that is, of public hygiene in early industrial France—illuminates with uncommon clarity the unresolved tension haunting the hygienists' accomplishment and the irreducible ambiguity in what they, their contemporaries, and many subsequent commentators have regarded as a program of unqualified humanitarianism.

To view Villermé and his intellectual associates as apologists of class interests is perhaps exact but in itself is merely a claim, not an exposition of the precise terms in which that apology was expressed. Most hygienists belonged to the bourgeoisie and the rising professional orders, the great beneficiaries of the economic expansion unleashed in this golden age of liberalism, and a generous expression of self-interest is only to be expected. I have attempted to describe and analyze the endeavor of the French public health movement without placing particular emphasis upon such acts of self-justification. These have not been ignored, certainly, but neither are they allowed to command the argument. I have adopted throughout this work a subdued tone, one that is best suited, I believe, to portraying the central drama of this story, namely, the persistence of the discord between what one science, sociomedical investigation, presumed to teach and the action that another science, political economy, refused to countenance. The Paris hygienists were cognizant of this discord, and their views regarding its inevitability shifted as the social world they knew itself changed. Villermé's own outlook evolved between 1815 and 1848 from optimism to pessimism, an evolution also marked by an increasing harshness in his estimate of the intrinsic moral and therefore economic capacity of the laboring class. The system of beliefs comprising political economy, when translated as it was under the constitutional monarchy into social convention, administrative practice, and the very law of the land, long precluded serious public action in the realm of improving the sanitary condition of labor. Only too obviously ideology, whether conscious or unconscious, has its unexpected consequences. These can be traced in detail, and it is the challenge of doing so that brings public health and political economy together in this volume.

Sociomedical investigation drew its advocates principally from the new medical community of Paris. It was from Paris also that Say and his associates waged their campaign for political economy. The capital shared, too, the remarkable demographic and economic changes then sweeping

France. These diverse developments, essential elements in the creation of a public health interest, I describe in Part I of this volume. The reader should note that I do not intend or attempt a biography of Villermé (though happy circumstance does allow this book to be published on the two-hundredth anniversary of his birth). My purpose is to allow his investigations and conclusions to provide guidance through the vast domain which was the French public health movement. In my discussion I do not seek to frame an apology for the hygienists-economists' own apologetics but attempt instead to expound the reasons that that apology, for such it was, took the form that it did. I have tried to read Villermé in such manner that the intellectual and social assumptions by which he and like-minded contemporaries made sense of their world become evident. Villermé was but one amongst the large body of this first major generation of bourgeois intellectuals. While eschewing, therefore, a strictly biographical approach I have nonetheless tried to respect the autonomy of his person and views. But I also strive to suggest how the social group necessarily and importantly molded these views, it doing so above all by presenting in forcefully reasoned form a set of alternative understandings of the proper constitution of the social and economic order, a set from which a definite and deliberate choice was made.

Chapter 3 ("Political Economy") thus plays an important role in this book, for there the divergent views of Say and Sismondi are examined in detail. My aim is not to summarize in a few paragraphs the science of political economy but to indicate how the principles of that science defined economic man, the ultimate actor on the social and hygienic stage, and how Sismondi rebelled at the extreme consequences of this approach. The terms of his rebellion constantly informed the thought of the hygienists and usually gave them pause even when their instinct for rigorous doctrinal assertion rode high.

In Part II I offer an extended analysis of the diverse objectives and the distinctive method—the numerical method—of the Paris hygienists. The contemporary term *hygiéniste* or its English equivalent is employed throughout. In the 1830s and 1840s English usage was moving towards "public health" as the most appropriate global expression for the emerging ensemble of thought and action regarding sanitation. French practice favored *hygiène publique* or, occasionally, *salubrité publique*, and from the former expression I, like the hygienists, derive both substantive and adjectival forms. Villermé's empirical studies, which ranged from the prison to the urban slum and the factory, assume predominant position in this discussion. I seek to assay, through Villermé, the program and intentions of the French sociomedical observers. Death played the leading role in their drama, for the most striking feature of these empirical studies is the

hygienists' effort to express collective social condition in terms of differential mortality and to state differential mortality in the seemingly irrefutable language of number.

As noted above, while hygienic inquiry did disclose the extremes and
character of contemporary social dysfunction, it was frequently guided by
a clearly formulated political purpose. Too often the findings of empirical
investigation could not be reconciled with the needs of political and economic doctrine. The discoverer could not also be reformer; ideology overwhelmed inquiry. This matter is treated in Part III; there, I draw together
the varied elements of Villermé's conception of political economy and
provide an introduction to the views of other members of a veritable *parti
d'hygiène publique*.

Part I

A Changing Nation

Chapter 1

Medical Paris

Public hygiene deals with man in society and also with his biological nature. Religion, government, manners and customs, institutions, the relations of men with other men and of peoples with other peoples—all of this falls within its province. In short, public hygiene touches every aspect of our social existence. It does even more, for, as Cabanis had hoped, it tends to perfect human nature itself.

Jean François Rameaux, 1839

The medical profession that faced the challenges presented by the demographic and industrial changes transforming France after 1815 had itself been recently and dramatically transformed. Experience of a decade of revolution and reform, followed by another of incessant warfare, had created a large corps of seasoned physicians and surgeons. French hospitals had also been reorganized and the conduct of their institutional and medical affairs set upon a new path. The schooling of the profession and its practical training were being revolutionized. Physician and surgeon acquired equal rights to practice the medical art, and the hospital, now become the foundation for the study of pathological anatomy and for clinical instruction, moved to the center of medical inquiry and action. The hospitals of Paris provided, moreover, another arena for the observation of sickness and suffering on a large scale, providing thereby abundant cases for subsequent numerical analysis.

These changes in pedagogy and institutional structure were not introduced merely to further the knowledge and interests of the medical profession or to assure an adequate supply of military surgeons. They were overwhelmingly the consequence of the realization, however imperfect, of important and long-standing social concerns. The condition of the sick and the poor had been a matter of intense public and private interest during the final decades of the Old Regime, and it provided the focus for much significant social legislation enacted during the Revolution and Consulate.

EPIGRAPH: J. F. Rameaux, *Appréciation des progrès de l'hygiène publique depuis le commencement du dix-neuvième siècle* (Strasbourg: G. Silbermann, 1839), pp. 5–6.

The charitable instinct, the celebrated *bienfaisance* of the Enlightenment, was codified at this time and integrated into the administrative apparatus of the state. Public assistance entailed public care, first of those who were truly sick, incompetent or indigent and then, at a much later date, of the population at large. Like so many other hygienists, Louis René Villermé passed through several of these institutions and was then further instructed by years of active medical service in the Imperial armies. Well before he and his associates encountered the medical perils of an urban and industrial society, they had gained on the battlefield a thorough knowledge of human suffering and social chaos.

Louis René Villermé

By temperament and inclination Villermé was destined for a life of study. Born in Paris (10 May 1782) to the wife of a lawyer in municipal service, he soon moved with his family to a small village (Lardy) some thirty miles south of the city.[1] He there received his first schooling. Continued studies required the resources of the capital, and thence Villermé went, arriving in Paris apparently during the early years of the Directory.

1. There is no biography of Villermé but several brief notices exist; each provides a different perspective and often unique information. Of these the most useful are Alphonse Guérard, "Notice sur M. Villermé," *Annales d'hygiène publique et de médecine légale* 21 (1864): 162–77 (includes an indispensable but incomplete bibliography); Jules Béclard, "M. Villermé," in *Notices et portraits. Eloges lus à l'Académie de médecine* (Paris: Masson, 1878), pp. 73–105; Pierre Astruc, "Villermé, Louis-René," *Biographies médicales*, no. 7 (1933), pp. 225–44. Also [Joseph?] Naudet, "Mort et obsèques de M. Villermé," *Journal des économistes* 40 (1863): 488–91; A. L. [Alfred Legoyt], "L. R. Villermé," *Journal de la Société statistique de Paris* 5 (1864): 46–47; Marcel Delabroise, *Un médecin hygiéniste et sociologue: Louis René Villermé, 1782–1863* (Thèse de médecine, Paris, 1939); Michel Oger, *A propos d'une étude oubliée de Villermé: Le rapport de 1850 sur les accidents du travail*. Thèse de médecine, Paris, 1962). A concise record of Villermé's medical studies appears on his *inscription* at the Faculty of Medicine, Paris (Thèse no. 108, 22 August 1814, Archives de la Faculté de médecine de Paris, Archives Nationales). Erwin H. Ackerknecht's "Villermé and Quetelet," *Bulletin of the History of Medicine* 26 (1952): 317–29, provides invaluable information, as does the Villermé correspondence (utilized by Ackerknecht) preserved in the Bibliothèque royale de la Belgique; see Liliane Wellens-de Donder, "Inventaire de la correspondance d'Adolphe Quetelet déposé à l'Académie royale de Belgique," *Mémoires de l'Académie royale de Belgique: Collection in-8°* 37 (1966): 1–299 (Villermé, p. 140). Pierre de Calan offers a familial view of his great-great-grandfather in "Mon trisaïeul," *La Croix*, 2 December 1970. I have not seen Jacques-Yves Vincent, "La pensée du docteur Villermé" (Mémoire pour le D.E.S. de sciences politiques, Université de Rennes, 1968).

Not a biography but the first serious modern analytical study of Villermé's scientific work is B. P. Lécuyer, "Démographie, statistique et hygiène publique sous la monarchie censitaire," *Annales de démographie*, 1979, pp. 215–45.

The tumult of revolution continued to be felt in the educational domain. Institutions and programs were created, destroyed, and created again with ease and rapidity. As a consequence, Villermé's early instruction was disrupted and fragmentary, a situation he worked to correct during free hours in the army medical service.

Villermé entered the newly founded Ecole de médecine at Paris (probably in 1801) and three years later was graduated directly into the army medical service as a third-class surgeon. Only upon resignation from the army (June 1814) was he free to complete his medical studies, receiving the doctor of medicine degree from the Paris faculty in August of that year. It appears that the principal influence upon his medical studies was exerted by the surgeon Guillaume Dupuytren. Villermé had served Dupuytren as prosector and warmly acknowledged the surgeon's continuing support.[2] Presumably these studies were conducted at the Hôtel-Dieu sometime between 1801 and 1804. It was obviously at Dupuytren's suggestion that Villermé commenced and long continued his study of false membranes and of membranous tissue in general. Dupuytren reentered his life as one of the examiners set by the Faculty of Medicine for Villermé's doctoral dissertation, defended before the formidable assemblage of Jean Noël Hallé, Anselme Richerand, Nicolas Louis Vauquelin, Marie Alexandre Desormeaux, Alexis Boyer, and Dupuytren.

For ten years Villermé followed the French army, serving in Germany, Austria, France itself, and, worst of all, in the bloody and much dreaded Peninsular campaigns. All accounts agree that this service was a harrowing experience. It is clear that Villermé proved an exceptionally able army surgeon, receiving the personal approval of P. F. Percy, director of the military medical service, and slowly advancing to the rank of surgeon-major in 1813. Villermé's few recorded comments on his war experience simply reported the brutality and infinite suffering of all who were involved. Above all, he came to know intimately famine and its psychological and social consequences.[3] This was an experience to be encountered again, now in the great manufacturing centers during periods of economic depression, and one which, whether met within a military or a civilian setting, posed directly a central question of sociomedical investigation, the relation between means of subsistence, disease, and death.

The years 1814–18 proved to be the turning point in Villermé's career. His military service ended, and a very brief essay at medical practice in Paris having proved unrewarding, he determined to devote himself en-

2. Villermé, *Sur les fausses membranes* (Thèse de médecine, Paris, 1814).

3. Villermé, "De la famine et ses effets sur la santé dans les lieux qui sont le théâtre de la guerre," *Journal général de médecine, de chirurgie, de pharmacie* 65 (1818): 3–24.

tirely to a study of the basic principles by which society might further, even assure, the physical and moral well-being of its members. Supported by a legacy from his father, Villermé became a man of the city, inquiring into the most intimate details of its structure and functions. He made contact with both the multifaceted philanthropic movement of the period and the vigorous societal life of Paris medicine.

His closest early connection was with the Société médicale d'émulation, founded in 1796. Villermé served the society for a number of years and thereby won entree into the broader community of Parisian physicians. Between 1815 and 1824 he attended its meetings with great regularity and was elected to two secretarial positions. His greatest contribution to the society's affairs was as editor and financial guarantor, in both roles seconded by the collaboration of his friend, the clinician Isidore Bricheteau, of the *Bulletins de la Société médicale d'émulation*.[4] Especially active in the society in these years before the new Académie royale de médecine created an overwhelming distraction for men of talent and ambition were, in addition to Bricheteau and Villermé, the military surgeons Dominique Jean Larrey and Gilbert Breschet; the naval surgeon Pierre François Kéraudren; Jean-Jacques Leroux des Tillets, second dean of the Faculty of Medicine and editor of the important *Journal général de médecine, de chirurgie, de pharmacie*; the physiologist François Magendie; and the clinician François Victor Merat, senior editor of the *Dictionnaire des sciences médicales*.

Members of the society valued highly the clinical ideal of the Paris school, and they valued no less original research of all kinds. Led by Xavier Bichat, the Société médicale d'émulation had been founded by young men for the purpose of increasing medical knowledge: the society existed neither for social diversion nor to provide a gathering point for established leaders of the profession or members of the faculty. The latter were always welcomed but were also expected to contribute meaningfully to the advance of medical knowledge. The natural sciences were highly esteemed within the society, and in this can be seen the continuing hold

4. Villermé's activities at the Société médicale d'émulation may be traced in detail in the "Procès-verbaux de la Société médicale d'émulation, 1810–1831," MS. 2191, Bibliothèque de la Faculté de médecine de Paris. On the society see Jules-Omer Cherest, "Recherches historiques sur la Société: Son origine, ses fondateurs, ses travaux," *Recueil des travaux de la Société médicale d'émulation de Paris* 30 (1850): 5–47; on the societal life of Paris medicine in general consult Pierre Astruc, "Les sociétés médicales françaises de 1796 à 1850," *Le progrès médical*, 10 January 1950, pp. 28–30, and E. H. Ackerknecht, *Medicine at the Paris Hospital, 1794–1848* (Baltimore: Johns Hopkins Press, 1967), pp. 115–19. Care must be exercised to distinguish the *Bulletins* of the society, the title in the plural, (published from 1821 to 1823 under the auspices of Villermé and Bricheteau) and the society's *Bulletin*, issued both before and after this period.

exerted upon an important segment of the medical community by the doctrines of the idéologues. A primary witness to this passion for chemistry, anatomy, physiology, botany, and vital statistics as well as sustained concern for the full spectrum of practical medical concerns is the celebrated *Dictionnaire des sciences médicales*. Distinctive by its title alone, the *Dictionnaire* emphasized science along with medicine and received contributions from a host of members of the Société médicale d'émulation, stimulated no doubt by their associate Merat. Villermé himself contributed over thirty such articles, some of major proportions.[5]

Beginning in 1824 Villermé gradually withdrew from active participation in the society's affairs. Other interests and opportunities had presented themselves. Elected in 1823 *membre-adjoint* of the Royal Academy of Medicine, Villermé long remained an enthusiastic participant in the proceedings and investigations of this the most prestigious of French medical organizations. He received full membership in the academy's section of hygiene in 1835. It was to the Academy of Medicine that Villermé continued his reports on hygienic and statistical matters which he had begun for the Société médicale d'émulation. More significant, however, was his election to the refounded Académie des sciences morales et politiques. Here, in association with his friend Louis François Benoiston de Châteauneuf, he brought the ideals and results of sociomedical investigation to the very heartland of the school of political economy and received its approbation and support.

The Academy of Moral and Political Sciences, an original component of the Institut de France (1795), had quickly won notoriety by its outspoken political discussions and defense of liberal values. Bonaparte valued technical expertise but not liberty of expression; this *IIe classe* was suppressed in 1803 and remained so throughout the Restoration. Its reestablishment in 1832 was an act designed to display the liberal proclivities of the new regime, one seeking to enlarge and give assurance to its constituency. François Guizot created the new academy with very explicit social and political purposes in mind. Many years later he recalled his motives:

> It is no longer simply among the higher members of society but also within the lower orders that theories which inflame [*portent le dérèglement*] both minds and nations are favorably received and exercise a powerful influence; it is no longer merely in the learned world

5. These are cited by A.C.P. Callisen, *Medicinisches Schriftsteller– Lexicon der jetzt lebenden Aerzte, Wundaerzte, Geburtshelfer, Apotheker, und Naturforscher aller gebildeten Voelker*, 25 vols. (Copenhagen: the author, 1830–37), 20:144–45. The *Dictionnaire* as an enterprise of a school is described by J. L. Casper, *Charakteristik der franzoesischen Medicin, mit vergleichenden Hinblicken auf die englische* (Leipzig: F. K. Brockhaus, 1822), pp. 562–91.

but also amongst the ignorant [mob] that these theories are to be feared
and pursued. . . . The government may have confidence in the intellectual life of the higher orders; it should recognize there the promise of
greater assistance than risk. And may it be unrelenting in combatting
the intellectual disorder of society's lower ranks.[6]

The Academy of Moral and Political Sciences was conceived as an important instrument of public authority. Guizot hoped, and not in vain, that
his academy would not perpetuate the materialism, even republicanism,
of the old academy, but would become the semiofficial voice of new and
socially more conservative doctrines. Philosophical eclecticism, spiritual-
ism, and history as the witness of social cohesiveness came to dominate
the academy's considerations. The older idéologues, men of the Revolution such as Joseph Lakanal, Joseph Garat, the abbé Sieyès, and P.C.F.
Daunou, became an increasingly minor force in its proceedings.

Membership in the new academy was drawn first of all from the small
handful of survivors of the old academy and then from leading contemporaries. The latter included numerous representatives of the liberal
school. On 29 December 1832 Villermé entered the *classe* of political
economy, statistics, and finance at the academy. Save for a lateral move
(to the classe of moral science in 1851) this remained his intellectual home
until his death. Elected at the same time as Villermé were such notable
figures as the physician François Joseph Victor Broussais; the physiologist
William Francis Edwards, a member of the Milne-Edwards and Dumas
family dynasties in natural science, medicine, finance and public administration; and the economists and moral philosophers François Xavier Joseph Droz, whose humanitarian brand of political economy Villermé and
the hygienists favored, and Charles Comte, a stalwart in doctrine and publicity for the new school.[7]

Villermé's role at the academy, of which he was president in the unsettled year 1849, is perhaps the clearest external mark of his recognized
place in the campaign for political economy in the era of the constitutional
monarchy. He lent his hand freely, however, to various other enterprises

6. François Guizot, *Mémoires pour servir à l'histoire de mon temps*, 8 vols. (Paris:
Michel Lévy, 1860), 3:147, 148. On the new academy, see André-Jean Tudesq, *Les grands
notables en France (1840–1849): Etude historique d'une psychologie sociale*, 2 vols.
(Paris: P.U.F., 1964), 1:456–65; Yvonne Knibielher, *Naissance des sciences humaines:
Mignet et l'histoire philosophique au XIXe siècle* (Paris: Flammarion, 1973), pp. 309–26.
See also M. S. Staum "The Class of Moral and Political Sciences, 1795–1803," *French
Historical Studies* 11 (1980): 371–97.

7. Institut de France, Académie des sciences morales et politiques, *Notices biograph-
iques et bibliographiques*, 9th ed. (Paris: Didot, 1972), p. 395.

of the economists. Of these the most important was the *Journal des économistes*, a veritable party organ and an instrument of social propaganda.[8] Edited by Adolfe Blanqui (to be distinguished from his brother, the socialist revolutionary Louis Auguste Blanqui) the *Journal*, founded in 1841, spread liberal economic doctrine to interested readers across France. Villermé served on the editorial board of the *Journal* and contributed to it a number of articles and reports, addressed particularly to the progress of official statistics and to the populationist argument.

Except for his early years in Paris and for brief service during the cholera epidemic of 1832, when he joined with the entire medical corps of Paris in aiding the afflicted populace, Villermé neither practiced medicine nor engaged in study or teaching concerning clinical medicine. The latter was perhaps the greatest glory of Paris medicine. Its seat was the hospital, morgue, and dissection hall, and its principal contribution a vastly improved capacity to precisely diagnose diseases. Villermé and his fellow hygienists undertook instead social diagnosis, the object of their study being the city and its inhabitants. Not unexpectedly their procedure offered many features also characteristic of contemporary clinical investigation. The veneration of analysis, a passion for facts, acceptance of generalization when based upon the marshalling of large numbers of instances, insistence upon the immediacy of experience, a scepticism, albeit often reluctant, before theory writ large—here were grounds upon which, despite the disparity of their subjects, numerous clinicians and sociomedical investigators could meet and discover shared values.

The principal sources of information for sociomedical investigation were essentially three: printed materials, unpublished administrative documents, and personal on-site inspection. It was largely Villermé's capacity to discern the interplay of this diverse information that assured the fruitfulness of his approach. From the outset of his investigative career Villermé used numbers—both in simple sums and differences and, more persuasively, in proportions—as an essential instrument of medical and hence social analysis. This practice, simple though it was, was perfected by the Paris hygienists and applied to an increasingly wide range of social phenomena. The use of this numerical method, moreover, placed Villermé in friendly communication with Adolfe Quetelet and assured his role in the creation of a science of vital statistics. It should be noted that Villermé's purpose, like that of virtually all the early hygienists, was exclusively to

8. See Michel Lutfalla, "Aux origines du libéralisme économique en France: Le 'Journal des Economistes.' Analyse du contenu de la première série, 1841–1853," *Revue d'histoire économique et sociale* 50 (1972): 494–517.

reason with numbers. These investigators made no mathematical evaluation of the reliability of the data chosen for analysis or of the conclusions
drawn therefrom.

Contemporary English statisticians announced that their science had as
its principal purpose the collection of well-authenticated facts and their
arrangement in appropriate manner. They claimed that these facts were of
importance to the very articulation of a science of statistics and, an essential corollary, that statisticians with their numbers did not properly venture
upon overt social analysis, much less upon sharp social criticism. To be
sure, such objectivity was only an illusion, for the English, like the
French, worked their data for social purposes.[9] They, too, sought justification of the factory system and defense of private property, and they, too,
entertained the notion that science—that is, statistics—is an essential
guide in the delicate matter of social reform.

Villermé's first publications dealt with anatomical and surgical matters.
His report on the organization and sanitary conditions of prisons (1820)
revealed, however, a radically new orientation.[10] This work readily made
known its author's major concerns: the moral and physical condition of
the dispossessed and the unfortunate, criminality and destitution as a function of socioeconomic dislocation, and the redemptive power of rigorous
discipline and labor. Des prisons was, as its author recognized, an essay
in political economy.

In 1821 the prefecture of the Seine published the first volume of the
remarkable Recherches statistiques sur la ville de Paris et le département
de la Seine. Here appeared data worthy of the most assiduous analysis,
and these data formed the foundation of Villermé's first systematic consideration of the presumed connection between mortality and economic status, published in definitive form by the Academy of Medicine in 1828.[11]
In conception and general execution this memoir offers a concise résumé
of its author's expectations of vital statistics. It was this inquiry that established Villermé's reputation as the leading exponent of the application of
numerical reasoning to public health problems.

9. See V. L. Hilts "Aliis exterendem; or, The origins of the Statistical Society of London," Isis 69 (1978): 21–43. The illusory character of the English statisticians' stated aim,
one regularly contradicted by their importation of the doctrines of political economy, is
noted by J. M. Eyler, Victorian Social Medicine: The Ideas and Methods of William Farr
(Baltimore: Johns Hopkins University Press, 1979), pp. 22–23; see also the works cited by
Eyler.

10. Villermé, Des prisons telles qu'elles sont, et telles qu'elles devraient être; ouvrage
dans lequel on les considère par rapport à l'hygiène, à la morale et à l'économie politique
(Paris: Méquignon-Marvis, 1820).

11. Villermé, "Mémoire sur la mortalité en France, dans la classe aisée et dans la classe
indigente," Mémoires de l'Académie royale de médecine 1 (1828): 51–98.

Between 1828 and 1835 he published in rapid succession some two dozen studies on a wide range of topics. Virtually all of this work was numerical. The author's purpose, in fact, appeared occasionally to be only to test the scope of his new procedure. Mortality and natality served as primary indicators of social well-being or distress. Among these studies were articles dealing with the conjunction of conception (birth) and seasons of the year, the average duration of diseases at different ages, and the age-specific influence of marshes on human mortality. Two essays that have become classics in the literature of public health also date from this period. The first was, in reality, a sketch of Villermé's fundamental convictions regarding the necessarily social nature of all hygienic investigation, offering a brief statement of how medicine, guided by political economy, must and will become a social science.[12] The second essay constituted Villermé's contribution to the voluminous literature dealing with the cholera epidemic of 1832.[13] Here was vividly portrayed the movement of epidemic disease through the most miserable quarters and dwellings of a great city, an object lesson for public health and an apt occasion for moral reflection, which the author did not fail to provide.

These essays were products of the study, not of direct observation of social ills. Villermé by no means closed his eyes to contemporary events, but he had not yet, save for army experiences, turned to systematic, personal inspection of social life. While analysis of vital statistics permitted both novel and more rigorous assessment of many features of society, it was an approach that maintained, perhaps inadvertently, social distance between observer and observed. The indispensable intermediate step, the gathering of data, was in France taken by a large and disparate group of individuals, ranging from the administrative officers of the department of the Seine to numerically inclined clinicians of the hospitals of Paris. To Villermé, as to his fellow hygienists, number alone was without meaning, a mere mark on the mute documents. To give these marks meaning and to do so by relating them to concrete sociomedical phenomena was to make the documents speak and thus render them socially useful. Nonetheless, these studies of the 1820s and early 1830s stand in marked contrast to Villermé's next undertaking, his famed inquiry into the condition of the working class in France.

Responding to a request by the Academy of Moral and Political Sciences, Benoiston de Châteuneuf and Villermé began a comprehensive sur-

12. Villermé, "Des épidémies sous les rapports de l'hygiène publique, de la statistique médicale et de l'économie politique," *Annales d'hygiène publique et de médecine légale* 9 (1833): 5–58.

13. Villermé, "Notes sur les ravages du choléra-morbus dans les maisons garnies de Paris, depuis le 29 mars jusqu'au 1er août 1832," ibid. 11 (1834): 385–409, plus 2 tables.

vey of the medical and social conditions of the new industrial proletariat of France. Their investigations involved on-site factory inspection, systematic if discrete discussion with the *patronat* and supervisory personnel, and very close observation and interrogation of the worker. Thus did Villermé's mode of inquiry come to match that of Parent-Duchâtelet, whose direct observations of the hygienic condition of Paris and its population provided and continue to provide timeless models for sanitary investigation. Villermé's personal examination of the condition of the textile worker in the north, east, and southeast of France was conducted between 1835 and 1837. His findings were reported in a series of preliminary publications but are best known today through the *Tableau de l'état physique et moral des ouvriers employés dans les manufactures de coton, de laine et de soie* of 1840, a work whose scientific merits were instantly recognized and which contributed greatly to increased awareness of social injustice and potential disorder.[14] This recognition was accompanied in many quarters by acute anxiety and a sharpened fear for the survival and continued prosperity of the newly triumphant bourgeois society. Villermé shared this fear and realized, perhaps better than any of his medical contemporaries, the real and legitimate foundations for the grievances of the people. His political outlook, however, remained unchanged, and the events of 1848 caused not only shock but despair.

In 1848 Villermé was sixty-six years old. Progressive physical debility was beginning to place limits on the reach of his undiminished mental alertness, and his early resilience and adaptability to change were rapidly departing. Villermé held the government and principles of the July Monarchy in little esteem and felt that the revolution of February 1848 was less spontaneous than contrived by utterly corrupt interests. Family tragedies and misadventure made the years after 1851 increasingly somber. Whereas public affairs still dominated his concerns during the revolution and Second Republic, calling forth *Associations ouvrières* in 1849, after 1851 he turned to narrowly hygienic matters.[15] These continued until death was indeed near; a report on a major study in progress dealing with age at marriage was published in 1861. In September of that year he bleakly informed his friend Quetelet that "I hear only with difficulty, I do not see well, I can no longer walk and I am growing weak."[16] Deterioration thereafter was steady, and Villermé died in Paris on 16 November

---

14. Villermé, *Tableau de l'état physique et moral des ouvriers employés dans les manufactures de coton, de laine et de soie* 2 vols. (Paris: Jules Renouard, 1840).

15. Villermé, *Des associations ouvrières* (Paris: Pagnerre, 1849).

16. Quoted in Ackerknecht, "Villermé and Quetelet," p. 329.

1863, a few months short of having spent a half-century in the Parisian medical community.

Honest and unrelenting labor was the preeminent feature of Villermé's existence; work was his true passion. Military experience surely helped mold his personality. His forthright manner and "fierce and proud probity" have been remarked by virtually all biographers.[17] Blunt and incisive, ceaselessly inquiring, Villermé quickly acquired and always retained a reputation for scrupulous honesty and unmatched insight into both familiar and unfamiliar hygienic problems. He was not a distinguished speaker and played no public role outside the academic world of Paris. Behind the brusque manner, Villermé was cordial and, until his last years, receptive of new views. He elicited easy and well-placed confidence. This openness and unqualified benevolence, albeit strongly paternalistic in form and expression, made possible repeated contact and a frank exchange of views with what seemed another world altogether, that of the peasant and the urban worker, the latter commonly not a generation removed from the land. This was, of course, a world already familiar to an ex-surgeon who had tended the wounds of the heterogeneous and conscripted armies of Bonaparte.

Villermé's stated purpose was not mere investigation. He hoped and often expected that his inquiries would lead quickly to the alleviation of human suffering. His confidence in the persuasive power of scientific inquiry was very great and in the good will of men, at least of most men, even greater. As will be seen, this confidence not infrequently was misplaced. More importantly, the central claim of the party of political economy, absolute liberty in the marketplace, made it impossible even for men of the most benevolent disposition to contemplate serious interference, much less radical change, in the economic relations joining capital and labor. Villermé, like so many others dedicated to sociomedical investigation, might perhaps create a science but definitely would fail to transform society or even render its affairs more harmonious.

Sociomedical investigators sought particularly to establish in rigorous manner the hygienic consequences of destitution and human misfortune. These consequences were often expressed openly by the human frame, by disease and its bodily effects, and they thus quite naturally attracted the attention of the curious physician or surgeon. But they could also be expressed more subtly and indirectly. Mortality rates, for example, attracted the attention of observers, often, again, the physician or surgeon, to whom a population of men and women offered a reality of an interest and impor-

17. Béclard, "M. Villermé," p. 77.

tance equal to that of the individual patient. Mortality rates were a social phenomenon and turned the mind directly to society itself. Virtually by definition but, of course, also by inclination, students of public hygiene in the era of the constitutional monarchy were led to consider the fundamental economic and social issues confronting the French nation. Often their view of these matters was only implied or remained largely unexpressed: such was the case with the retiring Parent-Duchâtelet. Others, however, made explicit their conception of the interrelation between sociomedical investigation and contemporary socioeconomic concerns. Villermé was outspoken in this regard, and his conclusions consequently provide an unusually clear view of the interaction between the claims of seemingly dispassionate scientific investigation and the demands of deep-seated social commitments.

Public Hygiene and the Paris School

The Paris school of medicine emerged from the meeting of a new epistemology and a transformed institution.[18] The epistemology was the skeptical empiricism articulated by the medical *idéologues*, notably P.J.G. Cabanis and Philippe Pinel, and the institution, the several public hospitals of the French metropolis. A critical stimulus to the triumph of an empirical outlook in the hospital setting was the earlier success and continuing distinction of surgery. Paris medicine meant above all the correlation of physical lesion and clinical sign or symptom. It thus demanded that the discovery and description of the former receive no lesser attention than that traditionally given the latter.

The skill and prestige of the French surgeon had begun to rise by the mid-eighteenth century.[19] He had by that time acquired his own academy (1731), a critical step in social and official recognition, and had come increasingly to provide a broad spectrum of medical services. His parity with the physician was consecrated by the radical reforms of medical education introduced during the Revolution. By the law of 4 December 1794—which created medical schools at Paris, Montpellier, and Strasbourg—it became official doctrine that, in Antoine François de Fourcroy's

18. Ackerknecht, *Medicine at the Paris Hospital*, pp. 3–44.

19. Oswei Temkin, "The Role of Surgery in the Rise of Modern Medical Thought," in *The Double Face of Janus* (Baltimore: Johns Hopkins University Press, 1977), pp. 487–96; Toby Gelfand, "The Hospice of the Paris College of Surgery (1774–1793): 'A Unique and Invaluable Institution,'" *Bulletin of the History of Medicine* 47 (1973): 375–93; "From Guild to Profession: The Surgeons of France in the Eighteenth Century," *Texas Reports on Biology and Medicine* 32 (1974): 121–34. "A Clinical Ideal: Paris 1789," *Bulletin of the History of Medicine* 51 (1977): 397–411.

words, "medicine and surgery are two branches of the same science. To study them separately means to abandon theory to delirious imagination and practice to blind routine. To reunite them and to mel[d] them together means to enlighten them mutually and to further their progress."[20] Ideally, the graduate of the Paris school gained his knowledge of pathological anatomy in the dissection halls under supervision of an experienced surgeon-physician who had earlier followed the fatal course of the patient's disease in the hospital wards.

An emphasis upon basic surgical skills very quickly became evident. The last wars of the Revolution had stimulated the creation of the new medical schools, and continued warfare under Bonaparte made great claims upon its graduates. Save for short interludes of peace, most medical students at Paris moved quickly into military service. Military service provided many of these young surgeon-physicians an exceptional educational experience and, whether desired or not, opportunity. The army medical officer, even in smaller units, often had to cope with the full spectrum of medical care.[21] He encountered frequent epidemic disease and uncounted wounds and injuries. Death from many causes was his daily business. He had to recruit and often train his supporting staff, arrange transport of the wounded, organize formal and all too often rudimentary hospital services, and procure food and medical supplies by any means available. Medicine and surgery were thus only one dimension of his existence. During and after combat he became the center of a complex and frenzied system, and even in calmer periods he had to provide sustained care for the convalescent and the dying, an effort that required organizational ability and the capacity to perceive and control the interrelations between a large number of disparate needs and events.

The military surgeon acted, in short, within the framework of an elaborate social system designed to deal with vast numbers of men and women whose physical condition was weakened or precarious. In the lower ranks the surgeon dealt with his cases and no doubt ignored the structure and operation of the whole; at a higher level men such as Percy and Larrey won lasting glory by learning to dominate that whole, insuring that it serve, insofar as the medical and surgical arts permitted, the needs of the injured and the suffering. Many sociomedical investigators of the post-Imperial era received their introduction to widespread and severe famine,

20. Quoted in Ackerknecht, *Medicine at the Paris Hospital*, p. 32.

21. D. M. Vess, *Medical Revolution in France, 1789–1796* (Gainesville: University Presses of Florida, 1975), pp. 146–47. See D. B. Weiner, "French Doctors Face War," in *From the Ancien Régime to the Popular Front: Essays in the History of Modern France in Honor of Shepard B. Clough*, ed. C. K. Warner (New York: Columbia University Press, 1969), pp. 51–73.

social disruption, and desperate medical necessity in this hostile environment of battlefield and military hospital. In addition to Villermé they included Benoiston de Châteauneuf, Broussais, Kéraudren, René Nicolas
Desgenettes, Etienne Pariset, Nicolas Charles Chervin, Léon Rostan, and
Jean Etienne Dominique Esquirol.

The Paris medical school created in 1794 was provided with twelve
professors and an equal number of adjunct professors. The appointees
were in the main drawn from the old Faculty of Medicine and College of
Surgery (founded in 1724), both suppressed in 1790, and included numerous distinguished figures, among them François Chaussier, Percy, the surgeons Boyer and Pierre Joseph Desault, and the great clinician Jean Nicolas Corvisart, symbol of the school's focus on pathological anatomy and
clinical description.[22] Students numbered in the hundreds at the beginning
and in the thousands by the 1820s. Instruction was conducted by lectures
and, most importantly, in public and private dissection halls and in the
hospitals of the metropolis. Most members of the faculty were attached to
the medical services of one of the several Paris hospitals; others who also
participated in these services but lacked a faculty appointment offered independent instruction. Competition among the students was keen and
heartily encouraged by the authorities, principally by means of the famed
concours, upon which prestigious and instructive appointments as interns
or externs of the Paris hospitals depended.

Until the 1840s this great and complex machine for the production of
physician-surgeons prospered. It exercised a powerful attraction upon students across Europe and in the Americas and thereby spread the Paris view
of medicine throughout the world. But the school was truly dominated by
the clinical ideal and placed maximum value upon precise diagnosis. New
and promising ancillary sciences—chemistry, microscopy, experimental
physiology—found no home in the Faculty of Medicine (its formal title
after 1808). The quest to localize disease, to specify physical lesions,
contributed enormously to the discovery and clear definition of discrete
disease entities (for example, pulmonary tuberculosis, typhoid and typhus
fevers, and diphtheria) but contributed little at all to finding the cause(s)
of such diseases, an effort some held essential to the discovery of more
effective remedies for these and other afflictions. Therapy, with the exception of surgical practice, was not a strong point of the Paris school. Worst
of all, perhaps, the institution began to destroy itself by the common but
nefarious practices of cumulation of positions, permutation between
chairs, and widespread nepotism. At first gradually and then rapidly after
1850 the German universities rose to world ascendancy in the medical arts

22. The original faculty is listed by Ackerknecht, *Medicine at the Paris Hospital*, p. 35.

and sciences, now attracting those students who in an earlier generation would eagerly have sought their training in Paris.[23]

Among the chairs originally assigned the new school of medicine was that of medical physics and hygiene. This was indeed a new creation, having no forerunner in either the old Faculty of Medicine or College of Surgery. It reflected, however, many of the ambitions of the earlier Société royale de médecine. Created in 1776, the Royal Society represented the crown's interest in matters, broadly speaking, of public hygiene and the social dimensions of human and animal medicine.[24] The Royal Society was viewed with profound distaste by the old Faculty of Medicine, defender of traditional privilege and no less of traditional, primarily academic medicine. While the faculty's acerbic criticism could not destroy its increasingly important rival, the systematic suppression of corporate privilege by the Revolution did so in 1790. But the remarkable Félix Vicq-d'Azyr, the society's *secrétaire-perpétuel*, kept alive the program of the Royal Society and included in his celebrated plan for the reform of French medical education an important role for hygiene. Vicq-d'Azyr's views were essentially those which Chaussier and Fourcroy presented to the Convention in 1794 and which provided the formal plan for the new school. The wide responsibilities of the chair of hygiene were defined in the following manner by Chaussier and Fourcroy (the latter, a disciple of Vicq-d'Azyr, was the real author of the report to the Convention). The incumbent of the chair must profess, Fourcroy announced,

1. A knowledge of man and his needs when in a condition of health.
2. A knowledge of the *choses naturelles* of which the healthy man makes use; of the influences [*choses*] which surround him (applicata); of the *choses non-naturelles* which he takes into his system (ingesta), which he excretes (exreta), which he performs in his behavior (acta) and which he perceives (percepta).
3. A knowledge of regimen.
4. A knowledge of man as an individual (private hygiene) and of a man as a member of society (public hygiene).[25]

---

23. On the decline of the faculty, see ibid., pp. 121–27.

24. See C. C. Hannaway, "The Société royale de médecine and Epidemics in the Ancien Régime," *Bulletin of the History of Medicine* 46 (1972): 257–73; idem, "Veterinary Medicine and Rural Health Care in Pre-Revolutionary France," ibid. 51 (1977): 431–47; J. Meyer, "L'enquête de l'Académie de médecine sur les épidémies, 1774–1794," in J.-P. Desaive et al., *Médecins, climat et épidémies à la fin du XVIII⁰ siècle* (Paris and The Hague: Mouton, 1972), pp. 9–20.

25. Quoted by A. Proust, "L'évolution de l'hygiène et l'histoire de la chaire d'hygiène à la Faculté," *La lancette française; ou, Gazette des hôpitaux* 68 (1895): 486. Indispensable studies of French hygienic investigation and instruction are E. H. Ackerknecht, "Hygiene in France, 1815–1848," *Bulletin of the History of Medicine* 22 (1948): 117–55, and A. F.

The first three items reflect, of course, a long tradition reaching back to Greek medicine of formal instruction and guidance in matters of personal hygiene. Based on the technical notion of the six things nonnatural and directed towards those members of society who enjoyed both the intelligence and wherewithal truly to care for their physical and mental well-being, this hygienic advice was offered uniquely to the individual. In this form it proved to be no guide for improvement of the mass of mankind.[26]

But hygiene in the Paris school, while continuing to find frequent expression in manuals of personal hygiene, gradually brought the public dimensions of the subject to the fore. Hallé, the first incumbent of the newly founded chair and its distinguished occupant until his death in 1822, was instrumental in thus expanding the definition of the scope of hygiene. His successors in the chair (R. H. Bertin, 1822–28; Gabriel Andral, 1828–30; Desgenettes, 1830–37) often attended unduly to medical interests other than hygiene. With Hippolyte Royer-Collard (professor of hygiene, 1837–50), however, and especially his great successor, Apollinaire Bouchardat (professor of hygiene, 1850–86), the Paris faculty acquired hygienists of uncommon activity and insight.

Hygienic investigation, action, and instruction was, if anything, even more vigorous outside the walls of the faculty. Independent schools, municipal and regional institutions, and the national government were all involved in one manner or another with problems of public hygiene. And it was in 1829 that the *Annales d'hygiène publique et de médecine légale* first appeared.

Public hygiene was the subject of a long-continued series of popular courses at the Athénée de Paris. This school was one of the few institutions to continue its activity from the Old Regime across the Revolution and Empire into the Restoration and beyond. The lineal descendant of Jean François Pilâtre de Rozier's Musée, founded in 1781, the Athénée served throughout the Empire, Restoration, and July Monarchy as a municipal focus for popular scientific and medical instruction, drawing its auditors principally from the new professional and educated classes of the capital. Public hygiene was taught at the Athénée by Pariset in 1813–14 and again the following year.[27] Eusèbe de Salles repeated the series in

La Berge, "Public Health in France and the French Public Health Movement, 1815–1848" (Ph.D. diss. University of Tennessee, 1974).

26. See William Coleman, "Health and Hygiene in the Encyclopédie: A Medical Doctrine for the Bourgeoisie," *Journal of the History of Medicine* 29 (1974): 399–421.

27. A history of the Musée-Athénée is wanting and much needed, but see Charles De Job, "De l'établissement connu sous le nom de Lycée et d'Athénée et de quelques établissements analogues," *Revue internationale de l'enseignement* 18 (1889): 4–38. I draw my roster of lecturers from De Job's lists.

1824–25 and 1825–26. Upon Pariset's recommendation the young François Mélier, a major figure in later French sanitary investigation and administration, lectured at the Athénée in 1827–28. The following year (1828–29) Villermé presented the course. His subject was population in all its dimensions, and his lectures quite probably covered the several topics soon collectively to be designated demography.[28] Subsequent lecture series were offered by Achille Pierre Requin (1829–30) and Alphonse Sanson (1840–41, 1841–42).

Such courses simply testify to the continued public interest in the related matters of hygiene, population, and economic development. Far more important in inaugurating and sustaining a professional function for the era's growing hygienic expertise was the foundation of the Conseil de salubrité de Paris in 1802.[29] The Paris Health Council served its creator, the prefect of police of Paris, in an advisory role. Virtually all leaders of the Parisian public health community were members of the Health Council at one time or another, the roster including Parent-Duchâtelet, Esquirol, Pariset, Hallé, Jean D'Arcet, J. B. Huzard father and son, Charles Louis Cadet de Gassicourt, Adolfe Trébuchet, Villermé, and numerous others. The council's task was "to investigate various public health problems and requests for industrial authorizations, prepare reports on them, and then submit these reports to the prefect of police along with recommendations as to how the problems might be remedied."[30] Industrial investigation required much the greatest effort. The decree of 15 October 1810 ordered industries to be classified according to the hazard they were believed to present to the surrounding community. Each new establishment required official authorization, and this was based largely upon the findings of the council's investigators. Literally hundreds of requests were considered each year, and except for exceptionally hazardous operations, most applications appear to have been approved. The council's attention was also directed to many public health matters other than industrial authorization. The council was, moreover, particularly active in preparing the capital for the anticipated outbreak of epidemic cholera in 1832, devising a program for cleansing the city and providing medical aid that proved necessary when sanitary measures failed to halt the advance of the disease.

28. This work unfortunately was published only in fragments: Villermé, "Sur la population: Sommaire," *Journal des cours publics de la ville de Paris* 1 (1828): 189–90; "Population-Hygiène: Première Leçon," ibid. 2 (1829): 38–57; "Population-Hygiéne: II," ibid., pp. 24–27; "Population-Hygiène: III," ibid., pp. 125–28. The "première leçon" was also issued as a separate pamphlet (19 pp., 1829).

29. Essential are A. F. La Berge, "The Paris Health Council, 1802–1848," *Bulletin of the History of Medicine* 49 (1975): 339–52; D. B. Weiner, "Public Health under Napoleon: the Conseil de salubrité de Paris, 1802–1815," *Clio medica* 9 (1974): 271–84.

30. La Berge, "Paris Health Council," p. 343.

The Paris Health Council served as a model for comparable entities in major cities across France. Of equal if not greater importance was the fact that the Paris Council officially sponsored continuing investigation of all aspects of the urban scene. The Health Council members had, as it were, all Paris for their laboratory. Their inquiries and the widespread announcement of their findings and conclusions—vigorous publicity was an essential element in the council's activities—conveyed to the broader public an ever greater awareness of the sanitary shortcomings of the metropolis. Within the medical community the activity of council members served as a constant reminder of the social and economic dimensions of disease and death and provided repeated opportunity for further increasing knowledge of these connections. It was, lastly, principally members of the Health Council (Parent-Duchâtelet, D'Arcet, Esquirol, C.C.H. Marc, and Villermé) who joined together to create the *Annales d'hygiène publique et de médecine légale*, long the world's foremost public health publication and the enduring monument of the entire French public health movement.[31]

The central government, too, was active in hygiene. The national interest, however, was expressed in traditional terms and was countered by fierce and growing professional demands. The state's sanitary responsibility was essentially that of protecting the nation's frontiers against invasion by infectious disease; local action was left to local authorities. State agents acted upon contagionist assumptions and used quarantine and the sanitary cordon as their principal weapons. After 1820 the contagionist doctrine was heavily attacked by the combined forces of anticontagionist physicians, commercial opponents of quarantine, and liberal critics of the supposedly oppressive Bourbon regime. Throughout these conflicts, however, state machinery for sanitary surveillance and control of the frontiers continued in effect, even expanding in extent if not effectiveness during the Spanish conflict of the early 1820s.

The state dispatched physicians to observe foreign epidemics and also maintained a central sanitary commission.[32] State action was confused and much contested during the yellow fever scares of 1819 and 1821, years of epidemic outbreaks in Cádiz and Barcelona. It was far more coherent when dealing with the growing threat of cholera. Observers were then sent abroad, and close sanitary control of the frontiers was enforced. But cholera, of course, marched past both observer and border officer. Once in

    31. François Leuret, in A.J.B. Parent-Duchâtelet, *Hygiène publique; ou, Mémoires sur les questions les plus importantes de l'hygiène appliquée aux professions et aux travaux d'utilité publique*, 2 vols. (Paris: J. B. Baillière, 1836), 1:xiv.
    32. See esp. G. D. Sussman, "From Yellow Fever to Cholera: A Study of French Government Policy, Medical Professionalism, and Popular Movements in the Epidemic Crises of the Restoration and the July Monarchy" (Ph.D. diss., Yale University, 1971).

France it became fundamentally a local problem and was dealt with as such. In Paris responsibility for the prevention of cholera and the care of its victims fell to the city's Health Council.

Throughout the period 1815–48 there surfaced frequent opposition between functionaries of the national government and spokesmen for the medical profession. This was due in part to rival views of the nature of communicable disease and thus of the measures deemed most suited for control of epidemics. It was also due to clear-cut political differences dividing some (but by no means all) physicians and the restored monarchy. Many physicians shared the new liberal sentiment rising in opposition to the Bourbons, and later, when an Orleanist king occupied the throne, other physicians were active in the radical opposition to this the apparent apotheosis of the liberal state. Yet, while always subject to the doctrinal conflicts of the times, the state sanitary machinery remained largely in place. Quarantine and cordons were never without their advocates, however reduced the influence of the latter at times might become. The central government was thus also engaged in the great hygienic movement of the period, but its goal was essentially that of previous years—to keep disease from entering the nation—and its methods were no less traditional. Local authorities, especially those in the larger towns, were left to cope with the problems presented by epidemic disease once it had arrived—and no less with that new and vast host of problems ranging from destitution and famine to filth and endemic disease that had become a continuing and prominent feature of urban life.

The endeavors of the Paris hygienists showed many parallels with thematic developments in contemporary clinical medicine and pathology. As Paris medicine, under the influence of Bichat and Corvisart, moved away from reliance upon disease symptoms alone and sought out a more secure basis for diagnosis in pathological changes in the human body itself, so public health investigation began to shift from a mere description of phenomena to the pursuit of the underlying relations, or supposed causes, of those phenomena. No longer content with what was immediately apparent, the hygienist began to create a social pathology, one which sought palpable evidences of social dysfunction and which at first was expressed principally in the language of economics. It was concluded, moreover, that social disruption is not something radically new or utterly different, an external agent which, coming from without, caused one or another of society's ills. The upset was, as French pathologists were coming to insist, within the organism itself, be this the living body or society at large. Dysfunction was due to aberrations in the very structure and nature of the body or of society. These disturbances might perhaps be stimulated by external causes but could only be understood in their own terms. These terms, in turn, could be known only by direct and ever more probing investigation of the inner nature of the body and of society. Public health investigation consequently was the study of society as a single phenomenon that exhibited as part of its essential character a host of secondary, often contradictory, and occasionally pathological manifestations. The hygienist, like the physician, preferred to find the organism in a state of health but more commonly met it in a condition of distress or advanced dilapidation. The latter, of course, presented the principal object of concern to each.

The analogy between Paris medicine and Paris hygiene may be pressed even further. Certain therapists, notably Broussais, pursued an active therapeutic course, acting on the implicit assumption that sound medical theory (which Broussais and his numerous followers believed they had established) in itself dictated the needed therapeutic measures. In Broussais's case, these measures were bold and involved massive intervention in the physiological affairs of the human body.[33] Other physicians either followed a similar but much more moderate course of treatment or, by 1830, began to impune the very bases of Broussais's heroic therapy. These latter physicians simply reasserted the long-standing and, even in Broussais's day, strong French allegiance to expectant therapy, to placing medical confidence less in the physician's weapons than in the healing power of nature, whose course the truly sound physician would best know how to encourage.

Students of society recognized similar therapeutic options. Some, discontented not only by contemporary social problems but also by the conviction that nature heals nothing or does so too slowly to be meaningful, sought a rapid and thorough solution by means of complete social reorganization, even revolution. Others—and to this camp most hygienists belonged—recognized the perils that modern industrial society had created but were persuaded that such problems were inherent in the process of growth. What was called for was not rapid and massive intervention but, instead, a clear eye and much patience. Nature, if properly guided and, above all, not hindered by man, would cure the very problems that had arisen as a consequence of economic progress. At most, one or a few specific social or economic reforms were in order—and some held that even this modest intervention was probably excessive. The hygienists' position was marked by continuing tension. None knew better than they the nature and probable sources of human suffering in a rapidly urbanizing and industrializing society. But their remedies for these problems almost

33. E. H. Ackerknecht, "Broussais, or, A Forgotten Medical Revolution," *Bulletin of the History of Medicine* 27 (1953): 320–43.

always stopped short of requiring major social change. The people's interest was not alone at stake; the needs of commerce and industry, too, had to be determined and respected. While the community of physicians battled over rival therapies, often enough retreating to a sceptical or even nihilistic position, hygienists generally gave faith to the inviolate laws of nature and only with greatest caution and much reluctance accepted modification of the social organism, its structures and functions.[34]

For what reason or reasons was there so great an efflorescence of public health interest and activity in France and above all Paris during the period 1815–48? Erwin Ackerknecht has submitted several answers to this question.[35] Particular emphasis must be placed upon the military experience of the medical profession during the quarter century of war that separated the Restoration from the Old Regime. Military surgeons were accustomed to investigation and action that involved large numbers of persons and were habituated to the practice of preparing comprehensive reports upon their experience. Industrialization, moreover, was the cause or at least the concomitant of the greatest part of the popular destitution, sickness, and death that the hygienists examined. It is possible, and in many areas of the nation quite probable, that rural misery was objectively greater than that in the city. Hygienists, however, largely ignored the country, attending instead to the problems of what appeared to be an altogether new and truly dangerous social phenomenon, the industrial town and city. Ackerknecht has also pointed out that therapeutic scepticism and nihilism necessarily diverted attention to the possibility of anticipating, even preventing, the outbreak of disease. Personal hygiene, of course, had always had this goal as one of its paramount objectives; in France after 1800 a self-conscious effort was made to expand this goal to embrace not only the individual but society itself.

Ackerknecht emphasizes that this systematic and sustained concern for public hygiene emerged in a nation which at that time was more advanced than any other in the articulation of social theory. This was the age of Henri de Saint-Simon, Auguste Comte, P.J.B. Buchez, Charles Fourier, and, somewhat later, Karl Marx. The social phenomenon as such was very much before the public mind, and it began to receive in these years what authors and contemporaries together believed to be truly scientific treatment. Moreover, much but certainly not all of the new philosophy had been stimulated by and was particularly concerned to remedy the all-too-evident disharmony and lack of direction that informed French society.

34. E. H. Ackerknecht, *Therapeutics from the Primitives to the Twentieth Century* (New York: Hafner, 1973), pp. 103–8.

35. Ackerknecht, "Hygiene in France," p. 144.

Many hygienists were deeply involved in these intellectual developments, but only a very few, notably Buchez and François Vincent Raspail, subscribed to the nascent socialist implications of emerging social philosophy. Political economy, the programmatic instrument of the liberal improvers, also offered a coherent and prescriptive view of society. It was this view, not the hopes of the socialists, that gave theoretical coherence to hygienic inquiry during the period 1815–48. Finally, the new hygienic literature, itself as much social and economic as medical in orientation, provided the philosopher his fund of concrete empirical information regarding the character and problems of contemporary society. Hygienic inquiry was an integral element in and not simply an offshoot of the awakening concern with and explicit theoretical consideration of social problems in the early nineteenth century.

Public Assistance

Before the Revolution relief of the sick and the aged and, in a much more uncertain manner, of the unemployed was provided by a diverse array of institutions and individuals. While these institutions and individuals pursued their task with great seriousness, their activities too often proved inadequate in the face of the overwhelming need. In difficult times, such as those experienced in the last decades of the eighteenth century, relief measures often failed entirely. Major segments of the population were reduced to their own resources, resources which too frequently were nil. Such problems were not only social in nature and origin but by 1789 had moved to the forefront of public concern. Poverty and mendicity and ensuing bodily suffering and deterioration commanded the sustained attention of the revolutionary assemblies and of the governments of the Directory and Consulate. Major inquiries were conducted, and comprehensive legislation was drafted and occasionally enacted. Prerevolutionary charitable institutions were first suppressed and new and presumably more appropriate institutions then projected. France, however, had not only to carry the burden of its poor and sick but also to guide the events of a revolution and conduct war on many fronts. Administrative personnel and procedures were often in disarray, finances were usually insufficient, and public priorities remained unsettled. It was not until 1801 that the revolutionary process of destruction and tentative reconstruction eventuated in the definitive organization of public institutions in Paris for relief and medical care. These institutions not only provide concrete evidence of the pervasive charitable concern of the period but provided the indispensable bases for the perfection and pursuit of the clinical ideal of Paris medicine.

The *cahiers de doléances* prepared before the election of the Estates-

General of 1789, soon to be transformed into the first revolutionary assembly (the National Assembly, or the *Constituante*), frequently remarked poverty, mendicity, and misery as among the most serious flaws of contemporary society. The authors of the *cahiers*, however, offered no consistent or well-considered solution to these age-old problems. The National Assembly addressed the matter directly, creating in February 1790 the Committee for the Extinction of Mendicity, the first in a succession of famed revolutionary committees dedicated to investigating destitution in all its forms and consequences and to creating new institutions capable of dealing efficaciously with the problems thus described.[36] In so acting the National Assembly paid respect to cardinal political principles of the early Revolution. Liberal members of the National Assembly agreed that society was first constituted and is maintained by a circle of mutual obligations binding upon all citizens. The social contract lay at the root of this notion, and its bearing upon the idea of social responsibility for poverty and ensuing sickness and suffering was profound. Obligations implied rights, and rights imposed obligations. In the view of the duc de La Rochefoucauld-Liancourt, leading spokesman for matters of public assistance before the National (1789–91) and Legislative (1791–92) assemblies, society will properly expect all of its members to engage in productive labor. Work was a value in its own right; its praise went hand in hand with condemnation of the idle and wasteful existence of the nobility and of the otherworldly and utterly useless life of members of the religious orders. But if all citizens were obliged to work in order to assure their subsistence, society had the responsibility of assuring that work was available to all capable of employment.

This audacious claim led directly to essential qualifications. La Rochefoucauld, himself an entrepreneur of no small ambition and accomplishment, realized that, in fact, not all persons were capable of working.[37] This recognition was shared by other members of the committees of the

36. A large literature deals with this subject; a review, from which I draw much of the following discussion, and references are provided by George Rosen, "Hospitals, Medical Care, and Social Policy in the French Revolution," in *From Medical Police to Social Medicine* (New York: Science History Publications, 1974), pp. 220–45. Older works have not been superseded, notably Camille Bloch, "L'assistance et l'état en France à la veille de la Révolution" (Thèse de l'Université, Paris, 1908); Michel Bouchet, *L'assistance publique en France pendant la Révolution* (Paris: Henri Jouve, 1908); and S. T. McCloy, *Government Assistance in Eighteenth-Century France* (Durham: Duke University Press, 1938). The central issue is brought into sharp focus by D. B. Weiner, "Le droit de l'homme à la santé: Une belle idée devant l'Assemblée Constituante, 1790–1791," *Clio medica* 5 (1970): 209–23.

37. See Ferdinand Dreyfus, *Un philanthrope d'autrefois: La Rochefoucauld-Liancourt, 1747–1827* (Paris: Plon-Nourrit, 1903).

National and Legislative assemblies and was, indeed, responsible for the comprehensive nature of the proposals that they presented for resolving the interconnected problems of poverty and sickness. The individual's obligation to work for his living and the state's right to demand such labor had no meaning for those who, for one reason or another, were unable to work. Such reasons had long been evident: acute but especially chronic disease, malnourishment, a crippled condition, extreme youth or age, and general infirmities of a varied nature, including mental deficiency. The revolutionary committees gave these matters close attention and realized that effective public assistance would require simultaneous action on several fronts. Most importantly, it was seen that care for the sick and infirm must be regarded as a matter distinct from finding employment or providing relief, should it be deemed advisable, for the able-bodied. Legislative provision of separate institutions and personnel for these disparate purposes was envisaged as early as 1790 but was realized only in 1801 with the formal separation of the *hôpitaux* from the *hospices* and the agency responsible for home relief. All were united under a single administrative entity. Yet each could henceforth exert greatest effort in the area of its primary concern and no longer be burdened by the conflicting demands of multiple responsibilities. The scale and new efficiencies of the Paris hospitals and other institutions of public assistance were made possible by this division of labor and specialization.

Under the Old Regime charitable assistance was generally provided by private individuals or ecclesiastical and municipal authorities. The reach of such charity was local, not national. Financial support was also limited, not only in amount but in its designated beneficiaries, priority going to the needy of the immediate locality. The entire system depended upon moral imperatives and upon the claims exerted by the church on the generosity of the faithful. The latter had, in the course of centuries, created numerous endowments, often of significant size, the income from which was to be used for relief of the sick and the poor. These ecclesiastical foundations, together with institutions supported by towns and the crown, provided the principal instruments for public relief in France and especially in Paris in 1789.

The Revolution, however, shattered these arrangements. Inflation, economic uncertainties, and the flight of many wealthy donors rapidly reduced private contributions for charitable purposes. Most seriously affected, however, were ecclesiastical foundations. Hospital property, being primarily land that yielded a sizeable and regular income, was at first excluded from the sale (beginning in 1790) of nationalized property.[38] The

38. Louis Paturier, *L'assistance à Paris sous l'Ancien Régime et pendant la Révolution:*

Convention, in desperate financial need, reversed this exemption and in July 1794 ordered the sale of the endowments of the Paris hospitals. The Convention also assumed public responsibility for the operating revenues of the hospitals. This promise remained, not unexpectedly, unfulfilled. Within two years the hospital system was nearing collapse, its income from remaining endowments now yielding about one-quarter of that available in 1790 and the state by no means making up the difference.[39]

It was the Directory that began the difficult task of reconstruction. The first step was to order a halt (7 October 1796) to further sale of hospital properties and to demand reassignment of all remaining revenues to their original purpose, namely, support of the charitable activities of the hospitals. Moreover, seeking always the possible and not the ideal, the Directory restored the civil status of the hospital and thus in effect not only recreated the situation of 1789 but denied one of the great aspirations and accomplishments of the Revolution, establishment of the legitimacy of the claim of the needy upon the state itself. In the last years of the century even the sick and the poor seemed once again to have no state right to public assistance.

And yet it was, again, the Directory that laid the foundations for a solution to the dilemma, a solution that the Consulate would then formulate and impose and that governed without significant change the administration and finance of the Parisian hospitals throughout the nineteenth century. When reestablishing civil control of the hospitals, the Directory saw fit to preserve one new and crucial aspect of administration, namely, a central office and unified financial control for the entire Parisian organization. Care of the sick and aid to the deserving poor, whether in a public institution or at home, became *de facto* the responsibility of a single, all-encompassing authority. Of greater importance, the Directory assigned definite and sufficient revenues to the hospital system. In 1797 a special tax on amusements in the capital was levied in favor of the hospitals; the following year a priority share of the municipal *octroi* (the toll on goods imported into Paris) was made available.[40]

These several piecemeal actions were finally reduced to order in 1801.

Etude sur diverses institutions dont la réunion a formé l'Administration générale de l'assistance publique à Paris (Thèse de l'Université, Paris, 1897), p. 211; Jean Imbert, *Le droit hospitalier de la Révolution et de l'Empire* (Paris: Sirey, 1954), pp. 67–255. A fundamental instrument for study of the multitudinous changes in the early history of these institutions is *Table alphabétique, chronologique et analytique des règlemens relatifs à l'Administration générale des hôpitaux, hospices, enfans-trouvés et secours de la ville de Paris* (Paris: Madame Huzard, 1815).

39. Paturier, "Assistance à Paris," p. 239.
40. Ibid., pp. 239–40.

Three acts of that year created the Conseil général des hospices de la Seine. The council was placed under the presidency of the prefect of the department of the Seine and included among its members his principal administrative rival, the prefect of police. Eleven additional members were appointed. The interests of these members inclined predominantly towards the related problems of relief of poverty and maintenance of social order. Explicitly medical orientation was given the council only by Michel Augustin Thouret, dean of the Paris school of medicine, although La Rochefoucauld and the agronomist Antoine Augustin Parmentier, both active members, had long been concerned with such matters. The council thus represented above all *bienfaisance*, comprehensive concern for the many and varied needs of public welfare, and not the special desiderata of the medical profession.

The latter, however, were not overlooked. One of the council's first steps was to survey the several institutions for which it was henceforth responsible, a survey that provided grounds for assigning specific tasks to each institution. The classification then effected provided the basis for all subsequent institutional support for medical care and public relief in the capital. "The organization [established] in *an* IX [1801] is," Louis Paturier has stated, "the starting point for the course followed by the *Assistance publique* of Paris," the foremost social agency for the alleviation of poverty and sickness in nineteenth-century France.[41] A fundamental distinction was established by the council. The term *hospice* was henceforth reserved for the exclusive designation of institutions devoted to long-term care of the aged and the incurable, to orphans of either sex, and to maternity care. There were in 1801 eight such institutions, of which the Bicêtre and the Salpêtrière, both set aside principally for the care of the aged infirm, were the most important. Ten hospitals fell under the council's jurisdiction, *hôpital* now indicating an institution providing aid solely to those judged to suffer from an acute and presumably curable illness. It was in the wards and postmortem rooms of these hospitals that the basic studies of the Paris clinical school were pursued. Foremost among them were the Charité and Hôtel-Dieu, each providing general care and devoted especially to the so-called contagious diseases; the Pitié was added to this group in 1809. There were also specialized hospitals concerned with venereal diseases, skin disorders, and sick children.

Admission to these hospices and hôpitaux was determined by a central bureau of admission. Physicians in this office were chosen by competition and could expect a favored future in the Paris hospitals. Their decisions

41. Ibid., p. 248.

were crucial to the operation of the entire organism, for the diagnosis of the condition of each applicant for admission determined the hospice or hôpital that the patient would enter. Except for emergencies, where direct entrance to certain hospitals could be made, public medical care in Paris was rigorously centralized. Control was thereby effected from the moment of first patient or inmate contact. Thus was avoided the lamentable irrationality, caprice, and inefficiency held to have characterized public assistance under the Old Regime.

The council also supervised relief outside the walls of hôpital or hospice. Its twelve *bureaux de charité* made available in each *arrondissement* of the capital gratuitous medical advice, drugs, food, and clothing to those among the deserving poor whose condition or desires precluded their entering hospice or hôpital. This program of home relief was designated especially to aid widows with large families and the indigent aged without serious infirmities. The council also had responsibility for other indispensable operational entities, ranging from a central pharmacy and bakery, each serving all the hospitable institutions of Paris, to the administrative staff that assured the maintenance of building, oversaw the determination and support of medical and nursing appointments, and provided overall financial surveillance.

The fortunate culmination of a decade of effort marked by turmoil and contested ambitions, the Conseil général des hospices represented formal assertion by public authority of responsibility for the care of the aged and the indigent sick. The fundamental mission of the council was relief—symptomatic alleviation of the desperate problems facing the poor whose years or bodily affliction precluded their gaining a subsistence. The able-bodied unemployed had no claim on such assistance; no provision was made for them in the legislation of 1801. Almost certainly the council's programs did not bring relief to all who were entitled to it. Yet, in the judgment of foreign observers, the lot of the poor in France was clearly better than that of the poor elsewhere on the Continent. The New York physician F. C. Stewart, whose knowledge of French medicine and surgery was encyclopedic, commented that

> in no country of Europe, probably, is there more poverty than in France, and yet, owing to the precautions taken, and the benevolent care afforded by the Government, the utter destitution and squalid misery which are so common in some other European states, are rarely met with in that country. That there are thousands of individuals amongst the lower orders of French subjects, who experience all the privations of want and destitution, I do not pretend to deny; but, *as a class*, they

are far better off, and more prosperous, than persons of the same caste in many other parts of the old world.[42]

However the accomplishment of the institutions directed by the council be objectively judged, probably the most striking fact regarding these institutions is simply that of their existence. They testify to the persistence of the conservative ideals of the early Revolution, being the realization of the good will and reformist intentions of liberal members of the National and Legislative assemblies. They were not, and were not intended to be, a radical solution to the problem of poverty. Their target was what was deemed to be the truly needy, the deserving poor. The able-bodied could be expected to take care of themselves. Since restraints on trade and on the labor market were removed in 1791, it was believed that opportunities were created for all who sought employment to find it. The worker fit for labor had no place in the *hospices*.

The philosopher-physician Cabanis, whose views so deeply influenced the development of French medical thought and institutions, had insisted that the critical issue was that the poor did indeed exist and that they were "in general the creation of social institutions." This was, however, simply the unfortunate consequence of bad laws and poor administration. His charge to the new assembly in the winter of 1789–90 was therefore to reform public practice, keeping clearly in mind that it is the sick poor above all who require and deserve public care: "He who in health is already needy is all the more so when ill. It is thus an act of humanity, of justice, to assure that he is cared for and cured."[43] The hôpitaux, hospices, and bureaux de charité of Paris responded to this need. They were the creation of public authorities and provided strong precedent for continued and comprehensive state intervention into often the most intimate of human affairs. Being so closely tied to a gratuitous easing of the condition of the working class, however, they inevitably evoked unease in the minds of moralists addicted to intransigent economic liberalism. The matter required close attention and careful definition. In particular, assurance was needed that public services would not be made freely available to those who were capable of working—that is, of supporting themselves without state aid. Public support of the indigent sick was proper and necessary; society and common humanity demanded it. But the essential guideline was always to be individual responsibility; the state must encourage no

42. F. C. Stewart, *Eminent French Surgeons, with a Historical and Statistical Account of the Hospitals of Paris* (Buffalo: A. Burke, n.d.), p. xiii.

43. P.J.G. Cabanis, *Observations sur les hôpitaux*, in *Oeuvres philosophiques de Cabanis*, ed. C. Lehec and J. Cazeneuve, 2 vols. (Paris: P.U.F., 1956), 1:6.

one to escape the necessity of labor. Again, the able-bodied were cast to their fate.

Contemporary private charity shared these stern sentiments. Charitable organizations were numerous and active during the Restoration. Many were closely associated with crown or church or both, while others represented a continuation of the humanitarian concerns of the Enlightenment. A common theme in these societies was the encouragement of individual self-help. Workers in many parts of France had already made efforts to create local mutual aid societies *(sociétés de secours mutuels)*. These societies were usually organized by trade and were intended to provide family assistance at death and in times of need and also to assure limited sick benefits. Their treasuries on occasion provided resources for a strike fund, a gesture that struck terror into the hearts of statesman and entrepreneur alike and elicited quick suppression of the offending society. The Société philanthropique, the favored agency of well-intentioned *notables*, undertook to encourage these mutual aid societies but with the aim of exercising severe control upon them.[44] By providing central guidance and technical assistance the Société philanthropique furthered individual initiative and assured both employers and state authorities that the mutual aid societies would not evolve into political bodies representing the workers' interests. No philanthropist was more deeply concerned with these matters than Villermé's initial patron, the duc de La Rochefoucauld-Liancourt. It was the latter, moreover, who played a decisive role in the Société royale des prisons. This society enjoyed official patronage and was perhaps the most visible and active of major charitable efforts under the Restoration. Villermé, a member of the society, executed his first major inquiry under its auspices.

During the 1820s concern for these several problems also emerged in the Roman Catholic community. The church itself remained extremely conservative, merging its interests dangerously with those of the Bourbons and generally closing its eyes to any prospect of major social reform. Individuals, however, were less blind to the unhappy consequences of urbanization and gradual industrialization. To Roman Catholic observers as to others, the critical problem was perceived to be the suffering of those who could not live by their work alone.[45] Employment might be erratic,

---

44. See Octave Festy, "La Société philanthropique de Paris et les sociétés de secours mutuels," *Revue d'histoire moderne et contemporaine* 16 (1911): 170–96, and A. M. Péan de St.-Gilles, *La maison philanthropique de Paris: Histoire de cent dix ans* (Paris: Lemerre, 1892).

45. See J. B. Duroselle, *Les débuts du catholicisme social en France (1822–1870)* (Paris: P.U.F., 1951).

wages low, and public assistance nonexistent: what was to be done? Self-help was encouraged; charitable organizations were established (Société de Saint Joseph, 1822; Société de Saint Vincent de Paul, 1833); inquiry and commentary began. By 1830, however, a new note was being heard. Buchez, Félicité de Lammenais, Charles de Coux, and others emphasized that the source of the problem lay in a faulty distribution of wealth. Their remedies for the problem remained, however, no less disparate than those ventured by non-Catholic observers. Some stressed individual charitable acts, others demanded organized charity, and yet others demanded social and economic reform, a truly social Catholicism.

Only a few years later socialism began to attract vocal adherents. To moderate Roman Catholics and no less to almost the full range of the economists the socialist solution to the heart of the social problem—the dismal lot of the unemployed and underemployed, the absence of public provisions for their assistance, and the frequent inadequacy of the wages of those who did find work—was altogether too radical. Certain measured reforms might be in order but the restructuring of society and its economic activity was simply out of the question. The liberal truly believed in liberty, and the charitable liberal saw it to be his task to encourage all persons to exploit their capabilities to fullest advantage. This encouragement usually verged on fierce insistence. The worker, lacking both discipline and initiative, must be bent to the needs of the new society, and for this to be done it was essential that he learn the hard lesson of self-sufficiency. Genuine charity for such persons would best be devoted to furthering the development of their own powers of support. Measures for such beneficence were the hallmark of the times. Included amongst them must be sociomedical investigation, for sound knowledge of society seemed to investigators of the 1820s and 1830s the one prerequisite to intelligent and gradual reform. Little did Villermé at first appreciate the conflict between the deplorable social conditions so precisely documented by his inquiries and the impotence of the measures offered by the economists for their alleviation.

Sociomedical investigation as exemplified by the career of Louis René Villermé represented a response to a diverse set of challenges. The French nation was changing and, in certain areas, changing rapidly. Demographic transformation accompanied by urbanization and industrialization was in the process of creating utterly new social problems in many localities and of greatly exacerbating long-standing difficulties in others, notably Paris. Traditional charitable action proved inadequate to deal with the new needs of the nation, and by design the new organization of medical and domiciliary relief that emerged from the revolutionary era could not ease the lot of able-bodied men and women who on their own were incapable of finding or keeping regular employment. Widespread perception of these ills was due in no small part to the efforts of sociomedical inquiry, yet that inquiry, conducted in accordance with the scientific principles of political economy, appeared to some to make the problem only more desperate because probably irremediable.

Chapter 2

Population and Industry

I lose my way, I am lost in this vast city; I no longer even recognize the new quarters. The market gardens fall back and give way to buildings. Today we see Chaillot, Passy, [and] Auteuil closely linked to the capital. Soon Sèvres will also join Paris and, if one looks ahead a century, from Versailles to Saint-Denis, from Picpus to Vincennes, there will stand a city altogether Chinese in character.

Louis-Sébastien Mercier, 1782

To statesmen and social observers in early modern Europe population constituted the indispensable foundation of wealth and national power. By this measure France throughout the eighteenth century remained the richest and most powerful of European states. Notoriously a nation of peasants, France in 1789 possessed an estimated rural population of 21 million hard-working and, for the most part, poorly rewarded individuals. Another 4 to 6 million Frenchmen occupied small market towns, military, commercial, and administrative centers and the nation's unique metropolis, Paris. This basic structure persisted well into the nineteenth century.

The 1840s, however, brought clear signs of change. Just as the revolution of 1848 marked a hardening of class divisions and social perceptions in France, so the census of 1846 disclosed that a century and a half of steady population increase had come to an end. The multiple disasters of the later years of the reign of Louis XIV had been followed by an irregular but nonetheless definite and long-sustained period of growth in population. After 1846, however, the French population growth rate dropped sharply, and after 1880 the nation faced a threat of genuine depopulation.

Population figures from the Old Regime and, indeed, until the 1850s are generally to be received with great caution. Censuses of both France and Paris were attempted, but procedures for the collection of relevant data and standards for the evaluation and presentation of this data re-

EPIGRAPH: Louis-Sébastien Mercier, *Tableau de Paris*, 12 vols. (Amsterdam, 1783), 1:37–38.

mained unsystematized until well into the nineteenth century. Moreover, global population was often estimated (from birth or death rates) and not enumerated by name, the only truly secure guide to population. An informed estimate of 1697–1700 gave the population of France as 19 million (with a margin of error of about 10 percent).[1] On the eve of the Revolution the population had increased, contemporary evaluations suggest, to 25–27 million. The census of 1821 reported significant growth (population, 30,462,000) and that of 1846 still further increase (population, 35,402,000).[2] Even given the imprecision of many of these figures, the overall trend of population is nonetheless clear. Population growth during the eighteenth century was at the barest minimum 20 percent and may have been as high as 40 percent. Recovery immediately after the losses of the Imperial wars was apparently rapid. Growth between the census of 1821 and that of 1846, however, was only 16 percent. The population of France continued its growth, making the period 1750–1850 a "demographic whole," but the rate of growth was demonstrably slowing.[3] Increasingly France was becoming a smaller element in the Europe that it had dominated in 1700.

Parisian medical investigators such as Louis René Villermé and Jean Baptiste Parent-Duchâtelet were less concerned (if in fact they paid the subject the least heed) with the relative standing of France on the international scene than with the character and development of the population within the nation's frontiers. It cannot be overemphasized that their observations were made during a period of significant social and demographic change. This period, approximately 1815–48, was marked by a declining birth rate, the central factor in the contemporary drop in the population growth rate, and by the initiation of a major redistribution of the French population, signaled by the appearance of town and city as the principal foci for growth. The period, it should be stressed, merely constitutes a beginning. Rural depopulation on a massive scale came very late to France. Not until 1931 was more than 50 percent of the French population defined as urban; that proportion had been reached in Britain by 1851.[4]

Given a slowing of growth of the total population, the growth of the

1. Pierre Goubert, "La force du nombre," in *Histoire économique et sociale de la France*, vol. 2, *Des derniers temps de l'âge seigneurial aux préludes de l'âge industriel (1660–1789)*, ed. Fernand Braudel and Ernest Labrousse (Paris: P.U.F., 1970), pp. 12–13.

2. André Armengaud, *La population française au XIXe siècle* (Paris: P.U.F., 1971), p. 9.

3. Charles H. Pouthas, *La population française pendant la première moitié du XIXe siècle*, I.N.E.D., Travaux et documents, cahier no. 25 (Paris: P.U.F., 1956), p. 195.

4. André Armengaud, "Population in Europe, 1700–1914," in *The Fontana Economic History of Europe: The Industrial Revolution*, ed. Carlo Cipolla (London: Collins, 1975), p. 35.

French cities, a striking social phenomenon of the period, could proceed only at the expense of the more fertile countryside. Paris grew stupendously, roughly doubling in population between 1801 and 1846. Cities with traditional or mixed economic activity, such as Lyons, Rouen, and Toulon, also increased in size. Predominantly industrial towns—for example, Roubaix, St. Etienne, and Mulhouse—manifested high rates of growth. Yet none of these cities and towns, Paris excepted, exhibited the sheer size attained by contemporary British industrial cities such as Manchester, Birmingham, and Glasgow. In 1850 ten British cities, including London, numbered over 100,000 inhabitants each; in France, only Marseilles, Lyons, and Paris had attained such a population, and these cities were by no means centers of exclusively industrial enterprise.[5] Size alone, however, offered no insurance against the anxieties and misery incumbent upon rapid urbanization and industrialization; sociomedical observation proved this elementary yet fundamental point over and again.

The Rural Population and the Urban Phenomenon

In 1846 the vast preponderance of the French population (75 percent) lived on the land or in a village or *bourg* with a population of less than 2,000. Throughout the eighteenth century it had been a fertile population. The marriage rate was high and so was that for births. Now, unlike earlier periods, the high birth rate, a major feature of country life, led to a significant increase in population. There is general agreement that this growth was in large part due to a decline in the death rate, whose toll increasingly failed to act as a check on the steady and high fertility of the nation. The reasons for this decline in the death rate, however, are subject to far less agreement. Certainly the long period of relative peace beginning in 1715 and interrupted only by the mass destruction of young men during the Revolutionary and Imperial wars increased survival of members essential to a fertile society. Broad-ranging pestilence also declined, although the incidence of infectious disease remained very high and was consistently deadly, particularly in the not uncommon times of dearth and economic disruption. But real famine became increasingly rare in France. The appalling winter, and death, of 1709/10 was not repeated, not even after the critical harvest failures of 1787–88 and 1845–46.[6]

From 1800 onwards the death rate continued its moderate decline. The annual number of deaths remained relatively constant—about 800,000 per

---

5. Ibid., p. 33.
6. See Goubert, "La force du nombre," pp. 58–66; Thomas McKeown, *The Modern Rise of Population* (New York: Academic Press, 1976).

year save for periods of epidemic outbreak, dearth, or social and economic disorder, during which previous gains were often severely reduced. The annual number of births also remained reasonably constant (between approximately 950,000 and 975,000 per year), but began a slow decline towards 1830. The net effect of these trends was growth but at an ever-decreasing pace. Variations by annual average within five-year periods (the unit of the census) before 1850 were great, the natural movement of the population ranging from a maximum of 207,000 (1821–25) to a minimum of 119,000 (1831–35).[7] An ominous sign of the future became evident in 1854 and again in 1856 when, for the first time in the century, deaths exceeded births.[8]

The effects of this trend must not be anticipated. The general fact was that mortality remained in deficit until after 1850, natality pursuing it on a downward course but at a greater rate. As a consequence of these movements the population continued its increase and this not least in the country, the proverbial generator of children. It was during the 1840s that the rural population of France weighed most heavily upon the land. "Without doubt," André Armengaud concluded, "never in its long history had the French countryside been so densely populated as at the end of the July Monarchy."[9] Here, of course, is the critical fact behind internal migration and the beginnings of population concentration within the urban setting.

Rural growth rates were unevenly distributed across France.[10] Areas of established and continuing economic activity and relative ease, such as rural Normandy and the Garonne region, grew slowly. Regions in full development, where agricultural opportunities were or seemed abundant, grew more rapidly; such was the case for the Rhône Valley and for the central departments on and below the Loire from the Vienne to the Nièvre. Signs were already present that within regions containing an urban center of industrial activity, differential growth rates would prevail. Between 1801 and 1846 the population of the manufacturing department of the Nord increased 51 percent; the adjoining agricultural departments (Pas-de-Calais and Somme) grew only 31 percent. Within the Nord, a few industrial *arrondissements*, notably Lille, accounted for the preponderance of the recorded growth.

Before the Revolution unemployment and underemployment as well as vagabondage and widespread mendicity were acute rural problems. The general economic recovery and expansion after 1815 gave greater opportunity to these masses but only during years of prosperity. By the 1840s

7. Armengaud, *Population française*, p. 11, table 1.
8. Ibid., pp. 44–45.
9. Ibid., p. 25.
10. Regional variations are described by Pouthas, *Population française*, pp. 38–59.

the pressure of population on the land had become so severe that any climatic reverse or economic downturn had serious repercussions. Generally speaking, the survival of this increasing humanity was assured by two developments, both of long standing. On the one hand, surplus rural labor commonly migrated on a seasonal basis to regions of greater employment. Most often this meant the movement at harvest time of large numbers of young men to departments with more intensive agricultural exploitation. But seasonal movement to the city was also common, and as the century wore on, increasingly these migrants failed to return home, thus becoming permanent urban residents. On the other hand, rural employment was by no means confined to agriculture. In all regions of France small-scale manufacture of pottery, metal goods, articles using wood and leather, and other enterprises were common. Textiles were also widely produced. Spinners and weavers were found in most farm families, women and children contributing heavily to the task. Textile manufacture on the domestic system thus formed an intrinsic part of the rural economy and was doubtless responsible for significantly increasing the carrying capacity of the land.

Under the constitutional monarchy these well-established practices began to deteriorate, often rapidly and frequently with disastrous consequences. This proved a decisive event in the social history of France, just as a similar collapse of the domestic textile trades, joined with agricultural distress, marked critical turning points in the social changes ensuing upon industrialization in Britain, Germany, and elsewhere. A rural population heretofore sustained by combined exploitation of land and manufacture suddenly discovered one of its indispensable foundations being irrevocably brought to ruin.[11] By shifting and often destroying the bases upon which one might found a livelihood, such changes generated widespread and alarming rural misery. These evil conditions were exacerbated by a simultaneous increase in population. Peasants and artisans caught by this situation faced a fearful choice. They might remain in the country, still hoping to find there their fortune or at least to survive. Unfortunately, neither land nor sufficient employment was available in proportion to their numbers. The alternative was to seek a new life in town or city. This option proved compelling to many. Migration, the order of the day, accounted above all for the increase in population of the urban areas, be

11. See Robert Laurent, "Les mutations de la société rurale," in *Histoire économique et sociale de la France*, vol. 3, *L'avènement de l'ère industrielle*, ed. Fernand Braudel and Ernest Labrousse (Paris: P.U.F., 1976), pt. 2, pp. 739–67; Jean Vidalenc, *Le peuple des campagnes*, La société française de 1815 à 1848, I (Paris: Marcel Rivière, 1970), pp. 329–60; idem, *Le peuple des villes et des bourgs*, La société française de 1815 à 1848, II (Paris: Marcel Rivière, 1973), pp. 79–106.

these the smaller, predominantly industrial towns, the established regional centers of French life, or the incomparable enormity of Paris.

Movement to the city in nineteenth-century France was apparently a regular phenomenon. The overall urban population grew about 1 percent per year until mid-century; thereafter and until the 1880s the pace accelerated to approximately 1.75–2 percent annual growth. Even the crisis of 1846 did not disturb this development (except in Paris). Between 1811 and 1901 total urban population increased from 4,201,000 to 13,817,000, an increase of 300 percent; total population for France increased only 39 percent.[12] Further witness to the regularity of this process is the singular fact that until 1851 the pace of urban growth was closely paralleled by an increase in the number of towns qualifying for urban status (towns with a population of 3,000).[13] Obviously, the urbanization process in France occurred on a wide scale and tended initially to produce many cities of small size rather than a few of excessive proportions (Paris always excepted). The first phase of the concurrent processes of industrialization and urbanization thus produced in France a diverse array of small to middle-sized cities quite widely distributed across the face of the nation.

In 1851, as in 1801, the largest French cities were those with long-established and diverse social and economic functions. The rank order of the five largest cities (Paris, Marseilles, Lyons, Bordeaux, Rouen) remained unchanged over these years.[14] The next four cities (in rank order of 1851, Nantes, Toulouse, Lille, Strasbourg) also advanced together. Only one of the largest twenty-five cities in 1846 was truly a city founded upon massive industrialization. This was St. Etienne, whose manufacturing economy, based on coal, iron, and silk, had ancient origins but was vastly stimulated by railway construction and military supply in the late 1820s. St. Etienne in 1846 ranked fourteenth in size, its population having grown from 16,000 in 1801 to 50,000 in 1846.[15] The industrial city in France was thus a growing reality but it had not by 1850 assumed a preponderant national position.

Lille, whose name is synonymous with industrial France, in actuality acted as a regional center for urbanization. Its own growth was greatly below that of its immediate environs.[16] Lille was a military strong point of long standing and served also diverse commercial and administrative

12. Georges Dupeux, "La croissance urbaine en France au XIXᵉ siècle," *Revue d'histoire économique et sociale* 52 (1974): 180–83.

13. Ibid., p. 184, graph II.

14. Pouthas, *Population française*, p. 18, table 8.

15. Ibid., pp. 108–9.

16. Ibid., pp. 107–8.

functions. Its industrial vitality was already evident at the beginning of the period. Until 1831 both Lille and its department (Nord) grew rapidly. Thereafter, however, an important change occurred. The arrondissement containing Lille but excluding the city itself grew enormously. The department outside the arrondissement as well as the walled city of Lille exhibited only minor growth. Obviously, the zone of expansion had shifted and had come to focus on the environs of the city. It was, of course, these environs that after 1831 underwent explosive industrial development. The Lille *banlieue* contained two of the most expansive (yet still small) cities in all France—Tourcoing (with a population increase between 1801 and 1851 of 150 percent) and the great textile manufactory of Roubaix (with a population increase of 338 percent, the highest in France.)[17]

Such rates were not the product of a natural increase of the population. Birth rates in the Nord, for example, were high, but mortality was no less pronounced, especially in the urban areas. The city grew at the expense of the country (the Lille area drew upon both the surrounding department and nearby Belgium). Migration was the critical factor in large-scale urban growth. Unfortunately, internal migrations are exceedingly difficult to study. Not until later in the century (1861, 1891) did the French census record place of origin of new arrivals.[18] For any locality, therefore, as well as for the nation at large, the best that can be done is to establish the difference between population change as expected from natural increase, that is, the excess (or deficit) produced by total birth and death, and population as actually recorded. This difference can be attributed to immigration or emigration. From analysis of overall migrations of the French population Charles Pouthas concluded that until the 1850s net internal migration remained quite limited in extent, affecting perhaps only 1 percent of the population (later in the century that figure would rise to 20 percent).[19] Nonetheless, for those cities whose rates of expansion could not possibly be explained by their natural population increase, this small proportion of the nation's human wealth provided the substance of growth. There appears to have been, therefore, no nationwide emptying of the countryside before 1850. Population movement there was, real and widespread, but it was as yet limited in its impact. A quite small percentage of the truly vast rural population accounted for the steady but only occasionally spectacular urban growth of the period. It seems clear that the developing cities, especially those of industrial orientation, did not so much

17. But neither town exceeded 30,000 in population (ibid., p. 110).

18. Ibid., pp. 121–41.

19. Ibid., p. 141. Pouthas cautions, of course, against the possibility that in-migration was more or less balanced by out-migration. In such a case, net migration would be small but actual movement possibly very large.

Table 2.1. Population of the city of Paris, 1801–1851

1801	548,000
1817	714,000
1831	786,000
1841	936,000
1846	1,053,897
1851	1,053,261

SOURCE: Louis Chevalier, *Laboring Classes and Dangerous Classes in Paris during the First Half of the Nineteenth Century*, trans. Frank Jellinek (New York: Howard Fertig, 1973), p. 183.

attract immigrants as simply receive those who could find no future on the land. Rural hardship and lack of opportunity were in all probability the ultimate stimuli to the early-nineteenth-century beginnings of a population movement that reached mass scale only later. Nonetheless, urban growth in excess of that of the nation at large had made its first appearance, and nowhere was this more evident than in the changing scale of the capital itself.

Sociomedical investigators never tired of emphasizing the manifold singularities of Paris. Its level of commerce and scale and diversity of manufacture, its filth and noise, its crime and prostitution, were notorious. But these distinctive characteristics and numerous others were rightly recognized to be the product of a population without parallel in France.

The most striking fact regarding Paris in the early nineteenth century was its size, both in absolute terms and relative to France as a whole. The census of 1801, carefully taken, found 548,000 Parisians. The increase of the population of Paris in the following decades was spectacular, as the figures in Table 2.1 reveal.[20] Between 1801 and 1846, 506,000 persons had been added to the city's population, an increase of 92 percent in 45 years. Both the size of this population and its rate of change had been utterly transformed. The extraordinary conditions of 1848 and during the Second Republic caused an unprecedented halt in growth, even a small loss of population. But growth resumed rapidly after 1851: by 1911 the Parisian population had reached 2.8 million.

The Parisian birth rate was high, and after 1820, it stood consistently higher than that for France at large. The capital's death rate was also higher than that for the nation. The resulting natural rate of increase within the city, although not insignificant, could by no means account for the

20. These figures are taken from Louis Chevalier, *Laboring Classes and Dangerous Classes in Paris during the First Half of the Nineteenth Century*, trans. Frank Jellinek (New York: Howard Fertig, 1973), pp. 174–80, 183. The continuing demographic development of Paris is portrayed by Chevalier in *La formation de la population parisienne au XIXe siècle*, I.N.E.D., Travaux et Documents, cahier no. 10 (Paris: P.U.F., 1950).

enormous mass of new Parisians. Immigration thus provided the substance of Paris.[21] In net terms, between 1821 and 1846 an excess of births over deaths produced 78,000 new Parisians; immigration, however, yielded 263,000.

With a growth rate approximately three times that for France, Paris gradually absorbed an ever-greater proportion of the national population. But Paris, like metropolitan France, did not expand its geographical limits between 1815 and 1848. The city in 1815 was 34 km² in area. From rapid population growth and fixed urban limits arose an important demographic and social phenomenon of early-nineteenth-century Paris, namely, high and increasing population density. In 1801 this density stood at 15,900 persons/km²; it had reached 22,500/km² by 1831 and the enormous figure of 30,700/km² in 1846.[22] These, however, are global figures and obscure the varied experience of the different arrondissements and quarters of the capital. Until the 1850s the vast bulk of the Parisian population remained concentrated in the traditional core area of the city, that is, the islands in the Seine, the right bank from the Bastille to the Tuileries, and the central lower reaches of the left bank. Within this core, the old medieval city along the river, many of its ancient structural features not only still extant but in heavy daily use, presented the greatest concentration of population. In its quarters—Cité, Arcis, Marchés, Hôtel-de-Ville, Montorguel, Saint-Avoye—population density was already high in 1801, Arcis, the densest, holding at this time 125,000 persons/km².[23] Between 1801 and 1846 the tendency towards growth spread throughout the city. Population growth rates were highest in the large and relatively empty peripheral arrondissements and quarters. While these rates were remarkable in their own right, their very magnitude was largely a function of the low initial population. In the central quarters growth was less rapid but nonetheless real. As a consequence, the crowded center became ever more densely packed. Arcis in 1846 had reached the staggering density of 244,000 inhabitants/km².[24] Seven other central quarters had densities over 100,000/km². The population of Paris throughout the period remained concentrated within the *grands boulevards*. Space in this area was limited and, more importantly, was virtually filled by existing structures. The new population of the core simply had to find its place within a largely static urban framework.

The 1840s laid foundations for changing this situation. Circulation within the old city was seriously hindered by lack of thoroughfares. The

21. Pouthas, *Population française*, p. 173, table 21.
22. Ibid., pp. 160–62.
23. Ibid., p. 160.
24. Ibid., p. 162.

opening of the *grands boulevards* after 1815 scarcely improved movement within the center but did provide a new and wide focus for urban expansion. A critical decision made under the July Monarchy placed the several Parisian termini for the new railways at the outer margin of the city—that is, on the fringe of current development. Finally, the crisis of 1846 placed a definitive stop to continued population increase in the core.

Under the Second Empire a new Paris was created and much of the old either destroyed or modified beyond recognition.[25] While such developments may have relieved the pressures on the antiquated city core and, of course, served also to produce vast new areas whose squalor and misery measured up to earlier standards, the harsh consequences of urban overpopulation and underdevelopment perceived in the early nineteenth century were those presented especially by the ancient quarters along the Seine.

Recorded in vivid detail by Honoré de Balzac, Eugène Sue, and Victor Hugo, controlled with varying degrees of success by a large and sophisticated police apparatus, and patiently analyzed by both social and medical reformers, the new reality which was Paris provided a model, inescapable and alarming, for the unanticipated human consequences of those agricultural, industrial, and demographic changes that lay behind the formation of new, and the startling evolution of old, cities. Paris was vast, it was diverse, its toll of mankind seemed beyond both necessity and simple justice. The city, through its vital statistics, economic life, and public practices, was to become a laboratory, a center for social discovery if not yet social amelioration. The city thus gave the hygienists their great opportunity.

Early Industrialization

To the hygienist the principal concern was man in the mass. The hygienists dealt with populations and not individuals. Population is a relative term and one applicable to both large and small aggregations of men and women. The hygienist's reference, however, was unambiguous. Sociomedical investigation dealt with the hazards to health, life, and happiness posed by Paris and the emerging industrial towns. Those cities as well as many of the distinctive perils they presented were largely the product of novel economic endeavor.

Throughout the period of early industrialization (ca. 1800–1851) the

---

25. See D. H. Pinkney, *Napoleon III and the Rebuilding of Paris* (Princeton: Princeton University Press, 1958). Continuing transformation is recorded by Norma Evenson, *Paris: A Century of Change* (New Haven: Yale University Press, 1979).

underlying economic and social reality of French life—the predominance of agriculture—remained little changed. Agricultural interests had been well served by the Revolution and Empire. A major transfer of land had occurred, and more importantly, these holdings were now secured by property rights guaranteed by Constitution and Civil Code. Both large and small holders benefited from the high protective tarifs reintroduced by the Restoration. Despite a marked reluctance until the 1840s to introduce improved methods of exploitation, agricultural production slowly increased and rural prosperity ensued.

It was, nonetheless, an unstable prosperity.[26] Subsistence was not assured in all parts of France. Agricultural prices fluctuated, often widely, and rendered uncertain many aspects of the enterprise. Trade in foodstuffs was neither well organized nor placed on a national basis; genuine shortages still occurred. Means of communication were utterly inadequate. The numerous small holders at least had their land and could, in bad times, retain its product for themselves. Already, however, many such persons and, all the more, those inhabitants of the countryside who owned no land had become dependent on the additional income provided by the domestic system of manufacture. As this latter system was gradually undermined between 1815 and 1848 and was repeatedly shaken by the economic crises of the period, the traditional modest security of agricultural employment became increasingly precarious. Agricultural prosperity was thus a real but aggregate phenomenon. Large land owners and frugal or efficient small holders produced a surplus which, in a well-protected market, was sold at high prices. Those without property found employment when it was available, paid going prices for their necessities, and rarely possessed reserves with which to withstand a downturn in the economy.

The domestic system as developed by the textile trades was only one component, albeit an important component, in rural nonagricultural employment. Manufacture in France was characteristically dispersed.[27] It served a predominantly local market, and each region generally possessed a wide spectrum of producers of essential goods. Textile spinning and weaving were pursued in all parts of France; hundreds of forges, most of them small and employing few hands, were scattered in every corner of the realm. These and other essential undertakings were artisanal opera-

26. Henri Sée, *La vie économique de la France sous la monarchie censitaire 1815–1848)* (Paris: F. Alcan, 1927), pp. 44–47; Vidalenc, *Le peuple des campagnes*, pp. 350–69.

27. See Pierre Léon, "Les nouvelles élites" and "Morcellement et émergence du monde ouvrier," in Braudel and Labrousse, *Histoire économique et sociale de la France*, 2:601–49, 651–89.

tions. They rarely entailed the collection of a large number of workers in a single enterprise and were not, in general, highly capitalized.

This had been the nature of manufacture in France under the Old Regime, and it persisted in most sectors of the economy well into the nineteenth century. The value of the product of this *petite industrie* far outweighed that contributed by the developing *grande industrie*. Far more workers were employed in small shops than in large. Throughout the century the artisan remained the predominant force in the French economy. All the more striking, then, was the emergence, clearly visible by 1830, in selected sectors of the manufacturing economy of new forms of organization and an accelerating rate of development in these sectors. In this, the process of industrialization, leadership in France was taken by iron smelting and refining and by cotton finishing and spinning. Soon, however, the movement began to spread throughout the metal and textile industries and into the new chemical industries.

The iron industry modernized steadily after 1815. Smelting with coke and the use of blast furnace and the puddling process were well installed but by no means predominant by the 1830s. Pig-iron production rose from 174,000 metric tons in 1827 to over 500,000 tons in the mid-1840s. Between 1830 and 1850 coal production soared.[28] Just as French mining and metallurgy had adopted English production innovations, so the cotton industry in France sought to benefit by new machinery only available across the Channel. Even before the Revolution efforts had been made to introduce the new spinning machines and factory organization. Another and briefly successful attempt was made under the Empire. But definitive success came only after 1820. Between this date and 1845 the spinning industry was revolutionized, spinning by hand being almost eliminated. Despite difficulties in obtaining machines, particularly up-to-date machines, mechanical spinning by mid-century had spread from cotton to wool, linen, and silk. By that date mechanical weaving was making its appearance, and mechanized processes for printing and finishing were well installed. The demands of the textile industry proved a major stimulus to the development of an indigenous machine-tool and metal fabrication industry. The latter prospered no less from the belated start during the 1840s on a widespread rail network for France. Also closely associated with the textile industry was the emergence after 1800 of important chemical enterprises, often situated in leading textile regions but also in Paris.

28. N.J.G. Pounds and W. N. Parker, *Coal and Steel in Western Europe: The Influence of Resources and Techniques on Production* (London: Faber and Faber, 1957), p. 151 and p. 153, graph.

In those industries that adopted the machine as the primary basis of production and sought to exploit it and its unceasing improvements to fullest effect the results were striking indeed. Productivity increased dramatically. An average spindle in an Alsatian cotton mill in 1815 produced 4.5 kg of thread; by 1835 that production had risen to 10.6 kg and in 1845, to 15 kg. In 1806 each worker operated 20 spindles; in 1828 she controlled 45.[29] In the Alsatian cotton-printing industry annual production per worker increased 230 percent between 1827 and 1842. These increased yields were largely due, of course, to systematic exploitation of new machinery.

In the highly mechanized industries, notably cotton spinning and iron production, growth in productivity was directly translated into a steady yet dramatic decline in prices. The decline in the price of cotton goods between 1810 and 1845 has been estimated to have been 5.5 percent per annum; even woolen goods, whose production was less highly mechanized, witnessed a price decline of 1.3 percent.[30] The price of iron products was markedly lower in 1850 than it had been in 1820. Mechanization meant greater efficiency. It allowed the entrepreneur to reduce prices in hopes of expanding the scope of his business. In good times the overall profits from such undertakings were vast and were, naturally, retained by the *patronat*; the prospective benefit to the working class was employment, a cash income, and the ability to purchase goods heretofore inaccessible.[31] There was, to be sure, a startling disproportion between these respective rewards, a disproportion that lies at the root of the determination and concurrent perception of class differences. Medical investigators possessed an intimate acquaintance with these developments.

Consideration of only prices and profits, however, is inadequate, for the prospect of such great and rapid gain attracted emulation. The efficient manufacturer produced more goods for the same cost. To his product, which he found beneficial constantly to enlarge, was then added that of other manufacturers. For the most part the French market for textiles was an interior market. It was a market that was ill-organized except on the local level and one that coped poorly over a long span of years with the prodigious output of the new mills. Moreover, if cotton manufacture, and that of other textiles as they followed its example, promised satisfying profits it also posed great risks. Both *patron* and worker faced these risks,

29. Pierre Léon, "L'impulsion technique," in Braudel and Labrousse, *Histoire économique et sociale de la France*, 3, pt. 2:498–500.

30. Pierre Léon, "Le dynamisme industriel," ibid., pp. 598–99.

31. On profits, stated as a percentage return on equity, see Claude Fohlen, *L'industrie textile au temps du Second Empire* (Paris: Plon, 1956), p. 109.

the one knowingly, the other because without alternative. Economic crises repeatedly struck France, and each time grave consequences followed. Periods of depression were closely tied to crop failures (1817–19, 1846–49) or to international political and economic events (1826–32, 1837–42).[32] Agricultural decline was particularly serious, as it eroded or eliminated the buying power of the great mass of the nation and in effect closed the major market for what proved to be an excess of goods. Thus France, in common with other European nations in the early stages of industrialization, unwittingly found herself caught up in a skein of economic relations that tended to affect every member of the nation. Overproduction seemed to observers to be the greatest source of difficulty. To a society long accustomed to intermittent or continued shortages the notion that intense suffering can result from a surfeit of goods was surely bizarre. Yet such untoward events occurred frequently between 1815 and 1848, leading the prosperous entrepreneur to ruin and all too often reducing the discharged worker to misery and utter destitution.

Increased productivity was due not simply to exploitation of machines but to more effective organization of the entire production process in which they played so important a role. It was in cotton manufacture that the factory system first took form in France. Its major traits were nonetheless visible at an early date in the iron industry and perhaps also in chemicals. Capital, labor, raw materials, and machinery had all to be secured and organized in a manner both rational and consistent with the paramount goal, a high rate of return on investment. The central role in this process, providing initiative and subsequent direction, was played by the entrepreneur.[33]

Compared to the domestic system of production, the factory system was more energy- and capital-intensive. The individual productive unit suddenly increased in scale, expanding from the immediate family to assemblages of often hundreds of workers, an increase enjoined by mechanization and in itself a major factor in demanding the discipline and unceasing application characteristic of the factory system. From the outset observers, and not least among them medical investigators, recognized that whatever the virtues or faults of the new economic organization might be, the factory was effecting a profound social transformation and one not at all bene-

32. See François Crouzet, "An Annual Index of French Industrial Production in the Nineteenth Century," in *Essays in French Economic History*, ed. R. E. Cameron (Homewood, Ill.: American Economic Association, R. D. Irwin, 1970), pp. 276–78.

33. David Landes, "Religion and Enterprise: The Case of the French Textile Industry," in *Enterprise and Entrepreneurs in Nineteenth- and Twentieth-Century France*, ed. Edward C. Carter II et al. (Baltimore: Johns Hopkins University Press, 1976), pp. 41–86.

ficial to the physical and moral well-being of those employed therein. The factory caused unprecedented concentration of labor, at first in the workplace and then very quickly in place of residence. Housing virtually everywhere was inadequate to the task. The absolute size of such agglomerations and, worse yet, their rate of growth offered one of the most alarming visions of the age. To compound these problems of quantity, or population density, came the related problem of quality, for the mere fact that one possessed shelter became in itself an almost insignificant datum. The nature, maintenance, cleanliness, and cost of such shelter moved to the center of attention and has remained there throughout the subsequent history of industrial cities. The rapidity and scale with which the factory system implanted itself in certain areas of France in the early nineteenth century served to overwhelm the usually inadequate urban resources of the period. Large and dense populations were quickly created, these living under the most insalubrious circumstances. Villermé's *Tableau de l'état physique et moral des ouvriers* responds above all to the special problems of these populations concentrated in an industrial setting.

Most commentators remark that the period 1815–48 constituted the era of industrial beginnings in France; frenzied expansion and maturity followed in the boom years of the Second Empire.[34] Toward 1820 the most dynamic industries (cotton and iron) belonged to broader sectors that commanded approximately 21 percent of the total annual industrial and artisanal product; their share had mounted to 26 percent by 1840.[35] These figures embrace not only the emergent industrial component of cotton and iron but also the great artisanal effort in these areas. As other sectors of the economy either remained wholly artisanal or had taken only small steps toward industrialization, it is clear that the industrial phenomenon in France before 1848 was not widespread. This is further illustrated by the fact that employment continued to be concentrated in petite industrie, dominated by artisanal production, and moved only slowly toward grande industrie, its basis being the factory and large enterprise. The latter in 1851 numbered 124,000 *patrons* and 1.3 million workers, whereas petite

34. The pace, really the slow pace, of French industrial development has long been a matter for discussion, dispute, and implicit lament. John Clapham found the term "revolution" inappropriate to describe this development, and for those economic historians intent on giving rate of growth pride of place the French case has always proved annoying. A balanced and valuable account of these several issues is provided by Richard Roehl in "French Industrialization: A Reconsideration," *Explorations in Economic History* 13 (1976): 233–81.

35. T. J. Markovitch, "The Dominant Sectors of French Industry," in Cameron, *Essays in French Economic History*, p. 235, table II. My figures are the sum of Markovitch's categories 8, 9, and 16 (1815–24, 1835–44).

industrie gave employment to 1.5 million masters and 2.8 million workers, a proportion little changed in 1881.[36]

While it is clear that in 1850 agriculture and scattered rural manufacture continued to dominate the French economy, factory production had begun to claim a significant share of the aggregate national product. Furthermore, certain sectors of industry had moved triumphantly to new levels of growth and were establishing a model that others would follow. Extensive mechanization and rationalization were essential to this process. From the perspective of students of public health the great novelty of mechanized industrialization was neither the machine nor the singular economic arrangements that its systematic exploitation demanded but the social and physical framework within which the change was occurring. If the health conditions of those engaged in artisanal production were not good, and almost certainly they were not, that fact was of long standing and was, moreover, largely obscured by the diffuse character of such production. The factory kept no such secrets. The industrial novelty, and shock, of the age, its internal routine, assemblage of humanity, and complete domination over the lives of its laborers made the factory a central preoccupation of concerned social observers. Hygienists did scrutinize the factory, but they devoted far more attention to the new social world these enterprises were creating, namely, the industrial quarter or city and its physical setting and inhabitants. The factory was private property and was entered only by arrangement and usually with difficulty; the city at large was public domain, and its afflictions, unlike those within the factory, seemed to threaten general medical mayhem.

The economy of Paris as well as its population gave the capital a singular position within the nation. Until at least 1850 Paris remained first of all an administrative and only secondarily a commercial and industrial city. Yet, its scale, the diversity of its economic activities, and the disproportions of wealth of its inhabitants rendered the city a microcosm of changes then underway across France.

Because of its public functions, Paris had long attracted men and wealth. It was a consumption, not a production, center.[37] Given its size and wealth, the influence of Parisian consumption became ever more important. The reach for provisions exceeded the Paris basin, extending further and further across France. Financial resources increasingly were concentrated in the capital; and by 1850 central banking and exchange had

36. Pierre Léon, "Le moteur de l'industrialisation: L'entreprise industrielle," in Braudel and Labrousse, *Histoire économique et sociale de la France*, 3, pt. 2:519.

37. The following discussion is based on Bertrand Gille, "Fonctions économiques de Paris," in *Paris: Fonctions d'une capitale*, Colloques: Cahiers de civilisations, ed. Guy Michaud (Paris: Hachette, 1962), pp. 115–51.

become essential to national industrial development. Men of wealth, with their liquid assets, moved to Paris and gradually deprived the provinces of entrepreneurial leadership. Financial control of international trade and finance also shifted to Paris. Paris assumed, too, a decisive role in marketing on the national level. Even before the completion of a major rail network, an accomplishment of the 1850s and the indispensable basis for a truly national market, provincial manufacturers retained an agent in Paris to handle and promote their affairs.

While Paris thus established without threat of rival its premier role in the financial affairs of France, it also continued and expanded its industrial activity. The production and sale of *articles de Paris*, luxury goods produced by highly skilled craftsmen, was little diminished by years of revolution and war. The vast majority of manufacturing establishments in Paris were very small. Of 937 such shops in 1801, employing in all some 60,000 workers, only 24 employed more than 100 persons.[38] Enterprises having the greatest concentration of employment in 1807 were textiles (both the manufacture of fabric and the production of consumer goods), metal fabrication, and the production of wallpaper and tobacco. Most of these undertakings were private, although a few sizeable state enterprises were in operation (La Savonnerie, Gobelins).

Certain quarters became concentrated centers of industrial activity. Metal fabrication appeared at Chaillot (where steam engines were produced) and Batignolles (soon a major producer of equipment for the new railways). Chemicals were prepared at Javel and along the course of the Bièvre. Furniture was the traditional product of the Faubourg Saint-Antoine. An historical geography of industrial Paris has yet to be prepared, but a clear indication of the concentration of establishments in the city may be taken from a contemporary assessment of the sanitary situation in the valley of the Bièvre.[39] A small stream rising in the hills south of Paris, the Bièvre flows across the southeastern quadrant of Paris and enters the Seine just above the Pont d'Austerlitz. Its industrial function in the 1820s and 1830s began in the suburb of Gentilly. Here were located several establishments for the washing of wool, bleaching of cottons, manufacture of mineral acids, and preparation of soft white leather. Gen-

38. Jean Tulard, *Nouvelle histoire de Paris: Le Consulat et Empire, 1800–1815* (Paris: Association pour la publication d'une histoire de Paris, Hachette, 1970), pp. 72–74.

39. A.J.B. Parent-Duchâtelet, "Recherches et considérations sur la rivière de Bièvre, ou des Gobelins, et sur les moyens d'améliorer son cours, relativement à la salubrité publique et à l'industrie manufacturière de la ville de Paris" (1822), in A.J.B. Parent-Duchâtelet, *Hygiène publique; ou, Mémoires sur les questions les plus importantes de l'hygiène appliquée aux professions et aux travaux d'utilité publique*, with a biographical notice of Parent-Duchâtelet by François Leuret, 2 vols. (Paris: J. B. Baillière, 1836), 1:98–155.

Industrial concentration in Paris:
the valley of the Bièvre in 1765 and 1822
(see maps on following pages)

Over a period of approximately sixty years the market and cloister gardens of the Bièvre Valley in southeastern Paris gave way to a thriving but crowded and filthy industrial quarter. The two maps on the following pages portray this transformation, the first, that of Piganiol de la Force, exhibiting a largely agricultural landscape and the second, that of Parent-Duchâtelet, depicting only an occasional garden amidst a scene of vigorous manufacturing endeavor. Among the establishments recorded by Parent-Duchâtelet are the following (according to number key): 8, paper mill; 12 (old) and 13 (new), sewers from the Salpêtrière hospital (11); 15, sewer from the slaughterhouse of Villejuif (14); 18, Esquirol's hospital; 23, starch works; 31, Pitié hospital, with attached dissection hall for the Paris school of medicine (32); 40, brewery; 42, cotton spinning mill; 59–62, 73–77, and 94–97, tanneries; 66, chemical works; 71, wool spinning mill; 86, tanner, and also entrance of the major sewer running beneath rue Mouffetard; 1012, color grinder (with water wheel); 114, skin dresser; 117, color grinder (with steam engine); 122, dyeworks; 125, Gobelins tapestry factory; 126 and 142, stations for washerwomen; 132 and 136, stagnant pools; 133, gardens; 140, box manufacturer.

SOURCES: Piganiol de la Force, "Plan et description du quartier de la Place Maubert avec ses rues et ses limites," in *Description historique de la ville de Paris*, 10 vols., new ed. (Paris: Les Libraires associés, 1765), 5: facing p. 145. J. B. Parent-Duchâtelet, "Recherches et considérations sur la rivière de la Bièvre, ou des Gobelins," in *Hygiène publique; ou, mémoires sur les questions les plus importantes de l'hygiène appliquée aux professions et aux travaux d'utilité publique*, ed. F. Leuret, 2 vols. (Paris: J. B. Baillière, 1836), 1: facing p. 154.

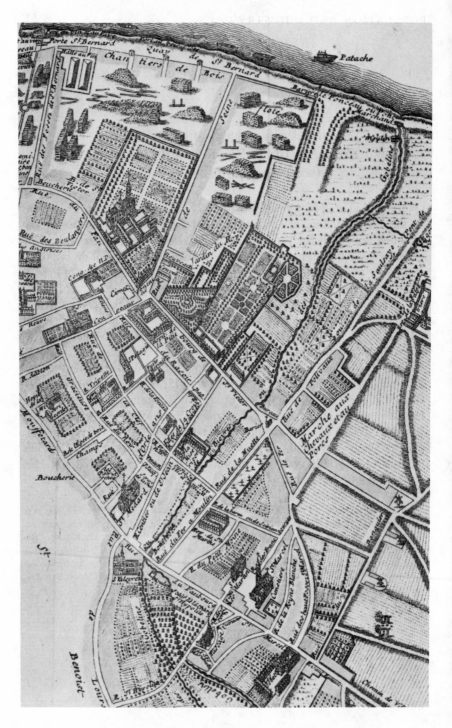

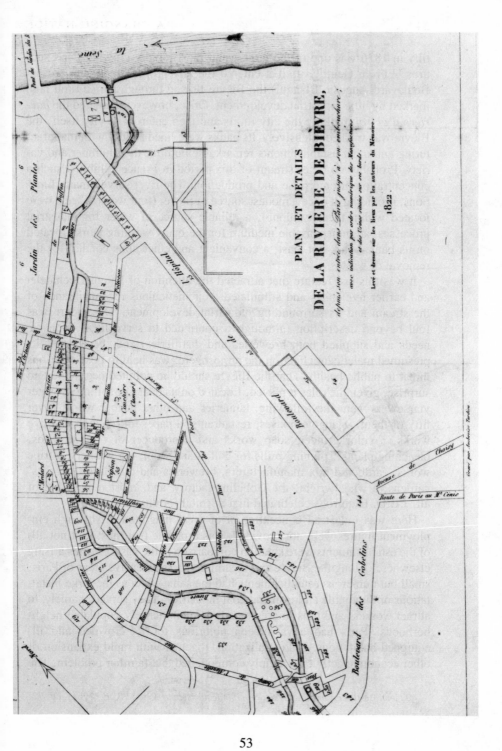

PLAN ET DÉTAILS
DE LA RIVIÈRE DE BIÈVRE,
depuis son entrée dans Paris jusqu'à son embouchure;
avec indication par ordre numérique des Manufactures
et des Usines situées sur ses bords.
Levé et dressé sur les lieux par les auteurs du Mémoire.
1822

Gravé par Ambroise Tardieu

53

tilly in 1836 was one of the largest and most rapidly growing Paris sub-
urbs.[40] From Gentilly until it entered the city proper (under the present
Boulevard Auguste Blanqui) the Bièvre flowed through agricultural land
marked by little industrial development. Once, however, it neared the *bar-
rière d'octroi* marking the city limits and then entered the city itself, the
Bièvre was worked intensively. Its banks were lined solidly with manufacturing and other establishments remarkable both for their number and variety. Probably no other stream of this period in France exhibited such a
concentration of enterprise and production. The river served many functions, providing at once a modest source of power (four water wheels were
located within the city alone), a reliable source of water for industrial
processes, an indispensable medium for the many washing works located
on its banks, and, not least, a convenient and efficacious conduit for the
removal of wastes.

It was this last feature that attracted the attention of Parent-Duchâtelet
and earlier hygienists and stimulated their meticulous reconnaissance of
the stream and its surrounding industrial development. The Bièvre was
foul beyond description (although it continued to serve local domestic
needs and supplied both breweries and distilleries) and, because of its
presumed maleficent effect on the atmosphere, was held to pose a serious
threat to public health. That the Bièvre should be polluted occasioned no
surprise, given the roles it played. Located on its banks or soiling its water
via sewers were the following: tanneries and other leather works (over
fifty of them), slaughterhouses, restaurants, a paper mill, starch and dye
works, a color grinder, soap works and a producer of organic acids,
bleaching plants, spinning mills for cotton and wool, rag washers, a tripe
works, cardboard-box manufacturers, breweries and distilleries, florists'
gardens, a wheelwright, the Gobelins factory, and, most remarkable of
all, J.E.D. Esquirol's celebrated first hospital for the mentally ill.

Here was industrial concentration of great magnitude. Although employment figures were not provided, it is probable that most (but not all)
of the establishments were small in comparison to the vast factories arising
elsewhere. Along the Bièvre and in similar if less extensive areas of Paris,
small but numerous establishments had the same effect as the large instal-
lations of the textile and iron and coal industries. They served, namely, to
attract workers and thus to create and maintain densely populated neigh-
borhoods. Paris had always been notorious for its crowded and ill-
equipped habitations. Industrialization, together with rapid expansion of
other economic activities, simply compounded that familiar problem. The

40. Jean Bastié, *La croissance de la banlieue parisienne* (Paris: P.U.F., 1964), pp. 92–
93.

Paris of Balzac and Hugo was not the invention of fiction but reflected fairly the contemporary reality described by Parent-Duchâtelet, Villermé, and other sociomedical observers. Economic Paris was different, to be sure, from the mill towns of the north or east, yet its effect on its population was strictly comparable. Whether in the capital or in the provinces, privation, suffering, sickness, and premature death on a massive scale were reliable indicators of the unanticipated but all too real consequences of frenzied economic expansion, most notably that based in the factory and urban setting.

It is a remarkable fact, and a further bond between Paris and the new factory towns, that leadership in cotton manufacture was first exercised by the department of the Seine. That leadership was soon lost, but during the Directory and Empire, Paris witnessed quick development of large-scale cotton spinning operations.[41] Not only did the Seine possess more spindles (136,000 in 1812) than any other department, but it contained a disproportionate share, 8 of 25, of the largest mills in France (those with over 5,000 spindles). Certain of these mills were truly vast: the celebrated Richard-Lenoir was utilizing 20,000 spindles in 1808. Already in 1801 Richard-Lenoir's works required almost 8,000 employees and made the entrepreneur by far the largest private employer in Paris and perhaps in the country.[42]

A large and cheap labor supply, numerous spacious and solid buildings, and the foundations of a machine industry made the spinning boom possible. But although the Paris mills were located near a large market for their product, their energy sources were limited, especially as coal began to replace wood. Worse yet, costs, especially wages, were lower in the provinces. Competition from the west, north, and east eventually destroyed cotton manufacture in Paris. By the 1840s the capital was utterly outclassed by these new centers; Paris now worked 56,000 spindles (requiring but 1,000 workers), while the Nord alone possessed 550,000.

The Crisis of 1846

The old demographic order governing France came to an abrupt end in the 1840s. A true exodus from the land then began. The urban areas became the foci of economic hope and of sustained population growth, and in consequence the long-standing balance between town and country was

41. D. H. Pinkney, "Paris: Capitale du coton sous le Premier Empire," *Annales E.S.C.* 5 (1950): 56–60; Louis Bergeron, *Banquiers, négociants, et manufacturiers parisiens du Directoire à l'Empire*, E.H.E.S.S., Civilisations et Sociétés, no. 51 (Paris and The Hague: Mouton, 1978), pp. 205–22.
42. Tulard, *Nouvelle histoire de Paris: Consulat et Empire*, pp. 81, 74.

altered. These changes were initiated by a complex of agricultural, commercial, and political crises. They left behind them not only a new political order but also a new demographic pattern for France. By the mid-1850s it had become clear that rapid population growth, a striking feature of other developing economies in Europe, would not be characteristic of France.

The harvest of 1845 had been poor, and food stocks were seriously depleted by the spring of the following year.[43] Such shortages had been common under the Old Regime but had become much less so during the nineteenth century. Shortages, however, were transformed in many areas into outright dearth by the terrible crop failure of 1846. Fundamental foodstuffs, wheat and potatoes, were particularly affected. Death by starvation was probably uncommon, but undernourishment became the rule in many rural areas. Its effects, especially notable among children, the sick, and the aged, were immediately evident. In the lush year 1845 the excess of births over deaths had been 240,000, giving a growth rate of 6.9 percent. By 1847 that excess had dropped to 52,000 (1.5 percent); in 1849 the natural increase of population virtually disappeared (12,000, yielding a growth rate of but 0.3 percent).[44] Mortality in 1849 was, it should be noted, exaggerated by a devastating return of the cholera. Recovery in 1850 gave a new peak but one which was never again reached during the nineteenth century.

Upon these events there followed in rapid order financial panic and commercial and industrial decline and stagnation. And then came the February Revolution, a new and short-lived Second Republic, to be followed by a more viable Second Empire. Recovery in agriculture proved no blessing. A glut was produced, prices were driven down, and small or marginal rural properties could not and did not survive. The net effect of these several blows was to undermine the economic foundations of rural life and to reveal with harsh clarity the limited prospects available to the massive rural population of France. If overall population growth slowed significantly, that of many departments, perhaps more than half, stopped altogether. Emigration became the rule. The seasonal movement of labor was transformed into a definitive settlement of the rural worker in the city.

The period 1846–50 thus represented a "demographic catastrophe" for France.[45] The collapse of rural industry could only mean starvation at home or movement to areas offering the prospect of employment or public relief (a traditional if unwelcome function of town and city). Yet France

43. See Armengaud, *Population française*, pp. 21–33.
44. Ibid., p. 30.
45. Ibid., p. 32.

in 1850 was on the threshold of two decades of exceptional economic expansion, stimulated by the construction and railway booms of the Second Empire and the unmistakable appearance of industrial activity now expanding well beyond coal, iron, and textile production. French industrial development was thus accompanied by very slow overall demographic expansion and rapidly increasing concentration of labor in urban regions. Nonetheless, the sheer initial mass of the rural population meant that, on the whole, it would preserve its majority position until century's end.

To the hygienist, the industrial city was the great novelty, its rate of growth (whatever its actual size) the preeminent demographic fact, and the manifold set of interacting physical, moral, and economic factors the foremost concern.[46] The new cities and the problems they presented were largely the product of a transformation of the rural world. A slowing rate of population increase did not check rural misery. Men and women endowed with initiative and those driven by simple despair saw in the developing cities either their opportunity or their salvation. The city was thus rapidly supplied with an increasingly large population of men and women unaccustomed to the exigencies of urban survival, persons often without fixed domicile and whose living conditions and employment opportunities were decidedly unattractive. By 1848 the urban poor had ceased to be an ill-defined minority deserving of private charity and occasional public support. The poor had become a large, perhaps preponderant mass within the city. They formed a populace whose political persuasion was volatile and whose propensity to violence was already an established feature of French life. This mass constituted a social problem; its creation generated, in fact, the very notion of the social problem. The hygienist-economist was well aware of these changes, and they filled him with great anxiety. The pursuit of individual interests had led, as Jean Baptiste Say and others had insisted it would, to extraordinary economic expansion. Yet the free marketplace had also created an army of dependents whose capacity for the exercise of

46. From the outset hygienic inquiry tended to ignore the countryside; a brief contemporary review of issues and a bibliography of marvellously obscure literature are provided by Ambroise Tardieu, "Rurale (hygiène)," *Dictionnaire d'hygiène publique et de salubrité; ou, Répertoire de toutes les questions relatives à la santé publique*, 2nd ed., 4 vols. (Paris: J. B. Bailliére, 1862), 3:542–60. Recent historians have paid the subject greater heed: see J.-P. Goubert, *Malades et médecins en Bretagne, 1770–1779* (Rennes: Université de Haute-Bretagne, and Paris: Klincksieck, 1974); Jacques Léonard, *La vie quotidienne du médecin de province au XIXe siècle* (Paris: Hachette, 1977); G. D. Sussmann, "Enlightened Health Reform, Professional Medicine, and Traditional Society: The Cantonal Physicians of the Bas-Rhin, 1810–1870," *Bulletin of the History of Medicine* 51 (1977): 565–84; Matthew Ramsey, "Medical Power and Popular Medicine: Illegal Healers in Nineteenth-Century France," *Journal of Social History* 10 (1977): 560–87.

economic initiative existed not in this world but only in the theorist's imagination. Rich and poor were now divided by a gap of unprecedented width; poverty meant not only lesser wealth but, it was now realized, serious and systematic degradation of the human biological condition. Such had not been anticipated by Say's science of wealth, but it was clearly foreseen by his first major opponent, Simonde de Sismondi. Between 1820 and 1850 the party of political economy generated its own critics, and to their voice the hygienists were particularly attentive.

Chapter 3

Political Economy

Today the well-being of the working classes in France is the rule and destitution the exception. This destitution has two causes: the usual and most frequent cause is the debauchery and sloth of the workers. Dissolute living is an individual vice that in no way can be imputed to our social organization. The other cause derives from social accidents and from flaws in our own nature. These are exceptions within the exception. Here are burdens that simply weigh upon a society, whatever its industrial and economic organization. . . . In each nation the poor will always exist; there will always be destitution, just as the sick are ever-present.

Théodore Fix, 1842

The French Revolution was accomplished in the name of liberty, with passing emphasis upon equality and fraternity. A high ideal, liberty also made quite specific constitutional and legislative demands. Nowhere was this more evident than in the economic domain. The destruction of the ancient corporations in 1791 made away with one of the most restrictive institutions of the Old Regime and gave new freedom for the expression of individual economic initiative.

The science of political economy, then still in its formative years, also adopted as its essential principle the supremacy of individual liberty. The party of political economy in France proclaimed that pursuit of individual interest, when unfettered by custom or law, necessarily furthered the general interest. The economists promised to transform the national economy and the nation as well. Their goal—to increase wealth—was a common enough ambition, yet the nature of such wealth and the means proposed for attaining it were both new. Wealth was no longer to be measured by a nation's population, its supply of precious metals, or its area of arable land, but by the products of farm and, most importantly, factory. Production became the fundamental preoccupation of French political economy,

EPIGRAPH: Théodore Fix, "De l'esprit progressif et de l'esprit de conservation en économie politique," *Journal des économistes* 2 (1842): 222, 237.

having been elevated to this position by Jean Baptiste Say, supreme apologist of industrial capitalism.

But industrial production not only created new and abundant goods; it gave birth to a problem-ridden social world. In contrast to the economists' claim that individual interests would silently merge, creating thereby prosperity and social harmony, France in the post-Imperial period exhibited continued poverty and new forms of destitution as well as heightened social tensions. Social classes were being formed; a large urban proletariat was coming into being. Conflict, not harmony, marked this society.

Critics of the rising industrial system also abounded, offering solutions that ranged from return to the corporate structure of the Old Regime to a radical, socialistic reconstruction of French society. Among these critics were persons who accepted certain of the major tenets of the economists. Simonde de Sismondi, the first writer systematically to publicize the enormous human cost of unregulated economic activity and rapid industrialization, belonged to this group. So, too, did Villermé and numerous other sociomedical investigators of the period. Villermé believed implicitly in the economic advantages of the factory system and of augmented production and in the supreme importance of complete freedom in all economic transactions. He discovered, however, that these advantages conferred benefits shared unequally if at all by differing members of society and that for many persons the reign of liberty meant no more than uncertainty, suffering, destitution, and early death. In an optimistic mood he held such misery to be merely a transient social phenomenon. In a later, more pessimistic frame of mind his thoughts approached the uncompromising words of Théodore Fix. Villermé, like Sismondi, was beset by the problem of reconciling the claims of liberty and the increase of production in a capitalistic economy with first-hand knowledge of the appalling reality of life amongst the laboring classes, above all amongst those persons newly engaged by the factory. His reconciliation of the conflicting demands was never complete, and it lacked logical rigor. The prospect of reform and despair of any solution at all alternated in his thought throughout the 1840s.

Say and the economists conducted an unceasing campaign to demonstrate that modern industry was not irreconcilable with the happiness and well-being of mankind. But to others the human and social costs of the factory system were very high. Sismondi wavered: he valued augmented production greatly but favored man even more. His solution thus denied large-scale industrialization and sought a return to the artisan operating on a basis of individual enterprise and close personal interaction. For this he earned Karl Marx's contempt as the foremost spokesman of petty bourgeois interests. Yet it was Sismondi who laid bare the dilemma of overproduction, of gluts and crises, and thus forced sensitive social observers to take their science of political economy not as a pure science but as a reflection, and this perhaps quite imperfect, of only one facet of human social experience. To liberty and production Sismondi added man.

In Part III I examine the relationship between Villermé's endeavors as a sociomedical investigator and the doctrines that he and fellow hygienists shared with the economists. My purpose will be to document and develop the claim that public health inquiry in France during the constitutional monarchy was closely allied to emerging industrial interests, but was also forced into a stance critical of significant aspects of industrialization by social facts then uncovered. In the present chapter I describe important features of the new industrial philosophy and present certain of the familiar views of its critics. Emphasis is given to the doctrines of Say and the criticism of Sismondi. Complicating their discourse was the challenge posed by Thomas Malthus. The early French economists did not read Malthus in unrelievedly pessimistic manner and neither did sociomedical investigators. The threat of overpopulation was nonetheless perceived and therefore also receives notice in my discussion.[1]

Liberty

The *Déclaration des droits de l'homme et du citoyen*, promulgated 27 August 1789, was among the proudest statements of the revolutionary period. It later stood as the preamble to the first revolutionary constitution (accepted by Louis XVI on 14 July 1790) and gave formal voice to the general call for liberty in France. Personal freedom, security of property, and the right of resistance were assured all citizens.

The *Déclaration* and constitution of 1790 expressed in positive manner the long-sought alternative to the perceived vices and inefficiencies of previous royal government. France would henceforth be rid of rule by privi-

1. I intend no comprehensive discussion of French political economy, only identification of that doctrine's principal bearings upon contemporary consideration of the social problem. The school has never received extended historical analysis; useful general accounts are Charles Gide and Charles Rist, *A History of Economic Doctrines from the Time of the Physiocrats to the Present Day*, trans. R. Richards (Boston: D. C. Heath, n.d.); Gunnar Myrdahl, *The Political Element in the Development of Economic Theory* (New York: Simon and Schuster, 1969); Marian Bowley, *Nassau Senior and Classical Economics* (London: Allen and Unwin, 1937). Jérôme Adolfe Blanqui provides an enthusiastic record of the thoughts of myriad long-forgotten economists in *Histoire de l'économie politique depuis les anciens jusqu'à nos jours, suivie d'une bibliographie raisonée des principaux ouvrages d'économie politique*, 2 vols. (Paris: Guillaumin, 1837). See also L. Le Vau-Lenesle, "La promotion de l'économie politique en France au XIXᵉ siècle jusqu'à son introduction dans les Facultés (1815–1881)" *Revue d'histoire moderne et contemporaine* 27 (1980): 270–94.

lege, caprice, and tyranny. The monarchy was preserved, but its powers were limited by explicit constitutional provisions. These texts were the creation of men of liberal persuasion, and their eager participation in the affairs of the early Revolution had aimed precisely at creation of a constitutional monarchy.

If liberty was dear to these statesmen, so too was the security of property. Property they designated an "inviolable and sacred right." Inheritances were thus confirmed and due recognition paid to the fruits of one's own labor. The Legislative Assembly, the first such body to function under a revolutionary constitution, created between December 1790 and June 1791 the fundamental legislation under which economic and especially industrial development in France was pursued until well into the nineteenth century. The task before the Legislative Assembly was a complex one. Previous privileges had to be denied and new rights simultaneously assured. The assembly's most celebrated enactment was the *loi Le Chapelier*, promulgated 17 June 1791. This, however, was but the third and final step in the series of economic acts that gave legal standing to the regime of laissez-faire.

The first step (decree of 31 December 1790) defined the rights of the inventor in his discovery.[2] These rights were fully his but were limited to the "exploitation and yield" of the invention; the invention itself remained the property of society, to which its benefits would return after a set period of years. A few months later followed a decree (2–17 March 1791) of greater significance. Within a framework of wide-ranging fiscal reform, the Legislative Assembly abolished not only certain long-standing fees but the very institutions giving rise to these fees. Thus perished before the law the powerful institution of the *corporation*, the assemblage of artisans gathered together in each separate trade to control the quality and quantity of production and to regulate all matters affecting each trade, including membership in the corporation. The corporation had received its exclusive privilege from the crown, and now that privilege, like others during the Revolution, was suppressed. Opportunity, it appeared, stood open to all men of initiative.

The first outlines of a new manufacturing order were also indicated in this decree. Manufacturers were henceforth to be licensed by the state, for which service a variable fee, the *patente*, was to be charged.[3] The patente

2. The following discussion is drawn from Marc Sauzet, "Essai historique sur la législation industrielle de la France," *Revue d'économie politique* 6 (1892): 353–402, esp. 890–929.

3. Adolfe Trébuchet, "Patentes (Administration)," *Dictionnaire de l'industrie manufacturière, commerciale et agricole*, 10 vols. (Paris: J. B. Baillière, 1833–1841), 8: 419–33; Sauzet, "Législation industrielle," p. 902; the importance of the *patente* for French social

provided contemporaries with a convenient dividing line between the worker and *petit bourgeois* and the world of entrepreneur and great wealth (Villermé later used this line in assessing the differential mortality of the arrondissements of Paris). Labor required no patente. The patente was the responsibility only of a master or entrepreneur, for apprentices, journeymen, and simple wage-laborers working in his shop or factory were now free economic agents. The primary intention behind this decree was, of course, to destroy the monopolistic privileges of the corporations, the latter, it was held, having long engaged in a multitude of nefarious economic practices. The creation of the patente, however, introduced a new distinction. Those who were patentés were not only men with great economic ambitions. They also possessed sufficient capital or commanded adequate credit to contemplate serious entrance into trade or manufacture. With fiscal intent, no doubt, but also with an eye to regulating such entrepreneurs, the state by means of the patente had given formal recognition to the spirit of enterprise. More importantly, by the exception of wage-labor from the patente the state also recognized the existence of a propertyless population whose sole resource was its ability to find and keep work that was offered only by another. One might view this exception as de facto public acceptance and admission of the utility of the proletariat.

The economic outlook of the men of the Legislative Assembly had been formed under the Old Regime. With but few exceptions, manufacture in France was pursued by numerous small-scale undertakings. Personal relationships were usually close. The reformers believed that had it not been for the artificial constraints imposed by the corporation and other privileged entities, these relationships would surely have compelled a constant interaction between master and man regarding all conditions of employment. Not least of these conditions, the legislators realized, was wages. What monopoly had prevented, liberty would now provide.

Already in 1774–76 A.-R.-J. Turgot had sought to break the monopoly. His attempt failed, as did the entire reform effort of the hopeful early years of the reign of Louis XVI.[4] Success came fully with the Revolution. The dissolution of the corporations created freedom and thus opportunity for all, and the loi Le Chapelier was designed to assure that no comparable restraints on economic liberty would arise in the future. The intent of the loi Le Chapelier was to prevent all associations or combinations, whether between workers or masters or between representatives of the two groups, for purposes of influencing the conditions of employment. Combination

---

and economic development under the July Monarchy is stressed by Robert L. Koepke, "The *Loi des patentes* of 1844," *French Historical Studies* 11 (1980): 398–430.

4. Douglas Dakin, *Turgot and the Ancien Régime in France* (London: Methuen, 1939).

in order to raise or diminish wages was the special target of the law.

The loi Le Chapelier has been in bad odor for almost two hundred years, and for good reason. Its effect fell quite differently on the intended parties. Combinations of workers were regularly and effectively suppressed. Associations of masters were also occasionally touched by the law. Masters, however, had lesser need to seek collective opinion and action. Capital, especially when concentrated in the hands of the larger and more successful entrepreneur, spoke with its own voice, dictating employment, wages, and virtually all factors bearing on the conditions of work. Combinations between entrepreneurs, more discrete than the mass organization required if labor were to act with effect, were more difficult for the law to discern, had its guardians in fact been observant.

The fundamental difficulty of the loi Le Chapelier, as Marc Sauzet has pointed out, was that its articles reflected the ideals of small industry and thus proved utterly inadequate (from labor's perspective) in dealing with the new manufacturing system that gradually arose after 1800.[5] The law assumed a true and absolute liberty and thus parity of will and economic power between participating individuals. The individual worker treated on completely open grounds with the individual entrepreneur. Personal contact was not only assumed; that notion was enriched by the (false) conviction that master and worker were dealing with one another as equally free agents. The human contact that the corporations had assured the few was now, it seemed, expanded to all working relationships. Even better, employment and wages would necessarily be just, for a contract had been struck which, in order to prevail, had to have the explicit agreement of two parties of equal standing.

The factory system, of course, made a jest of this benign suggestion. The isolated worker in no way exercised economic power commensurate with that of the successful entrepreneur. Liberty before the law remained; in the marketplace, however, the individual worker became increasingly impotent. And the loi Le Chapelier could be and was invoked to assure that workingmen did not combine in associations designed to gain their economic goals. One right that had not been assured by the *Déclaration des droits de l'homme et du citoyen* was that of association. The loi Le Chapelier was thoroughly consistent with this decision. All worker's associations, even those ostensibly devoted to nonindustrial and nonpolitical purposes, were suspect in the eyes of the police. They were closely watched and often dissolved. Charitable persons, including Villermé, found it sometimes difficult to persuade public authorities that philanthropic organizations devoted to assuring sickness insurance and death

5. Sauzet, "Législation industrielle," pp. 920–24.

benefits and including large numbers of workers were conducive to social order or public security.

The revolutionary assemblies did not reject all control over industry. Various regulations in force under the Old Regime simply continued under the new, and these were augmented during the Empire by further decrees and institutions, often imposed by the prefecture and not by the central government.[6] But this legislation and administrative initiative did not touch the heart of what might be called the negative labor legislation of the Revolution. Liberty in the labor market was sought, and liberty was *de jure* attained. The reality was far different. Sociomedical observation was thus directed to the condition of men, women, and children who were not only ill-housed, underfed, poorly clothed, sickly, and subject to an early and miserable death but who, in the name of liberty, had been rendered economically and politically powerless. Liberty had placed the burden of salvation, in this world as in the other, strictly upon the individual.

A Science of Wealth

In his *Traité d'économie politique* Say sought to expound the eternal laws that governed all economic transactions. The *Traité* served as the voice of economic liberalism and was perhaps the most popular textbook of economic doctrine during the early nineteenth century. While its first edition (1803) proved uncongenial to the emerging centralist economic ambitions of the late Consulate and Empire, the second (1814) and third (1817) editions provided the principal themes for the continued attack by liberals on the reactionary agrarian and mercantilist expectations of the Restoration government and *notables*.

By experience and conviction Say (1767–1832) was destined for leadership of the party of the economists.[7] An eager participant in the moder-

6. Exceptions pertaining to dangerous trades (dangerous, that is, to the community) had already been made in 1791 (Sauzet "Législation industrielle," p. 906) but became of major importance under the Conseil de Salubrité founded in 1802 in Paris by the Prefecture of Police: see A. F. La Berge, "The Paris Health Council, 1802–1848," *Bulletin of the History of Medicine* 49 (1975): 339–52. The decree of 15 October 1810 laid the foundation for further and elaborate development of such regulation of new manufacturing establishments: see Ambroise Tardieu, "Etablissements insalubres," *Dictionnaire d'hygiène publique et de salubrité*, 2nd ed., 4 vols. (Paris: J. B. Baillière, 1862), 2:225–56.

7. Biographical information regarding Say is given by Ernst Teilhac, *L'oeuvre économique de J. B. Say* (Paris: Félix Alcan, 1927). Say's *Traité* is available in a modern reprint edition, with a valuable preface by Georges Tapinos (Paris: Calmann-Lévy, 1972). Two studies by Edgard Allix are indispensable for understanding Say's intellectual and social purpose: "J.-B. Say et les origines de l'industrialisme," *Revue d'économie politique* 24 (1910): 303–13, 341–60; and "La méthode et la conception de l'économie politique dans l'oeuvre de J.-B. Say," *Revue d'histoire économique* 4 (1911); 321–60.

ate phase of the Revolution, he was also a leading figure among the idéologues, serving for a period as editor of their major propaganda instrument, the *Décade philosophique*. The rise of Bonaparte halted this publicity, and Say turned to private affairs, becoming a prosperous cotton manufacturer in the north and thus a leader in the introduction of the factory system into France. When he repeatedly pronounced ever-increasing production to be the supreme economic good, he spoke not only from a well-reasoned doctrinal position but on the grounds of extensive personal experience.

Say loathed equally Bonapartist and Bourbon. Both wanted to deny the freedom for which France had suffered a revolution, and neither emperor nor restored monarch appreciated the central role of production in the creation of national wealth. Bonaparte devoted his career to destruction, not production, and had lived by means of war and spoliation. The Bourbons were, if anything, worse. They represented the interests of landed wealth, of privilege and monopoly. The yield of the land was steady but small in comparison to equivalent capital invested in manufacture. Such great potential wealth seemed to Say idle and misdirected. Moreover, landed wealth severely restricted the entrepreneurial opportunities of others and thus hindered the increase of national wealth. In England, always the implicit ideal in such discussions, liberty was a reality, and the prodigious development of manufacture in that nation was incontrovertible witness to the power and desirability of the new economic organization.

Say intended political economy to provide a rationale for, indeed, to become, the science of industrial wealth. Grounded in unvarying laws of nature, economics, too, would come to possess that certainty and timelessness held to be characteristic of the exact sciences. The task of economic science was to discover these laws and to develop their consequences for the tangled and seemingly inexplicable phenomena presented by the world of production, distribution, and consumption of goods. Economic activity was thus to be understood once and for all on the grounds of (familiar but unfortunate phrase) the nature of things. "The general facts constituting the sciences of politics and morals," which together embraced economics, "exist independently of all controversy," Say observed. "They as certainly proceed from the nature of things as the laws of the material world."[8] Classical political economy accepted this point of view as a fundamental methodological postulate. The nature of things, albeit

8. J. B. Say, *A Treatise on Political Economy; or, The Production, Distribution, and Consumption of Wealth*, trans. C. R. Prinsep, 4th American ed., (Philadelphia: John Grigg, 1830), p. xxviii.

often variously understood, provided the indispensable ultimate argument to which there was no recourse.

To the economist wealth was not at all an abstract good. It was a real and very proper goal of human behavior. The doctrines of political economy in France were based upon psychological foundations prepared by Etienne Bonnot de Condillac and, more especially, by the idéologues. Their views were expressed in detail by Say's contemporary, A. L. C. Destutt de Tracy, whose influential *Elémens d'idéologie* (1800–1815) provided both a summary statement and a name for the new psychology.[9]

Man, Destutt de Tracy asserted, is both a sensible and a rational being. Sensory impressions give rise to perceptions, and the mind develops these, seeking generality by establishing their relations to one another. Perceptions also create within us needs (*besoins*), and these we consciously attempt to satisfy. Satisfaction of our needs requires an act of will, and such satisfaction—that is, human happiness—is a function of our act of will. Destutt de Tracy's theory of mental activity proved, not unexpectedly, to depend entirely upon liberty. "The nature of every being endowed with will," he wrote, "is such that this faculty of willing causes his happiness or unhappiness, he is happy when his desires are accomplished, and unhappy when they are not; and happiness or misery are proportioned in him according to the degree of his gratification or disappointment."[10] *Liberty* was simply the term that described this freedom of choice and action. It was silent on the matter of what our particular desires might be and how they will change with time, which Destutt de Tracy insisted they would do. The important matter was that liberty at all times and under all forms of government be preserved. "The government under which the greatest liberty is enjoyed, whatever may be its form, is that which governs the best, for in it the greatest number of people are the happiest; and when we are as happy as we can be, our desires are accomplished as much as possible."[11]

The decisive factor in this calculus of happiness was the individual. Happy individuals created a happy state; under the reign of liberty the

9. See Sergio Moravia, *Il pensiero degli idéologues: Scienza e filosofia in Francia (1780–1815)* (Florence : La Nuova Italia, 1974); Edgard Allix, "Destutt de Tracy, économiste," *Revue d'économie politique* 26 (1912): 424–51; Emmet Kennedy, *A Philosophe in the Age of Revolution: Destutt de Tracy and the Origins of "Ideology." Memoirs of the American Philosophical Society*, vol. 129 (Philadelphia: American Philosophical Society, 1978).

10. A.-L.-C. Destutt de Tracy, *A Commentary and Review of Montesquieu's "Spirit of Laws,"* quoted in Walter Simon, ed., *French Liberalism, 1789–1848*, (New York: John Wiley, 1972), p. 40.

11. Ibid., pp. 41–42.

successful pursuit of individual ambition contributed inevitably to the ever greater happiness of society at large. The individual was endowed with sensation, reason, and volition; he was charged to exercise these faculties as fully as he was able. It was reason and volition that defined the nature of man and thus truly set him apart from all other animals. It was again these faculties that, leading a man always to attend first to his own interests, also led him into necessary and repeated intercourse with fellow human beings. By his nature man was a social animal, not the irrational savage that Say and the economists tended always to find in the doctrines of that lamentable misanthrope Jean Jacques Rousseau.[12]

Intrinsic to this analysis was the further and all-important proposition that while liberty grants the individual opportunity to attain true happiness, it also insists that responsibility for meeting so obviously desirable a goal is uniquely an individual consideration. We succeed or we fail by acts of our own will. Society in general is not and should not be directly concerned with assuring our prosperity and happiness. Save for the maintenance of peace and the assurance of justice and, to more advanced members of the school, insistence upon those rudiments of education which would inform the masses of their responsibilities, the state had no role and must avoid the sphere of economic activity.

To bring buying and selling, producing and consuming, human acts *par excellence*, within the hallowed domain of modern natural science seemed to the economists the supreme challenge to a philosopher's ingenuity. While economic science portrayed the structure and functions characteristic of human industry, it did not demand that an individual in fact direct his actions in accord with stated principles. Political economy was a certain and a descriptive science, but it claimed not to be a prescriptive one. Nonetheless, what reasonable man, the economist must have asked, would not seek happiness for himself and those dependent upon him. Unfortunately, however, the new science failed to consider not only whether all men did indeed act exclusively in accord with their individual interests but, more importantly, whether all men in reality possessed the opportunity to do so if the inclination were truly present.

Say returned often to the nonprescriptive character of political economy. With regard to action by public authorities, he observed in the *Traité* that "all that can be required from political economy is to furnish governments with a correct representation of the nature of things, and the general laws necessarily resulting from it."[13] He left it to the administrator to determine

---

12. Man's social nature was, Say held, the *sine qua non* of the production of wealth and thus of civilization itself (*Cours complet d'économie politique pratique*, 2nd ed., 2 vols. (Paris: Guillaumin, 1840), 1: 497–508.

13. Say, *Treatise on Political Economy*, p. lv.

whether or not a particular decision was in accord with science and to assume responsibility for making that decision. He was more emphatic in his *Cours complet d'économie politique pratique*:

> It is wise, I believe, to refrain from a pretension of a great number of economists who view this science merely as the art of governing or of directing the government on the road to public well-being. I believe they have erred with regard to the purpose of our science. No doubt it is quite suited to guide the actions of men, but [*économie politique*] is not, properly speaking, an art; it is a science. It informs us of those things which constitute the social body and of what ensues from the action of these parts upon one another. . . . The nature of things [that is, nature itself], as proud and disdainful [of inexact procedure] in the moral and political sciences as in the physical sciences, at the same time that it allows its secrets to be seized for the benefit of whoever studies [nature] with constancy and in good faith also pursues its [own] course, whatever this may be and independently of whatever may be said or done. . . . Everyone, depending upon the circumstances in which he finds himself, is called upon to take counsel of the science; no one is authorized to give directions.[14]

These themes offer a résumé of the liberal economist's conception of man, a conception of capital importance to subsequent discussion of the social and hygienic dangers of industrialization and to the modest remedies proposed for their reduction or elimination. The liberal sincerely believed that a reasoned set of choices should be put before every man but that each person must then be left to make the decision. At most, rational persuasion might be attempted; any form of compulsion was rejected. True enlightenment meant clearly perceiving one's individual interest and taking action—all men and women now being free—to attain that end. Such was the rational course of behavior, such by definition was what all men and women as rational beings would desire and do. Those who failed to plot their course in this reasonable manner were *ipso facto* irrational and deserved to be treated, as indeed many were, like dumb beasts incapable of exercising informed wills.

Say, nonetheless, by insistence upon the distinction between the rigorous science of political economy and the varied and often conflicting requirements of public administration, preserved considerable analytical flexibility. He was not, of course, altogether pleased with the distinction thus drawn. He hoped that his new science would "embrace the entire social system," its appropriate designation thus becoming *économie sociale*.[15] The ideals of natural science—certainty, comprehensiveness, even

14. Say, *Cours complet*, 1: 25.
15. Ibid., p. 4; ibid., 2:557 (*économie sociale*).

prediction—might then pass into the total social domain and mere economics expand into genuine social science. To the myriad transactions that create and transfer wealth were added intellectual life and necessary administrative functions as well as all "the reciprocal relationships between individual and social body."[16] But Say restrained himself. Not wishing thus to launch on "a career extending into infinity," he elected to "circumscribe the object of [his] research" to strictly economic activity.[17] It was not merely the scope of the projected *économie sociale* that induced restraint. Say realized that human activity was always influenced by time, place, and person (the very purpose of a science of wealth was to discover unchanging principles that abstracted at least economic affairs from this chaotic flux), and he understood that contemporary science was simply inadequate to the task of transforming such vague considerations into hard doctrine. The consequence of his reflections was that Say left to his numerous readers both the ideal of a rigorous science of wealth, together with its essential psychological presuppositions and radical individualism, and also the recognition that the phenomena presented by individual existence and by society are, for better or worse, not fully embraced by that science. Science as the ideal and society as the recalcitrant reality would give later economists endless vexation. But it also left them scope to entertain seemingly heretical proposals. To those who followed Say in this his generous construction and avoided the rigidity and outright hostility of the doctrinaire economists of the 1840s (of whom Théodore Fix provides an excellent example), the "nature of things" proved more pliable than at first glance it might appear.

Occasional proposals were made that the government intervene in the affairs of industry by means of explicit legislation. The worker, to be sure, was enjoined to lead a more sober, peaceful, and productive life, and the master was sternly admonished to moderate his exactions and even take an active role in the moral and economic improvement of his employees. Political economy, even in the quasi-geometrical and seemingly rigid form given it by Say, still preserved a flexibility that permitted its adherents to call for efforts at social reform by both individual and the state. Say's science was not dismal; amelioration by human intervention was possible and, in the eyes of man, desirable.

All the same, his principal objective remained always to prepare the way for increased industrial production. Industry and especially modern manufacture he held to be the combined product of three parties.[18] The worker provided, of course, direct labor. But he had no work without the

16. Ibid., 1:4.
17. Ibid.
18. Ibid., pp. 92–102.

entrepreneur, literally the hero of the factory system. The entrepreneur either possessed or, more commonly, obtained from others the capital necessary to purchase plant and equipment and acquire raw materials. He recruited and organized his labor force, supervised actual production, and then with the finished goods plunged into that great testing ground, the market. The entrepreneur represented initiative; he took the risks; he had fair claim to the proceeds of the endeavor. If work and industriousness were ornaments of the human condition and if industry was really only the systematic combination of reason and resolute effort, then in his person the entrepreneur was the critical dynamic element in industrial capitalism—in Say's eyes, the most important actor on the economic stage. He was the embodiment of the success that came to a responsible individual wisely using his forces. He drew on his own resources and talents, to be sure, but also upon those of others. Thus entered the third industrial party, the *savant*, whose inquiring mind perfected familiar learning and made new discoveries, both of which were important to manufacture. Throughout his career Say insisted on the economic value and social utility of intellectual work and, no doubt spurred on by the views of Henri de Saint-Simon, came to accord ever greater importance to this function in industrial affairs. Technical innovation was a powerful and most desirable goal to industrial development.

The necessary effect of entrepreneur, savant, and worker was to augment industrial output. Now the consumer now entered: his desires were the spring that sustained the entire productive process. "Wants multiply as fast as they are satisfied," Say happily noticed; "a man who has a jacket is for having a coat: and, when he has his coat, he must have a great coat too."[19] But desires, idéologue psychology had explained, are manifestations of reason, of self-interest, expressed by the will. Under the reign of liberty, reason and intelligently conceived desires no longer faced any but internal impediments; desire thus increased with the growth of reason. Say celebrated production, but he realized fully that prosperity demanded, on balance, complete consumption of the industrial product. The entrepreneur, the producer, thus existed to serve the consumer.

Yet, because of Say's view of the nature of exchange, these two roles almost became one, and this, in turn, allowed the dilemma of overproduction to be resolved. Money was not a value to be carefully saved, on the pretense that here in fact was real wealth. Money was simply an efficient and indispensable means for furthering the exchange of goods. The production and actual exchange of these goods constituted genuine wealth. Thus, should the desires of an individual or a nation not yet be

19. Say, *Treatise on Political Economy*, p. 373.

satisfied, the recourse of each was obvious. To acquire goods one must produce goods, the greater the production the greater the means available for acquisitions. New or expanded production thereby assured consumption of other goods. Desire, naturally great and enormously stimulated by reasoned consideration of individual self-interest, was virtually unlimited. How then, Say's doctrine asked, save by despotism and the destruction of liberty—in short, by abandoning all that had been won in the name of *civilisation*—could one seriously contemplate a situation in which production regularly surpassed consumption?

"It is because the production of some commodities has declined," he observed, "that other commodities are super-abundant."[20] Say recognized, of course, that industrial gluts were real and were economically and socially disruptive. But they were local and transient phenomena. Their remedy consisted in further reducing constraints on the economic engine, following which the market inevitably would once again allocate rewards in a just manner. To this cure would also be added the encouragement of a high level of production by all other parties of ever higher levels of production, Say finding therein assurance that effective demand would be kept high. Exchange, hence continued prosperity, must ensue.

Say well understood that overproduction and the resulting economic crisis affected more than the mere parameters of the business cycle. The prudent master might safely weather the storm; his workers, however, were exposed to immediate and grave risk. As business slowed, wages declined and hours were shortened. Unemployment constantly threatened. The worker's reserves were usually slight, and destitution came swiftly. Say did not evade the difficulty.

He insisted, first of all, that neither principle nor the law required that such persons, however desperate their situation, receive private or public assistance. The unemployed and the utterly destitute had no legitimate claim upon the state or, indeed, upon the more fortunate members of society. Nonetheless, while law and principle thus stood in opposition, he admitted that common humanity and, careful inclusion, the "social interest," a euphemism for the preservation of social order, did require judicious assistance be provided the needy.[21] But only the deserving poor— abandoned or orphaned children, the aged, and the genuinely infirm—had a claim to such support. Nothing could induce the economists to favor the English Poor Law, in 1830 still unrevised and widely considered in France, as in Britain, a marvellously efficient device for the propagation

20. Ibid., p. 79; Allix, "Say et les origines de l'industrialisme," p. 311.
21. Say, *Cours complet*, 2:361–70.

of immorality, sloth, and disorder and a splendid stimulus to unregulated reproduction by the lower orders of society.

The deserving poor, however, were a minority, and the greatest need in hard times was felt by the working poor. To them, Say and fellow economists merely counselled foresight and forbearance.[22] Early marriage was strongly discouraged. Reproduction, like family expenditure, was to be held within strict limits. The individual was admonished to assume responsibility for his own welfare and for that of his family in bad times as well as good. These were utterly unrealistic demands in an era of low wages, uncertain employment, and imperfect savings institutions; and the vast extent of hunger and sickness during times of crises made evident to those who would see just how misdirected such solutions must be. In fairness to Say and in agreement with the optimistic mood of the first decades of industrialization in France, it may be noted that he consistently maintained a rudimentary sense of distributive justice. Liberty was not a license for the rich to exploit the poor. Say's was a philosophy of growth, and it was important to him that the benefits of increasing production reach all industrious members of society, the worker as well as the entrepreneur. On what other grounds could it be fairly demanded that the worker and his family make provision in good times for the periodic if passing difficulties that lay ahead? Say read this singular moral lesson to the newly rich whose sense of sharing was as yet ill-developed:

> The comforts of the lower classes are, therefore, by no means incompatible with the existence of society, as too many have maintained. The shoemaker will make quite as good shoes in a warm room, with a good coat to his back, and wholesome food for himself and his family, as when perishing with cold in an open stall; he is not less skillful or inclined to work, because he has the reasonable conveniences of life. . . . It is time for the rich to abandon the puerile apprehension of losing the objects of their sensuality, if the poor man's comforts be promoted.[23]

Such preaching served to maintain, of course, the preeminent role of entrepreneur and capital and thus to preserve, at least in principle, distinct class lines and overall social order. Evidently, the growing wealth of industrial society was not being distributed in equitable manner; that was simply in the nature of things. But the entrepreneur had responsibilities broader than his personal economic interest. Faith in an ever-increasing product and hence total wealth assured Say that economic development need not place master and man in a zero-sum situation. Their rivalry was

22. Ibid., pp. 366–67.
23. Say, *Treatise on Political Economy*, p. 373.

real but could be tempered. It was up to the master to seize the initiative in this matter. It would be his deeds that showed the mark of genuine benevolence and humanitarianism, above all, of sincere paternalistic concern. Paternalism presupposed the authority of the master-father and demanded the submissiveness, even the gratitude, of the worker-child. It also reassured the master and his associates of their own goodwill and reaffirmed for all to see the structurally inferior social status of the working class. Most importantly, paternalism as praised by the economists and enthusiastically endorsed by Villermé defined a relationship based in the workplace and guided by the same improving spirit that had inspired the entrepreneur. Paternalistic intervention was not identical with charitable concern or action. The latter tended to be indiscriminate, whereas paternalism was thoughtfully yet aggressively discriminating. Biological survival, like social improvement, was really possible only for those who would help themselves.

Mankind, Not Science

With the Revolution France had won liberty, and under the Empire she had lost it again. What could be expected of the restored Bourbons? At the very least, the economists hoped, the Charter of 1814 assured that the government would follow a policy of nonintervention. The charter guaranteed the security of all property, however acquired during the tumultuous years since 1789, and presumably would continue to do so. Rapid economic development followed the return of peace. Economic growth and expansion of the factory system were soon interrupted, however, by the first of a long series of crises that characterized the period of the constitutional monarchy. The suffering caused by this depression, France's first taste of the negative side of the business cycle, was vastly compounded by the harvest failure and calamitous winter of 1816–17. Simonde de Sismondi was a close and increasingly critical observer of these events. His *Nouveaux principes d'économie politique* (1819) made evident to all that wealth alone, whatever the scientific principles by which it might be justified, was too limited an objective for political economy. Sismondi's "new principles" demanded that the human actor be restored to a central position in economic discourse.

Sismondi (1773–1842) is best known as an historian. The son of a Huguenot family of Geneva, he fled to Tuscany during the 1790s to escape the spreading turmoil of the French Revolution. There he began the study of the history of Italy, as well as making his first efforts in political economy.[24] Again settled near Geneva, he devoted himself to large schol-

---

24. On Sismondi's economic views see Mao-Lan Tuan, *Simonde de Sismondi as an*

arly enterprises, publishing a history of the literature of south Europe and launching a vast history of the French nation. An article on political economy contributed to an encyclopedia in 1818 forced him to reconsider the foundations of his science.[25] From this article grew the *Nouveaux principes d'économie politique*.

Sismondi confronted the reassuring social harmony portrayed by other economists with a vigorous report on the conflict and class struggle that seemed inevitably to result from the new system of untempered liberty and ferocious competition. He persuaded few contemporaries that these were remediable problems. His solutions for economic inequality and ensuing social conflict were modest and generally conservative, and they exerted slight (but as yet little explored) influence. Nonetheless, his presentation of the problem marked an epoch in social analysis and its relation to economic development. The *Nouveaux principes* returned French political economy to concrete social reality, challenging both the optimism and pertinence of the scientific credentials of that woefully abstract science. There is little doubt that the French school of sociomedical investigation during the constitutional monarchy worked directly in the Sismondi tradition.

Sismondi observed that the consequences of the commercial crisis of the immediate postwar years and the "cruel suffering of the workers" in the industrial establishments of Europe simply demanded a new view such as his. Governments, ignorant of the nature of these problems, by their action or neglect merely aggravated an already difficult situation. They pursued false goals. Some sought to augment production; others, to increase population; and they did both because convinced that greater wealth or a larger population meant greater national prestige and power. Power, it appeared, was in itself a satisfying national goal. Sismondi viewed the matter quite differently. "The true problem of the statesman," he observed, "is to find that combination and proportion of population and wealth which will guarantee the greatest happiness of mankind in a given locality."[26]

The ultimate source of social conflict and the degradation of labor Sismondi found in the collapse of the traditional form of the organization of work, spurred on by the advance of economic liberty. In the competitive

---

Economist (New York: Columbia University Press, 1927); Albert Aftalion, *L'oeuvre économique de Simonde de Sismondi* (Paris: Pedone, 1899); and Octave Festy, "Sismondi et la condition des ouvriers français de son temps," *Revue d'économie politique* 32 (1918): 46–72, 118–146.

25. Sismondi, "Political economy," *The Edinburgh Encyclopedia*, ed. David Brewster et al., 18 vols. (Philadelphia: Parker, 1832), 16: 39–78; also reprinted separately (New York: Augustus M. Kelley, 1966).

26. Sismondi, *Nouveaux principes d'économie politique; ou, De la richesse dans ses rapports avec la population*, 2 vols. (Paris: Delaunay, 1819), 1:v–vi.

arena that the economists viewed as the unique dynamic element in economic progress, Sismondi saw nothing but a frightening and corrosive force, a force degrading the close personal relationships that alone maintained harmony among men and women. He found the example of England alarming; competition there seemed to be destroying the very social fabric.

> This nation, in many ways an example to be copied, so extraordinary even in its faults, has seduced all the statesmen of the continent. And, if [my] reflections can no longer be useful to England itself, I may at least hope to have served humanity and my compatriots by revealing the dangers of the path she is pursuing and by demonstrating on the basis of her own experience that to found the whole of political economy on the principle of unlimited competition is to authorize an attack on society by each individual and to sacrifice the interests of humanity to the simultaneous expression of the individual cupidity of each and all.[27]

Sismondi's fond hope was to reestablish the intimate regime of small-scale production and thereby assure that production was paced by consumption. But contemporary reality, he fully realized, was founded on opposite principles. The factory system had vastly expanded both the productive process and the product itself. Sismondi simply denied Say's essential premise that ever more abundant goods would find their consumer if only artificial impediments to manufacture and exchange were reduced. To the contrary, Sismondi held the new system to be structurally incapable of absorbing its own products.[28] A major reason for this situation was the necessary diminution of effective demand that the capitalistic system had engendered.

All wealth not immediately needed for individual or family consumption, maintaining thereby for each a modestly comfortable existence, was a surplus subject to exchange. The factory system and above all the introduction of more efficient machinery tended to increase this surplus and constantly pushed it beyond, Sismondi remarked, often far beyond, real human needs. In modern society luxury goods assumed a larger share of total production, and the balance between labor and capital shifted in favor of the latter. "Man living alone amasses [wealth] in order to make use of it; man in society sees the product of his sweat accumulate for the benefit of [another], who will enjoy it."[29] This dangerous tendency towards concentration of capital and debasement of labor was, in Sismondi's eyes, the proximate cause of social disharmony.

27. Ibid., 2:366.
28. Ibid., 1:79.
29. Ibid., p. 81.

The respective powers of the two protagonists, capital and labor, had been dramatically changed by industrialization. The machine, a marvelous instrument for increasing production and for easing the burden of labor in many an arduous or dangerous manufacturing operation, was also the instrument that imposed a division of labor, often extreme, on the workplace. Sismondi assigned primary responsibility for the impotence of labor before the growing demands of capital to the division of labor.[30] The laborer required work in order to survive. His skills, however, had been eroded by machine manufacture (if he had, in fact, ever had an opportunity to develop such skills). He knew but one or a few operations; he faced numerous others whose capacities were equally limited and whose need for work was equally great. The employer could and did exploit this situation, profiting from the competition for employment by driving down wages and selecting his workers by whatever criteria he chose.

In a fierce indictment of the modern factory system Sismondi pointed out that while the master took great risks, he also expected rich rewards. The worker, by contrast, worked simply to stay alive. His salary, one would suppose, must be adequate to cover not only subsistence but to make provision for unemployment, sickness, leisure, and old age. It fell, of course, far short of such needs. "The first effect of competition," Sismondi observed, "has been to depress wages and at the same time increase the number of workers."[31] A nation can be said to be truly rich when its wealth not only has increased but is ever more equitably distributed. The purpose of political economy must never be simply to defend the wealthy, much less their too frequent spoliation of labor; its goal is to seek the benefit of all citizens, the worker as well as the master. Yet, the competitive ideal forced its way into the economic sphere of action and had virtually assured the triumph of destitution and disorder. Consequently, Sismondi concluded, my view

> contradicts decisively one [actually two] of the axioms most emphasized by political economy, that free competition assures the most favorable progress of industry, this because each person better understands his individual interest than could an ignorant and inattentive government, and that the interest of each contributes to the interest of all. Both axioms are true, yet the conclusion is false. Individual interest, restrained by that of the others, would in fact [lead to] the general interest, but each person seeking his own interest at the expense of the others as well as by the development of his own capacity, is not always held in check by forces equal to his own. The strongest find it in their interest to take, and the weakest, in their interest not to resist the

30. Ibid., pp. 90–92.
31. Ibid., pp. 374–75.

strong, for a desire for the least evil as well as for the greatest good is the aim of human behavior [*politique de l'homme*]. Injustice can often triumph in this struggle of all interests against the others, and in such a case, injustice will almost always be aided by the public authority. The latter, believing itself impartial, in fact is so, since, without examining the issue at hand, it will always take the side of the strong.[32]

The surest indicator of the dysfunctional nature of laissez-faire was that new and terrifying event, the business crisis. Here was evidence—Sismondi was writing in the aftermath of the collapse of 1817—that unrestrained competition was vicious and literally inhuman.

Yet, although Sismondi's anatomy of crises remains the most celebrated aspect of his contribution to economic analysis, even here he found himself in an ambiguous situation. The evil caused by rapid industrial development was patent; the remedy for that evil, far less certain. It was important to condemn both the doctrinal and organizational causes of such unparalleled suffering; it was also necessary, Sismondi admitted, to concede and even try to retain certain indisputable advantages of the new manufacturing system.

Our industry, he lamented, booms. As long as demand remains high, new factories are erected and labor is attracted to the city. Production and urban population swell. But once, he sarcastically observed, the "market of the Universe is sufficiently provided for," an inevitable prospect, the entire fabric unwinds in devastating manner.[33] Production drops; unemployment rises and this is only hastened by the continued, ever more frenzied effort by manufacturers to introduce more efficient machinery in order to capture some share of the remaining market by means of lower prices. "Distress then [rises] to its peak, and one even [begins to regret] the progress of a civilization that has, by gathering together in one place a greater number of persons, only compounded their suffering; in a lonely wilderness misery would at least touch a smaller number of victims."[34] For tangible illustration of these events Sismondi merely called his reader's attention to the industrial and commercial situation then prevailing in England, a depression of wide dimensions.

Sismondi nonetheless was baffled. He realized that increased production was also the sign of prosperity, and this he regarded as a social good. One and the same process—rapid industrialization based largely upon the introduction of new and more efficient machinery—was at one and the same time a source of great wealth and of unparalleled suffering. Although often

32. Ibid., pp. 378–79.
33. Ibid., 2:328.
34. Ibid.

inconsistent, Sismondi most commonly emphasized the latter fact and thereby self-consciously adopted a severely critical stance with regard to the factory system. Industrial distress, he also realized, was a genuine social creation, one made by man and hence presumably remediable by man. It was not at all the inevitable consequence of the nature of things.

He was convinced that the principal sign of contemporary industrial malaise was the disjunction of labor and the totality of the productive process. Under the traditional corporate system the newcomer faced a prolonged period of apprenticeship. In this subordinate status he acquired not only the full range of skills required by his chosen craft but also the tools of production and an intimate acquaintance with the potential market for his products. The latter was all-important. The craftsman produced for expressed demand; factory-based industry, Say held, assumed that a product would create its own demand. The craftsman produced less but did so always with reasonable assurance that his work would in fact be purchased.

The most remarkable aspect of Sismondi's analysis is that it assigns greater rationality and certainty to corporate economic organization than to the new industrial system, which, in the view of its apologists, represented the ultimate application of reason to production. Sismondi saw that the factory system truly divorced producer and consumer; the former could no longer adjust production to suit the needs or desires of the latter.[35] A vast impersonal market was being created. It promised wealth to some, notably entrepreneur and capitalist. But they, too, were only men and therefore capable of misjudgment or perfidy. The modern tragedy was that their errors brought grief not only to themselves (although some among their number would surely have reserves by which to live or even start anew) but to those who possessed nothing, the workers whose only support was the continuity of labor. Industry was creating a new class, propertyless, economically and socially impotent, and useful only in reproducing itself, assuring thereby the wealth of others. Thus, Sismondi declared in a notable passage,

> the more the poor man is deprived of all property the greater is the danger that he will tend to misjudge [the magnitude and, above all, the security of] his revenue; this will encourage the increase of a population which, no longer corresponding to the demand for labor, will be unable to assure its subsistence. This observation is of sufficient an-

35. Ibid., pp. 256–65. At issue here were the consequences of unrestrained liberty as compared with those eventuating from a conservative constitutional view of liberty and equality; see H. O. Pappé, "Sismondi's System of Liberty," *Journal of the History of Ideas* 40 (1979): 251–66.

tiquity to have entered common language and has passed from Latin to the modern tongues. The Romans designated as proletarians those persons who owned no property, as if they, more than all others, were called upon [merely] to produce children: *Ad prolem generandam.*[36]

This degradation was perpetuated by the system itself. The proletarian, a member of a distinctive social class, had contracted the "habit" of owning nothing. His notion of wealth was "simply to exist"; his conception of poverty was "to die of hunger." How, then, expect such a debased human being to make plans for the future? Why expect him to limit his numbers when his view of the future was but anticipation of more of the same suffering? Say and his followers had set in opposition the producer (entrepreneur-savant-worker) and the nonproducer (government functionary-soldier-clergy) and believed that the producers, in their triumph over the nonproducers, would assure prosperity and put an end to petty strife between nations.[37] Sismondi, too, sensed the reality of a social struggle and its importance for the reestablishment or prevention of social harmony. But he saw production as the problem and not the solution.

The Malthusian Challenge

The program of political economy seemed doomed, however, by unrestrained human reproduction. The proletariat was accomplishing its mission too successfully, reproducing (and dying) far more rapidly than the other social classes and expanding overall population at a rate that appeared to threaten labor's well-being and survival as well as dampen national prosperity. In his early economic writings Say had largely dismissed the challenge posed by Malthus. Say's faith in production being well-nigh absolute, he held that population would seek and maintain a level commensurate with industrial activity. The factors that favored an increase in population also encouraged an increase in production, agricultural as well as industrial, and this latter assured support for new hands. Although Say later tempered his sanguine view, he nonetheless continued to discount the Malthusian peril.[38]

Malthus' arguments were widely discussed in France.[39] While some adopted the most pessimistic reading of his claims, most observers chose a more moderate stance. To be sure, they admitted, a serious problem

---

36. Sismondi, *Nouveaux principes d'économie politique*, 2:262–63.
37. Allix, "Say et les origines de l'industrialisme," pp. 311–12.
38. Ibid., pp. 309–10.
39. See J. J. Spengler, "French Population Theory since 1800: I," *Journal of Political Economy* 44 (1936): 577–611, 743–66; Joseph Garnier, "Population," *Dictionnaire de l'économie politique*, ed. Charles Coquelin and G.-U. Guillaumin, 2 vols. (Paris: Guillaumin, 1852–53), 2:383–402.

threatens society, and the possibility even exists that, here and there, most probably in the industrial districts of England and a few cities in France, the threat of overpopulation had become a reality. But as Malthus himself had indicated, there was nothing necessary about this dismal outcome. Most economists felt that population growth should be limited and, more importantly, could be limited. The solution to the problem had been stated by Malthus himself. Individual responsibility must be exercised, marriage delayed, and moral restraint practiced within marriage.[40]

Even granting the efficacy of moral restraint, a euphemism for sexual abstinence, population continued to grow. But growth would be gradual, not explosive. It marked social and economic progress, not decline. Only when preventive checks (moral restraint) failed, Joseph Garnier noted, did repressive checks become operative.[41] Garnier's repressive checks were Malthus' "positive" checks—famine, disease, and war. Michel Chevalier, M. T. Duchatel, and numerous other unflagging publicists of political economy shared Garnier's hopeful outlook. Frédéric Bastiat, in his extravagant *Harmonies économiques* (1850), brought optimistic Malthusianism to its culmination.

Yet few of these authors, save perhaps Bastiat, pretended that the danger of a population exceeding its means of subsistence was unreal or doubted that the consequences of overpopulation would prove disastrous to a large proportion of the nation. Their qualified optimism was based upon the conviction that each citizen could pursue a rational course of behavior, even in matters of sexual passion. The task of the statesman and social observer was to inform the individual of his responsibilities and let him know that upon his choice depended not only his own well-being but also that of his family. His choice was, in fact, a social act. Population does not exceed subsistence unless man so wills. If weak, or of evil intent, or worst of all, merely ignorant, mankind will reproduce excessively, and widespread misery will quickly manifest itself. Should an individual refuse to be educated or to act as advised, Malthus had truly described the inevitable outcome. Here science was imperious and permitted no trimming before its stern dictates.

These arguments meant, of course, that moral choice could be exercised only by the individual. The economists firmly rejected intervention by public authorities. Charity for the able-bodied, whether public or private, was, they held, a social scourge. It created false expectations, encouraged greater fecundity, and provided safe harbor for the lazy or incompetent.

40. William Petersen, *Malthus* (Cambridge: Harvard University Press, 1979), pp. 50, 54–57.
41. Garnier, "Population," p. 388.

Employment by means of public works, which Garnier approved and Sismondi attacked, provided at best a small and uncertain income and encouraged a sense of dependence in precisely those persons whose initiative most needed awakening. Individual freedom and responsibility also meant that the citizen who sincerely desired regular employment had to perfect his or her talents and make an individual effort to seek and retain work. The right to work, increasingly under the July Monarchy the foremost demand of labor, was anathema to the economists who viewed that claim as a flat contradiction of liberty. Citing Louis Napoleon ("Perhaps the greatest danger of modern times comes from the false notion implanted in many minds that a government can do everything"), Garnier in classic liberal manner withdrew public authority from the domain of public happiness.[42] "Good governments," he wrote, "are quite incapable of assuring the happiness of their citizens, for the latter are the unique agents controlling their fortune, their comfort and their station in life."[43] The economists' reply to Malthus was thus fundamentally individualistic. Given liberty and an informed populace (education thus became a panacea), the economist found it obvious that the rational individual would seek a course that increased his or her long-term pleasure and diminished immediate as well as long-term pain.

The economists were not alone in facing Malthus' challenge. A singular perspective was provided by J.P.A. de Villeneuve-Bargemont, whose service in the royal administration in the Nord and Tarn, important textile departments, gave him a very clear notion of the human suffering caused by the factory system.[44] Villeneuve-Bargemont, however, spoke not only for man, for the worker, but also for throne and altar. His response to the new problems of threatening overpopulation and industrial degradation was castigation of modern industry as a godless and un-French importation from Protestant England and an exhortation to achieve a thoroughly Christian moral regeneration of the laborer. His ideals were charitable, his favored agents the landed proprietor and the church official, his objective the restoration of the presumed harmonies of agricultural society. Luxurious tastes would thus be countered and a spirit of brotherhood and sacrifice engendered. Prudence, including sexual restraint, necessarily ensued.

42. Ibid., p. 398.
43. Ibid., p. 399.
44. See Octave Festy, "Le Vᵗᵉ Alban de Villeneuve-Bargemont et la condition des ouvriers français aux environs de 1830," *Revue des sciences politiques* 42 (1919): 78–98, 234–61; Georges Cahen, "L'économie sociale chrétienne et la colonisation agricole sous la Restauration et la Monarchie de Juillet," *Revue d'économie politique* 17 (1903): 511–46; Jean Baptiste Duroselle, *Les débuts du catholicisme social en France (1822–1870)* (Paris: P.U.F., 1951), pp. 59–71.

This was a moral, that is, a Roman Catholic, answer to the accursed "parson Malthus." Villeneuve-Bargemont's great strength was his sincere regard for the worker as a human being and hence his demand, shared with Sismondi, that political economy concern itself with more than the mere increase of wealth. He ignored, however, the numerous strictly economic factors—above all, those pertaining to the level and surety of wages—that were contributing to the emerging struggle between the social classes, and therefore he sought no solution to the social problem from within an industrial organization whose very character he abhorred.

In numerous respects Villeneuve-Bargemont's views reflected those propounded a decade earlier by Sismondi. Both authors viewed the triumph of radical individualism with alarm; both sought to restore certain main features of earlier forms of economic organization: and both, beyond all else, responded passionately to the plight of men, women, and children captured without hope by the early industrial revolution. Their differences, however, were more profound. Sismondi, a Protestant (as were Say and numerous other economists), would have none of Villeneuve-Bargemont's recreation of a paternalistic landed aristocracy, defenders, no doubt, of both Roman and royal authority. Moreover, Sismondi could not rid himself of a certain admiration for the productive capacity of the modern factory. It was really its dysfunction, its remedial injustices, that so disturbed him. Above all else he wanted each individual to have the opportunity to measure fairly his own means and ends. Large-scale capitalist enterprise destroyed this opportunity. In defending the small peasant proprietor and arguing for a revival of the corporate organization of manufacture, Sismondi was seeking to find a scale of economic endeavor suited to individual responsibility. His models came, of course, from the past. But, unlike Villeneuve-Bargemont, who verged upon calling for a restoration of the Old Regime, Sismondi made appeal to the celebrated independence of the farmer under the Roman Republic and to those who in his day seemed to perpetuate this myth of vigorous freedom and moderation in all things.

Here was the basis for Sismondi's response to Malthus. The latter, who had gathered facts of indisputable importance, had also committed a "fundamental error in his reasoning." Sismondi found Malthus' idea of a geometrical increase of mankind of dubious merit; it was an abstraction, not a demonstrated reality. To set this wholly hypothetical increase in opposition to a lesser increase in the means of subsistence, thereby establishing the notion of an inevitable biological limit to population, was "completely sophistical."[45] Malthus' equation described a situation which, Sismondi

45. Sismondi, *Nouveaux principes d'économie politique*, 2:268.

was confident, had never occurred in the past and was most unlikely to take place in the future. In the first place, such a limit could refer only to the carrying capacity of the entire globe or to that of a closed nation. The former, however, had never been tested, even approximately, and the latter was strictly a fiction (trade makes its way into all lands).

But these were mere passing observations. Sismondi's principal argument against Malthus was that economic constraints will always be encountered before biological limits are reached.[46] Over the years and generations the land always produces, food is always available and commonly is available in abundance even in hard times for those with the means to procure it. The means of subsistence exist, but money to purchase them often is lacking among those most in need. To Sismondi the Malthusian dilemma had to be understood in terms of available revenue. One can and, indeed, under the modern industrial system, often did starve in the midst of plenty. Owners of productive land, of course, exercised ultimate control over the price and availability of foodstuffs and therefore over population. In Sismondi's view, this was an acceptable situation; it reflected, after all, the interests of lawful holders of property. What was unacceptable was the other side of the coin, namely, the insufficient revenue of the worker and his family. Whereas the property-owning farmer could estimate the demand for his crops, the industrial worker exercised control over neither labor nor market, and as observed above, this to Sismondi constituted the major flaw in the new organization of production. Food existed, as did other human necessities; both eluded the worker's grasp because he lacked the means to purchase them. Population was thus constrained by the means of subsistence in only an indirect and remote manner. So far as Sismondi was concerned, the issue was better discussed in economic than in biological terms.

Sismondi's analysis of population reasserts forcefully the claim that political economy must be more than the science of the increase of wealth. Reading Malthus and David Ricardo in a pessimistic light made it appear that natural law and hard facts condemned many men and women to destitution and early death. Such seemed the inescapable dictate of the convergence of Malthus' geometrical and arithmetical rates of growth. Whatever Sismondi may have thought of this extreme formulation of the Englishman's view, he most certainly concluded that it was not really pertinent to the issue at hand, namely, the causes and means for the alleviation of human suffering in industrial society. Those causes had human origins. They were due to men, men expressing their collective will by means of

46. Ibid., pp. 270–78.

legislation and public institutions. As such, *misère*—suffering and destitution—was not predestined in the laws of nature but literally manufactured by the laws of men. But legislation is open to change and amelioration. By assigning economic, that is, social, causes and rejecting
biological, that is, natural, determinants, Sismondi brought the somber
condition of the laboring classes before his readers as a human problem
that might be remedied, not simply regretted but ignored.

Bold Diagnosis and Conservative Therapy

Astute diagnostician, Sismondi was a conservative therapist. Indeed, to
some contemporaries his remedies seemed outdated and futile. They were
even pernicious, for, because of the self-deception upon which they were
raised, they diverted attention from other and perhaps more efficacious
solutions to the critical problem that their author had so strikingly portrayed. No one spoke more directly to this point than did Karl Marx and
Frederick Engels, writing with well-aimed polemical intent at the outset
of their public career:

> In countries like France, where the peasants constitute far more than
> half of the population, it was natural that writers who sided with the
> proletariat against the bourgeoisie, should use, in their criticism of the
> bourgeois *régime*, the standard of the peasant and petty bourgeois, and
> from the standpoint of these intermediate classes should take up the
> cudgels for the working class. Thus arose petty-bourgeois Socialism.
> Sismondi was the head of this school, not only in France but also in
> England.
>
> This school of Socialism dissected with great acuteness the contra-
> dictions in the conditions of modern production. It laid bare the hypo-
> critical apologies of economists. It proved, incontrovertibly, the disas-
> trous effects of machinery and division of labour; the concentration of
> capital and land in a few hands; overproduction and crises; it pointed
> out the inevitable ruin of the petty bourgeois and peasant, the misery
> of the proletariat, the anarchy in production, the crying inequalities in
> the distribution of wealth, the industrial war of extermination between
> nations, the dissolution of old moral bonds, of the old family relations,
> of the old nationalities.
>
> In its positive aims, however, this form of Socialism aspires either
> to restoring the old means of production and of exchange, and with
> them the old property relations, and the old society, or to cramping the
> modern means of production and of exchange, within the framework
> of the old property relations that have been, and were bound to be,
> exploded by those means. In either case, it is both reactionary and

Utopian. Its last words are: corporate guilds for manufacture, patriarchal relations in agriculture.[47]

Marx and Engels, of course, celebrated increased industrial production as
much as did the most enthusiastic of liberal political economists and on
this ground alone were destined to oppose both Sismondi's diagnosis
(large-scale manufacture is at fault) and his remedies (return to traditional
economic organization). Their purpose was to create a new and harmonious industrial world; Sismondi's, to temper the untoward social effects of
industrialization, even if this occasionally threatened to reject modern
manufacture itself.

All particularities and qualifications aside, Sismondi held that work
alone might resolve the social problem. The great contemporary dilemma
was the manner in which work was now organized, if indeed "organization" was the appropriate designation for the chaos of the labor marketplace of early industrial France. Sismondi ventured no claim that labor
enjoyed a right to work. He demanded measures that gained the same
effect, namely, entrepreneurial assurance of both steady employment and
a fair wage. It was, Sismondi claimed, the "call for work" that determined
population size and thus exercised ultimate control over individual well-
being and social harmony. Work provided revenue and thus encouraged
optimistic expectations and increased reproduction. Let employment decline and those expectations were proved false. The worker, his fellows,
and, above all, his children, fleeting prosperity's increment to the population, then quickly fell into one or another degree of destitution, often
profound. In short, national prosperity depended upon the "demand for
labor, but a demand [that must be] regular and continued." Anything less
than this simply meant "suffering and death" for the worker; "far better"
in such a situation "that he never have been born."[48]

Sismondi's scrutiny of the factory system had convinced him that human ingenuity could devise no better scheme for assuring labor's insecurity. Effective economic power had passed almost entirely into the hands of
the capitalist, whether landed proprietor or factory owner. Control of production, the sale or exchange of whose yield assured the steady revenue
that alone permitted a confident and happy existence, had passed into
hands other than those of the actual producer.[49] Sismondi did not, as socialist thinkers soon would do, deplore this event in itself. It was its consequences that he so fiercely condemned. Of these one stood supreme,

47. Marx and Engels, *Manifesto of the Communist Party*, in Karl Marx and Frederick
Engels, *Selected Works*, 2 vols. (Moscow: Foreign Languages Publishing House, 1962),
1:56–57.
48. Sismondi, *Nouveaux principes d'économie politique*, 2:285.
49. Ibid., pp. 304–5.

namely, the producer in losing direct contact with the consumer lost also his capacity to measure output by real demand.

Moreover, capitalism and technical innovation constantly and dramatically stimulated this breakdown of traditional economic relations. Cupidity joined the simple desire for survival in a harshly competitive environment and drove the capitalist constantly to expand his production and seek to command ever larger markets. Among his most powerful instruments for this purpose was labor-saving machinery. Machines proved more efficient than massed hand labor. Reduced costs and, presumably, lower prices appeared to create a better competitive position for the innovative entrepreneur. Even in 1819 these conclusions presented little novelty. Sismondi spoke nonetheless in a manner quite different from that of most contemporary economists when, instead of celebrating the arrival of mechanized manufacture, he pointedly indicated that the machine created not only wealth but widespread destitution and social disharmony.

The vice was in the socioeconomic setting of the machine.[50] An admirable addition to the arsenal of production when demand exceeded supply, the machine became the devil's own device for the worker when demand declined. In hard times, the machine guaranteed continued production but also virtually assured reduced or uncertain employment. Sismondi's views on the matter quite contradicted those of Say and his followers. Without effective demand, and this a preexisting demand, the machine only made worse the always uncertain calculations of the entrepreneur. The worker, having lost control over the process of production, had become the passive victim to fluctuations in the pace of economic activity. The high cost of machinery virtually ensured that few workers under the factory system had a realistic opportunity to remedy their situation by advancing into the ranks of the entrepreneur. Sismondi's condemnations of industrial mechanization did not, on balance, touch the machine or technical innovation itself. Repeatedly he insisted, even when calling for a halt to such invention (including a demand to suppress the decree [1791] that had established the patent system), that it was not the machine itself, often a quite marvelous device, but its too extensive or too rapid application that should be blamed.[51]

Naturally, one expects that an observer so passionately concerned with destitution and so astute in his perception of its nature and probable causes would propound a reasoned solution for elimination of the problem or at least alleviation of its worst symptoms. The charge that Sismondi's efforts were devoted primarily to observation and description and not to change

---

50. Ibid., pp. 312–34.
51. Ibid., pp. 331–34.

is fundamentally correct, yet it requires careful qualification. Often the charge means nothing more than that the critic disagrees, sometimes violently, with the proposed remedy. Such, surely, was the case of Marx and Engels, whose respect for their Swiss predecessor was real, however it might be obscured by immediate political needs.

Sismondi's specific remedy for the dilemma of the deserving poor was simple indeed, even simplistic, and as he soon realized, it was more an expectation based on shared good will than a practical proposal for industrial reform. Legislation provided the basis and sanction for reform; the entrepreneur, willingly or otherwise, was to be the agent of reform; the role of labor was nil. Sismondi called for certain positive steps.[52] To the magistrate, the natural "protector of those who have no other," he assigned the task of prohibiting the marriage of parties who lacked an income that was adequate and sufficiently secure to provide for the children that inevitably would follow. Because marriage was a "public gesture, a legal act," it quite properly fell within the domain of public scrutiny and control. The entrepreneur was enjoined to guarantee a new husband's wages for a given period of years (a demand, obviously, that touched dangerously near to labor's claim to the right to work). An effort was to be made, using local resources reserved for this purpose, to encourage and aid the diligent worker and father to "ascend the social scale." Persons trapped at the bottom of the scale—and Sismondi accepted the continued existence of the truly poor—paupers, as they were called by the English, were to be refused the rite of marriage. It was the deserving poor, those willing and able to work but who, because of the industrial system, lacked a just and assured income, who alone deserved the solicitude of legislator and magistrate and their probably very reluctant associate, the entrepreneur.

Sismondi admitted that his plan might increase vice amongst those to whom marriage was prohibited. That problem was outweighed, he assured the clergy and other interested parties, by the diminished number of "young girls who, born without resources, are led by destitution to vice" of their own.[53] Given the incidence of prostitution in this period and the replenishment and active recruitment of its corps from the most impoverished classes, Sismondi's claim may not have been unjust. Some members of the entrepreneurial class, furthermore, would have another and substantial complaint against the proposed reform. Sismondi did not trim before their greed. He assured them that, yes, they might well have to guarantee their workers an annual wage or perhaps even invite labor to share the profits of their establishment. Like it or not, the entrepreneur had social

52. Ibid., pp. 307–9.
53. Ibid., pp. 308–9.

responsibilities that reached beyond and might occasionally even contravene his personal interests. He was, Sismondi held, morally committed to raise the worker from his "more than servile condition" and assure him and his family the means whereby an orderly and happy life could be conducted. "This before all else," the economist declared, "is the reform that the legislator desires, even if it prove fatal to a number of manufacturers. Such entrepreneurs are not worth the trouble of saving if this can be done only by the sacrifice of human victims."[54] As for the worker's estimate of these proceedings, little was said save for the following: "It is possible that such legislation would first of all excite protests from the workers; soon these complaints would change into expressions of gratitude."[55] Self-deception, perhaps, but common enough and never put to the test.

Reform was thus to be initiated by legislation but put into effect by the *patronat*. By assuring a regular wage and by moral example and exhortation, the *patron* caused the worker susceptible of improvement (of course, not all were thought to be so) to be gradually elevated in social station. The implied goal, obviously, was not to invent new and rival entrepreneurs but to create a class of sober and self-sufficient laborers, secure in their lives, an asset to their employer, and hopefully, no threat to the peaceable order of society. Sismondi, however, utterly failed to provide any indication of how such legislation might be introduced, defended, and adopted and ventured no word as to how to persuade the recalcitrant manufacturer to abide by either the letter or spirit of such laws. He offered the core of a solution to industrial and social problems, whatever might be thought of its merits, but ignored all aspects of the equally great problem of how to launch even so modest a plan. In 1827, in the second edition of his *Nouveaux principes*, he simply abandoned all hope. While still accepting the above principles as his "goal," he admitted that "we dare not undertake to indicate how it is to be attained."[56] The risk was so great because he realized full well that such legislation had no prospect whatsoever of being accepted by the legislative assemblies of the constitutional monarchy.

Between 1820 and 1850 Sismondi's work was widely read and discussed. His attack on the vices of early industrial capitalism was comprehensive and impassioned. He aimed truly, first sensing and then exploring in knowing manner the phenomenon which, before all others, was transforming English society and was now making its entrance upon the Continent. He focused on the faults of industrialization, on the physical suf-

54. Ibid., p. 309.
55. Ibid., p. 308.
56. Sismondi, *Nouveaux principes d'économie politique*, 2nd ed., 2 vols. (Paris: Delaunay, 1827), 2:309.

fering and moral degradation that seemed always to accompany it. He drew upon his observations and reflections to compose the first truly comprehensive indictment of modern industrial civilization, a text that ruthlessly contradicted many of the by then sacred symbols and allegiances of the improving classes in France and in England. But Sismondi offered too limited and too ineffective a program to mark a stage in the extraordinarily rapid development of philosophies of social reform and revolution in the era of the constitutional monarchy. His influence was largely that exerted by publicity: working France, and Europe, is suffering as never before and we, men, are responsible for this crime. Publicity making the same claim continued in the work of leading figures in the French hygienic movement, in whose hands the nature of the problem was subjected to ever-more-detailed empirical examination and to whom a genuine solution seemed equally unrealizable.

Sismondi's analysis offered sustained criticism of the central tenet of economic liberalism, the theory of possessive individualism. Yet his attack was indirect and often muted, a reflection, no doubt, of his own participation in the privileges of capital and of his profound conviction, the mark of a man from Geneva, of the importance of individual responsibility, not least in the marketplace. Battle was truly joined between the economists and their most determined critics only in the 1830s and 1840s. The principal issue by then was obvious to all: should economic activity, and thus legislative action and social organization, continue to be based upon defense of individual initiative and property, or has modern industry so transformed the conditions of labor and so concentrated socioeconomic power that a new organization of society must be invented and called into being? If the latter, collective action must replace individual initiative. In the name of *association*, whose very mention struck fear into the economists, were taken the first steps towards the organization of labor for economic purposes under the July Monarchy.

Sismondi's response to the issue was essentially an exercise in nostalgia and one quite incommensurate with the intent of the advocates of association during the 1840s. The latter, thoroughly disillusioned by the action and especially inaction of proprietor and entrepreneur and expecting nothing at all from the state, saw Sismondi's notion of a class struggle evident in every aspect of daily life and called upon labor to marshal its forces, via association, first to oppose the propertied classes and then to seize mastery of the social order. February 1848 put these aspirations at the center of French political life.

The rapid defeat of the Second Republic perhaps reassured the economists, but their confidence if not their faith had been seriously shaken. Political economy now more than ever had to contribute to the reassertion

of sound ideas and the restoration of a healthy social order. Essay upon
essay in the *Dictionnaire de l'économie politique*, supreme voice of the
party, was designed with this end in view. Charles Coquelin, coeditor of
the great project, found it necessary to call none other than Say into order.
During the 1820s and probably because of the stimulus of Sismondi's initial critique, Say had been tempted to redesign, temper, and redesignate
his science. The proposed new denomination, *économie sociale*, agreed
with an expansion of concerns that would probably drive political
economy well beyond the rigid and limited abstractions of production,
distribution, and consumption. The adjectival "social" indicated that men
and women, their physical and moral well-being, must constitute an intrinsic element in any discussion of the increase of the wealth. To Coquelin, Say's new expression was both misapplied and premature. "As to the
word *social*," he wrote,

> it may be applied to political economy only when it is well stated and
> understood that the word applies to human society at large, to that kind
> of universal association that industrial connections create among men,
> and in no way to political society which is merely a fragment of that
> great society. Besides, men have so abused this word *social* in recent
> years, it has been used as a shelter by so many mad imaginations, a
> cover for so many antisocial and inhuman doctrines, that it is perhaps
> necessary to avoid its use in serious works for a long time to come.[57]

The irrepressible Garnier added that only political economy might teach
the people to separate the possible from the impossible. The possible,
based upon a knowledge of "things as they are, as they can be according
to the laws of nature," was also the desirable; seeking the impossible had
only led to social catastrophe, that is, to the revolution and bloodshed of
the spring of 1848. "Political economy," Garnier advised, "protects the
people against those moral epidemics caused by philosophical adventurers
who cast all the world into a chaos of truth and error."[58] In the years
between the First and Second Republics the struggle for power in France
had shifted. The Revolution of 1789–99 had pitted new and frustrated
interests against the traditional holders of power. Say represents well this
new world, composed of *bourgeois*, reform-inclined aristocrat, and entrepreneur, fighting together in defense of liberty and also, in the name of
economic opportunity, against patriarchal agriculture, the closed world of
the *corporations*, and the constitutional system that had supported both.
Their victory was won only slowly, and throughout the contest the new

57. Charles Coquelin, "Economie politique," *Dictionnaire de l'économie politique*,
1:666.
58. Garnier, "Population," p. 402.

men and probably most members of yet lower social orders, a third interest, believed that the contest was one in which all who were engaged had
a common interest. By 1820, however, it was becoming clear that that
alliance, if such it had been, was a false one and that the interests of
bourgeois and *le peuple* were very different and rapidly diverging.[59] Agriculture had either retired from public life or had been co-opted by the
spirit of enterprise. Moreover, the landed proprietor faced essentially the
same problem as the ambitious industrial entrepreneur. His property produced a revenue only when worked, and for this purpose abundant and
docile labor was essential. Apparent community of interest thus dissolved
into disagreement and misunderstanding and then open conflict. Insurrec-
tions in Lyons and Paris between 1831 and 1834 unmistakably announced
the arrival of this new world; the events of 1848 soon demonstrated the
true depth of the divisions that had been created within French society
since 1789. Fraternity was daily contradicted and equality was a patent
falsehood. Liberty alone survived, and that, to many observers, seemed
the real source of the problem, for liberty—genuine liberty whose benefits
could be enjoyed by all—was unequally given the nation. The economist,
nonetheless, faced with social conflict of unparalleled ferocity, aghast at
the spreading appeal of the socialist alternative, and himself weary and
more than ever inflexible, continued to proclaim the victory of 1789 and
the progress of civilization that had resulted from the rise of modern industry. He also urged patience on the part of those who had not yet, it
seemed, received their share. In this frightened atmosphere of self-justification even hygienists were pressed into the campaign. Villermé, for example, contributed a semi-official and, of course, critical report on workers' associations, a vigorous statement of the doctrines of political
economy. His essay of 1849, the culmination of a career that had combined sociomedical investigation with economic advocacy, turns attention
directly to those remarkable inquiries that defined in so exacting a manner
the condition of labor during the constitutional monarchy.

59. Articulation by an economist of this break in political outlook is described by Edgard
Allix, "La déformation de l'économie politique libérale après J.-B. Say: Charles Dunoyer,"
Revue d'histoire économique et sociale 4 (1911); 115–47.

Part II

Sociomedical Investigation

Chapter 4

The Prison and Social Inquiry

It is not sufficient merely to reform the prisons; one must go to the root of the problem and create new generations [of men]. Education forms our moeurs and work preserves them; idleness degrades them and misery corrupts them. It is thus by means of work that we must form our citizens.

Duc de Plaisance, 1819

The vital condition of a circumscribed population, that of the prison and penitentiary, provided both data and problems that induced Villermé to pursue a career in sociomedical investigation. These several populations, each prison or penitentiary presenting a society in miniature and each exhibiting distinctive morbidity and mortality, offered the initial factual basis for melding consideration of populations and their health status. Society at large posed numerous, formidable, and interrelated problems that challenged the ingenuity and patience of the investigator. The prison and penitentiary were less comprehensive social units, but they, too, set countless methodological and substantive difficulties before their observer. Villermé began with the army and ended with society at large; it was the study of the hygienic character of the prison and penitentiary that provided the transition between these disparate sets of human phenomena.

In the study of prison populations Villermé first made use of the nascent numerical method; that method I examine in Chapter 5. After the prison studies he turned first to the differential mortality of rich and poor (Chapter 6) and then to a diverse collection of hygienic and populationist problems (Chapter 7). With the shift to factory investigation and consideration of the working class that began in the mid-1830s (Chapter 8) Villermé's effort returned to direct inspection of hazardous institutions. All of this work continued themes that had first become manifest in the assessment of the health condition of prison inmates, and it is precisely these prison investigations that, by combining a medical perspective with assiduous attention to the distinctive features of the social setting, authorize repeated use

EPIGRAPH: Quoted in Charles Daru and Victor Bournat, "La Société royale des prisons, 1819–1830," *Revue pénitentiaire* 2 (1878): 71.

of the expression "sociomedical investigation." Villermé's *Des prisons telles qu'elles sont et telles quelles devraient être* (1820) stands creditably amongst the growing number of such descriptive and programmatic essays concerning prison conduct and reform that characterize the years after 1815.

The Prison and Society

In 1820 the penitentiary was still a new institution. The creation of philanthropic activists of the late Enlightenment, its purpose and functions were complex. The penitentiary was to replace the vengeful punishment of antisocial behavior characteristic of the Old Regime with a planned program of isolation, work, and education. Incarceration, not bodily revenge, defined the new ideal. This was a program designed not only to remove the delinquent from society but to remake him or her into a new and responsible citizen. Upon discharge, philanthropists imagined that the prisoner would assume a useful role in society. He would also be submissive to strict social discipline; the penitentiary offered training for this role also.

The reduction of the inherited tangle of law and judicial practice to a single, rational code was a paramount concern of the eighteenth-century legal reformer. Reformers anticipated that this reduction would diminish long-standing inconsistencies and prejudices in the law.[1] Of equal if not greater importance, it might help eliminate outright illegalities in the law's application to offenders. With one coherent code of law, its terms applicable to all citizens, it seemed possible both to determine with exactitude the relative seriousness of each infraction and to prescribe with equal precision the appropriate penalty. The judicial operation thus rationalized was also depersonalized: the offense determined the punishment; the offender was merely its recipient. Intrinsic to the conception of the penitentiary, however, was a new and far more individualized view of the condemned. The prisoner, in contrast to the offender, was the object of sustained and exhaustive observation. His early biography, intentions, and actions and his behavior in prison were all deemed of major importance to the central function of the penitentiary. This was reform of the delinquent. Reform demanded novel administrative techniques. The penitentiary assured constant surveillance and isolation of the prisoner, moral and secular instruc-

---

1. My discussion follows Michel Foucault, *Discipline and Punish: The Birth of the Prison*, trans. Alan Sheridan (New York: Pantheon, 1977), pp. 248–56, 273, 276. See also Michael Ignatieff, *A Just Measure of Pain: The Penitentiary in the Industrial Revolution* (New York: Pantheon, 1978). Ignatieff emphasizes British prison reform, noting particularly the revival of the reform spirit after the Napoleonic wars.

tion, and obligatory labor. The stated function of the penitentiary thus melded deprivation of liberty (for purposes of punishment and for the presumed protection of society) and the basic instruments of moral regeneration.

Complete control of the moral and physical circumstances surrounding the inmate was the reformer's first desideratum. In keeping with the views of many philosophes and with basic tenets of the idéologue party, he held that the character and thus the possible reform of a prisoner depended essentially upon the influences surrounding that prisoner. Such physical and moral influences could be discovered; their study and exploitation would provide the bases of the technique by which the penitentiary must be administered.

Classification of the prisoner was the indispensable first step.[2] This was an act whose contribution to the repression of delinquency far outweighed its possible aid to administrative efficiency. Men and women themselves were among the most potent influences that determine human behavior. This being so, careful characterization of persons being incarcerated— young or old, experienced criminals or first offenders, male or female, accused or convicted, healthy or sick—and distribution of members of each category to a specialized institution or distinct subunit of a general prison was a matter of great importance. In Restoration France this problem was acute, one of the worst vices of the French penal system being indiscriminate mixing of prisoners. Not only did disorder and sexual depravity result from this practice, but the very purpose of the institution, moral regeneration, was grievously harmed. Few examples could be set in such prisons, save for the worst, and even fewer could be followed. The penitentiary without classification of its inmates was simply a school for crime.

Within the penitentiary, isolation of the inmate was necessary. Nothing, it was believed, was more conducive to self-reflection than sustained separation from the sight and word of fellow human beings. Self-reflection, of course, led to intense consideration of one's moral bankruptcy and life in crime. Such consideration, in turn, elicited remorse within the prisoner and gave him or her a secure beginning for a new life, a now virtuous and productive life. While this sanguine conviction was widespread, the most effective means for assuring its application remained in dispute. French reformers were sharply divided over the kind and degree of isolation required within the penitentiary. They argued for decades over the relative merits of the Philadelphia and Auburn systems, each offering a distinctive model for isolation of inmates, and they reached no consensus. Nonethe-

2. Foucault, *Discipline and Punish*, pp. 236–44.

less, isolation, whether assured by overt physical boundaries or by rigorous control over behavior, seemed indispensable if hegemony over the prisoner were to be assured.

This general control had an avowed purpose. The prisoner must be remade according to society's demands. Through education and work the new citizen gained an awareness of the moral demands that society imposed upon him and a familiarity with the discipline required of labor in modern society. Education sought less to impart information and the capacity for independent reasoning than to inculcate sound habits, among which regularity and obedience, of course, stood foremost. The penitentiary, formed on the model of the military hierarchy, was, like the contemporary hospital and factory, a representative institution of modern bureaucratic society. It was devoted to training and using productive individuals. To its proponents the success of incarceration was to be measured by attainment of these goals. Unhappily, the high rate of recidivism quickly revealed how narrow were the limits of their dreams.

Upon such principles prison reform developed rapidly after 1780. Surveys were conducted, notably the influential review of the condition of European prisons by John Howard, and projects for new prison design proposed, of which Jeremy Bentham's terrifying Panopticon is surely the most notorious.[3] The first realization of these amibitions occurred, however, across the Atlantic in the American republic. In the years following the war for independence the Pennsylvania legislature greatly reduced the number of capital crimes, replacing them with prison terms and periods of hard labor. In part this was a reaction against the harsh British criminal law that had been imposed on William Penn's colony during the eighteenth century; in part it was a reassertion of the Quaker ethos in the context of Enlightenment humanitarianism. In 1790 a society of philanthropists, with approval of the legislature, created in Philadelphia the Walnut Street Jail. This celebrated institution seemed the concrete realization of the reformers' dreams. Its goal was reform of the prisoner; its methods were isolation and labor.[4] Prisoners were classified and separated by sex, age, and offense. The facilities of the Walnut Street Jail, however, were soon overwhelmed, and plans were made for its replacement. Opened in 1829 Cherry Hill—that is, Eastern State Penitentiary—continued and developed the earlier ideals. Each prisoner was kept in an individual cell, to

3. Ibid., pp. 200–209; Philip Hilmore Person, "The Penology of Jeremy Bentham" (Ph.D. diss., University of Wisconsin, 1929): Max Grünhut, *Penal Reform: A Comparative Study* (Oxford: Clarendon, 1948), pp. 23–42.

4. On the American prison systems see D. J. Rothman, *The Discovery of the Asylum: Social Order and Disorder in the New Republic* (Boston: Little, Brown, 1971), pp. 30–108; also Grünhut, *Penal Reform*, pp. 43–63.

which was joined a private exercise yard. Remunerative work, organized on a handicraft basis, was offered each inmate. All contact between prisoners was prevented. Self-reflection was further encouraged by a corps of visitors, upright and God-fearing citizens, who brought moral guidance to the inmates in their solitary chambers. This, the Philadelphia, or Pennsylvania, system, was immediately examined and praised by foreign observers, not least of whom were numerous French visitors abroad to escape the rigors of the revolution then in progress in their homeland. The duc de La Rochefoucauld brought the Walnut Street Jail to the attention of French readers in 1796; its central features governed Villermé's conception of correct prison administration.[5]

In contrast to the Philadelphia system stood the Auburn, or New York, system. Inaugurated at the Auburn and Sing Sing prisons, the New York system, while retaining single-cell accommodations, enforced behavioral isolation by means of fierce disciplinary measures. Work was undertaken in common, but silence was rigorously enforced. Advantages of scale were sought: the lock step, lash, and chain gang were essential instruments of social control. With occasional modifications leading to less brutal discipline, American prison practice largely adopted the New York system. European practice was more impressed with the Philadelphia system and particularly with its seeming capacity of preventing the infection of crime from spreading from one inmate to others.

French interest in matters of prison construction and administration reached back into the eighteenth century. Committees of the revolutionary assemblies, notably those devoted to mendicity, had their attention constantly diverted to problems of the workhouse and prison. While long years of war submerged this concern, it returned with undiminished vigor during the Restoration. The postwar years were a period of great turmoil. Unemployment was high, the business cycle irregular, harvests unsure. Vagrancy, mendicity, and crime seemed to abound; the state found it could not ignore these problems.

Administrative responsibility for prisons remained uncertain. While the central government had authority over the Paris prisons and projected or operating *maisons centrales* (maximum security penitentiaries), provincial incarceration was in the hands of numerous and unregulated local officers. Even in Paris there was no comprehensive and well-executed plan of prison administration. The famine and social turbulence of 1817 called forth concerted agitation for genuine prison reform. Governmental officers, notably the comte de Decazes, minister of Interior, heard and en-

---

5. [François, duc de La Rochefoucauld-Liancourt], *Des prisons de Philadelphie, par un Européen* (Philadelphia: Moreau de St. Méry, 1796; also Paris: Du Pont, an IV).

couraged these appeals. As a device to further this agitation as well as to
gain invaluable assistance from private individuals in the reform campaign, there was created (9 April 1819) under joint private and ministerial
initiative a major charitable organization, the Société royale pour
l'amélioration des prisons.[6] The society's membership was drawn principally from the aristocracy and from other *notables* of the period. A sizeable annual contribution was imposed and, for the more serious members,
considerable effort required. The society's primary mission was to "cooperate with the public administration" in all that concerned prison reform.[7] The comte de Decazes, whose ministry had at the same time as the
founding of the society received exclusive authority over the prisons of
Paris, indicated in a memorandum to his prefects the essential purposes of
the society. The society, he wrote, will serve to "ease the lot of the prisoners, make the prisons more salubrious, and provide more abundant and
substantial nourishment; provide clothing for the prisoners and assure
them of work that will destroy their idleness; provide resources against the
day of their release; organize infirmaries; prevent prisoners from becoming yet more depraved; and restore them to sound moral standards with
the aid of religion."[8]

The society's principal activities involved inquiry and inspection. It immediately launched a detailed investigation of the French prison establishment and quickly published its conclusions.[9] Over the decade of its existence (it perished with its creator, the Bourbon monarchy) the Société
royale des prisons made a major financial contribution to prison improvements and played an important role in certain reforms which were then
effected. Larger and better-designed prisons were constructed; clothing
was provided for the indigent; food and bedding were upgraded. Some
progress was made towards the classification and separation of inmates,
and widespread employment in the larger institutions was assured by outside entrepreneurs.[10]

The society's role was always an advisory one. Its members had the
leisure and were given the right to explore at will the condition of any and
all prisons and report not only their findings but also their recommendations to the minister of interior. Villermé was among the early members of

6. See Daru and Bournat, "Société royale des prisons," pp. 54–72, 288–301, 443–64,
729–51.

7. Ibid., p. 57. See also Ferdinand Dreyfus, *Un philanthrope d'autrefois: La Rochefoucauld-Liancourt, 1747–1827* (Paris: Plon, 1903), pp. 475–512.

8. Quoted in Daru and Bournat, "Société royale des prisons," p. 60.

9. Alexandre de Laborde, *Rapport à S. Exc. le ministre de l'Intérieur sur les prisons de
Paris et les améliorations dont elles sont susceptibles* (Paris: Imprimerie royale, 1819).

10. Daru and Bournat, "Société royale des prisons," pp. 744–48.

the society and followed with close interest its investigatory procedure. His own inquiry, conducted independently, followed very closely that pursued by the society, and his conclusions as well as his evidence reflect those published by the society. Important differences nonetheless exist, bearing especially on the role of secular education and the emphasis given to productive labor, and these differences indicate the need Villermé felt to make publicly available an alternative view of prison reform, one that gave, he insisted, due place to hygiene and political economy.

Villermé Examines the Prison

Villermé dedicated his first major publication "not to a duke or peer of France" (La Rochefoucauld was both) but to that "citizen who, upon his return from the city of William Penn, made known in his homeland and to all Europe the principles that must govern [the administration of] prisons."[11] To Villermé, and indeed to most of his contemporaries, La Rochefoucauld was the supreme representative of a life devoted to the service of mankind. *Des prisons* is first witness to Villermé's commitment to the same ideal. The work also exhibits, albeit in unperfected form, the essential character of its author's subsequent sociomedical investigations. *Des prisons* presents a distinctive juxtaposition of direct and indirect investigation of social conditions; assertion of the great importance of numerical data (but without meaningful use thereof); philanthropic concern marked, in keeping with the times, with a nice sense of the social and economic utility of such sympathy; and a keen appreciation for making widely known the results of the inquiry, that is, an awareness of the power and necessity of intelligently conducted publicity.

Of course, Villermé's principal object was the health of the prison population. He recognized, however, that this was a matter altogether dependent upon the entire range of conditions that govern admission to and conduct of the penitentiary. He knew well that the purpose of the penitentiary was no longer mere incarceration but the moral regeneration of the prisoner. Maintaining sound health, both moral and physical, was important to both objectives; but it was absolutely essential to the second. Moreover, it was not sufficient simply to "assure the health" of prisoners, the victims of vice; one must "tear vice itself from their hearts."[12] This must

---

11. L. R. Villermé, *Des prisons telles qu'elles sont et telles qu'elles devraient être: Ouvrage dans lequel on les considère par rapport à l'hygiène, à la morale et à l'économie politique* (Paris: Méquignon-Marvis, 1820). pp. i–ii. An abstract of this work was published as "Prison (hygiène publique)," *Dictionnaire des sciences médicales*, 60 vols. (Paris: Panckoucke, 1812–22), 40 (1820): 208–63.

12. Villermé, *Des prisons*, p. 174.

be done by means of just and fair treatment, giving proper attention to matters of housing, discipline, education, and labor. These several obligations of the administrative authorities existed because of the very purpose of the penitentiary. Moral reform was not meant to create a better yet continuing prison population; its goal was to create new men and women who should and, one hoped, would return to society, there to lead a law-abiding and useful existence. All of Villermé's reflections upon penitentiary and prison were informed by this expectation.

Des prisons was devoted to description of the physical and moral conditions existing in contemporary French, and particularly Parisian, prisons. The medical implications of these conditions were regularly noted and observation often directed to the conduct (and misconduct) of the prison authorities and their employees. Description was designed to support prescription: scientific knowledge assured control over the prison, and only firm control could guarantee amelioration of institution and inmate.

Virtually no aspect of the contemporary prison proved satisfactory. Particularly serious was the limited space available for the varied functions held indispensable for the preservation of the health and for the rehabilitation of prisoners. Most prisons occupied buildings that had been constructed for other purposes, often defense. To the ideal of security had been sacrificed all concern for salubrity. Walls were thick and constructed of stone; the spaces they enclosed were perpetually damp and cold. Subsoil dungeons continued in use, an abomination to the very notion of civilization. Access of light and air to all areas was severely limited. Windows were commonly mere slits in the wall or a remote and small opening to the sky. Into such chambers, occasionally spacious but usually quite small, were introduced pell-mell men, women, and children in numbers beyond all reason. Overcrowding was a major flaw in prison administration. An inevitable concomitant of such confinement was the absence of adequate and appropriate exercise areas.

All of these circumstances contributed to a characteristic feature of the prison, the inveterate filth of the structure and the spectacular uncleanliness of the prisoner. Clothing was commonly poor in quality and inadequate to the season as well as being filthy and vermin-infested. Villermé found this situation utterly wrong. Some kind of clothing being always required, it seemed to him quite reasonable that in clothing, as in fact in all matters of prison administration, one could easily be "more humane without being less frugal."[13] Contributing to these foul circumstances were the latrines. The latter were the "source of infection" in hospice and hos-

13. Ibid., p. 27.

pital as well as in prison; in the former, however, given the freedom of movement of the sick, one could at least remove the latrine from close proximity to sleeping and working areas. The prison imposed other demands. Villermé's solution, unlike that of imaginative forerunners and contemporaries, who sought via elaborate design immediate and definitive separation of the body and its wastes, was less architectural than homely.[14] Prisoners were to be provided, on a regular basis, with buckets, brooms, and water and compelled to make use of them. Chamber pots were to be emptied frequently and their contents not left to bake malodorously in overheated rooms under the eaves.

Among the measures leading to improved hygienic regimen within the prison, water, not surprisingly, was viewed as a panacea. Water could control the evil of latrine and chamber pot. It could also secure a notable innovation, namely, the washing or at least rinsing of the inmates' clothing. Not least, it could serve a dual hygienic and moral purpose; indeed, it acted so as to render the hygienic and the moral one and indissoluble. Water—and here indeed was a radical demand—could and must be used to assure the cleanliness of the prisoners' own bodies. Face and hands were to be washed daily (inspection was needed, of course); a monthly bath and shave was prescribed; new inmates were to be thoroughly cleansed upon admission. Cleanliness, in short, was to Villermé an indispensable preliminary to moral reform and thus to the achievement of the purpose of incarceration. His experience among the armies had obviously convinced him that the inducement of "habits of cleanliness leads to sobriety and orderliness and contributes to the elimination of several physical and moral vices."[15] Of course, contemporary prisons were desperately flawed, for the vast preponderance thereof lacked a plentiful supply of fresh water.

A further influence upon the prisoner was diet. Its effects upon the inmate were, with one important exception, more physical than moral. Dietary problems in the prisons were only those that are chronic in all large impersonal institutions designed to operate at minimal cost. Food was generally insufficient, bread and vegetables being the mainstays and meat a great rarity. Foodstuffs were commonly of poor quality, and meals, if such they could be called, were served at table and in common (a violation of the Pennsylvania practice). Strictest silence between prisoners was demanded, however. Most emphatically, alcoholic beverages were to be

14. See Pierre Saddy, "Le cycle des immondices," *Dix-huitième siècle* 9 (1977): 203–14; Bruno Fortier, "Architecture de l'hôpital," in Michel Foucault et al., *Machines à guérir* (Paris: Institut de l'environnement, 1976), pp. 71–86.

15. Villermé, *Des Prisons*, p. 3. John Pringle, John Howard, and others were cited in support of this claim.

banned from the prison. Here was a utopian proposition, one in accord with the Philadelphia system but flatly in contradiction of long-standing Continental usage. Villermé's purpose was, again, moral improvement. He held that abstinence from alcohol not only tempered violence, an obviously well-grounded contention, but also led to a change in the prisoner's viewpoint and thus to his social redemption. The American system came to be seen as favoring moral reform via dietary practice and was thus to be doubly encouraged: it led to sustained bodily health, and it acted directly and favorably upon the spiritual affliction that had originally brought the prisoner to crime.[16]

So infelicitous an institution as the prison did not fail in placing the health and indeed the life of the prisoner at risk. John Howard is said to have observed that one could estimate the length of a prisoner's incarceration by his physical condition. Disease was endemic amongst prison populations, and epidemics fell upon them both frequently and with devastating effect. Villermé's catalogue of the common prison afflictions—including rheumatism, diarrhea, persistent respiratory complaints, scurvy, and general debilitation—offered no surprises.[17] Certain measures might be taken to alleviate this situation. Vaccination, for example, conferred protection against smallpox. Villermé insisted that all prisoners, whether only accused, standing trial, or convicted, must be vaccinated, preferrably upon admission to prison. Since, under French judicial procedure, the accused and those standing trial were also incarcerated, usually with the convicts themselves, and since only rarely were these truly distinct categories of inmates segregated, the innocent accused or defendant stood a good chance of gaining his liberty but losing his health and often his life. Special care, therefore, must be exercised with regard to the accused, as well as for pregnant women and those suffering from acute disease.[18] An obvious step towards solution of this problem presented itself. Every important prison must be provided with an infirmary which, suitably isolated from other prison facilities, would possess appropriate facilities and staff

16. Ibid., p. 53. On later moral reform in America as furthered by diet, see J. B. Blake, "Health Reform in the Rise of Adventism," in *Religion and Society in Mid-Nineteenth-Century America*, ed. E. S. Gaustad (New York: Harper and Row, 1974), pp. 30–49; J. C. Whorton "'Christian Physiology': William Alcott's Prescription for the Millenium," *Bulletin of the History of Medicine* 49 (1975): 466–81; Stephen Nissenbaum, *Sex, Diet, and Debility in Jacksonian America: Sylvester Graham and Health Reform* (Westport: Greenwood, 1980).

17. Villermé, *Des prisons*, p. 9. Curiously, no reference was here made to typhus fever, probably the predominant infectious disease of the prison. Villermé was, of course, thoroughly acquainted with the problem: see his "Prisonniers de guerre (santé de)," *Dictionnaire des sciences médicales*, 40 (1820): 263–77.

18. Villermé, *Des prisons*, p. 127.

for the care of those placed in its charge.[19] Lesser prisons might utilize special hospital wards. Lastly, due caution would need to be exercised to apprehend malingerers feigning illness.

These reflections introduced a brief but suggestive numerical excursus (*Des prisons* offered little more numerical analysis than this). Infirmaries might be expected to command a not unimportant share of prison resources. But what share? And how determine it? Arguing on the basis of a loosely drawn proportion of sick to sound inmates in Parisian prisons established by the inquiries of the Société royale des prisons, Villermé claimed that an infirmary must be prepared to receive about one quarter of the total prison population.[20] Such reasoning must obviously lead to numerical assessment of the state of the prisons. But here, at precisely the point where the subtle art of reasoning upon numbers must begin, the data failed.

Etienne Pariset, a medical jack-of-all-trades and an able publicist, was also a member of the Société royale des prisons. He had contributed to the society's inquiry and report of 1819 and had insisted in the latter that the systematic and regular collection of vital statistics within the prisons was essential to their improvement and correct administration. His views were reported by the society but clearly seemed futile if not foolish to its leadership.[21] Villermé, however, presented them as the indispensable foundation for correction of the medical condition of the prisoners. Pariset had asked that prison physicians be required to keep exact records of morbidity and mortality within each institution.[22] Average life span could thus be determined; disease incidence by sex, age, and type of labor established; and the most common diseases and least healthful establishments discovered. It was important that this data be collected regularly and without interruption, for only then could it be put to use. Pariset felt that determination of the movement of disease(s) through this diverse yet controlled population would provide clues to means of improving both general health within the prison and of rendering more salubrious the manufacturing processes conducted therein and, one may presume, in society at large. Moreover, these vital statistics might also be used to learn something of the relationship between disease and population. Given a good series of numbers over a period of years, one might discover whether the "diseases of the prisoners are stationary and always the same, or whether they change

19. Ibid., pp. 128–32.
20. Ibid., p. 125.
21. Daru and Bournat, "Société royale des prisons," pp. 451, 460–61. See George Sussmann, "Etienne Pariset: A Medical Career in Government under the Restoration," *Journal of the History of Medicine* 26 (1971): 52–74.
22. Pariset's demand is cited in Villermé, *Des prisons*, p. 126.

in stages and what might be the sequence of these stages," and, further, whether such diseases are tied to determinate climatic circumstances (*constitutions établies*) or are independent thereof.

Pariset had outlined the bare essentials for establishing a fund of dependable vital data suitable for further analysis. Villermé clearly perceived this fact and therefore lamented all the more that such information was not already at hand. It was not, except for a brief period of four years (1815–1818 inclusive) for prisons of the department of the Seine and for the *bagne*, or maximum-security prison, at Brest. This data was presented to the reader of *Des prisons* in a single concise table pertaining to Paris and an even more rudimentary summary table plus a listing of mortality and morbidity at Brest.[23] The author's discussion of this data was confined to the terse conclusion that "with regard to mortality, I leave it to the reader to deduce whatever consequences he will from the many facts that I have reported."[24] This was, in truth, neither abdication of responsibility on the part of the author nor an effort to avoid influencing unduly the reader's own conclusions. Villermé's recognized that what Pariset had demanded—one or several series of reliable data—simply did not exist in 1820. Later in the decade such material became more abundant and could then be fairly exploited for assaying, albeit still in a limited fashion, the medical situation within the prison. Villermé's essay on prison mortality, published in 1829, truly exhibited reasoning with numbers; *Des prisons* merely discussed the possibility and stressed the desirability of doing so.

The perils of prison life were not simply physical. The moral corruption therein outraged Villermé's sensibilities perhaps even more than did the abundance of preventable disease. Moral corruption meant but two things. Indiscriminate contact between the experienced criminal and the novice, as was usually inevitable in contemporary prisons, made incarceration a superbly efficacious training ground for new recruits to serious criminal behavior. Death, the young learned from seasoned offenders, was but a "difficult half-hour," whereas a long prison term, given the severity of treatment to be expected, meant perpetual misery.[25] Here Villermé followed Bentham's and other reformers' view: laws demanding capital punishment were but an invitation to eliminate victim or witness, an outright inducement to murder. A better deterrent would be the surety of a long term in prison—but only in a well-conducted prison. These confused themes of barbarous laws and the prison as a school for crime Villermé

23. Ibid., facing p. 133, pp. 162–63.
24. Ibid., p. 133.
25. Ibid., pp. 98–100. The moral hazards of the prison had been especially emphasized by John Howard; see his *The State of the Prisons* [1777] (London: J. M. Dent, 1929), pp. 5–6 et passim.

did not explore in depth. He was content merely to indicate that such was the daily reality of justice and its administration, a reality whose effect, of course, precluded the regenerative function that was, in his eyes, the only proper function of such institutions.

Another form of moral degradation could be more easily remedied, but only if prison administrators admitted the notorious truth of the problem and set about relentlessly to keep separate the offenders. You would think, Villermé laconically declared, that sexual desire would diminish as the tedium of prison life took hold. Alas, it was not so. The prison was society's very center of pederasty and masturbation. "With what terms can I describe for you," he declared, "the situation that obtains when, lacking a partner of the opposite sex, one prisoner will *marry* (that is the accustomed word in prison) another?"[26] Although the author's shock was doubtlessly exaggerated for the benefit, or moral horror, of his reader—as an experienced military surgeon he was surely familiar with these practices—he nonetheless found the subject both loathsome and demanding of stringent countermeasures. One obvious solution—namely, to allow a mingling of the sexes, a common practice in all too many prisons—simply led to other forms of depravity and particularly to the total debasement of the body and morals of the younger inmates, most of them female and many of them scarcely out of childhood. Here was foulness indeed, created in large part by the institution itself and thus a product of society's own neglect of the welfare of its potentially happy and productive members.

The prison need not be a house of horrors. Its purpose was not to torment the prisoner; it was to "bring a halt to his career in crime and to frighten those who might be tempted to imitate him."[27] And in most cases, a prison term was a limited affair. The prisoner would return to society and must be prepared for that return. Villermé's description of the maladministration, vice, and unrelieved violence of prison life was merely a prelude to the major message he wished to impart. His true object of study was not the individual prisoner or a particular act of humanity or knavery; it was an institution, in this case, the prison and the rising penitentiary. The prison, like society, presented man in the mass. Unlike society, however, it seemed to offer a controlled or at least controllable situation whose parameters could be assayed and mastered and then directed towards definite ends.

What, then, was Villermé's program for reform and upon what premises did it depend? To the question, To what is criminal behavior due? the

---

26. Villermé, *Des prisons*, p. 95. Villermé found prison homosexuality to be more common and less easily halted among the female prisoners than among the male (ibid., p. 96).
27. Ibid., p. 74.

source and the intention of his response were unmistakable. Arguing in the tradition of the idéologues, Villermé stressed the importance of external influences in the formation of moral character. The interaction of the moral and the physical was incessant and profound. Man was not by nature a soiled creature but was led to antisocial behavior by inadequate or improper education or by the example and stimulus of persons already grown corrupt. Poverty eventuating in destitution was perhaps the best invitation to such degradation. Under the encyclopedic rubric of "Other means of restoring prisoners to sound morality" Villermé indirectly provided a capsule psychological foundation for moral reform. As his analysis expanded into the world outside the prison, this foundation served also as the basis for social reform. Rudiments of a utilitarian ethical calculus were employed. Two motives guide all human behavior. Fear (pain) can assure control over men, but alone it offers little prospect for moral regeneration. Hope, however, exploits the pleasure principle and thus constitutes the bedrock of intelligent prison administration.[28] Hope (pleasure) appeals to self-interest; and to Villermé and fellow economists self-interest was the interest that truly mattered. Prison routine offered an excellent opportunity to apply these principles. The prisoner could be guided to virtue. Offer him, subject to demonstrable improvement in his conduct, the hope of early release (but, Villermé carefully added, "maintain the fear" that failure to reform would mean a full term). Reform, it was confidently expected, would follow. If, throughout *Des prisons*, the carrot received pride of place, the stick was never forgotten, for each was a critical element in social control, each an instrument of moral improvement.

Villermé was sincere in these ambitions. He saw no point at all in merely securing peace within the prison. Means must be provided for the elevation of moral standards and provision made for useful labor; naturally, measures must be instituted to compel the prisoner to receive benefit from them. Foremost amongst these instrumentalities was education, to be seconded by work and isolation. Instruction in reading and writing provided only first foundations. Of greater importance was the need to inculcate the prisoners with "a sense of the dignity of man, to provide instruction in political economy, to persuade them that security and happiness belong to those who fulfill their obligations, and finally, to address oneself to their intellect and to those sentiments of honor which they may still preserve."[29]

Members of the Société royale des prisons expected religious instruction to assume a paramount position within the prison. Given the zealotry

28. Ibid., pp. 109–23.
29. Ibid., p. 113.

of official French Catholicism under the Restoration, this is not surprising. From this demand Villermé, a loyal if not impassioned Roman Catholic, dissented sharply. His social outlook was stern, realistic, and secular. The zealots, he held, totally misunderstood the conditions of prison life. What possible good could repeated catechization of dogma do in a world in which housing, diet, discipline, work, and the most elementary instruction were in disarray? The first step was to improve the conduct of daily life in the prison and to let that life itself serve as an example of other improvements to follow. Only then should religious instruction begin, for only then would it have the faintest chance of a sympathetic reception.[30]

Work stood before religion as a moral influence in the eyes of the eighteenth-century social philosopher and speculative historian. The support of steady labor separated the civilized condition from that of the savage; Adam Smith noted that the "produce of the whole labour of [a large] society is so great, that all are often abundantly supplied, and a workman, even of the lowest and poorest order, if he is frugal and industrious, may enjoy a greater share of the necessaries and conveniences of life than it is possible for any savage to acquire."[31] With regard to labor men and women in prison were of many sorts. Some had lost the habit of work and had turned to crime; others had worked and continued to want to work but found none available and fell into criminal habits; and others had never acquired either the habit of or a desire for labor—crime was their sole occupation. These options, commonplaces of the period, offered recognition that lack of regular productive employment usually led to conflict with the law and often enough to prison. If lack of work, be it due to moral or economic failing, was thus a stimulus to crime, so might a heightened respect and capacity for useful labor serve as a remedy for the lawless life.

No one adopted this truism of prison reform more fervently than Villermé. "A well-run prison," he enthusiastically announced, "should appear to those who visit it less of a house of repression [*lieu de contrainte*] than a workshop."[32] Work and isolation, he had previously asserted, constitute the very core of prison regimen. Work is the primary agent of redemption. It not only prevents the lassitude too often encountered amongst prisoners but places them on the path of social righteousness. Well-directed and regular labor reduced debauchery, of course, but far better was the fact

30. Ibid., pp. 114–15.

31. Adam Smith, *An Inquiry into the Nature and Causes of the Wealth of Nations*, 2nd ed., 2 vols. (Oxford: Clarendon, 1880), 1:2. See T. M. Adams, "Mendicity and Moral Alchemy: Work as Rehabilitation," *Studies on Voltaire and the Eighteenth Century* 151 (1976): 47–76.

32. Villermé, *Des prisons*, p. 66.

that it replaced disorder with "order, decency, and sound habits [*moeurs*]."[33]

The supposed advantages of labor in prison had many ramifications. In the first place, it taught the untutored and the inexperienced a profession. This was an acquisition that was presumed to return with the discharged prisoner when he or she reentered society. An honest existence amidst his fellow workers seemed thereby assured. Here was philanthropy in the truest sense of the term: prison had made a man or a woman self-sufficient. This was a noble aspiration and one, it was believed, easily met by the proper organization of labor. The reality, of course, was far different, for employers were shy of men with criminal experience (Jean Valjean being only the most celebrated victim), and in prison discipline was imposed more than independent skills were imparted.[34] At best, the whole argument and its imperfect realization probably offered only another contribution to the formation of an acquiescent industrial proletariat, well-regimented hands for the new factories of France.

Villermé condemned the exploitation of prison labor. Prisoners, he argued, were to be paid a fair wage for their efforts and were to receive, as was the custom, one-third of that wage in cash (a second third was held in reserve for the day of discharge, and the final third reverted to the prison administration for the inmate's keep). Corruption on the part of prison officials, obviously the rule, was fiercely condemned. Payment of the first third was to be made in full and when due: how else would undisciplined persons learn the tangible advantages of labor? Once again, work offered hope, with steady wages as the continuing temptation placed before the malefactor, and through the encouragement of hope came promise of moral regeneration.

The system thus conceived offered advantages to others outside the prison. Villermé recognized that most prison production was organized on a handicraft basis, focusing especially upon clothing and shoes. He also realized that another approach was possible, and it was one that he clearly preferred. *Des prisons* was in no small part an earnest invitation to the rising entrepreneurial class to seize a neglected opportunity. Manufacturing operations should be moved within the prison walls. Such large-scale enterprise was already in profitable operation in the penitentiaries at Clairvaux and Melun. Villermé identified three principal economic advantages of prison production. Gathered in one convenient place were large numbers of hands, always ready to work and accustomed to discipline. The theft of raw materials and finished goods, a major problem from the ear-

33. Ibid., p. 60.
34. Ibid., p. 65. Lower prison wages were not appreciated by all: Victor Hugo, *Les misérables*, ed. Maurice Allem (Paris: Gallimard, 1951), p. 203.

liest years of industrialization, was virtually impossible in the prison. Lastly, and this no doubt constituted the greatest inducement of all, wages might be kept somewhat lower than in the outside world.

The creation of regular habits, the moral stimulus of the prospect of an income, the useful occupation of all the prisoner's days—such were the advantages of the workshop-prison. But the prison, like the world itself, had its misfits whose faults and misdeeds could not be overlooked. Their behavior demanded punishment. Villermé was modern indeed in dealing with this matter. Traditional penalties, being generally one form of physical assault or another, he would not tolerate. The purpose, as always, was moral reform, and so the means must suit the end. The only punishment in prison was to be "solitary confinement for a number of days scaled according to the seriousness of the infraction."[35] A few European prisons followed this practice, but in most cases it merely meant confinement in insalubrious dungeons. The Philadelphians, however, seemed to have perfected solitary confinement. A clean, well-heated cell, Villermé discovered, gave the prisoner but "the sky and four walls" for his diversion; most cried for release within a few days. Here was a moral instrument by which to touch even the most serious offender. "The guilty party, his communication with other inmates now severed, can no longer be influenced by them; his thoughts are turned inward, and the reflections which he is thus forced to entertain give him over to remorse."[36] Thus was born a new man, one endowed with the first rudiments of self-awareness and one who could recognize and follow socially acceptable actions that might also further his own interests.

Lost in a sea of similar and often far more substantial publications Villermé's *Des prisons* appears to have attracted few contemporary readers and remains little known today.[37] Its principal interest is its place in the formulation of the thoughts and investigatory procedure of an ex-army surgeon who very quickly was to become and would long remain the foremost sociomedical investigator in France. Villermé did not lack experience with social ills; what needed to be found, and was found, was a focus for his philanthropic instinct. That focus he discovered within the context of the prison reform movement of the early Restoration. It was more sharply defined by the activities of the Société royale des prisons and received sustained inspiration from La Rochefoucauld and from other investigators of the period, notably Benoiston de Châteauneuf and J. B.

35. Villermé, *Des prisons*, p. 117.
36. Ibid., p. 119.
37. An enthusiastic notice was published by Villermé's associate Gilbert Breschet: "Des prisons telles qu'elles sont et telles qu'elles devraient être," *Journal complémentaire des sciences médicales* 7 (1820): 63–71.

Parent-Duchâtelet. In *Des prisons* the reader meets first-hand description, skillful use of reports prepared by other observers, an as yet ill-formulated but nonetheless pronounced allegiance to the party of political economy, and an unqualified faith that reasonable men of good will, once come into possession of numerous reliable and pertinent facts, would prove invincible before any hygienic evils—in fact, any social evil whatsoever—that they might encounter.

A Simple Numerical Lesson

Numerical data allowed distinctions to be drawn between subgroups within a given population. One could then attempt to ascertain the conditions that determined or were regularly or commonly associated with the characteristic features of each subgroup under consideration. With regard to the nature of the prison population(s) of the 1820s, this calculus consisted simply of relating categories of prisoners and prison administrations to inmate mortality and of seeking to contrast life expectancy within and without the prison.

The data that Villermé analyzed in a new memoir published in 1829 were taken from diverse sources. A table of prison population and mortality for Paris (1815–18), drawn from *Des prisons*, provided a base point for comparison with officially collected mortality data for the same prisons for the years 1826–27. Departmental censuses were consulted, personal inquiries made, and vital statistics solicited from various administrative offices. Innumerable problems remained: data were usually not collected in the same manner, completeness was always uncertain, figures were given that could not properly be compared, and sizes of the prisons varied greatly. Villermé was cognizant of all these flaws and of the fact that in some cases the situation was beyond repair. His primary purpose, however, was to use this data for social analysis and persuasion; he did not seek a mathematical justification for his procedures, nor did he pursue, as William Farr was soon to do, a more careful definition of the kinds of data to be collected.

Villermé's memoir on mortality in the prisons[38] addressed itself to three basic topics. These involved a comparison or series of comparisons, each now to be effected by "valid and well-established facts," that is, by number. Not by chance did this remarkable memoir stand as the first contribution to appear in the celebrated *Annales d'hygiène publique*. Villermé sought to demonstrate, firstly, that different kinds of prisoners, presumably

---

38. L. R. Villermé, "Mémoire sur la mortalité dans les prisons," *Annales d'hygiène publique et de médecine légale* 1 (1829): 1–100.

because of their distinctive condition, had different mortality rates. Once admitted to prison, the prisoners of each group, he noted as his second point, exhibited death rates that varied with the institutions in which they were held; the conduct of prison affairs was thought to be displayed by these numbers. The third theme was to show how the mortality of prisoners, who constituted a segregated society, compared with that of comparable members of the nonprison population. Once again, number was used, now to show the presumed diminished life expectancy of the prison inmate (see Table 4.1).

Table 4.1. Annual mortality rate in selected Parisian prisons
(per 1,000 inmates)

Prison	1815–18	1819–27
Grande Force	24.5	17.4
Saint Lazare	55.7	41.7
Dépôt de Saint-Denis	251.9	177.3

SOURCE: L. R. Villermé, "Mémoire sur la mortalité dans les prisons," *Annales d'hygiène publique et de médecine légale* 1 (1829): 35. Restated. Figures for the years 1819–27 were as yet unpublished, Villermé consulting them in the office of the statistical department of the Seine. They later appeared in the *Recherches statistiques sur la ville de Paris et le département de la Seine* (Paris: Imprimerie Royale, 1829), vol. 4, tables 70–74.

Comparing death rates in the various Parisian houses of detention, Villermé found extraordinary differences, the worst case exhibiting ten times the mortality of the best. For the years 1815–18 mortality in the Grande Force was 24.5 per 1,000 in contrast to 251.9 per 1,000 in the infamous *dépôt de mendicité* at Saint Denis. Other prisons showed gradations of mortality, reaching 55.7 per 1,000 with Saint Lazare before increasing precipitously to that of the disastrous condition at Saint Denis.[39] The first clue to understanding such disparate experiences was found in the prison destination itself: each received a definite category of inmate, and his or her condition upon entrance seemed a critical factor in determining the overall mortality of each separate institution. The Grande Force served the Paris area as the holding house for males accused of crimes. The period of incarceration was often brief, many inmates had sufficient money to procure food and bedding from without and thus not be wholly dependent on the prison's own services, and no doubt most individuals who entered

39. Data from ibid., p. 3. Villermé's fractional expressions (e.g., 1 death per 40.88 inmates in the Grande Force) have throughout been restated in rates expressed in deaths per thousand inmates (thus, 24.5 deaths per 1,000 inmates in the same prison). The convention of expressing mortality as number of deaths per thousand population was probably introduced, and was consistently used from the 1830s onwards, by William Farr; see John M. Eyler, *Victorian Social Medicine: The Ideas and Methods of William Farr* (Baltimore: Johns Hopkins University Press, 1979), p. 69.

were in reasonably sound physical condition at date of admission. Saint Denis, on the other hand, was a house of last resort, the bitter end for the utterly destitute. Villermé recognized this clearly: "The mortality that one encounters at the *dépôt* in Saint Denis, mortality so high that proportionately there die no more soldiers in a murderous war, seems to have its source in the often degraded [physical] condition of the poor, brought on by privations and by suffering experienced before entrance into prison, and also in the impossibility these persons face in obtaining the necessities of life."[40] New data from other *dépôts de mendicité* showed that Saint Denis was no exception. Average annual mortality at Laon was 231.3 per 1,000 between 1814 and 1826, and at Auch over a five-year period more than 330 per 1,000 per annum; and during one dreadful year at Metz (1801), it reached 454.5 per 1,000.[41] In the *maisons centrales* mortality was less elevated: at Beaulieu (Caen) between 1814 and 1825 it reached an annual average of 86.3 per 1,000, and at Melun between 1817 and 1825 it attained 67.5 per 1,000.[42] The model prison at Ghent, a house for intermediate periods of detention, consistently presented lower mortality: 38.8 per 1,000 in 1789, 49 per 1,000 in 1801, and 22.7 per 1,000 in 1826.[43] The most severe prison regime in France was that governing the four maximum security and forced labor institutions (*bagnes*) operated by the naval ministry. Yet the condition of their inmates, as measured by mortality, was among the best in the nation (Rochefort, average for 1816–27, 86.9 per 1,000; Toulon, 1827, 55.6 per 1,000; Brest, average for 1816–27, 37 per 1,000; Lorient, average for 1816–27, 25.5 per 1,000).[44]

These data presented an obvious moral. Few persons, perhaps, doubted (or cared) that prison mortality was high. Some surely suspected that there were real differences in mortality and that these followed prisoner category and prison regime. Villermé, however, converted this suspicion into a demonstration, despite the woefully rudimentary nature of his data. If it stands to reason that he who is malnourished and ill stands a greater chance of dying than he who is well-fed and in good health, be he in prison or at liberty, one cannot by reason alone determine for each what the relative chances of life and death are. Villermé's mode of analysis

40. Villermé, "Sur la mortalité dans les prisons," p. 5.

41. Data from ibid., p. 9; see also pp. 42–43, table 1 (Laon) and table 2 (Auch), from which slightly different figures are obtained. Restated.

42. Data from ibid., pp. 44–45, table 4 (Beaulieu) and table 5 (Melun). Restated. In both *dépôts*, Villermé noted without comment, the death rate for males was notably higher (ca. 33 percent or more) than for females.

43. Data from ibid., p. 10. Restated.

44. Data from ibid., pp. 13–14. Restated. The *bagne* at Rochefort, lying in the low, humid reaches of coastal Charente Maritime, occupied a peculiarly unhealthy site.

assured that those chances could be computed with ever greater exacti-tude. That the poor, the exclusive candidates for the *dépôts de mendicité* as well as prime candidates for criminal conviction and therefore for a period in *maison centrale* or *bagne*, died more frequently than the wealthy or the regularly employed was, as has been often remarked, an ancient truism. Villermé's assessment of the differential mortality of prisoners was part of his concerted effort during the 1820s to convert this easy verbalism into apparently objective science.

Great caution was expressed regarding the causes of the sorry fate of the prisoner. "I do not claim," Villermé declared, "that the admitted differ-ences with regard to mortality in the diverse prisons of the department of the Seine must be attributed exclusively to the differences existing be-tween individuals, their health at the time of entrance into prison and their pecuniary resources; the location of each prison and the good or poor conduct of its affairs must also count for something in this matter."[45] Such judicious inclusiveness opened a further perspective on the effect of incar-ceration upon mortality. Just as prisoners vary in their moral and physical resistance, so prisons will vary in their effects upon their inmates. Villermé believed that number again most persuasively revealed this effect. Prisons dedicated to similar objectives declare their poor conduct by their high mortality.

Unfortunately, data regarding prison administration across France were difficult to obtain. Great weight was placed on selected cases, notably the contrast between mortality in the workhouses of the Low Countries and in the *dépôts de mendicité* of France and the improvement in the vital ex-perience of the prison of Vilvorde. Throughout the Low Countries (the Netherlands and Belgium) workhouse mortality at no time between 1811 and 1822 reached the dismal standard of France. Gradual but steady im-provement characterized the period, save for the bad year of 1817, when mortality rose—yet even then it did not reach France's usual level. For the seven workhouses in the Pays-Bas mortality was 112.9 per 1,000 in 1811, 107.9 per 1,000 in 1816, 182.1 per 1,000 in 1817, 107.6 per 1,000 in 1819, and 68.9 per 1,000 in 1822.[46] There was great variation between these workhouses: between 1811 and 1822, inclusive, mortality at Mons was 149.7 per 1,000, at Hoogstraten 124.8 per 1,000, at Lacambre (Brux-elles) 73.7 per 1,000, and at Reckheim 26.5 per 1,000.[47] None of these institutions ever approximated the appalling record of the French *dépôts de mendicité*. Here, certainly, were striking differences in mortality, yet

45. Ibid., p. 8.
46. Data from ibid., p. 17. Restated.
47. Ibid.

Villermé seemed incapable of explaining them. At best he concluded that in the Low Countries "the lot of beggars is or was less difficult than in our land [France] and the workhouses much better."[48] This, in fact, was only a conclusion, and it failed entirely the stated objective, namely, to provide via number precise discrimination between the condition of the entering prisoner and the conduct of the prison in their respective contributions to mortality.

Villermé's argument fared somewhat better with the prison of Vilvorde, an unparalleled case of horror and demonstrable improvement. Vilvorde (Brabant) had been governed, the author casually remarked, with "great negligence," evidence thereof being the death rate of its inmates. An X (1802) was the worst year for mortality and, Villermé noted without additional consideration, for the conduct of its internal affairs. Mortality that year reached an "almost unbelievable" rate of 789.5 per 1,000. Ergot-tainted bread may have accounted for part of this loss of life. In each of the following five years mortality was as follows: an XI (1803), 593.7 per 1,000; an XII (1804), 521.2 per 1,000; an XIII (1805), 128.8 per 1,000; an XIV (1806), 62.7 per 1,000; and 1807, 32.9 per 1,000.[49] In 1805 unspecified "ameliorations" had been introduced by new administrators; an immediate and abrupt drop in mortality ensued. This occurred in a prison which continued to hold the "same classes of prisoners" and whose average population had risen from 668 in 1802 to 1,185 in 1807. It appeared self-evident that an improved regime within the prison of Vilvorde, a regime presumably affecting matters of clothing, exercise, cleanliness, and above all, diet, was the cause of this happy development.

A hint of the real source of these improvements had been given elsewhere in the essay. What made the prisoner's lot more secure was work, for it was their own labor that had assured other improvements in the prisons of Metz. In these prisons mortality had declined significantly, although remaining very high. In 1801 the death rate stood at 246.9 per 1,000, in 1802 196.9 per 1,000, and in 1803 142.5 per 1,000, a diminution of almost 60 percent in three years.[50] "Do you wish to know what has been the cause of this progressive amelioration?" our author asked. If so, hear the words of the prefect of the Moselle, under whose authority the change had occurred: "One sees . . . mortality diminish in proportion to the introduction of sound prison administration [bonne police], more healthful and abundant nourishment, and cleaner clothing." And this was

48. Ibid., p. 18.
49. Data from ibid., p. 55, table 14. Restated. Annual population was determined by averaging the number of inmates on 1 January and 31 December of each year. The figure for 1 January 1807 is an obvious misprint.
50. Data from ibid., p. 16. Restated.

made possible because "all the inmates were placed under the obligation of working." Villermé merely reemphasized this point: "Thus, such great advantages for the health and life of the prisoners seem to be due simply to the introduction of work, or, in reality, to a decision taken by the local administration."[51]

The most telling instance, however, of the positive effects of improved administrative action was given by the prisons of Paris. By 1829 it had become possible to compare two time series of mortality data, the first being that already cited in tabular form in *Des prisons* and covering the years 1815–18 and the second made available in manuscript form to Villermé by his friend Frédéric Villot, director of the statistical office of the department of the Seine. The second series covered the years 1819–27 and, in a separate set of figures, 1819–25. These data revealed that a significant reduction in mortality had occurred between the two periods in every penal institution in the department (see Table 4.1). For the departmental prisons as a whole, including the *dépôt* of Saint-Denis, mortality had declined from 83.3 per 1,000 in 1815–18 to 65.4 per 1,000 in 1819– 25 (a decline of 21 percent); if the *dépôt* is excluded from the computation, the improvement is even more marked, falling from 43.5 per 1,000 in 1815–18 to 30.7 per 1,000 in 1819–25 (a decline of 29 percent). The most improved institution in the entire system was the Conciergerie, where the rate declined 55 percent in a mere six years (1815–18: 31.2 per 1,000; 1819–25: 14.1 per 1,000).[52] The two time series were divided by what to Villermé was a critical event in the life of the French prison system, namely, the foundation of the Société royale des prisons. It was to the investigations, propaganda, and financial support of the society, always seconded by a handful of astute and capable administrative officers, that he assigned responsibility for the improved mortality experience of the prisons. Better food, clothing, and bedding had been assured, and in 1825, a major administrative change was introduced. Thereafter the accused were to be as well-treated with regard to food and lodging as were those who had been convicted of a crime. Given the fact that the perversities of the law until then had assured convicts of basic support from public funds but denied this support to the accused, who were most likely only transients in the judicial system, this measure could not fail to improve the condition of men and women who had just been arrested or were awaiting or standing trial.

To those who believed that the prison should serve a regenerative function, it counted as a major vice if that institution not only fell short of its

51. Ibid.
52. Ibid., p. 35.

goal but imposed unequal burdens upon its inmates. Yet this was precisely what contemporary French prisons were doing. They destroyed the health of prisoners and thereby increased their mortality far beyond that of comparable groups in society at large. Proof of this contention appeared to be provided, once again, by number. It is well to emphasize at the outset that Villermé's analytical procedure in this instance was utterly wrong. The absence of data regarding the age distribution of the prison population and also of the class or economic origins of the prisoner vitiate his whole course of reasoning; subtracting average ages at death in order to determine years of life lost in two or more populations is slight of hand and gives no meaningful results. On the other hand, the entire operation is most revealing of the principal purpose behind such argument, namely, emphasis on extreme cases with the aim of persuasion. Villermé did not again attempt such a faulty investigation, but he returned repeatedly to the exemplary use of extreme cases.

The presumed demonstration required comparative data on life expectancy of age groups within and without the prison. Reliable figures regarding both groups were largely unavailable, although life tables for the latter group had been greatly expanded and improved since their introduction in the late seventeenth century.[53] Life tables for a prison population were, it appears, simply nonexistent. Lacking a series of any kind for age-specific mortality within the prison, Villermé sought instead to designate a common standard, a given age, and then to examine comparatively mortality and life expectancy of members of the free and incarcerated populations of that age. Immediately a dilemma arose: What is the age distribution of prisoners? No one knew. What, then, is the average age of prisoners in the system? Again, no one knew—but a conservative approximation could be given. In making his estimate Villermé sought to err on the high side; he estimated that the average age of French prisoners was 35 years.[54] Turning then to the life table prepared by E. E. Duvillard, he found that at age 35, 1 person in 58.5 in the nonprison population could be expected to die—

53. See D. V. Glass, *Numbering the People: The Eighteenth-Century Population Controversy and the Development of Census and Vital Statistics in Britain* (London: Gordon and Cremonesi, 1978), pp. 120–26; Eyler, *Victorian Social Medicine*, pp. 70–90.

54. But available data suggested that most prisoners were quite young. In the Philadelphia jail between 1822 and 1824 the "average age" of all inmates was less than 30 years (86 percent were younger than 40 years; 63 percent, younger than 30). In 1827 41 percent of new entrants to London's Millbank prison were less than 21 years old. Moreover, convicts in the *bagnes*, men usually condemned for recidivism and sentenced to the longest terms in prison, between 1820 and 1827 presented an average age of 34.5 years; 57 percent were 34 years or younger, and 82 percent were 44 or younger. Data from Villermé, "Sur la mortalité dans les prisons," pp. 23–25, and p. 98, table 17.

that is, the death rate for the 35-year-old age group was 17.1 per 1,000.[55] With this datum he then thought to compare the death rates in various French prisons, each of whose populations would have an average age, at most, of 35 years. It is just this comparison that vitiates the entire argument; no consideration was given to age-specific mortality and to the age distribution of prisoners; and, of course, there were no data available had comparisons in fact been contemplated.

The comparison, false in detail, was perhaps valid in its overall bearing. Of the fourteen prisons examined (all of the Parisian penal institutions were considered as one) only one, and this only for a given four-year span, exhibited lower mortality. In all of the other prisons and for every time period examined, the inmates died much more frequently than members of the standard 35-year-old civilian age group. High prison mortality was, of course, the central theme of the 1829 memoir and had already been examined from diverse points of view. Villermé now bent this same data to a new argument. He inverted Duvillard's life table, using now the death rate in a population to estimate the average age of such a population. Duvillard's life table had shown that on average at age 35, 17.1 persons per 1,000 population will die; inverted, his table reports that a population with mortality of 17.1 per 1,000 will average 35 years of age. Villermé possessed mortality data for prisons; now he sought to learn at what average age those tables would be equalled in the nonprison population.[56] The difference, he thought, would represent the excessive mortality of the prisoners.

But average age cannot be used for such purposes. Even worse was the extension of such reasoning to determining years of life "lost" because of incarceration. If, as was assumed, the average age of the French prison population was 35, then mortality within a prison greater than 17.1 per 1,000 (Duvillard's 1 death for each 58.5 members of the population) stood in excess of that of the nonprison population. Men and women on average, it appeared, died younger in prison than without. Their life expectancies were, Villermé claimed, seriously reduced by the prison experience, and their loss could be expressed in seemingly unequivocal number. Thus, at Toulouse 17 and 41 years were, on average, lost; at Paris, whose prison system was superior to most others in France, 25 years were lost; in the infamous château at Pau, a prison for the accused and not the convicted, the loss was a full 60 years. Alas, in such an analysis average age is

55. See Werner S. Jonckheere, "La table de mortalité de Duvillard," *Population* 20 (1965): 865–74.

56. Villermé's data are presented in "Sur la mortalité dans les prisons," pp. 26–27.

meaningless; without age-specific mortality data for both populations the argument collapses. Villermé thought he had illustrated in remarkable manner the meaning of "excessive mortality" and this due to incarceration alone; in reality he had demonstrated nothing but faulty reasoning.

Such cavalier treatment of vital statistics was not typical of his procedure. But it must be reemphasized that number was always a tool to be exploited by the sociomedical observer and rarely if ever a matter worthy of independent consideration. Those who in these early years did seek a more sophisticated mathematical approach to population phenomena—men such as Jules Gavarret, Joseph Fourier, and Adolphe Quetelet—spoke to an unhearing audience of physicians and social observers. Villermé was painfully aware of the inadequacies of the data that he attempted to manipulate. He knew that available figures were insufficient in number and were often presented in a manner incompatible with the analysis to be based upon them. He recognized that some data were inconsistent and that other figures were plainly erroneous. He sought to avoid, not always successfully, the great perils that these shortcomings presented. His task was not terribly difficult, for his mathematical analyses, however ingenious their social focus, were very simple. Regular reliance upon sums, differences, and especially averages could occasionally lead to serious technical error—but also to novel social insight.

The greater prize, in fact, was not the ultimate precision of number but the social purpose that might be furthered even by approximate numbers. The murderous state of affairs within the prison was well-known to social observers and had already been insisted upon by Villermé in *Des prisons*. Filth, crowding, psychological torment, sexual depravity, lack of air and exercise had there been cited, and were remarked again in 1829. In the memoir of the latter year, however, particular stress was placed upon diet and its insufficiency in both kind and abundance. Virtually all data showed a sharp rise in prison mortality and also civilian mortality following the famine of 1817. The famine was intimately related to the dearth of foodstuffs in the prisons. While not an unexpected conclusion it was one that could now be illustrated or, more boldly, proved by concrete figures. Soup, water, and bread (one and one-half pounds per day) were simply inadequate to the task of maintaining health.[57] Even in prisons where labor was required and the diet improved to include meat, the rations were often insufficient. A prisoner's only recourse in such a situation was to purchase additional food. But many inmates had no money to do so. Labor and its

57. Ibid., pp. 30–34. The "official" diet of the *bagne* and prison is noted ibid., p. 13, n. 1.

modest pecuniary yield were still the exception and not the rule in the overall system; prison administrators were often incompetent or corrupt and commonly both; the accused was still exposed to greater deprivation than the convicted. The 1829 memoir makes clear that, in Villermé's opinion, insufficient diet, from which ensued fatigue, systematic debilitation, rampant disease, and excessive mortality, was the paramount problem in prison administration. Diet was not simply a biological matter but a problem that demanded consideration on the economic and administrative fronts as well. The prison was a social system and society's own creation; it demanded the attention of every social interest.

In retrospect, it might appear that Villermé had proved what was obvious to all. In a narrow sense this observation is valid: his was not the first discovery that generalized misery and excessive mortality were the inevitable fate of the prisoner. His contribution was, however, more than mere reiteration of that conclusion. There were still few students of prison affairs, their inquiries were based largely upon visitation of the prisons, and their reports consisted principally of verbal description and exhortation. Villermé sought an additional means by which to give vivid and, hopefully, equally persuasive voice to the reformers' concern. His numerical approach allowed ruthless adherence to the seeming facts of the matter.

Yet the notion of an apolitical or uncommitted science of society was remote from his mind and from the minds of other sociomedical observers. Villermé's purpose was not merely to acquire knowledge of the prison. He sought the acquisition of such knowledge for a specific purpose, namely, reform of the prison to bring its practices into accord with its stated objective. This objective was to receive and remake the prisoner, and return him or her to a productive role in society. In the strict sense of the word, sociomedical observation was interested observation, and it was just this constant conjunction of social interest and social observation that united public health and political economy during the Restoration.

Thoughts regarding prison reform provided a foundation for later thought regarding society at large and for correcting society's vices and malfunctions. The target of Villermé's argument was only indirectly the prisoner. Prison administrators and their superiors in the central government bore the responsibility for the sorry condition of the prison. Villermé used strong language to publicize his claims: "The interest and the importance of the subject have demanded that I make known the general insouciance [of those responsible for] the lot of the prisoners. I have thus felt it my duty to expose how frequently they are murdered (that is not hyperbole) by the conduct of the prisons and to show that governments themselves lend their authority to that evil genius which, in so many places, directs these temples of justice."[58] Villermé refrained from ascribing evil intent to prison administrators. Their fault was a worse one: they acted from ignorance and made little or no effort to correct their shortcomings. Sociomedical investigation promised the first stage of the remedy, that is, reliable knowledge. Prison investigators had shown that prison administration not only should be reformed; it could and must be reformed. Their program for reform was addressed to the administrative corps itself, and their principal weapon was publicity. Intelligent men of good will are open to persuasion and will listen to the lesson of reason as it confronts the prejudices and ignorance handed down by tradition and too often incorporated into the routine conduct of social institutions. So it was believed.

In shared values and procedure Villermé, although of independent means and without official connections, was a member of the reform-minded administrative elite. He condemned only maladministration, not vigorous administration per se, and held optimistically to the faith that informed reason when placed at the disposal of determined hands would not fail to alleviate a desperate situation. Nowhere is this central conviction more apparent, and its ideological implications so patent, as in the assignment of remedies for assisting those unfortunates who were probably destined for a career in prison. Numbers had shown that prison administration had a direct effect on the well-being of the inmate. This was amenable to corrective action. But numbers had also shown that the condition of the prisoner upon entry into prison contributed to his or her life span within prison. Unhappily it appeared that "administration is virtually impotent" against those causes that decide the strength or weakness of the individual.[59] Prison administration, of course, was here intended, but the conclusion really extended to the full spectrum of direct state intervention into the multifarious conditions of human existence. In a limited number of discrete realms of concern it appeared to Villermé and his associates that state intervention was both legitimate and probably efficacious (if wisely conducted). But this intervention was not understood to reach to the point at which the state—meaning its administrative arm—assured all citizens the fundamental needs of biological existence.

In *Des prisons* as in other of Villermé's inquiries into the medical ramifications of the social condition, the themata of political economy informed both structure and execution of the work. Although *Des prisons* was only implicitly a political tract, its message was clear. Social problems exist. They are open to study and should be investigated. The stated

58. Villermé, *Des prisons*, p. 173.
59. Villermé, "Sur la mortalité dans les prisons," p. 40.

imperative rested upon the conviction that the use of reason is an inescapable obligation of being human. This exercise of intelligence is as applicable to society, to man in the mass and to his institutions, as it had been and remained the instrument for comprehending the individual and his thoughts. Moreover, intelligence as here construed had been both narrowed and rendered more powerful. The new ethos of the natural sciences played an increasing role. Facts, based upon direct observation and preferably expressed numerically, would decide all questions. Compassion, too, was demanded. Where economic interests were in question, however, the facts proved amenable to their defense, and compassion required tempering. An assertive insistence upon self-reliance dealt with this problem. Emphasis upon work in prison was one contribution to this end.

Social order, self-reliance, labor—it was within the framework of these rubrics that Villermé conducted his sociomedical investigations. Their presence is felt throughout his writings of the 1820s and early 1830s. This was Villermé's statistical period, a brief span of some fifteen years during which he made his principal contributions to the numerical analysis of the relation between society and its afflictions, most notably disease. The lesson of the prison provided essential guidance in this work. Distinctions were to be drawn and comparisons effected, the relative roles of wealth and poverty, topography, climate, and social condition itself were to be assayed. With these inquiries Villermé moved to the forefront of contemporary concern for the problems of public health and assumed his lasting role as intellectual leader of the French hygienic movement.

Chapter 5

Number in Medicine

Deaths and causes of death are scientific facts which admit of numerical analysis; and science has nothing to offer more inviting in speculation than the laws of vitality, the variations of those laws in the two sexes at different ages, and the influence of civilization, occupation, locality, seasons, and other physical agencies, either in generating disease and inducing death, or in improving the public health.

William Farr, 1839

A characteristic feature of early public health inquiry and propaganda was use of the numerical method. More often than not, a blunt form of the numerical instrument was employed, most observers simply ignoring the cautions stated by contemporary mathematicians. Those who would extend the calculus of probabilities from the physical to the social domain were warned against the peril of inadequate sample size and urged to compare their conclusions with the calculated probabilities for the results in question. Yet the numerical method followed a simpler, less difficult course. Mathematical reasoning by Paris physician and sociomedical investigator was largely confined to the computation and comparison of averages and to argumentative exploitation of simple proportions. A further, more serious, and widely recognized problem was the uncertainty, frequent noncomparability, and insufficient number of data actually available.

The numerical method was applied to analysis of diagnostic, therapeutic, and sanitary problems. An important element in the reasoning of the Paris clinical school, the numerical method promised sound generalization in place of undirected empiricism and vain speculation. Reasoning from numbers required an extensive and secure fund of medical fact. The needed clinical information was collected in the hospitals and postmortem rooms of Paris; data pertaining to matters of public health were garnered

EPIGRAPH: William Farr, *First Annual Report* of the Registrar General, quoted in J. M. Eyler, "William Farr (1807–1883): An Intellectual Biography of a Social Pathologist" (Ph.D. diss., University of Wisconsin, 1971), p. 66.

from a broad range of sources. The numerical method long remained an unsophisticated analytic tool, one whose flaws were constantly exposed and condemned. Nonetheless, in the hygienic domain it proved an effective agent for purposes of demonstration and publicity, and until the later 1840s, these remained its primary point of application. It was in this, its original form, that the numerical method was employed by sociomedical investigators in early-nineteenty-century Paris.

Of Certitude and Probability

The logical progression from a commitment to social amelioration to the acceptance and exploitation of the numerical method was direct. The reformers of the 1780s and Revolutionary period were persuaded that man is the product of his own institutions. If, in fact, a residual influence was left to inanimate environmental forces, priority of place increasingly was assigned to the formative power of human action itself, a power as much moral as physical. This was education, construed in the broadest possible manner, the common inheritance of the 1790s and the legacy of J. J. Rousseau, Etienne de Condillac, C. A. Helvétius, and a host of lesser prophets of the late Enlightenment.[1]

Sensationalism, which owed its extreme development to Condillac, provided the basic epistemology and ethics for the reform program. It being given that man is reasonable and that he can and should devise such social arrangements as will best assure his prosperity and happiness, the fundamental problem he faces is that of gaining an intimate and reliable knowledge of society. Social data are numerous and complex; indeed, they seem infinitely complex. The Condillacian method of analysis provided a means for gaining knowledge of these social facts. Analysis required both that primitive sensations be reduced to their irreducible elements and that these elements be reassembled, via comparison with one another and with other simple ideas, to produce complex notions. Knowing was a genetic process; it followed a method and demanded complete self-awareness on the part of the thinker.

Social facts offered a major challenge to analysis. Their number was forbidding, their scope vast, their interconnection extreme. To reduce society in all its diversity to a set of simple ideas seemed difficult; to rebuild society on the basis of such ideas appeared to be an even more arduous task. Yet, no matter how great the difficulty, it was a task that had to be undertaken. Reform always entailed some degree, often considerable, of

---

1. The "spirit of education in ideology" is emphasized by C. H. van Duzer, *Contributions of the Ideologues to French Revolutionary Thought* (Baltimore: Johns Hopkins Press, 1935), pp. 84–114.

reconstruction. The Revolution had either cast old institutions and practices into disarray or had destroyed them altogether. A new and presumably better society was to be created; its creators were the legislators of the revolutionary assemblies and the growing corps of public servants that provided administrative continuity in France from the reign of Louis XVI into that of Louis XVIII.

The assemblies adopted an openly rational and educative position. France would not only have a new form of government, but it would create new men and women. Subjects now became citizens. In their collective person they represented the power and glory of the new nation. Translating such high ideals into reality proved notoriously difficult. War, economic chaos, sharply opposed interests, and blatant opportunism created a political maelstrom from which emerged a new but scarcely regenerated nation. Reason—above all, reason following the deliberate course of Condillacian analysis—only rarely guided the ship of state. Nonetheless, the ideal itself, the reformer's dream of inaugurating an era of continuous improvement of the human condition, was not diminished. This dream had launched Condorcet earlier in his career on a quest for a new and scientific basis, a probabilistic basis, for social reform, and it gave him the assurance late in life and in desperate circumstances to create the celebrated *Esquisse d'un tableau historique des progrès de l'esprit humain*, the fullest witness of the period to a faith in man's own capacity for social and moral regeneration.[2] That same conviction was shared and expounded by Condorcet's younger associate, the physician and philosopher P.J.G. Cabanis.

It was Cabanis's special concern to estimate the degree of certainty that human intelligence could attain when dealing with natural and, in particular, medical phenomena.[3] Geometrical reasoning represented the attain-

---

2. See K. M. Baker, *Condorcet: From Natural Philosophy to Social Mathematics* (Chicago: University of Chicago Press, 1975), pp. 171–94, 343–82.

3. See Martin Staum, *Cabanis: Enlightenment and Medical Philosophy in the French Revolution* (Princeton: Princeton University Press, 1980); Sergio Moravia, *Il pensiero degli Idéologues: Scienza e filosofia in Francia (1780–1815)* (Florence: La Nuova Italia, 1974), pp. 13–288. Also George Rosen, "The Philosophy of Ideology and the Emergence of Modern Medicine in France," *Bulletin of the History of Medicine* 20 (1946): 328–39; Georges Gusdorf, *La conscience révolutionnaire: Les idéologues* (Paris: Payot, 1978), pp. 451–76. Further dimensions of medicine and *idéologie* are examined by Owsei Temkin, "Gall and the Phrenological Movement," *Bulletin of the History of Medicine* 21 (1947): 275–321, and E. H. Ackerknecht, "Broussais; or, A Forgotten Medical Revolution," ibid. 27 (1953): 320–43; for an earlier period, Moravia's essay "Philosophie et médecine en France à la fin du XVIIIᵉ siècle," *Studies on Voltaire and the Eighteenth Century* 89 (1972): 1089–1151, is indispensable. The programmatic piece by Philippe Pinel and Isidore Bricheteau, "Idéologie (Application de l'idéologie à la médecine)," *Dictionnaire des sciences médicales*, 60 vols. (Paris: Panckoucke, 1812–22), 23:473–83, also requires attention.

ment of complete certitude and so it should, for here, Cabanis believed, "there are only creations of the mind which, having put them there, can always find them again."[4] All other notions, not being the product of pure reason itself, were necessarily less certain. Moreover, they presented the greatest fund of subject matter with which the human mind had to deal. Nature, man, and society belonged to this realm; and their study demanded patience, skill, and uncommon application. This was the sensible world. We might perhaps be able to offer an exact description of it, yet, at the limit of our power of generalization, we discerned only the relationships between the phenomena that the sensible world placed before us. These relationships might be expressed in number, in degrees of probability.

This viewpoint, one first conceived with regard to medical matters, Cabanis soon applied to social issues. In an address expounding the brilliant promise of the new Consulate, from whose leader, Bonaparte, he expected a renewal of the ideals of the early Republic and continued support for the philosophical and technocratic reconstruction of France, Cabanis stated that

all of our knowledge and particularly our practical knowledge is the product of observation and experience and of reasoning directly exercised on each. It is from these materials that arises the entire edifice of rigorous certainties we have been able to establish in certain areas of theory. So also arise the probabilities, be they great or small, which, in the familiar arts and, more generally, in the conduct of life, suffice to guide and fix our conclusions. The social art belongs without doubt to this second class [of the sciences], and it is here that the objects of observation are most varied in their nature and temporal relations. It is here that experiments prove most difficult and full of risk and here also where phenomena can most easily be viewed in false light.[5]

It was clear to Cabanis that medicine had long been illuminated by a variety of false lights. From false principles had been created one medical system after another, dogma had vied with caprice, and medicine was left a morass of conflicting theories, virtually none of which was in accord with observation or of demonstrable utility.[6] Cabanis also condemned radical empiricism, for the empiric eschewed all hope of achieving generality.

4. [P.J.G. Cabanis], "Lettre à M. F. sur les causes premières" [written 1806–7, published 1824], in *Oeuvres philosophiques de Cabinis*, ed. Claude Lehec and Jean Cazeneuve, 2 vols. (Paris: P.U.F., 1956), 2:268.

5. Cabanis, "Quelques considérations sur l'organisation sociale en général et particulièrement sur la nouvelle constitution" [1799], ibid., p. 468.

6. Doctrinal controversy in medicine declined little in the generations following Cabanis; see Erwin H. Ackernecht, *Medicine at the Paris Hospital, 1794–1848* (Baltimore: Johns Hopkins Press, 1967), esp. pp. 101–13, 121–27.

Experiment, too, was rejected: it interfered too deeply with the very phenomena themselves, the vital processes, to serve as a reliable guide to their nature.

In this desperate situation only one solution remained. Experience must become our master. But we cannot be content with simple if sure observation. We must constantly correlate our observations, focus them upon one another by means of comparison, and thus win an ever more detailed perception of the endless complexity of medical and social realities. These steps tell us, Cabanis wrote,

> how the mind advances when we follow sound procedure—and such is the procedure that we must compel ourselves always to follow. The theoretical part of a science must thus be the simple statement of the interconnection, classification, and relationships of all the facts that constitute the science; theory should be, so to speak, the summary expression of the science. If theory does not strictly hold itself to these narrow limits, it will no longer offer systematic representations [*tableaux méthodiques*] of real objects; rather, there will arise assemblages of results that are strangers to the facts, theory will give birth to vain phantoms.[7]

Such an investigation required close adherence to the method of analysis. Most importantly, the pertinent facts had to be presented in as simple and clear a manner as possible. Cabanis had already suggested the minimally satisfactory form that all scientific exposition should follow, namely, direct portrayal or representation (*tableau*) of the elementary facts. On the one hand, *tableaux* offered "complete and well-ordered collections of observations"; on the other, they provided a set of "short theoretical expositions wherein can be reported (1) the manner [*esprit*] in which these collections are and must be assembled and (2) the most immediate results that can be drawn from these different observations."[8]

Cabanis recognized that most such information would not attain the status of certain knowledge (even though the facts themselves might appear to do so) and that all conclusions drawn from these facts would be probable conclusions only. Yet constant conjunction in space and regular succession in time must, he felt, persuade even the sceptical of the great likelihood of various recurring events, be they the daily passage of the sun or the efficacy or failure of frequently administered remedies.[9] One can,

    7. Cabanis, "Coup d'oeil sur les révolutions et sur la réforme de la médecine" [1804], in *Oeuvres philosophiques de Cabanis*, 2:183.
    8. Ibid., p. 184.
    9. Ibid., pp. 196–97.

one must, and one does take action upon such knowledge. Cabanis's suggestions regarding the evaluation of therapeutic measures quickly found their mark in the work of Philippe Pinel, which gave first outline to the clinical use of the numerical method in Paris medicine. Cabanis did not, by contrast, explicitly refer to the possible application of his views to an analysis of problems of public health. Nonetheless, I suggest that his proposals did in fact define the singular virtue of applying the method of analysis to investigation of the social dimensions of disease. In the first place, Cabanis's perspective was relentlessly social: he recognized and stressed the importance of the distinction between the individual and the mass. Of what use to statecraft, he asked, are those legislators who "only know man and not the people, their government, and their revolutions?" The legislator possessed a more assured, a social approach. Were he to combine an awareness of the many "experiments" made upon (and "at the expense of") the "masses of mankind"—the reference, no doubt, is to the long history of changing forms of government—with the "more exact notions" now available regarding the "nature of man," he would be able to draw more certain conclusions, that is, "results that increasingly approximate the ultimate degree of probability, the only kind of certainty admitted of by the practical sciences, particularly those that deal with man as a moral being." [10]

The legislator and all others who dealt with the conduct of public affairs, not least those administrators whose responsibilities extended to questions of population, poverty, and sanitation, were thus instructed that their first task was to acquire secure scientific knowledge of man as individual and in society. For the latter purpose, no method seemed as promising to sociomedical investigators as the numerical method. One may claim, in fact, that the abundant social statistical tables prepared by Villermé's generation provided a numerical expression of the "short theoretical expositions" that Cabanis had called for and whose utility was soon to be so widely appreciated. If number provided the most dependable means for the expression of important social facts, then the *tableaux* of the social statisticians offered the most concise and reliable means for making generalizations from those facts. It deserves emphasis that sociomedical investigators, as well as contemporary statisticians such as Quetelet, employed the term *tableau* and not *table*. The latter denoted only a list or catalogue of numbers. It did not, because it could not, convey any sense of the many possible meanings of such numbers. A *tableau*, however, was a reasoned list, one thoughtfully composed to suggest the interrelation of the often numerous variables being represented. Such visual presentation of data, an abstract

10. Cabanis, "Quelques considérations sur l'organisation sociale," ibid., pp. 465–66.

of the raw data themselves, was itself a generalization, perhaps the most important and surely the most striking that the sociomedical investigators offered their audience.[11]

Cabanis had posed a continuing problem. Committed to sensationalism and induction, utterly sceptical of the possibility of applying rigorous mathematical analysis to social and medical phenomena, he with others of his generation (above all, Condorcet and P. S. de Laplace) saw that another form of mathematical reasoning might offer important benefits. Probability replaced certitude; yet this, sociomedical observers realized, might be seen as a gain and not a loss. It meant that a reasoned and critical mode of generalization could now be introduced into the study of society and medicine. The method reasserted a cardinal tenet of the idéologues and their successors—direct experience received via the senses is the foundation of all our knowledge—and also allowed an inquirer to advance towards generalization with an assurance that a known degree of certainty might be attained. Where the complexity of the situation precluded other modes of analysis, the numerical method appeared to provide a sound, flexible, and fruitful technique for assessing problems of foremost contemporary concern.

The Numerical Method

This book offers an extended description of the application of the numerical method to outstanding sociomedical problems in early-nineteenth-century France as well as a commentary upon the intentions and practices of a leading investigator of the period. It is unnecessary, therefore, to provide a separate discussion of these issues here. Contemporaneous application of the numerical method to clinical diagnosis and to the evaluation of therapeutic procedures does, however, require brief consideration. Whether applied to problems of public health, to diagnosis, or to assessment of the efficacy of different remedies, the argumental form taken by the numerical method was largely one and the same. In all cases the claim was made that sound reasoning must be based upon the collection of a number, preferably a large number, of instances. This required not only the creation of a sizeable data base but also demanded constant vigilance and discernment in order to assure that the facts gathered were authentic and reliable and were recorded in a manner appropriate to subsequent

11. On this topic, unfortunately little explored, see H. G. Funkhouser, "Historical Development of the Graphical Representation of Statistical Data," *Osiris* 3 (1937): 269–404; Erica Royston, "A Note on the History of the Graphical Representation of Data," *Biometrika* 43 (1956): 231–47.

analysis. In both the clinical and sanitary domains that analysis was focused upon the correlated changes, usually of frequency, of two and occasionally more variables.

French medical thought after 1800 was populated by a small legion of fiercely defended and usually irreconcilable therapeutic beliefs.[12] Therapeutic activists could choose among numerous weapons. The recent triumphs of pneumatic and analytic chemistry had restored enthusiasm for the time-honored practices of iatrochemism. Mesmerism was discredited, but galvanism was on the rise. Stimulation and counterstimulation had become the rage elsewhere in Europe. Broussais had launched his antiphlogistic campaign, and the demand for leeches rose beyond all expectation. On the other hand, expectant therapists, still probably the dominant group in the Paris school, preferred only mild interventions and commonly no intervention at all. Every effort was made, always in the name of Hippocrates, to encourage the healing power of nature.

Depending on one's point of view this situation could be described as utterly irrational or—and this appeared to amount to the same thing—as the inevitable consequence of excessive reliance upon reason alone. A fundamental question was thus posed: By what means can the efficacy of one or another therapeutic measure be objectively demonstrated? The school of analysis, or, as it came to be called in the 1830s, the *école d'observation*, provided an answer and attempted to translate it into practical medical terms. A model for this mode of reasoning had been given by Cabanis's friend and fellow idéologue Pinel. Pinel had found it difficult not only to cope with the problem of classifying mental disorders, these being his primary professional concern since appointment at the Bicêtre in 1793, but also to evaluate the efficacy of his own therapeutic measures. He offered moral treatment—that is, an orderly, friendly, and supportive regimen—to his patients. But to what effect? he asked. His analysis of the question, published in 1807, defines the program of those who, two decades later, brought the numerical method to the center of medical discourse.

The problem was to draw sound conclusions from one's experience. The solution was to determine by enumeration the relative weight of favorable and unfavorable instances and to let number, the simplest possible expression of fact, speak for itself. Pinel observed:

> It is difficult to reach agreement in medicine if one does not attach a precise meaning to the word *expérience*, for everyone speaks highly of his own experience and cites a medley of facts in its favor. Experience, if it is to be authentic and conclusive and is to serve as the solid foun-

12. See Ackerknecht, *Medicine at the Paris Hospital*, pp. 129–38.

dation for any method of treatment whatsoever, must be drawn from a large number of the sick, subjected to certain general rules, and followed through in a determinate order. It must also be based upon a regular succession of observations which are established with extreme care and are repeated over a certain number of years in a constant manner.[13]

This method Pinel called, improperly, the "calculus of probabilities," and he observed that, since it had already served with good effect for the study of "objects of social life," it could surely provide medicine with a "sound foundation" for its reasoning. In this way alone could the healing art finally escape from "blind empiricism," not to mention ill-grounded speculation, and thus become a "true science."[14]

Pinel offered more than programmatics. He reported observations on patients made over a period of four years. By collecting therapeutic experience (in two categories: cured and discharged; not cured) with patients at the Salpêtrière hospital, he hoped to be able to compare these results, the product of moral treatment, with those obtained by other methods of dealing with the mentally ill. But this, Pinel sadly recognized, was an impossible ambition: comparable data simply did not exist. It was not, in fact, until the late 1820s and early 1830s that the numerical method made its triumphant entry into clinical medicine.[15] In the hands of P.C.A. Louis and his students, number was used for diagnostic purposes (phthisis, typhoid fever) and then to assay the effectiveness of particular therapies

13. Philippe Pinel, "Résultats d'observations et construction des tables pour servir à déterminer le degré de probabilité de la guérison des aliénés," *Mémoires de l'Académie des sciences* 8 (1807): 169.

14. Ibid., pp. 169–70.

15. Remarkably, no comprehensive history of the numerical method as used in medicine exists. A broad view is provided by George Rosen, "Problems in the Application of Statistical Analysis to Questions of Health: 1700–1880," *Bulletin of the History of Medicine* 29 (1955): 27–45. French use of the method is described by Ackerknecht, *Medicine at the Paris Hospital*; Paul Delaunay, "Les doctrines médicales au début du XIXᵉ siècle: Louis et la méthode numérique," in *Science, Medicine, and History: Essays on the Evolution of Scientific Thought and Medical Practice Written in Honour of Charles Singer*, ed. E. A. Underwood, 2 vols. (London: Oxford University Press, 1953), 2:321–30; M. Bariéty, "Louis et la méthode numérique," *Clio medica* 7 (1972): 177–83; and Roger Huron, "La statistique médicale en France à l'époque romantique," *Mémoires de l'Académie des sciences, des inscriptions et des belles-lettres de Toulouse* 137 (1975): 121–39. Of major importance in determining the origins and development of this movement is Ulrich Tröhler, "Quantification in British Medicine and Surgery, 1750–1830, with Special Reference to Its Introduction into Therapeutics" (Ph.D. diss., University of London, 1978). Always critical of statistics was Claude Bernard; see Joseph Schiller, "Claude Bernard et la statistique," in *Claude Bernard et les problèmes scientifiques de son temps* (Paris: Editions du Cèdre, 1967), pp. 155–71.

(venesection, emetics, and blisters). By the middle 1830s the numerical method, which Louis enshrined as the doctrinal heart of his new Société médicale d'observation, had become probably the most fiercely contested proposition in all of French medicine. Louis's grounding in fact occasionally proved slight indeed.[16] In testing the efficacy of bloodletting, he used only two series of cases, one of 78 patients (of whom 28 died) and another of 29 patients (4 of whom died). Those sanitarians who dealt with vital statistics and relied upon large masses of official and unofficial documentation were fortunate in comparison.

But Louis was also an inspired propagandist who could clearly articulate the purpose and advantages of the numerical method even while exploiting it in ambiguous manner. His statements exhibit the unbroken continuity in the French medical world of the tradition of Condillac and Cabanis. Louis's was once again the method of analysis; he required both clear and simple facts and reasoned generalization based uniquely thereupon. In 1837 he replied to his critic Jean Cruveilhier that "all [knowledge] comes from experience, it is true but experience is nothing if it does not form collections of similar facts. Now, to make collections is to count."[17] Two years earlier, in his famous study of venesection (*Recherches sur les effets de la saignée dans quelques maladies inflammatoires, et sur l'action de l'émétique et des vésicatoires dans la pneumonie*, 1835), he had declared: "Between he who counts the facts, grouped according to their resemblance, in order to know what to believe regarding the value of therapeutic agents and he who does not count but always says 'more or less rare or frequent,' there is the difference between truth and error, between something that is clear and truly scientific and something that is vague and without value—for what place is there in Science for that which is vague?"[18] In such forthright claims lay the provocation, welcomed by the many enemies of the numerical method, for the impassioned academic disputes that surrounded that method in the later 1830s.

One critic in particular, while favoring the extensive use of number in many areas of medicine, nonetheless pointed out the grave shortcomings of the numerical method as it had been employed by Parisian pathologist

16. See E. B., review of *Researches on the Effects of Blood-Letting*, etc., by P.C.A. Louis, *American Journal of the Medical Sciences* 18 (1836): 102–11. Major Greenwood, *The Medical Dictator and Other Biographical Studies* (London: Williams and Norgate, 1936), pp. 123–42, emphasizes the insufficiency of Louis's data. The program of medical *observation*—that is, the school of thought stimulated by Louis—is briefly described by Pierre Astruc, "Le centenaire de la médecine d'observation," *Le progrès médical*, Supplément illustré 9 (1932): 73–79, 81–87.

17. Quoted in Bariéty, "Louis et la méthode numérique," p. 181.

18. Quoted in Huron, "La statistique médicale en France à l'époque romantique," p. 127.

and therapist alike. Jules Gavarret possessed the advantage of rigorous training in mathematics and the physical sciences as well as in medicine. He brought Denis Poisson's recently published statistical analysis of jury voting patterns directly to bear on the physician's numerical method and found—as he had expected—little resemblance between them. To Gavarret his medical colleagues had simply engaged in a semantic exercise: they merely attempted to replace "more" and "less" with seemingly more precise number. Yet they had failed entirely to realize that the manipulation of numbers for such purposes depended upon the properties and size of the sample that was under consideration. The calculus of probabilities was not, emphatically, to be identified with the numerical method. The latter proffered simple sums and proportions but treated problems of sample size and variation with abandon, if at all.

Gavarret insisted in particular that, if one is to claim that an event (say, successful administration of a given remedy) has actually occurred, it must be shown that in two (or more) comparable and very large series of data the probability of the event in question exceeds a limit of error that is itself a function of the number of data observed.[19] Only when this criterion is satisfied is one in a position to assert (within the limits of the applicable probability) that the trial has been successful, that the desired result has indeed occurred. Of course, the proponents and critics of the numerical method had evidenced no awareness of this requirement. They had transgressed, too, on another ground. Gavarret followed Laplace in declaring that even the correct mathematical approach ("statistical medicine") could provide only a high probability (in some cases verging on certainty) that a particular conjunction of events had occurred. Louis and his followers had assumed that the connection, for example, between a given therapy and a cure (or noncure) was a real connection; it was held to be causal, and the remedy in question was spoken of as being the cause or not the cause of a discrete succeeding event. Gavarret flatly condemned such thinking, especially among those who pretended to use the mathematics of large numbers as their essential demonstrative tool.[20] The connections thus established, he pointed out, were probable connections, the degree of probability being stated by the limits of the system under consideration. No probable cause could ever give that "exact and rigorous translation" of the influence of A upon B which the clinicians pretended to make. Thus, Gavarret concluded, "it is especially because they [have] failed to sense the real importance of these considerations and because they [have] be-

19. Jules Gavarret, *Principes généraux de statistique médicale; ou, Développement des règles qui doivent présider à son emploi* (Paris: Bechet jeune et Labé, 1840), p. 98.
20. Ibid., pp. 24–25.

lieved, wrongly, in the absolute truth of the numerical relations they established (which were, moreover, founded on too few numbers), that the partisans of the numerical method have reached the most contradictory results."[21] In Gavarret's view the entire exercise, vitiated by false method, had been futile.

That Gavarret's critique was needed is merely witness to the gap that separated physicians entertaining numerical ambitions from the advances already made in the study of the calculus of probabilities. Since the 1770s leadership in this domain had been provided by French mathematicians.[22] Laplace had developed Thomas Bayes's notion of inverse probability (given a particular event or set of events, what can be determined regarding the probable causes involved?) and showed how it might be applied to the study of varied natural phenomena. It seemed an approach as suited to the analysis of human behavior as it was to the determination of celestial motions, and it was an essential complement to increasingly sophisticated techniques for determining the probability of future events, the traditional objective of the calculus of probabilities. Condorcet, stimulated by Laplace, had made the application of the probabilistic outlook to social phenomena the program of his later scientific career.[23]

The Bayesian question might have provided an essential perspective for those who favored an empirical approach to the study of social phenomena. But this was not, of course, the goal of those Parisian physicians who either supported or contested Louis's claims regarding the efficacy of various therapeutic measures. As Gavarret emphasized, the calculus of probabilities, had it guided both the experimental trials and the analyses made thereof, might have proved relevant to these clinical investigations. All the more, then, would it have served a valuable role in early public health investigation, an endeavor which in conception and execution was being pursued in the joint name of humanity and natural science. But here no more than in the testing of rival therapeutic measures or in diagnostics did the calculus of probabilities find early acceptance. This happened despite the fact that sample size and authenticity of data were no doubt occasionally suited to its application. The cause of this neglect—which occurred under the very eyes of the *doyen* of French science, Laplace, and the leading younger statistician of the period, Poisson[24]—can probably be

21. Ibid., p. 25.
22. The following discussion draws upon Baker, *Condorcet*, pp. 129–71.
23. Ibid., p. 171. See also pp. 225–44.
24. That Laplace was familiar with medical needs is revealed by the following comment: "The calculation of probabilities can make appreciable the advantages and the inconveniences of the methods employed in the speculative sciences. Thus in order to recognize the best of the treatments in use in the healing of a malady, it is sufficient to test each of them

assigned to two reasons. In the first place, the leading French sociomedical investigators under the Restoration and the July Monarchy had been recruited from among practicing surgeons and physicians. They had received little formal instruction in mathematics and almost certainly none at all in the higher mathematics involved in probability theory. Gavarret gave excellent witness to this problem: considering his audience, he still found it advisable in 1840 to banish all algebraic operations from his text (although a "démonstration des principes" was provided in six extensive notes that concluded the volume). Villermé and Benoiston de Châteauneuf passed directly from military service into Parisian medical life, and both quickly turned to social investigation: Parent-Duchâtelet appeared to move without interruption from medical studies to sanitary investigation. The former two certainly could not have been wholly unaware of developments in the mathematical treatment of large numbers. Benoiston de Châteauneuf was a close associate of Poisson, and Villermé was the intimate friend of Quetelet, seeing the latter's classic monograph, Sur l'homme, through the press.[25] But they did not learn the expected lesson. Their utilization of numerical data showed great insight and gives abundant evidence of awareness, and avoidance, of hazards intrinsic to the process of analysis, but they made no attempt to control their conclusions by means of the calculation of probable error.

If aptitude thus seems to have been lacking, commitment to this special form of mathematical rigor almost certainly was absent. It deserves repetition in this context that the paramount objective of sociomedical investigation was improvement of the physical and moral condition of the nation, above all, the condition of members of the working classes. Sums and proportions obtained from archives, published reports, and direct observation easily persuaded these practical men that their conclusions were valid beyond any reasonable doubt. Precision, even that special precision afforded by the calculus of probabilities, would surely have struck these investigators as an abstraction and an unnecessary burden. Furthermore, while niceties of computation were lacking, in many instances the size of the population being considered was quite large, and the comparisons based on such ample denominators carried persuasion in their own right.

---

on an equal number of patients, making all the conditions exactly similar; the superiority of the most advantageous treatment will manifest itself more and more in the measure that the number is increased; and the calculation will make apparent the corresponding probability of its advantage and the ratio according to which it is superior to the others" (Pierre Simon, Marquis de Laplace, A Philosophical Essay on Probabilities, trans. F. W. Truscott and F. L. Emory [New York: Dover, 1951], pp. 105–6).

25. Adolfe Quetelet, Sur l'homme et le développement de ses facultés (Paris: Bachelier, 1835), p. ii.

Villermé and his associates were devoted to concrete social and economic objectives and believed that the data at hand, despite its limitations, permitted and indeed assured the drawing of conclusions such as could not be denied by reasonable men. The latter, from whose number they themselves were drawn, constituted their primary audience, and it was an audience that, like the medical community in general, was untutored in mathematical analysis.[26] Sociomedical investigators addressed the political and economic nation, not the savants, and they used discourse familiar to or at least comprehensible by their auditors. The desiderata stated by Gavarret began to be met in the domain of vital statistics only much later in the century.

Sources of Statistical Information

Hygienic investigation in France, as in England, commonly utilized information that had been collected for other purposes. This information was supplemented, particularly after 1830, by the findings of special investigations devoted directly to problems of epidemic disease, poverty, and the conditions of existence of the general population. Such investigations were usually conducted by private parties acting on their own authority or, when under the shelter of a learned academy or society, with semi-official sanction. In no European country before the 1830s were systematic, effective, and truly national inquiries made into matters concerning public health and the biological condition of the population. As a consequence, the information available to sociomedical investigators was incomplete and often inexact, quite diverse in character, and subject to many and serious limitations.

The base point for reliable demographic analysis is regular civil registration of at least births and deaths and a well-conceived and carefully conducted periodic census of the population. With one exception, none of these criteria was consistently satisfied in France, or elsewhere, until well into the nineteenth century. Periodic national censuses executed according to the definite and appropriate rules were a late creation and began to gain authority only after 1840. Local censuses had been more common, yet their reliability was uncertain or altogether doubtful, and given their idiosyncratic character, they offered little ground for comparative analysis.

Statecraft in the eighteenth century, particularly in those nations still adhering to the mercantilist principle of national economic and military

26. English statisticians, not least Farr himself, did little to pursue the study of the mathematical bases of statistical reasoning; see J. M. Eyler, *Victorian Social Medicine: The Ideas and Methods of William Farr* (Baltimore: Johns Hopkins University Press, 1979), pp. 18, 67.

autonomy, had required comprehensive assessment of the nation's strengths and weaknesses. Surveys were consequently made (many others were merely projected) of the manifold assets of the state. Their purpose, the chemist A. L. de Lavoisier noted, was to provide an exact and concise view of "the situation of the realm, its wealth in men, in production, in industry, and in accumulated capital."[27] For this reason it was essential that a national survey comprehend all matters of public concern, ranging from topography and mineral deposits to commercial and manufacturing activity, administrative organization, means of communication, religious and educational institutions, and population itself. Such surveys, the embodiment of the original conception of *Statistik* and a distinctive feature of eighteenth-century German administrative literature, produced catalogues rather than reasoned analyses of the various factors presumably underlying national power.[28] Nonetheless, many observers already regarded population size as the ultimate measure of the nation's strength. It seemed essential, therefore, to gain an exact appreciation of the number of men, women, and children living within one's own borders. Unhappily, it long proved difficult if not impossible to gain even a fair estimate of the desired figures. As direct enumeration was widely regarded as impracticable, the population was often assayed indirectly by calculation. Such estimates were based upon extrapolation to the nation at large of a basic ratio determined originally for a selected locality or small group of localities. The usual ratio (whose numerical value varied with the author) stated the relationship observed between the number of recorded births and the total population in a given locality. Obtaining, then, a figure for the total number of births in the nation in a given year, one easily calculated a figure that was boldly offered as a good approximation to the total population.[29] Given the absence or inadequacy (or, more commonly, both) of registra-

27. Antoine Laurent de Lavoisier, *Résultats extraits d'un ouvrage intitulé, "De la richesse territoriale du royaume de France,"* in *Oeuvres de Lavoisier,* ed. Eduard Grimaux, 6 vols. (Paris: Imprimerie nationale, 1864–93), 6:405.

28. See George Rosen, "Cameralism and the Concept of Medical Police," *Bulletin of the History of Medicine* 27 (1952): 21–42; idem, "The Fate of the Concept of Medical Police, 1780–1890," *Centaurus* 5 (1957): 97–113. A set of review essays by Michel Friedlander made the intention and much of the data of the statist-statisticians available to the Parisian medical community; see his "Mortalité," "Population," and "Statistique médicale," all in *Dictionnaire des sciences médicales,* 34 (1819); 348–95; 44 (1820): 304–17; 52 (1821): 487–96.

29. The process is best exemplified by the calculations of Auget de Montyon ("Moheau") in his *Recherches et considérations sur la population de la France* (1778), pp. 32–48, 61–70. See William Coleman, "L'hygiène et l'état selon Montyon," abridg. and trans. J. Guillerme, *Dix-huitième siècle* 9 (1977): 101–8, to appear in complete form as "Inventing Demography: Montyon on Hygiene and the State," in *Festschrift for I. B. Cohen,* ed. Everett Mendelsohn (forthcoming).

tion of births, this procedure allowed at best only a very qualified guess at population size. The French crown for generations had insisted that exact vital records (births, deaths, marriages) be maintained by every parish in the realm. Yet even such records as were regularly maintained posed serious problems. Baptism, not birth, was the event of concern to the parish priest; many a newborn child that died before reaching the font thus passed unrecorded. In provinces or nations where sizeable elements of the population did not belong to the established church, all vital records seriously underestimated contemporary demographic events. Such was the case for Protestants and Jews in France and for Nonconformists in Britain. Of course, census by estimation also assumed a stable national population; the procedure was especially precarious in times of social unrest, sizeable migration, and changing birth and death rates. All in all, the possibility for error in census by estimation was understandably great, and it only increased as analysis of this data was extended into the domain of marriage rates, age distribution of the population, and that most interesting indicator of social well-being, mortality.

French administrators of the Old Regime were aware of these problems and sought in vain to institute a true census and to enforce the call for exact and all-inclusive vital registration. Their campaign continued through the Revolution: registration was extended to Protestants in 1787 and divorced from the church in the early 1790s. Renewed efforts were made to create a national statistical service. In 1794, a group working in Gaspard Prony's Bureau du cadastre, situated in the Ministry of Interior, undertook a comprehensive survey of the economic activity and population of France and collected much data from various provinces and departments. No overall series of data was prepared, however, and the local series were of variable quality. A new regime demanded better or at least more comprehensive results.[30] J. A. Chaptal, acting on orders from the

---

30. I follow hereafter M. R. Reinhard, "La statistique de la population sous le Consulat et l'Empire," *Population* 5 (1950): 103–20. An overview of the collection and publication of official French statistics is provided by E. Levasseur, "L'organisation, les travaux, et les publications de la statistique officielle en France," *Journal de la Société statistique de la France* 26 (1885): 225–84, and especially Claude Legeard, *Guide de recherches documentaires en démographie* (Paris: Gauthier-Villars, 1966), pp. 94–105, and Pascal Gaston Marietti, *La statistique générale en France* (Paris: P.U.F., 1949), pp. 3–25. See also the various articles in the collection by F. Bédarida, *Pour une histoire de la statistique, I. Contributions* (Paris: Institut National de la Statistique, n.d.); and see Louise A. Tilly and Charles Tilly "A Selected Bibliography of Quantitative Sources for French History and French Sources for Quantitative History since 1789," in *The Dimensions of the Past: Materials, Problems, and Opportunities for Quantitative Work in History*, ed. Val R. Lorwin and Jacob M. Price (New Haven: Yale University Press, 1972), pp. 157–75; Frank Lorimer, "The Development of Demography," in *The Study of Populations: An Inventory and Appraisal*, ed. Philip M.

recently installed minister of interior, Lucien Bonaparte, who in the summer of 1800 had created a *bureau de statistique* within his ministry, immediately launched a quest for vital and other information upon which to build for the First Consul an encyclopedic view of French economic and human strength. This hasty inquiry, completed within three months, constituted the basis of the first French census, the results being published in 1801. While this census offered a broadscale view of France, it was primarily an exercise in statecraft. The bureau had no demographers, categories for collection of data were defective, and the results offered much confusion and uncertainty.[31] Despite efforts, notably those of E. E. Duvillard, to improve the rubrics of the census and to increase the accuracy of the collection of data, the bureau was not a success. The foremost concern of the Imperial government was economic prosperity and the capacity of the nation's economy to support the demands of continuous warfare. Bonaparte cared not or was unaware that depopulation might pose a threat to the state. The collection of economic statistics, however, was continued, responsibility therefor being transferred to the new Ministry of Manufactures and Commerce in 1812. The old bureau de statistique at the Interior Ministry, which had sustained the government's interest in vital statistics, was abolished in the same year.

Chaptal well appreciated the profound importance of a census to the state. He also understood that the only useful census is an accurate census. Give me facts, he wrote his associates, "that which is, and not that which might be . . . ; facts, and not what has been written."[32] Only on such foundations can "good administration" be established. While Chaptal's own experience with the first census did ultimately eventuate in a classic study of French industry, the census itself as a national endeavor disappeared from the French scene for almost a quarter century. Perhaps the government of the Restoration saw in the census and its technical personnel too great an Imperial influence; perhaps the new regime, whose central preoccupation was the restoration of legitimacy and immediate assertion of political power, felt a lesser need for a numerical assessment of national strength. In any case, except for publication of specialized ministerial series beginning in the 1820s, national statistics regarding population were not a matter of official concern until, again, a new regime was installed. One of the first acts of Adolfe Thiers as minister of commerce under the

---

Hauser and Otis Dudley Duncan (Chicago: University of Chicago Press, 1959), pp. 124–79.

31. Reinhard, "La statistique de la population," p. 111.
32. Quoted in ibid., p. 112.

July Monarchy was to create (1833) a new bureau de statistique.[33] His model was apparently the statistical department of London's Board of Trade, created in 1832 with the purpose of providing a means for collecting and correlating statistical reports from across the nation.[34] Placed under the direction of Alexandre Moreau de Jonnès and located in the Commerce Ministry, the new bureau was again charged with collection of both economic and vital data. A set of important retrospective volumes was soon issued, and plans were formulated for a new census, first conducted in 1836 and continued thereafter on a quinquennial basis.[35] Thus was launched the continuous history of a central statistical office and of the French national census. These events, of course, and, more importantly, the publication of a regular series of national census reports postdate the principal statistical activities of the leading Parisian sociomedical investigators. Their work depended, not upon national statistics, however desirable if unattainable these were seen to be, but upon local data. To Villermé, and for good reason, by far and away the best material for the numerical analysis of sociomedical problems was that which dealt with the capital itself and which first became available in 1821.

A strong wave of enthusiasm for regional statistics had swept France during the Revolution and early Empire.[36] These inquiries, fashioned on the German model, sought in particular a comprehensive inventory of the natural resources, social institutions, and population of the provinces and regions of France. By the later Empire this extreme particularism had been discouraged, and even official attention to the size and evolution of national population was, as noted above, allowed to disappear in a ministerial reorganization. The first era of French enthusiasm for vital statistics thus passed into oblivion.

The administration of Paris, however, followed another course. Under the guidance of G.J.G. Chabrol de Volvic, prefect of the department of the Seine, a municipal statistical office was created that gathered and published in exemplary manner demographic and economic data pertaining to the capital. Chabrol de Volvic, an *ancien polytechnicien*, veteran of the Egyptian expedition, and tried and trusted senior officer of the Empire,

33. Levasseur, "L'organisation, les travaux, et les publications de la statistique officielle," pp. 252 f.

34. See M. J. Cullen, *The Statistical Movement in Early Victorian Britain: The Foundations of Empirical Social Research* (London: Harvester Press, 1975), pp. 19–27.

35. *Statistique générale de la France: Territoire et population* (Paris: Imprimerie royale, 1837).

36. See the comprehensive account by Jean Claude Perrot, *L'âge d'or de la statistique régionale française: an IV—1804* (Paris: Société des études robespierristes, 1977).

was also endowed with great administrative talent and remarkable political flexibility.[37] Named prefect of the Seine by Bonaparte in 1812, he retained this position until 1830 despite repeated cries for his dismissal mounted by the returned foes of all Revolutionary and Imperial innovations and personnel. He had quickly won and clearly retained the unshakable confidence of both Louis XVIII and Charles X. That confidence was well-placed, for Chabrol proved an inspired administrator. Paris gained under his leadership major additions to its physical and economic infrastructure (notably canals, quays, and the new Halles aux vins) as well as greatly improved organization of its administrative staff and procedures. The statistical office constituted an integral part of these improvements.

Chabrol issued a call in 1816 for a thorough census of his city. He was no doubt concerned by the conjunction of the extraordinary economic development and population increase of Paris and the effects that were both felt and anticipated from the poor harvest and severe winter of 1816/17. In 1816 and 1817 there was no statistical office within the prefecture.[38] Outdated administrative documents and older materials regarding vital registration, which, with one major exception, had been carefully and continuously executed in the capital since the time of Colbert, were the responsibility of the "Garde des archives." Another office, devoted to "Personnel, Etat civil et politique, Cultes," prepared instructions for continued vital registration and saw to the "preparation of decennial tables [and to] the classification and preservation of the records of civil condition."[39] But 1818 witnessed the appearance of a new administrative entity, at first located outside the usual divisional structure of the prefecture and given its own director. Its title, Bureau spécial des archives et de la statistique, indicates that full centralization of municipal statistical services was already being contemplated. Frédéric Villot was made director of the new bureau spécial.[40] Finally, in 1822 the statistical office won regular organizational status within the Third Division ("Instruction publique, Hospices et Secours"). The archival function was retained and so was the charge, first noted in 1821, of attending to "the statistical work of the city of Paris and the department [of the Seine]."[41] With the arrival of yet another regime an important relocation of the bureau occurred. In 1831 it was removed from the domain of education, hospitals, and public welfare

---

37. Roman d'Amat, "Chabrol, Gilbert-Joseph-Gaspard de, qualifié de Volvic," *Dictionnaire de biographie française* (Paris: Letouzy et Ané, 1933–).

38. I know of no history of the statistical department of the Seine and city of Paris. The following information is gathered from the *Almanaches royales* for the period 1816–33.

39. *Almanache royale* (Paris: Testu, 1817), pp. 741–742.

40. Ibid. (1818), p. 754.

41. Ibid. (1822), p. 765.

and added to the broader administrative responsibilities of the First Division.[42] There, the new *troisième bureau* lost its original primary association with matters of public health and economic and social distress and became essentially a demographic office serving the general needs of vital registration, urban statistics, jury selection, electoral roles, and intraservice personnel matters. Thus did official Parisian vital statistics early begin its separation from its roots in sociomedical investigation.

The Bureau de statistique et archives (its title after 1822) perpetuated ideals that had inspired the foundation in 1794 of the foremost scientific school in France. The mission of the Ecole polytechnique was to create a corps of military and civil engineers, men who, thoroughly versed in mathematics and the physical sciences and indoctrinated with the great social need for practical application of their knowledge, would form the teachers and administrators upon whom national regeneration depended.[43] Among the early teachers at the Ecole polytechnique was the mathematician J.B.J. Fourier, and among his students was Chabrol de Volvic. Fourier's public career during the Empire was a brilliant one and brought him great rewards, but it rendered him vulnerable to the purge of the public administration that accompanied the Restoration. Deprived of public office and income, Fourier was rescued by Chabrol. He became mathematician in the emerging departmental bureau de statistique.[44] Without doubt much of the success of the bureau was due to Fourier. He contributed not only a sophisticated analysis of the need for and problems in dealing with average values in figures pertaining to the census but also offered extraordinarily perceptive remarks concerning central factors affecting demographic movements and population age structure.[45] Fourier's steady surveillance of both the conception and execution of the census of 1817

42. *Almanache royale et nationale* (Paris: Guyot, 1831), p. 737.

43. See Maurice Crosland, *The Society of Arcueil: A View of French Science at the Time of Napoleon I* (London: Heinemann, 1967), pp. 192–208.

44. Not director as reported by J. R. Ravetz and Ivor Grattan-Guiness in "Fourier, Jean Baptiste Joseph," *Dictionary of Scientific Biography* (New York: Charles Scribner's Sons, 1970–80).

45. Fourier's essays, cited hereafter, were omitted from the *Oeuvres* edited by Gaston Darboux (1888–90) and are not discussed by recent students of Fourier's scientific career; see I. Grattan-Guinness and J. R. Ravetz, *Joseph Fourier, 1768–1830* (Cambridge: M.I.T. Press, 1972), and John Herival, *Joseph Fourier: The Man and the Physicist* (Oxford: Clarendon Press, 1975). Fourier's four statistical essays, all published in the *Recherches statistiques sur la ville de Paris* (cited below, n. 46), are "Notions générales sur la population," 1 (1821): 1–94; "Mémoire sur la population de la ville de Paris depuis la fin du XVIIe siècle," 2 (1823): xiii–xxvii; "Mémoire sur les résultats moyens déduits d'un grand nombre d'observations," 3 (1826): ix–xxxi; "Second mémoire sur les résultats moyens et sur les erreurs des mesures," 4 (1829); xi–xlviii.

assured the remarkable quality and abundance of the data then obtained and helped assure that that data would be presented to the public in its most effective form.

This remarkable combination of scientific administrators—the prefect Chabrol, the statistical director Villot, and the mathematician Fourier— produced the first volume of the *Recherches statistiques sur la ville de Paris*, a collection of demographic data without parallel in its time and the model for many a subsequent census. Perhaps the most important decision taken by Villermé in his early career was to devote himself to determining the sociomedical implications of this data and of that contained in later reports issued by the bureau de statistique.

The first volume of the *Recherches statistiques sur la ville de Paris*, published in 1821, was an abstract of the 1817 census of Paris and inaugurated a series of statistical publications dealing with the capital, each more detailed and comprehensive than its forerunner.[46] In volume 1 Chabrol reported in detail how the census had been conducted.[47] Nominative lists were prepared for each house or dwelling place in the city. Age, sex, marital status, and profession were recorded for each person. Special agents were trained and used for the task; their work was scrutinized daily by other agents, who also undertook to repeat on a random basis 10 of every 100 reports filed. Chabrol was confident that his staff had missed very few indeed of the regular inhabitants of Paris, that errors in recording were few, and that cross-checking, which the nominative lists (in contrast to the usual numerical lists) permitted, would help to assure the accuracy of the results obtained. The transient population, always sizeable in Paris, was recorded by number, not name. However, the speed with which the operation was conducted (all returns were gathered in about 40 days) promised to reduce this source of error to manageable proportions. Hospitals and hospices as well as military establishments were carefully assessed. Two groups, however, posed especially serious problems and were therefore omitted from the census. These were the aged indigents in public institutions and children of Parisians sent to wet-nurses outside the city walls; the latter group was probably a sizeable one.

46. The *Recherches* were published as follows: *Recherches statistiques sur la ville de Paris et sur le département de la Seine, recueil de tableaux dressés et réunis d'après les ordres de Monsieur le comte de Chabrol, conseiller d'Etat, Préfet du Département* (Paris: Ballard), vol. 1 (1821), vol. 2 (1823), vol. 3 (1826), vol. 4 (1829), vol. 5 (1844), vol. 6 (1860). Prefatory matter to volume 6, prepared under the direction of Baron Haussmann, contains a brief history of the endeavor and an indispensable index (pp. 693–708) to all six volumes of the collection.

47. [Chabrol de Volvic], "Extrait d'un rapport fait à son Excellence le Ministre de l'Intérieur," *Recherches statistiques . . . Paris*, 1: 95–113.

Chabrol observed that the accuracy of this census, by far and away the best made to date of the French capital, was admirably suited to the administrative needs of the city even if it might not meet the strict standards set for scientific exploitation of the data.[48] Villot, who had provided direct supervision of the census, repeated this sentiment, adding that administration can be satisfied with a general, if not exact, knowledge of the facts.[49] No doubt both Chabrol and Villot were put on guard by their associate, Fourier, and, while proud of their accomplishment and cognizant of its public utility, were careful not to put forth excessive claims.[50]

Villot invited further scrutiny of the figures. While the census had been taken in order to provide a factual basis for routine administrative action, its sponsors felt that its publication would also lead to its use by members of the general public for forming "sound opinions" and presenting "useful proposals."[51] The very form of publication of the data was directed to this end, and that form was justified by a familiar argument, namely, that statistics is an instrument for analysis and comparison. Obviously, Villot observed, the raw data themselves should not be published: they are both too numerous and too varied. A means that was concise and that lent itself to direct comparison of facts was required. For this reason, the census results from Paris were presented in tabular form (63 such tableaux appeared in the first volume of the series). Villot's words return one to the continuing tradition of the idéologues. Statistics is an "observational science," he noted; it is not given to "discourse and conjectures." Thus it follows that the "preparation of tableaux has the advantage of excluding useless discussion and of directing all research towards its principal objective, namely, the methodical enumeration of facts."[52]

Naturally, upon the method informing this enumeration depended the importance of the entire undertaking. If composed wisely, the tableaux enabled the establishment of correspondences between seemingly disparate phenomena and the discovery of "constant laws" by which one set of facts is generated from another. But the bureau de statistique, Villot confessed, must restrict itself to the collection and publication of statistical data. He noted that the "study of causes is slow, difficult, and uncertain";

48. Ibid., p. 105.

49. [Villot], "Introduction," ibid., p. ix.

50. Thus Fourier ("Notions générales," ibid., p. 2): "The degree of precision that inquiries regarding population require depends upon the viewpoint of the inquirer. The knowledge of all the elements of the population that is needed for public administration does not always demand an evaluation as rigorous as that which is needed by the [natural] sciences or political arithmetic."

51. [Villot], "Introduction," ibid., p. vi.

52. Ibid., pp. vii–viii.

it demands "prudence, understanding, and long meditation." Lavoisier's consideration of public finance provided an admirable example of such analysis; the certainty of his procedure had simply put out of court "all superfluous discussion."[53] Public servants, however, could not indulge a taste for such extended investigations. Limits of time, space, and money prevented it. But the bureau de statistique could and did marshall its data in a manner that lent itself to closer analysis by other persons. Villot's public invitation, seconded by close personal encouragement and support, was essential to Villermé's singular exploitation of the published and unpublished material gathered by the bureau.

The census as published in 1821 provided information regarding births, marriages, and deaths for 1817 and calculations for 1818. It thus offered a view of the population at a fixed point in time. The bureau de statistique was not content with such inert figures. With the second volume, published in 1823, began an effort to capture the annual and long-term movement of the population. Procedures employed for this purpose varied. Reports of civil registration continued to be recorded. The census was repeated—but with important variations. The so-called census of 1826 was not a census at all but an extrapolation based upon annual population movements (computed from births) in the years immediately preceding that date. The census of 1831 and those which followed under supervision of the bureau de statistique (1836, 1841, 1846, 1851, 1856) were carried out strictly in accord with the principles laid down in 1817.

Villermé's major statistical studies of differential urban mortality also drew importantly on unpublished materials. He required information that was indeed being collected by public authorities but which, it seems, was either deemed insufficiently central to the principal concerns of the bureau de statistique to merit systematic publication or was published in a manner that inadvertently concealed its bearing on matters of sociomedical interest. It appears that the members of the bureau themselves only realized with some astonishment that the material they had been collecting and were in the process of publishing could be applied to such analyses. An incidental note buried deeply in the third volume (1826) in the *Recherches statistiques sur la ville de Paris* remarked that the material now being published (notably, mortality by *arrondissement*), when joined with that which had appeared in the second volume (1823) dealing with the distribution of wealth by arrondissement, suggested comparisons of "the greatest interest to several branches of the public administration."[54] By 1826,

53. Ibid., p. viii.
54. *Recherches statistiques . . . Paris*, vol. 2, no pagination: passage cited appears at foot of second page of "Enumération des Tableaux . . . 1817, 1818, 1819, 1820, et 1821," that is, the preliminary listing of tableaux numbers 42–50.

however, Villermé was already well along in establishing the comparisons that demonstrated the differential mortality of rich and poor. This was the kind of reasoning on numbers that Villot and his associates had hoped to elicit through publication of statistical information pertaining to Paris. Data of a similar nature provided the factual foundation for Villermé's assessment of cholera mortality in Parisian lodging houses. Here the unpublished materials were those gathered by the police in the course of controlling the movement of transients within the city. Such information Villermé compared with official published mortality figures in order to obtain a clue to the socioeconomic bases of differential mortality during the great cholera epidemic of 1832.[55]

The *Recherches statistiques sur la ville de Paris* proved to be an invaluable tool for social analysis. They were not, any more than were the incomplete and inexact national statistics then available, perfected examples of the collection and presentation of vital statistics. Their shortcomings were legion. For example, causes of death were unstated or indefinite. Yet the *Recherches* showed a major advance in reporting age-specific mortality. Embracing a population of some 750,000–800,000, age-specific mortality reports were provided by year for ages 1–10 and by five-year intervals for ages 10–100. Vital registration itself was progressing unevenly. Its procedures were revolutionized in Britain by the General Registration Act of 1836 and the ensuing creation of the Registrar General's Office, whose secretary, William Farr, began to transform the whole scope and purpose of the collection and analysis of vital statistics.[56] If in France municipal officers by the 1820s had generally replaced the parish priest as the recording agent (and this was not accomplished without long and disrupting disputes), still there existed only a central office (Bureau des longitudes) to prepare a national abstract of this data, but no census was conducted. The city of Paris fared better, for these statistical functions were executed by the experienced officers of the prefecture of the Seine. No statistical reports of the period, however, handled in appropriate manner the critical issue of migration. Movement into and away from the larger and rapidly developing cities was particularly important, yet it largely escaped the grasp of statisticians. Even the distinction between urban and rural populations remained uncertain, the designation of both civil entities usually resting on an arbitrary definition of maximum or minimum population size.

55. Villermé, "Note sur les ravages du choléra-morbus dans les maisons garnies de Paris, depuis le 29 mars jusqu'au 1er août 1832 et sur les causes qui paraissent avoir favorisé le développement de la maladie dans un grand nombre de maisons," *Annales d'hygiène publique et de médecine légale* 11 (1834): 385–413.

56. See Eyler, *Victorian Social Medicine*, pp. 37–65.

But to many students of city and countryside, population size and movement were not the greater objective. Their goal was to assess the quality of the population. To assay the relative well-being of the different elements of an urban population required, of course, close attention to population size and movement. It also required consideration of innumerable other matters, and of paramount importance, it demanded personal involvement in the outstanding social issues of the day. The latter seemed always to return the observer to one issue, to the "social question," the condition and prospects of the laboring population of the city and of the nation. Such was the stimulus for the explosion of statistical studies and societies in Britain in the 1830s, and such was the commitment that Villermé and his fellow sociomedical investigators brought to their inquiries throughout the 1820s.[57] Villermé used numbers to discover unsuspected or previously unconfirmed relationships. His goal was not to increase the mathematical subtlety and rigor of this kind of analysis but to translate his findings into socially useful commentary. His purpose was to know the social world, at first its medical condition and then, inevitably, the economic and other relations that bound it together and assured its continuity.

Villermé stopped short of Karl Marx's proud claim that our intellectual purpose is not simply to know the world but to change it. Villermé's political and economic allegiances allowed no sympathy whatsoever for the kind of change that Marx and other early socialists envisaged. Yet his knowledge was in fact largely their knowledge, and his investigations were decisive in removing the social question in France from the realm of mere discourse and placing it before the reading public in its harshest reality. The contradictions between his perception of the problem and his remedies therefor will be examined below, but it may be pointed out here that his perception was grounded in number, and number it was—despite the limitations of the sources from which it was drawn—that appeared to lend scientific authenticity to the endeavor. If the socialists thought history stood on their side, the political economists were pleased with their own cool view of social reality—best expressed in number. They had facts; their opponents, they felt, only opinion.

57. See Cullen, *Statistical Movement in Early Victorian Britain*, esp. pp. 135–49.

Chapter 6

Inequality before Death: Paris

The average life span is very short in places that civilization has not yet reached and it is much greater under the influence of intelligent governance. In this advance, far more than in the growth of total population, must be sought one of the most certain indications of public prosperity.

Joseph Fourier, 1821

The overriding objective of Villermé's statistical investigations of the 1820s and 1830s was to join number and social fact. The principal social fact placed in question was the differential mortality of the rich and the poor; the relevant number was the respective death rate of each group. Mortality and its close associate in the domain of vital facts, average duration of life, depended upon biological parameters that determined the strength and weakness of the individual organism and upon environmental factors with which each individual or group had to contend. But Villermé shared Fourier's conviction. "Civilization"—that is, modern European society—was also a factor, probably the most important factor, in matters of life and death. This premise had to be tested and traditional etiological assumptions weighed. Villermé first sought the hygienist's measure of civilization in the inequality before death of the people of Paris. The poor, he learned, die both more frequently and at a younger age than the wealthy.

This unsurprising conclusion was presented as a demonstration and not as a mere claim. It faced an earlier argument, one formulated in the aftermath of Jean Jacques Rousseau and still entertained by members of the medical profession, that the wealthier members of society are truly at risk. The idleness of the rich, physicians argued, their habitual overindulgence and moral laxity, reduced them to misery and brought them to an early grave. But this was a claim founded only on words. What was needed were facts, numerous facts and facts whose bearing could be turned di-

EPIGRAPH: Joseph Fourier "Notions générales sur la population," in *Recherches statistiques sur la ville de Paris et sur le département de la Seine, recueil de tableaux dressés et réunis d'après les ordres de Monsieur le comte de Chabrol, Conseiller d'Etat, Préfet du Département*, 1 (Paris: Ballard, 1821): 56.

rectly to the issue of differential mortality. Such were the facts, the numbers, that Villermé discovered in the *Recherches statistiques sur la ville de Paris*. Thereafter he began to apply methods he had developed for assessment of prison mortality to the study of a broader social issue and was thus launched on a career of comprehensive sociomedical investigation.

I deal with Villermé's statistical investigations in three chapters. He first came to wide public notice by publication of a study of the relative mortality of the wealthy and indigent classes of society. This memoir (1828), its antecedents, and its immediate offspring represent the burden of Villermé's work of the 1820s and early 1830s and offer a complete view of his method and intentions; I examine these memoirs in the present chapter. Simultaneously Villermé was exploring other vital patterns made evident by large numbers. These studies, closely paralleled by those of Adolfe Quetelet, again pointed to a connection between man's biological condition and his social status. These themes, notably body size and age specificity of death, are discussed in Chapter 7. After 1834 Villermé's predominant concern was direct assessment of the condition of the working classes in France. His study involved both on-site inspection of factory and factory worker and exploitation of numerical data; it repeated, of course, the central theme of earlier work, namely, life is more precarious, demonstrably more precarious, for the lower orders of society. These researches, presented en masse in the *Tableau de l'état physique et moral des ouvriers* (1840), are the subject of Chapter 8.

Rich and Poor

The recently founded Royal Academy of Medicine took seriously its responsibility towards the government to which it owed its existence. This concern was formalized when in 1825 Frédéric Villot presented to the academy a set of manuscript tableaux dealing with the movement of population in Paris. These tableaux reported on the years 1817–21 and were ultimately published in 1826. As part of its public health responsibilities the academy created a statistical commission, the commission charging Villermé, still only a *membre-adjoint*, to examine the tableaux and to prepare an official report. This report was also published in 1826 and represents Villermé's first systematic presentation of his notions regarding the differential mortality of the rich and the poor.

Villermé's report left many questions unanswered, however. Most notably, it failed to allow close geographical specification and economic characterization of differences in mortality. Villermé soon addressed himself to this matter in his celebrated "Mémoire sur la mortalité en France, dans la classe aisée et dans la classe indigente" (1828). This study was also based upon the census of 1817 and on reports on mortality for the years 1817–21; additional material was gathered for city quarter and street. The publication in 1826 of a new census raised hopes that the analysis could now be based on two sets of independent yet strictly comparable data. The new census, however, was only an evaluation, not an enumeration, and was deemed unreliable. Villermé's hopes were disappointed, and extension of the analysis to the years 1822–26 therefore provided, as he himself insisted, only the most uncertain results. A memoir of 1830 reporting these facts concluded his publications based on the Chabrol-Villot *Recherches*.[1]

In taking Villot's tableaux of 1825 under consideration, the academy's commission sought straightaway to indicate the "relation of these facts to the causes that have induced them."[2] Degree of wealth or poverty was immediately cited as foremost among these causes. It was important, however, to establish that the facts in question reflected "constant" and not "accidental" causes. This was Pierre Simon de Laplace's distinction, probably introduced into the commission's proceedings by Fourier and one subsequently to become essential to Quetelet's conception of social statis-

1. The history of the academy's, and Villermé's, study of the Chabrol-Villot reports is a complicated matter. To recapitulate, volume 1 of the *Recherches* was published in 1821 and was immediately reviewed in depth by Villermé ("Rapport sur un ouvrage intitulé: *Recherches statistiques* . . . ," *Bulletins de la Société médicale d'émulation*, 1822. pp. 1–41). Villot by 1825 had drawn up manuscript tableaux based on data in volumes 1 and 2 of the *Recherches*. These tableaux were submitted to the academy, which created a "Commission de statistique," for which Villermé was *rapporteur*. His report was read to the academy in 1825 and published in 1826 ("Rapport fait par M. Villermé, et lu à l'Académie royale de médecine, au nom de la Commission de statistique, sur une série de tableaux relatifs au mouvement de la population dans les douze arrondissements municipaux de la ville de Paris pendant les cinq années 1817, 1818, 1819, 1820, et 1821," *Archives générales de médecine* 10 [1826]: 216–47). The tableaux were then published in volume 3 (1826) of the *Recherches* (nos. 42–50). Thereafter Villermé continued his assessment with "Mémoire sur la mortalité en France dans la classe aisée et dans la classe indigente," *Mémoires de l'Académie royale de la médecine* 1 (1828): 51–98, and "De la mortalité dans les divers quartiers de la ville de Paris, et des causes qui la rendent très différente dans plusieurs d'entre eux, ainsi que dans les divers quartiers de beaucoup de grandes villes," *Annales d'hygiène publique et de médecine légale* 3 (1830): 294–341. The last item offers (p. 294) a brief synopsis of these events. Records of the Commission de statistique, if still extant, could not be located in the Archives of the Academy of Medicine. Commission members included N. R. Desgenettes, J. E. D. Esquirol, Fourier, Villermé, and three others. The reader should compare these studies with those prepared by William Farr and published beginning in 1839; the contrast in sophistication in data collection and analysis is striking, yet the objectives of the two observers were largely the same. See John M. Eyler, *Victorian Social Medicine: The Ideas and Methods of William Farr* (Baltimore: Johns Hopkins University Press, 1979), pp. 123–58.

2. Villermé, "Rapport . . . sur une série de tableaux" (1826), p. 216.

tics.[3] It was also an essential premise of all of Villermé's reasoning with numbers. He shared Laplace's conviction that a "series of events indefinitely prolonged" would *ipso facto* give evidence of the "action of regular and constant causes."[4] To Laplace the interaction of sun and planets and, particularly, between the planets offered best witness to the existence of constant causes. Here, where irregularity had long seemed to prevail, renewed analysis exhibited a long-term periodicity in which chance events played no part. This constancy of phenomena dictated a constancy of cause. Later in his career Laplace, like the Marquis de Condorcet, attempted to extend his reasoning to biological events, namely, the cause underlying the by then classical observation of the near equality of male and female births.

Laplace's starting point was thus an analysis which, by establishing the regularity of events, authorized investigation of causes.[5] Regularity strongly suggested the operation of invariable and therefore constant causes; deviations from regularity gave reason to explore a not yet evident cause or set of causes. The regularity perceived ruled out the operation of so-called accidental causes. Laplace required that regularity be tested, that is, that it be assessed by mathematical means in order to determine its margin of error. Fourier and Quetelet were sensitive to this demand; other investigators were not. "It was easier and more tempting," Victor Hilts has observed, "to suggest possible constant causes for observed differences than it was to calculate whether the differences themselves were really important."[6]

Medical observers, particularly those who collaborated with Fourier, were not altogether unmindful of the problem. The academy's investigators tested their material empirically, not mathematically. As will be seen, the essential data were presented as five-year averages of mortality by arrondissement. The question posed at the outset was this: were the differ-

3. See V. L. Hilts, "Statistics and Social Science," in *Foundations of Scientific Method: The Nineteenth Century*, ed. R. N. Giere and R. S. Westfall (Bloomington: Indiana University Press, 1973), pp. 206–33; Robert André, "Quetelet et la démographie," in Académie royale de Belgique, *Adolfe Quetelet, 1796–1874: Contributions en hommage à son rôle de sociologue*, Mémorial Adolfe Quetelet, no. 4 (Brussels: Palais des Académies, 1977), pp. 74–86; Frank H. Hankins, "Adolfe Quetelet as Statistician" (Ph.D. diss., Columbia University, 1908), esp. pp. 83–105.

4. Pierre Simon, Marquis de Laplace, *A Philosophical Essay on Probabilities*, trans. F. W. Truscott and F. L. Emory (New York: Dover, 1951), p. 62. Laplace, of course, only proclaims the faith of all social statisticians and numerically inclined hygienists: see the important analysis by Eyler, *Victorian Social Medicine*, pp. 32–33, 69, 81.

5. Hilts, "Statistics and Social Science," pp. 209–11.

6. Ibid., p. 211.

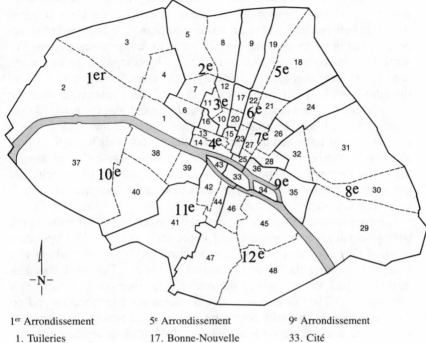

1er Arrondissement

1. Tuileries
2. Champs-Elysées
3. Roule
4. Vendôme

2e Arrondissement

5. Chaussée-d'Antin
6. Palais-Royal
7. Feydeau
8. Faubourg-Montmartre

3e Arrondissement

9. Faubourg-Poissonnière
10. Saint-Eustache
11. Mail
12. Montmartre

4e Arrondissement

13. Saint-Honoré
14. Louvre
15. Marchés
16. Banque

5e Arrondissement

17. Bonne-Nouvelle
18. Porte-St.-Martin
19. Faubourg-St.-Denis
20. Montorgueil

6e Arrondissement

21. St.-Martin-des-Champs
22. Porte-St.-Denis
23. Lombards
24. Temple

7e Arrondissement

25. Arcis
26. Mont-de-Piété
27. Sainte-Avoie
28. Marché St.-Jean

8e Arrondissement

29. Quinze-Vingts
30. St.-Antoine
31. Popincourt
32. Marais

9e Arrondissement

33. Cité
34. Ile-St.-Louis
35. Arsenal
36. Hôtel-de-Ville

10e Arrondissement

37. Invalides
38. Faubourg-St.-Germain
39. Monnaie
40. St.-Thomas-d'Aquin

11e Arrondissement

41. Luxembourg
42. Ecole de Médecine
43. Palais de Justice
44. Sorbonne

12e Arrondissement

45. Jardin du Roi
46. St.-Jacques
47. Observatoire
48. St.-Marcel

Paris before 1860: the 12 arrondissements and 48 quarters. Redrawn from *Recherches statistiques sur la ville de Paris et le département de la Seine* vol. 6 (Paris: Imprimerie administrative de Paul Dupont, 1860), "Tableau des 48 quartiers de Paris . . . ravagés du choléra . . . en 1854" (unpaginated).

ences thereby made evident due to "accidental causes"? An affirmative response to this question could only mean, of course, that the differential mortality between rich and poor was due to chance, it being a fictive appearance of numbers and therefore unsuited to further investigation. Villermé's commission responded to the charge by comparing figures representing five-year averages of mortality with others that expressed annual mortality (1817–21) in each arrondissement.[7] They discovered that the five-year trend in mortality in each arrondissement was the same (downward), and with slight variations, the rank order by mortality for each arrondissement remained the same over the period. This in itself seemed sufficient authorization to conclude that "constant causes" were always acting "in the same direction" and to permit enunciation of the principal question: "What are the causes that seem to assign to each quarter of Paris a characteristic degree of salubrity?"[8]

The commission proceeded by comparing mortality by arrondissement with a seemingly exhaustive set of explanatory options. The operation required numerous assumptions, not least of which was that which was thought to counter the effect of internal migration. The commissioners treated, as had Villot, each of the twelve arrondissements of Paris as a "distinct city." They then assumed, without reasoned justification and no doubt erroneously, that such migration as takes place almost always occurs among members of the same social class.[9] Migration therefore was assumed to have little net effect on social structure in each arrondissement, a matter of major importance to investigators who were seeking to relate the incidence of disease and mortality to degrees of wealth and poverty.

Villot's data revealed that in general the western arrondissements were significantly healthier than those in the city center and those to the east. The commission's reworking of his tableaux is given in Table 6.1.[10] These figures referred strictly to deaths that occurred at home (à domicile). As a large proportion of deaths in Paris took place in the hospitals, these especially among the indigent, the data presented in Table 6.1 provided only a first approximation of the tendency towards differential mortality among the twelve arrondissements. They nonetheless show that the highest rate was almost 50 percent higher than the lowest.

There were numerous possibilities for explaining the demonstrated pattern of mortality, derived principally from ancient medical theory. The

7. Villermé, "Rapport . . . sur une série de tableaux," tables, pp. 218–19.
8. Ibid., p. 220.
9. Ibid., p. 217.
10. Ibid., p. 218.

Table 6.1. Average annual mortality *à domicile*, by arrondissement, 1817–1821

Arrondissement	Quarters	Number of inhabitants per 1 death	Deaths per 1,000 inhabitants
2	Chaussée-d'Antin, Palais-Royal, Feydeau, Faub.-Montmartre	62	16.1
3	Montmartre, Faub.-Poissonnière, Saint-Eustache, Mail	60	16.7
1	Roule, Champs-Elysées, Vendôme, Tuileries	58	17.2
4	Saint-Honoré, Louvre, Marchés, Banque	58	17.2
6	Porte-St.-Denis, St.-Martin-des-Champs, Lombards, Temple	54	18.5
5	Faub.-St.-Denis, Porte-St.-Martin Bonne-Nouvelle, Montorgueil	53	18.9
7	Sainte-Avoie, Mont-de-Piété, Marché St.-Jean, Arcis	52	19.2
11	Luxembourg, Ecole de Médecine, Sorbonne, Palais de Justice	51	19.6
10	Monnaie, St.-Thomas-d'Aquin, Invalides, Faub.-St.-Germain	50	20.0
9	Ile-St.-Louis, Hôtel-de-Ville, Cité, Arsenal	44	22.7
8	St.-Antoine, Quinze-Vingts, Marais, Popincourt	43	23.3
12	Jardin du Roi, St.-Marcel, St.-Jacques, Observatoire	43	23.3
All arrondissements		51	19.6

SOURCE: L. R. Villermé, "Rapport fait par M. Villermé, et lu à la Académie royale de médecine, au nom de la Commission de statistique, sur une série de tableaux relatifs au mouvement de la population dans les douze arrondissements municipaux de la ville de Paris pendant les cinq années 1817, 1818, 1819, 1820, et 1821," *Archives générales de médecine* 10 (1826): 218.

environmental hypothesis, best expressed in the Hippocratic treatise *Airs, Waters, and Places*, was widely entertained in the later eighteenth and early nineteenth centuries.[11] This hypothesis was gradually divorced from

11. See J. N. Hallé, "Hygiène," *Dictionnaire des sciences médicales*, 60 vols. (Paris: Panckoucke, 1812–22), 22: 508–610; and William Coleman, "Health and Hygiene in the *Encyclopédie*: A Medical Doctrine for the Bourgeoisie," *Journal of the History of Medicine* 29 (1974): 399–421. A splendid discussion of the history of environmentalist hypotheses is given by C. J. Glacken, *Traces on the Rhodian Shore: Nature and Culture in Western Thought from Ancient Times to the End of the Eighteenth Century* (Berkeley: University of California Press, 1967).

its original context and made the foundation of much of the basic work of
the first generation of hygienic reformers. These reformers were generally
opposed to the notion of a living contagion as the source of disease, pre-
ferring instead to find its cause in the superbly unsanitary conditions that
characterized the early industrial cities. Edwin Chadwick elevated filth to
the level of a major explanatory principle, and numerous French sanitarians, notably less concerned with dirt, nonetheless became fervent anticon-
tagionists or, more commonly, paid the contagionist issue little attention.[12]

The academy's commissioners first tested a set of environmentalist options. If increased mortality is due, for example, to proximity to excessive
humidity, differences of altitude, soil character, or prevailing winds, then
the influence of these factors should manifest itself in regular manner over
the several arrondissements of Paris. Comparison of mortality and geographical location, however, revealed no such pattern. Some considered
the Seine, a major and constant source of dampness, an important source
of disease and death. But the commission's figures revealed that among
the arrondissements whose populations lived most removed from the river
some (second and third) exhibited a minimum mortality and another
(eighth), the maximum. On the other hand, of the arrondissements lying
close to the Seine, the fourth manifested a low mortality, the ninth a high
rate, and the tenth a middling degree.[13] The commission's conclusion was
stated cautiously but firmly: if an influence on mortality due to humidity
existed, it was not "sensible" and could not, therefore, be demonstrated.
The insensible was not a matter for scientific discourse.

This form of reasoning was then applied *seriatim* to other presumed
environmental features. No pattern was discerned that joined altitude and
mortality: the lowest districts of Paris bordered the Seine, yet mortality in
these arrondissements (first, fourth, seventh, ninth, and tenth) ranged
widely. Elevated areas also revealed no consistent pattern; mortality was
lowest in the second arrondissement and greatest in the twelfth, each of
which included much high ground. Surface soil provided no better correlation: save for paved areas and buildings, virtually the entire surface of
the city was composed of the debris left behind by generations of inhabitants. It offered no pronounced variations with which to correlate
mortality.[14]

12. See S. E. Finer, *The Life and Times of Sir Edwin Chadwick* (London: Methuen,
1952), pp. 297–313; E. H. Ackerknecht, "Anticontagionism between 1821 and 1867," *Bulletin of the History of Medicine* 22 (1948): 562–93.
    13. Villermé, "Rapport . . . sur une série de tableaux," p. 220.
    14. Ibid., pp. 220–21.

The movement of air in Paris was a function of the prevailing winds and the configuration of buildings, streets, and river. When these several factors were taken into consideration, once again no discernible overall pattern was revealed. Crosswinds dominated some sections of the city; winds sweeping over "infected" areas (notably the *voirie* of Montfaucon) seemed not to cause excess mortality; and those arrondissements exposed to steady air movements (first, eighth, tenth) revealed great differences in mortality.

These several examples convinced the commission that one could not find in the "layout of the city and in meteorological conditions the causes of the differences in mortality in the various arrondissements of Paris."[15] A closely related factor, however, had yet to be examined, namely, the water supplies of the city. Parisian water sources were numerous, including aqueduct, canal, spring, well, and river. The commission arbitrarily characterized these various waters by quantity of dissolved salts (no figures were given) and vaguely related their use to arrondissement. More telling, however, was the case of the Seine. That river's foul waters, happily if falsely characterized as the "lightest, purest, and best of all," served some three-quarters of the city, yet the arrondissements involved presented great differences in mortality. Again, no regular correlation could be established.[16]

Thus were exhausted the traditional environmental categories of disease causation. The exercise had been in vain: no one factor or combination of environmental factors could be matched to the demonstrated patterns of mortality. But the city presented another and distinctive feature with which the correlation might be attempted. This was congestion, the imposition of a massive population upon a relatively confined area. Some medical observers claimed that urban mortality was density-dependent.[17] The academy's commissioners scrutinized this possibility with especial care and established two bases for comparison.[18] The first provided the ratio,

15. Ibid., pp. 223.
16. Ibid. The role of water in the transmission of disease became one of the obsessions of nineteenth-century hygiene; see the discussions by S. C. Prescott and M. P. Horwood, *Sedgwick's Principles of Sanitary Science and Public Health* (New York: Macmillan, 1935), pp. 124–67; and C.-E. A. Winslow, *Man and Epidemics* (Princeton: Princeton University Press, 1952), pp. 52–111.
17. Claude Lachaise, *Topographie médicale de Paris; ou, Examen général des causes qui peuvent avoir une influence marquée sur la santé des habitans de cette ville, le caractère de leurs maladies, et le choix de précautions hygiéniques qui leur sont applicables* (Paris: J. B. Baillière, 1822), pp. 203–25, made this claim but then surrounded it with numerous qualifications.
18. Villermé, "Rapport . . . sur une série de tableaux," pp. 223–26.

by arrondissement, of built-up area to open space (streets, gardens, un-developed terrain). Stated in percentage terms, these figures ranged from 46 percent in the fifth and eighth arrondissements to 59 percent in the fourth, 60 percent in the ninth, 64 percent in the twelfth, 75 percent in the second, and 82 percent in the seventh. These figures represent housing density, not population density, and were offered, it turned out, as renewed contradiction of the environmental thesis. They seemed to show that breadth of street and amount of planted open space were irrelevant to degree of mortality; the densely built seventh arrondissement exhibited only moderate mortality, while the popular eighth arrondissement, whose working-class population shared the highest death rate in the city, was relatively little developed.

Villermé realized the peril of this argument. The open spaces were generally uninhabited and could not be considered an integral part of the daily experience of the average Parisian. A second set of density-related figures was required. Streets, *places*, and gardens were now eliminated from consideration, and the ratio of population to area occupied by housing alone was computed for each arrondissement. Once again no regular correlation with mortality was obtained. In the affluent first arrondissement each person occupied 65 m^2 of city surface, in the eighth 47 m^2, in the twelfth (whose mortality was highest) 37 m^2, in the second (which presented the lowest mortality) 27 m^2, and so on, down to the bursting fourth arrondissement, whose residents occupied 7 m^2 of city surface each but enjoyed relatively good health. A serious complicating factor in this analysis was the fact that Parisian housing was generally multistoried. If this tended to expand the space actually occupied, that expansion, Villermé noted, had to be weighed against the countervailing facts of the pattern of residence. Throughout Paris, rich and poor resided in close conjunction. The wealthy, however, tended to command a disproportionate amount of space, usually on the lower floors, and thus left the less wealthy, the poor, and the almost indigent to find their place in that order in the increasingly crowded upper stories.

Now, such results, the commission's *rapporteur* observed, "could not have been anticipated."[19] Environmental factors, the traditional medical explanation of the salubrity or insalubrity of localities, however chosen,

19. Ibid., p. 226. English observers, notably William Farr, ignored this conclusion at the next incursion of cholera (1848–49), insisting with renewed vigor that environmental factors, and above all, elevation, were the crucial correlates of the incidence of the disease. See J. M. Eyler, "William Farr on the Cholera: The Sanitarian's Disease Theory and the Statistician's Method," *Journal of the History of Medicine* 38 (1973): 79–100, esp. pp. 88–90.

could not be fitted to the facts, that is, to the numbers that expressed mortality and which provided the standard by which all supposed causes of death were to be judged. This rejection was consistent with the cautions expressed earlier by certain philosophes and idéologues, notably C. A. Helvétius and C. H. Volney, regarding the influence of climate on human affairs. By much diminishing the direct influence of climate, they opened other opportunities for man's own intervention in regard to his political, social, moral, and, perhaps, medical condition.[20] Density, too, whether of housing or of population, could be placed in no better accord with stated mortality. Yet, where the commission's analysis thus seemed to have reached an impasse, it had in reality come to a crucial turning point. Traditional explanations had been presented and tested and proved inadequate. It was necessary to reconsider the problem, approaching it now on a new and perhaps more fundamental biological and social level. Perhaps the basic conditions of human biological existence contributed most greatly to determining whether one group lives better or longer than another.

The very statement of such a possibility is impressive by its obviousness. Most certainly the novelty of the commission's ultimate argument is not to be found in its premise. What is striking, however, is the commissioners' willingness to accept this premise as the basis for an orderly assessment of the chances of life and death amongst a set of discrete populations. French observers, like their counterparts in England, had been forced by circumstances of war and poor harvest to examine more closely the relationship between availability of necessities of existence (particularly basic foodstuffs) and the physical and moral condition of the affected population. François Benoiston de Châteauneuf had provided a startling portrayal of the dietary lot of the Parisian population in 1817.[21] It was no doubt he who was primarily responsible for introducing this theme into the purview of sociomedical investigation. Foodstuffs and related necessities offered a common denominator between the economic and medical domains and suggested to contemporary observers a number of novel possibilities for measuring the well-being of a given nation or population.

---

20. See the notable essay by L. J. Jordanova that defines this problematic, particularly the organism-environment relationship and the connection of this relationship to contemporary historical understanding: "Earth Science and Environmental Medicine: The Synthesis of the Late Enlightenment," in *Images of the Earth: Essays in the History of the Environmental Sciences*, ed. L. J. Jordanova and R. S. Porter (Chalfont St. Giles: British Society for the History of Science, 1979), pp. 119–46.

21. Benoiston de Châteauneuf, *Recherches sur les consommations de tout genre de la ville de Paris en 1817, comparées à ce qu'elles étaient en 1789* (Paris: the author, 1820).

One such possibility involved the correlation of mortality with the movement of prices; another possibility required comparison of mortality with the overall financial condition of a population or set of populations.[22] Of necessity, the academy's commissioners chose the latter approach.

"The cleanliness or uncleanliness of clothing, [the quality and availability of] foodstuffs, drinks, and the like," the commission observed, "are other conditions whose influence it is very important for us to know." They are causes that, depending upon the beneficent or detrimental influence they exercise, "must certainly contribute to the prolongation or abbreviation of life."[23] The commissioners' problem was to discover a summary measure of these diverse factors. Nothing seemed more difficult—and yet nothing was more easily resolved. The *Recherches statistiques* again provided a clue. The *Recherches* recorded much more than figures of demographic interest. Amongst the numerous economic facts reported was a brief table that listed categories of rent paid in each arrondissement. The definition of each category provided the crucial criterion by which to separate the social classes. This definition was given in terms of the tax liability that followed upon the amount of rent paid. Rents under 150 francs were untaxed, this sum indicating that such renters lived in very reduced circumstances. Rents over 150 francs suggested at least a reasonably assured competence on the part of the renters; some of the latter, of course, would be persons of great wealth. All such individuals paid a tax. Upon this distinction rested Villermé's entire analysis by arrondissement of the differential mortality *à domicile* of rich and poor. He felt that Villot had provided "positive documents that indicate the degree, expressed in numerical terms, of all the conditions in question."[24] Taxed or untaxed thus became the decisive *differentia* between rich and poor and did so because

22. François Mélier, "Etudes sur les subsistances envisagées dans leurs rapports avec les maladies et la mortalité," *Mémoires de l'Académie royale de médecine* 10 (1843): 170–205. See William Coleman, "Medicine against Malthus: François Mélier on the Relation between Subsistence and Mortality (1843)," *Bulletin of the History of Medicine* 54 (1980): 23–42.

23. Villermé, "Rapport . . . sur une série de tableaux," p. 226.

24. Ibid., p. 227. Villot's tableau appears as no. 102 in volume 2 (1823). Without doubt, this measure of economic condition is inexact and perhaps wholly inappropriate; Edmonde Vedrenne-Villeneuve, "L'inégalité sociale devant la mort dans la première moitié du XIXᵉ siècle," *Population* 16 (1961): 672n, summarily notes the difficulty. While probably destructive of the utility of Villermé's discussion as a representation of objective reality, this being Vedrenne-Villeneuve's concern, Villermé's vice only serves further to illuminate its author's procedure and intentions, and these are my concern. A brief description of other contemporary efforts to gain a measure of the economic condition of the working classes is given in Coleman, "Medicine against Malthus," pp. 30–32.

Table 6.2. Average annual mortality *à domicile* of rich and poor, by arrondissement, 1817–1821

Arrondissement	Untaxed rents (%)	Number of inhabitants per 1 death	Deaths per 1,000 inhabitants
2	7	62	16.1
3	11	60	16.7
1	11	58	17.2
4	15	58	17.2
11	19	51	19.6
6	21	54	18.5
5	22	53	18.9
7	22	52	19.2
10	23	50	20.0
9	31	44	22.7
8	32	43	23.3
12	38	43	23.3

SOURCE: Villermé, "Rapport . . . sur une série de tableaux," p. 227.

the tax burden appeared to offer in resumé a statement of group financial condition and thus of group capacity to provide for essential biological needs. The commission now sought to compare Parisian mortality data with this new criterion. Villot's information was restated to display the proportion that untaxed renters commanded of the total number of renters in each arrondissement. This figure, expressed as a percentage, provided an admittedly crude measure of the overall wealth or poverty of each of the twelve arrondissements. These percentages were then juxtaposed with the mortality rates expressed in Table 6.1; thus was created Table 6.2. The "quite remarkable result" of this comparison was to show that, with one exception, average mortality by arrondissement followed directly the estimated degree of poverty of the arrondissements.[25] Here was displayed vividly a correlation of the kind that the commission had previously sought in vain. It permitted a far-reaching, if qualified conclusion. Thus, wrote Villermé, "wealth, a competence, and misery are, for the inhabitants of the diverse arrondissements of Paris and under the conditions which these arrondissements impose upon them, the principal causes (we do not say the unique causes) to which must be attributed the great differences noted among the mortality rates."[26] For the moment this conclu-

25. Villermé, "Rapport . . . sur une série de tableaux," p. 228. The exceptional arrondissement (the eleventh) was explained by its apparently disproportionate number of aged residents.
26. Ibid.

Table 6.3. Average annual combined mortality (home and institution), 1817–1821

Arrondissement	Number of inhabitants per 1 death	Deaths per 1,000 inhabitants
1	45	22.2
2	43	23.3
3	38	26.3
10	36	27.8
6	35	28.6
7	35	28.6
5	34	29.4
4	33	30.3
11	33	30.3
8	25	40.0
9	25	40.0
12	24	41.7
All arrondissements	32	31.3

SOURCE: Villermé, "Rapport . . . sur une série de tableaux," pp.233–34.

sion—a "truth," it was called—was merely stated; its further exploration was reserved for a future occasion.

This correlation, it should be noted, was based upon only a portion of the total mortality of Paris. To deaths *à domicile* had to be added those that occurred in public institutions, namely, the civil hospitals and hospices of the capital. The data necessary for this operation proved deficient. Moreover, it was necessary to make certain assumptions regarding the distribution by arrondissement-of-origin of the inmates of these institutions and, again, the proportion of deaths among these inmates. Villermé nonetheless did offer a very cautious view of the distribution by arrondissement of the now combined and therefore presumably overall mortality of Paris. Total mortality—that *à domicile* and in hospital and hospice—is given in Table 6.3. Although the death order of the arrondissements has shifted slightly (see Table 6.2), the original conclusion was confirmed. Taken together, the wealthiest arrondissements (first, second, third) exhibited a distinctly lower mortality than did the three least wealthy (eighth, ninth, twelfth). More striking is the fact, granting always the uncertain character of the figures being manipulated, that the introduction of institutional mortality increased the death rate in the poorer areas much more than it did that of the wealthier sections of the city. This simply confirmed by number what to Villermé and others was "easy to foresee," that is, hospital and hospice represented the retreat and defeat of the poor, their peculiar place to die.[27]

27. Ibid., pp. 234.

Mortality is the principal actor in the 1826 report to the academy. It did not stand alone, however. Data regarding other vital phenomena were also extracted from the *Recherches statistiques sur la ville de Paris*, and an attempt was made to correlate these, too, with the socioeconomic condition of the arrondissements. These correlations, involving the number of births and marriages and ratio of the sexes and legitimacy-illegitimacy, gave additional but less decisive evidence that wealth and poverty exerted profound sway over the human biological condition. Wealth tended to reduce the number of births, increase abandonment of natural children, and preserve life; the poor, by contrast, tended to reproduce more abundantly, lose more children to death, recognize their natural children, and themselves die younger.[28]

Other correlations were envisaged but, since Villot's volumes were silent on the matter, could not be executed. It would have been useful, the commission observed, to have compared mortality by profession or by the floor occupied in a dwelling. Given the available information, however, such was quite impossible. Even more interesting would have been to increase the resolution of the analysis. All of the correlations stated, and the deductions drawn therefrom, pertained to the arrondissement. The arrondissement was a large administrative unit, homogeneous neither in physical character nor in population. Would it not prove useful, Villermé inquired, to extend the commission's procedure to lesser and presumably more homogeneous units, to quarters or even to streets?

> If, instead of taking results from entire arrondissements, each of which is like a complete city, we would have compared the results from a much smaller quarter or a single street that offers either by the nature of the exposure of its lodgings, by the kinds of professions therein practiced, or by other factors, a set of clear-cut conditions with the results obtained from another quarter or street that offers, other things being equal, conditions equally well defined but different, we should *very probably* have found differences in the proportion of deaths, just as these occur for diseases. For each profession, each trade, every condition in this life presents its own dangers and opportunities, and these must have a bearing on differences in mortality.[29]

Such differences, he added, are not yet known, but surely they, too, could be submitted to numerical analysis. Here an investigator might find a "new career, difficult to pursue but into which one could throw oneself with the hope of making a great contribution to the improvement of the lot of the

28. Ibid., pp. 236–44.
29. Ibid., p. 236.

people."[30] This statement was more than empty rhetoric; it was a self-invitation to and the public announcement of the beginning of an important undertaking. The fruits of Villermé's next inquiry—for he became that new investigator—were published in 1828 by the Academy of Medicine in the inaugural volume of its famed *Mémoires*.

Several forms of evidence were marshalled to prove the differential mortality of rich and poor. Of these, however, most striking and novel was the analysis of mortality by quarter and street. Villermé opened his argument by recalling a major conclusion of 1826, namely, the sharp difference of mortality exhibited by the first arrondissement (wealthy) and the twelfth (poor). These figures were recomputed after the introduction of numerous assumptions and corrections. Restated they are: mortality in first arrondissement, 24.3 deaths per 1,000 (1826: 22.2 per 1,000) and in the twelfth arrondissement, 41.3 per 1,000 (1826: 41.7 per 1,000).[31] This difference was enormous (70 percent), and it seemed impossible to attribute it to chance. (Such were the advantages of choosing extreme cases, especially as the statistical significance of these numbers was left untested.)

Villermé's purpose, however, was to move beyond such crude generalizations and to assign mortality figures to geographically more circumscribed and economically better defined areas. But now Villot's data began to fail him; while useful (with reservations) for analysis of mortality by quarter, it could not be applied to analysis by street. The major difficulty in the entire enterprise lay in clearly separating those areas for which census and mortality data were available into zones of exclusive or at least preponderant occupancy by either the rich or the poor. Villot's report on taxes paid on rents gave only a rough approximation. Moreover, probably very few areas of Paris were truly an exclusive preserve of either rich or poor; in the 1820s residential segregation, to judge by Villermé's vexations in seeking to separate clearly the worlds of the wealthy and the poor, had not yet advanced far.

In response to these difficulties Villermé sought out new information. Of primary importance was an unpublished series of bills of mortality for the ninth arrondissement prepared monthly for the mayor of the arrondissement and dispatched by him to the Medical Society of Paris (Société de médecine de Paris) in whose offices, presumably, Villermé consulted them. These bills permitted, first of all, a comparison of two selected quarters in the ninth arrondissement. Their socioeconomic character was not stated, but it seemed clear that the residents of the Arsenal quarter lived in much less easy circumstances than the inhabitants of the nearby

30. Ibid.
31. Villermé "Sur la mortalité en France" (1828), p. 56.

quarter of the Ile-Saint-Louis. This fact was simply reasserted (no more, surely, could be claimed, lest the author be caught in circular argument) by the mortality figures for each quarter. After expressing many and serious reservations about his calculations (all of them just), Villermé reported that mortality in the Arsenal quarter was at least 1 in 38.4, that is, 26 deaths per 1,000 population per annum.[32] On the Ile-Saint-Louis, mortality was markedly lower: 1 in 46.4, that is, 21.6 per 1,000 per annum. Here, in an arrondissement whose overall corrected mortality (à domicile and in institutions combined) was among the worst in Paris (1826: 1 in 25, or 40 per 1,000), was manifest a difference in mortality as striking as that which separated the first and twelfth arrondissements.

A final comparison seemed required, however, and thus entered hygienic literature the famed rue de la Mortellerie, whose name alone conveyed the necessary lesson. Lying in the fourth arrondissement, the rue de la Mortellerie, today part of the rue de l'Hôtel-de-Ville, was one of those streets where "the poor are heaped together in confined, filthy, dark and ill-ventilated lodgings."[33] Across the river lay the more spacious apartments of the quays of the Ile-Saint-Louis, whose occupants, if not wealthy, lived in some comfort. Mortality à domicile alone (pertinent hospital and hospice data were unobtainable) sharply divided these streets: on the quays it was 1 in 52.4 (19.1 per 1,000); in the rue de la Mortellerie, 1 in 32.7 (30.6 per 1,000).[34]

Almost certainly the difference thus revealed was in actuality far worse. Villermé wanted to insure that the rue de la Mortellerie would not be forgotten, that it would stand as a symbol for the appalling mortality that affected the poor. He wished to emphasize that that mortality, now held to be social in origin, was potentially reducible. The above calculation had excluded death in the hospitals. But, the author noted, lodgings in the rue de la Mortellerie were in large part taken by single workers who shared a room with 10 to 20 others. It was a singular fact that not one of these persons appeared on the bills of mortality, which reported only death à

---

32. Ibid., p. 59. The difference in mortality between the two quarters was probably even greater, for Villermé was unable to include figures for the death of the poor in *hospices*, an operation that would have surely increased the death rate more in the Arsenal quarter than in that of Ile-Saint-Louis.

33. Ibid., p. 60.

34. Ibid. Of the inhabitants of the rue de la Mortellerie, Lachaise wrote (*Topographie médicale de Paris*, p. 172): "The indigent class is composed of port and shipyard workers, numerous masons, roofers, bakers' men, wood and iron workers, water carriers, and the like. Their rendezvous is the rue de la Mortellerie and the rue de la Vannerie, both of which are filthy and ill-built."

domicile. "They always [went] to the hospital to die," and there their records disappeared.[35] If these officially invisible figures could be included, the true death rate of the residents of the street would necessarily be elevated. Moreover, aged persons were relatively few in the rue de la Mortellerie. On the one hand, the bills of mortality for the ninth arrondissement grossly understated the number of deaths befalling the residents of the rue de la Mortellerie; on the other hand, this mortality touched a population containing remarkably few aged men and women. Poverty was slaughtering above all the young and, perhaps even more, given the nature of occupancy on the street, those in the prime of age. Villermé guessed that, were corrections possible, the death rate in the rue de la Mortellerie would be shown to be at least double that on the quays of the Ile-Saint-Louis or in the entire first arrondissement.[36] Of course, both of the two quarters and two streets that had been selected for comparison with one another had been chosen to present almost idential environmental conditions, thus precluding the attribution of differential mortality to their action.

It is this analysis of mortality by arrondissement, quarter, and street that is best remembered of the many related arguments presented in the memoir of 1828. The shortcomings of Villermé's procedure are real, and they disallow use of his conclusions as an objective representation of social conditions in Paris in the 1820s.[37] But surely these examples—and the author knowingly was presenting only examples—approximated the truth of the situation. And that was sufficient. The memoir of 1828 was contentious; its author demanded only evidence that was adequate for his purpose, and he found it. Sociomedical investigation was not disinterested but focused forthrightly on certain of the most conspicuous social vices of the era. Villermé found support for the picture thus formed in a variety of unexpected and often unsure sources.

In the memoir of 1828 he attempted to provide a comprehensive view of the kinds of evidence that indicated that rich and poor are defined by more than just financial condition. Differential mortality across the administrative entities and streets of Paris was but the first, albeit the favored, item placed in the balance. To it was added, first, the now familiar conclu-

35. Villermé "Sur la mortalité en France," p. 61.
36. Ibid., p. 62.
37. Vedrenne-Villeneuve has insisted upon this difficulty ("L'inégalité sociale devant la mort," pp. 674, 682). The crucial shortcoming was a failure to establish age-specific death rates and thus be assured that differences in mortality were not due to factors other than crudely estimated economic condition (for example, a disproportionately large number of children in a given street, quarter, or arrondissement).

sions drawn from mortality in the prisons.[38] For this purpose Villermé merely reiterated the principal points made in his volume of 1820. Prison mortality varied enormously, but death struck most frequently those who were weak, indigent, and given minimal care. Prisoners in the *bagne*, closely held but properly provided for, fared better than the population of any arrondissement in Paris; the neglected and debilitated indigents at the *dépôt* of Saint-Denis perished at a rate almost seven times greater than that of the worst arrondissement in the capital.

An attempt was made to extend the analysis beyond Paris to the nation at large. Various measures of the presumed wealth of the departments were gathered and contrasted to the (computed) movement of population for the years 1817–22 (a datum furnished by the Bureau des longitudes). The comparison showed that mortality in a set of 14 wealthy departments was 1 in 46.3 population per annum (21.6 per 1,000), whereas that in 14 impoverished departments was 1 in 33.7 per annum (29.7 per 1,000).[39] Thus, concluded Villermé, "whether we consider large populations or small, populations which are concentrated or are dispersed, the same truth emerges": the poor die earlier than the rich.

It was even possible to gain a first indication of mortality by profession. Here data were sorely lacking. Villermé relied upon a single document, a manuscript report on admissions to and mortality in the Paris hospitals for the year 1807. Professional categories therein were inclusive, and the distinctions drawn were very broad. Nevertheless, this document showed that for 1807 at least hospital mortality varied by trade. Of 1617 dressmakers received ill by the hospitals, 190 died (1 in 8.5, or 117.6 deaths per 1,000); shoemakers fared somewhat worse: 807 admitted, 108 dead (1 in 7.5, or 133.3 per 1,000); a heterogeneous group of lamplighters, woolcarders, bootblacks, and others had an even higher death rate: 1,277 admitted, 309 dead (1 in 4.1, or 242.1 per 1,000); worst of all were porters, men and women with only daily employment and subjected to heavy burdens, and their children: 130 admitted, 43 dead (1 in 3.0, or 333.3 per 1,000). By contrast, the more skilled workers (butchers, carpenters, jewelers, and the like) as well as those employed in the foul and seemingly perilous trade of night-soil removal had a much lower death rate: 1,239 admitted, 117 dead (1 in 10.6, or 94.3 per 1,000).[40]

Here, in one of the earliest statistical reports on the health of the professions, is already made plain that one's prospect of life and death, particu-

38. Villermé "Sur la mortalité en France," pp. 64–69.
39. Ibid., pp. 72–73.
40. Ibid., pp. 73–74.

larly when once taken ill, is very much a function of economic condition. The figures presented were for one year only; the categories hopelessly confounded quite different trades; and no attention was paid to the prior experience of the victims. Obviously these flaws radically limit the objective validity of Villermé's analysis; no less obviously they were inherent in the evidence he exploited. The exercise is of importance, nonetheless, for it points directly to one of the subsequent and central preoccupations of the Parisian sociomedical investigators. In the detailed study prepared in 1834 by a commission of the academy of the distribution of cholera among the residents of Paris, distinction by class and trade was already being insisted upon. By the later 1830s and 1840s this mode of analysis, an obvious response to contemporary social preoccupations, had become both commonplace and specialized. Villermé's own *Tableau de l'état physique et moral des ouvriers* was devoted not only exclusively to the condition of the laboring population but, more particularly, only to those employed in the manufacture of cotton, woolen, and linen goods.

There was still other evidence that proclaimed the inequality before death of the rich and the poor. Utilizing unpublished materials provided by the minister of interior, Villermé was able to construct (with what accuracy?) life table mortality for the rich departments compared with the poor. Of 10,000 recorded births, 2,031 individuals had died in the rich departments by the end of the first year and 2,242 in the poor. That disproportion continued: at the end of four years, mortality among the wealthy was 3,091, among the poor 3,474; in ten years, 3,760 compared with 4,406; and in forty years, 5,438 versus 6,226. The gap was greatest at sixty years (6,873 versus 7,804).[41] Quite clearly the poor died younger than the wealthy.

This point was reaffirmed by the devastating evidence contributed to Villermé's memoir by Benoiston de Châteauneuf. The latter had extracted from the bills of Parisian mortality for the years 1817–1823/24 the record of child mortality in the first arrondissement (wealthy) and the twelfth (poor) and in selected and presumably extreme sections of each arrondissement. Here were numbers whose message was both horrifying and irrefutable. The essential figures are given in Table 6.4.[42] At no time was the measure used—infant mortality—less than one-third greater among the poor than among the wealthy; at worst, the percentage of deaths

41. Ibid., p. 77.
42. Benoiston's measure, a comparison of two numerators only, is a cruder measure than the infant mortality rate shown in Villermé's life table construction. The social meaning of both indices is the same, however.

among young children of the poor was two and one-half times higher than the percentage among the rich. The rue Mouffetard joined the rue de la Mortellerie as the symbol of the poor faced by a hostile urban environment, an environment now defined primarily by economic condition and no longer exclusively by quality of air, water, or local circumstance.

Table 6.4. Comparative infant and childhood mortality among the wealthy and the poor, 1817–1823/24

Location	Percentage of all deaths	
	0–1 yr.	0–10 yrs.
Wealthy		
Arrondissement 1	17	37
Rues du Faub.-St.-		
Honoré and du Roule	14	32
Poor		
Arrondissement 12	25	50
Rue Mouffetard	33	59

SOURCE: Restated from François Benoiston de Châteauneuf, "Supplément au Mémoire sur la mortalité en France," in L. R. Villermé, "Mémoire sur la mortalité en France dans la classe aisée et dans la classe indigente," *Mémoires de l'Académie royale de médecine* 1 (1828): 97.

The memoir of 1828 was intended to be a diagnostic of the social condition. Using number as his principal instrument, Villermé attempted to sort through a set of familiar but unconvincing etiological alternatives in order to ascertain the primary cause of the alarmingly high mortality of Paris. The memoir also served a muted hortatory function, and this will be recorded in Chapter 9 below. It suffices for the present to note that sociomedical investigation, as exemplified in this celebrated study of 1828, found that assignment of a social cause for disease and death also entailed an optimistic view of the problem. The social world, unlike the fixed parameters of the physical environment, was man's creation and was thus open to improvement. Villermé's original position regarding contemporary social problems, a position only gradually modified and never wholly abandoned, was strongly melioristic.

Little new was added to Villermé's essay of 1830 that concluded this series of analyses of the differential mortality of Paris. Indeed, much the greatest part of the new memoir was reprinted verbatim from that of 1826. The great expectation of the new study was that the assessment of urban mortality could now be extended over a greater span of years and thus the advantages of larger numbers and a longer period be gained. Previous interpretation had been based on the census of 1817 and abstracts of the

Paris bills of mortality for 1817–21. Now the bills for 1822–26 were assayed and joined to the new census of 1826. Sociomedical investigators appeared to possess an unparalleled resource for the analysis of mortality and population movement.

Regrettably, they did not. Although Villermé did indeed compute new figures for mortality by arrondissement, he immediately cast doubt on his own work. The 1826 census, he noted, was a command performance. The government wanted results quickly: evaluation of the population was ordered and enumeration by name prohibited. Using 1817 as the base year the ratio of population to number of births was established, and this ratio then used to establish the population for 1826.[43] Villermé had only scorn for this procedure, and even Villot, who was charged with the operation, was dubious of both its accuracy and utility.

On the basis of the new data Villermé calculated mortality à domicile for each of the twelve arrondissements. He found that the arrondissements continued to stand in the same rank order, and he also found that average mortality for the period 1822–26 was noticeably lower than it had been for the period 1817–21.[44] This result could only have pleased the Restoration government, by the late 1820s increasingly forced to seize any and all arguments in its own defense. But Villermé disallowed the claim. The base figure—that is, the census of 1826—was, he believed, thoroughly unreliable. No sound basis for comparison was available and thus "it could well be that for the recent [period] calculations [of the relation of mortality to population] have very much exaggerated the improvement that appears to result from the figures."[45] In short, it was impossible to draw any sound conclusions regarding the period 1822–26 and consequently also impossible now to extend over a full decade the method of analysis so fruitfully applied to the earlier period, 1817–21.

Nonetheless, the 1830 memoir provides perhaps the best overall view of Villermé's endeavors during the 1820s. It exhibited the scope of study made possible by a novel and altogether remarkable source of social fact, the first volumes of the Recherches statistiques sur la ville de Paris, and it also pointed out the vice that had entered with the census of 1826. Quite probably the consequences of this census, a vexation to Villot as well as to his friend Villermé, discouraged further interest in this manner of assessing the vital condition of the population of the capital. In any case, an extraordinary event soon overwhelmed Paris and commanded the virtually exclusive attention of the medical community. The cholera epidemic of

43. Villermé, "Mortalité dans les divers quartiers de Paris" (1830), pp. 316–21.
44. Ibid., pp. 296–97.
45. Ibid., pp. 320–21.

1832 not only induced widespread terror and caused a singularly rapid rise in urban mortality, but it provided statistical material which seemed peculiarly apt for proving beyond the least doubt that a special and additional burden of poverty was sharply increased mortality.

Cholera in Paris

Asiatic cholera, or *cholera morbus*, is endemic to the Ganges Valley. In 1817 the disease began the long march that spread sickness and death around the world. China, the Malay peninsula, Persia, and the Caucasus region had been attacked by 1823. In 1830 Moscow and St. Petersburg were reached; then came the turn of Poland, Germany, and Britain. Cholera entered England at Sunderland, County Durham, in late October 1831; early in the following February it was in London.[46]

Observers in France, although remaining hopeful until the fatal moment, had, like their counterparts elsewhere in Europe, carefully studied the advance of the disease. Medical opinion was divided as usual, but united sufficiently to launch numerous warnings to the profession and to the nation at large and to provide, so far as was possible, concrete advice regarding prevention and therapy. But with the cholera in England and above all in London, it seemed inevitable that France, too, would suffer. The wait was not long. *Cholera morbus* entered France at Calais on 15 March 1832 and entered Paris in an altogether spectacular manner in late March.

46. The literature on the cholera epidemic of 1832 is large and continues to grow. A readable overview is provided by Norman Longmate, *King Cholera: The Biography of a Disease* (London: Hamilton, 1966). See also R. J. Morris, *Cholera, 1832: The Social Response to an Epidemic* (London: Croom Helm, 1976), and C. E. Rosenberg, *The Cholera Years: The United States in 1832, 1849, and 1866* (Chicago: University of Chicago Press, 1962).

France poses an exception: there is no detailed historical account of the 1832 cholera epidemic in that nation. The following narrative is drawn from the official report: *Rapport sur la marche et les effets du choléra-morbus dans Paris et les communes rurales du département de la Seine, par la commission nommée par MM. les préfets de la Seine et de Police* (Paris: Imprimerie royale, 1832). A suggestive discussion of the epidemic but one that does not depart significantly from the *Rapport* is provided by Louis Chevalier, "Paris," in *Le choléra: La première épidémie du XIXᵉ siècle*, ed. Louis Chevalier (La Roche-sur-Yon: Imprimerie centrale de l'Ouest, 1958), pp. 3–45. Other essays in this pioneer volume deal with cholera elsewhere in France and in Russia and England. See also the recent contributions by Catherine Rollet and Agnès Souriac, "Epidémies et mentalités: Le choléra de 1832 en Seine-et-Oise," *Annales E.S.C.* 29 (1974): 935–65, and by Patrice Bourdelais and Jean-Yves Raulot, "La marche du choléra en France, 1832 et 1854," ibid. 33 (1978): 125–42.

Four fatal cases were authoritatively diagnosed in Paris on 26 March; the following day six victims took ill. Thereafter, the epidemic advanced with prodigious speed and devastation. By the thirty-first of March, but five days after its first appearance, some 300 persons, living in 35 of the city's 48 quarters, had been afflicted. Morbidity and mortality were both high. By 14 April the disease had touched ca. 12,000–13,000 Parisians, and of these 7,000 had died. Hundreds (765 on 14 April) were dying each day.[47] City services, notably those providing for burials, threatened to be overwhelmed. City authorities launched a massive clean-up campaign and continued their generous support of the stations providing asylum and free medical aid in each quarter of the city. After a period of remission the epidemic reached a second but lower peak during midsummer (225 persons died on 18 July). It then lingered on, taking the life of some 25–30 individuals each day, until the end of September. The epidemic lasted 189 days and killed 18,402 residents of the city.

Such an event could not and did not pass without official notice. Appointed by the minister of interior, a special commission was charged with examining the course of the epidemic and considering the many causes to which medical and popular opinion attributed its outbreak. The commission's report constitutes one of the great documents in the history of public health investigation and empirical social inquiry.

The *rapporteur* for the commission was Benoiston de Châteauneuf; among the other nine members were Jean Baptiste Parent-Duchâtelet, Adolfe Trébuchet, chief of the health office at the prefecture of Police, Villot, and Villermé. The commission represented the apotheosis of public medicine in the years of the constitutional monarchy. Not a single member was a practicing physician, and there was no representative from academic medicine, then at the height of its fame. It was a commission composed predominantly of independent investigators (Parent-Duchâtelet, Villermé) and public officials. Nothing was inadvertent about this arrangement. The ministry quite clearly was hoping that its commissioners would be willing and able to eschew medical controversy, an art in which the Paris school was exceptionally skilled and which the cholera epidemic only encouraged, and would do so by adhering narrowly to the facts of the case, however these might run. "To gather facts, to give an account of them and to deduce conclusions therefrom," wrote Benoiston de Châteauneuf, "was

47. Average daily mortality in Paris during a nonepidemic period (1822–26) was at least 67 persons per day (only deaths à domicile being reported): see Villermé, "Mortalité dans les divers quartiers de Paris," table on p. [340] (24,546 deaths ÷ 365 days). Seasonal variations no doubt rendered this average a rare figure for any given day.

[the commissioners'] duty; they would have thought they ventured beyond their responsibilities by entering the domain of the [medical] art."[48]

The commission, uncertainly faithful to its charge, not so much avoided as discredited alternative medical explanations of the epidemic.[49] In doing so, its members followed closely the procedure of their associate Villermé. Even more striking, the ostensibly neutral document they produced did indeed reach its own conclusions. These were stated only lamely and without development. Yet, since other options had been weighed and rejected, these conclusions appeared to represent the collective opinion of the full commission. Astonishingly, the commission, the creation of a minister of a new regime dedicated to economic liberty and rapid industrial development, assigned a social cause to the differences in the pattern of suffering and death imposed upon Paris by cholera. The disease, it was noted, fell most heavily on certain distinctive quarters of the city. "In general, wherever a poor wretched population was pressed into filthy and inadequate lodgings," the commissioners noted, "there the epidemic multiplied its victims." Cholera, it seemed, struck especially "the professions that enjoyed least affluence."[50]

The commission ventured no stronger claim than this. Its inclination, however, was made clear by the fact that it provided in an appendix a remarkable tabulation of cholera mortality by profession. Here the categories employed provided both a vivid portrayal of the economic structure of Paris and of the varying risk within each station in life before an epidemic that found its victims in every corner of the city.[51] The commission's report was intended not only for an official and scientific audience but was especially directed towards the general reader and concerned citizen. It constituted, as inevitably it must have done, only an orderly abstract of the vast abundance of data collected for assessment of the epidemic and its consequences. Such data rested, in the form of notes and reports, in the files of the administration and in the oral communications that responsible public officials were capable of offering to an interested interrogator.

48. *Rapport sur la marche . . . du choléra-morbus*, p. 190.
49. Thus, correlations of sex, age, temperature, humidity, wind exposure, altitude, population density, and density of improvements with the incidence of cholera were attempted—and all were disallowed.
50. *Rapport sur la marche . . . du choléra-morbus*, pp. 188–89.
51. Chevalier, "Paris," pp. 38–43. While the *Rapport sur la marche . . . du choléra-morbus* reports the number of deaths in each profession, it does not give the total number of persons employed in these professions; the respective proportion of total mortality for each can thus be calculated but not the death rate.

Here, once again, Villermé found a new task peculiarly to his liking. Using unpublished official documents and inquiries made of public officials he undertook the study that concluded his researches on the problem of unequal mortality in Paris. He thus impressed upon his reader's mind, far more than the commission's timid report had done, that epidemic disease as well as accustomed causes of death (such as were recorded in resumé in the *Recherches statistiques*) demands a disproportionate toll from the poor and indigent members of society. Mortality, normal and epidemic, was a class-dependent phenomenon.

Villermé selected a special population for analysis, examining cholera mortality among the inhabitants of the furnished lodging houses (*maisons garnies*) of the capital.[52] Because of staff changes in the police administration, data were available only from the onset of the epidemic until 1 August. Although this prohibited comparison of total mortality in lodging houses with that of the city, it did not hinder the kind of analysis that Villermé had in mind. He would show, once again by quarter, that cholera mortality varied with the economic condition of the population at risk.

Lodging houses were divided by the police into five categories.[53] Large and small hotels (classes 1 and 2) received travelers for short periods and charged from 30 sous to 6 francs per night. Their occupants were principally visitors in Paris on either business or pleasure. These hotels were generally comfortable to luxurious and were well-maintained. Boarding houses predominated in class 3. They were the favored residence of students and military personnel, were occupied ordinarily by the year, and cost 15–40 francs per month. With classes 4 and 5 one entered a new world. Here were found sober workers, transients of all kinds, persons of uncertain or no calling, and prostitutes. Workers favored class 4 lodgings, occupying these on average for 8 months and paying 5–6 francs per month for their shelter. The others gravitated towards class 5 lodgings. Here rooms or a bed, or simply space on the floor, was taken by the night for the price of 5–15 sous. In addition to prostitutes (a major portion of the population of these dwellings), class 5 lodgings attracted the poorest and least settled of the residents of Paris. They were notorious as the repair of the city's sizeable criminal population.

This classification obviously reflected both the condition of the house in question and of its usual inhabitants. Lodging houses of classes 4 and 5

---

52. Villermé, "Notes sur les ravages du choléra-morbus dans les maisons garnies de Paris, depuis le 29 mars jusqu'au 1er août 1832, et sur les causes qui paraissent avoir favorisé le développement de la maladie dans un grand nombre de maisons," *Annales d'hygiène publique et de médecine légale* 11 (1834): 385–409, plus two tables.

53. Ibid., pp. 386–87, and "No. 2. Tableau numérique" (unpaginated).

were customarily crowded establishments, ill-ventilated, filthy, damp, and concentrated, often remarkably so, in particular sections of the city. Those located in the quarters of the Jardin des Plantes, Hôtel-de-Ville, and Cité were notorious for their insalubrity. Such dwellings housed the unfortunate residents of the rue de la Mortellerie. Villermé's task, and it proved to be a not difficult one, was to discover if cholera struck with disproportionate severity the men and women who occupied these miserable dwellings.

In the summer of 1832 there were some 3,100 lodging houses in Paris. Of these, many were quite small, being in actuality but a set of rooms within a larger edifice. The average population of all lodging houses was 32,434. Within this population there appeared 2,342 recorded cases of cholera, and of the latter 1,033 died of the disease. The morbidity rate within the lodging houses was thus 1 in 13.8 (72.5 per 1,000), the fatality rate 1 in 2.3 (434.8 per 1,000, at the lower end of the usual fatality induced by untreated cholera), and the mortality rate minimally 1 in 31.4 (31.8 per 1,000).[54] Mortality in Paris at large for the same period (26 March–31 July) was, at a minimum, 1 in 46 (21.7 per 1,000). Here was a sure indication that residents of the lodging houses were collectively almost half again more prone to death by cholera than were other residents of the city. But lodging houses, as their official classification revealed, were anything but homogeneous. Villermé would now show that, in addition to the official criteria, death itself was an excellent classificatory criterion.

Simple tabulation by class of the lodging houses revealed a remarkable fact. Of the 3,106 lodging houses in Paris, 965 (or 31.1 percent) contained at least one cholera victim. By class, however, the incidence of cholera in the houses was quite different (see Table 6.5). The progression thus revealed followed inversely that of the relative wealth of the inhabitants in the various classes of lodging. Class 1 hotels and inns received men of distinction and wealth and diplomats. Deputies to the assembly, major landowners, men in the wholesale trade, and the like favored class 2 establishments. To class 3 houses went merchants, small proprietors, students, workers with steady employment, and salesmen. Class 4 lodgings contained above all poor workers, most spending only a fixed period of each year in Paris and all usually crowded together in common sleeping rooms. Class 5, as noted above, embraced the *maisons à la nuit* and thus gathered in the intemperate, the immoral, and the destitute.[55]

This broad pattern, which showed unequivocally that cholera followed

54. Ibid., pp. 388–89.
55. Ibid., pp. 405–6.

Table 6.5. Cholera incidence in Paris, 1832, by class of lodging house

Class	Total houses	Houses attacked by cholera	% attacked
1	102	4	3.9
2	227	19	8.4
3	1,566	289	18.5
4	955	499	52.3
5	256	154	60.2
All classes	3,106	965	31.1

SOURCE: L. R. Villermé, "Notes sur les ravages du choléra-morbus dans les maisons garnies de Paris, depuis le 29 mars jusqu'au 1er août 1832, et sur les causes qui paraissent avoir favorisé le développement de la maladie dans un grand nombre de maisons," *Annales d'hygiène publique et de médecine légale* 11 (1834): "No. 2. Tableau numérique" (unpaginated).

poverty, reemphasized the conclusion that Villermé had already reached by examining the incidence of the disease in each quarter of the city. The first arrondissement provided an exemplary case. Generally very wealthy, the arrondissement nonetheless contained concentrations of the poor and even destitute. The Tuileries quarter was exceptionally prosperous. Of its 80 lodging houses, 73 belonged to classes 1, 2, and 3, and only 7 belonged to classes 4 and 5. (By contrast the Cité quarter, located in the ninth arrondissement and to most observers the very nadir of Paris life, had 34 lodgings in classes 4 and 5, 18 in class 3, and none whatsoever in classes 1 and 2.)[56] In the quarters of the Champs-Elysées and the Place Vendôme, however, one encountered more noticeable areas of poverty; and one section of the Roule quarter, known as Petite-Pologne, stood high among the capital's worst built and ill-policed corners. Villermé saw a definite rank order among these four quarters of the first arrondissement, a rank order based with equal validity upon the filthiness and insalubrity of the lodging houses or upon "the increasing proportion of *misérables* who occupy them," both being subjective measures, and hastened to compare this order with that established for cholera morbidity and mortality in their lodgings (see Table 6.6). This correlation appeared to authorize an important conclusion: "The ravages of cholera in the lodging houses seem to have occurred," for the period under review (26 March–31 July), "in direct relation to the poor situation [*tenue*] of these houses, that is, [as a function of] the destitution and number of the poor who have found lodging there."[57]

56. Ibid., "No. 2. Tableau numérique" (unpaginated).
57. Ibid.

Table 6.6. Cholera in the first arrondissement

Quarter	Cholera morbidity (Restated per 1,000)	Cholera mortality (Restated per 1,000)
Tuileries	9.1	5.5
Champs-Elysées	34.5	8.7
Place Vendôme	33.3	9.5
Roule	62.5	27.8

SOURCE: Villermé, "Notes sur les ravages du choléra-morbus," "No. 2. Tableau numérique" (unpaginated).

Other cases reaffirmed this conclusion. In adjoining quarters of the fourth arrondissement cholera mortality in their respective boarding houses was separated by a factor of 12 (Banque de France, 7.2 per 1,000; Louvre 87 per 1,000). The ninth arrondissement displayed, as usual, its special horrors. The Ile-Saint-Louis had a lodging house population of only 61, none of whom were destitute; not one of these was lost to cholera. In the quarter of the Arsenal mortality was 59 per 1,000, in the Hôtel de Ville 75.9 per 1,000, and in the Cité 116.4 per 1,000.[58] The experience of the latter, the worst in Paris, was appalling. The quarter lost by death over 11 percent of its population to one disease alone and this in a period of but four months; moreover, this loss was that incurred only by residents of its lodging houses (other residents of the quarter also perished). Villermé recognized that such figures might easily be skewed by intense foci of attack by the disease. In certain quarters a major portion of the total mortality could be assigned to one or a few unusually affected houses. Thus, in the Jardin des Plantes quarter, among the poorest in the city, almost one-half of the total cholera mortality (31 of 70 deaths) occurred in only 9 (of 57) lodging houses.[59]

Villermé always placed special argumentative weight on extreme cases. The contrast between the mortality experience with cholera in the lodging houses of the Tuileries and the Cité has already been noted. Lest these seem exceptional cases, and the populations affected appear too small, he provided, as he had done when utilizing the *Recherches statistiques sur la ville de Paris*, a more general measure. This was obtained by taking as a first group the three wealthiest arrondissements (first, second, third) and as a second, three of the poorest (seventh, ninth, twelfth), the whole embracing approximately one-half of the population of the city, and comparing the aggregate experience of their respective lodging houses during the

58. Ibid., "No. 1. Tableau récapitulatif" (unpaginated).
59. Ibid., p. 403, and "No. 2. Tableau numérique" (unpaginated).

epidemic. In the second, poorer group, average morbidity for the four-month period was 1 in 9 (111 per 1,000) and mortality 1 in 19 (52.6 per 1,000); for the wealthier group the comparable figures were 1 in 31 ill (32.3 per 1,000) and 1 in 97 dead (10.3 per 1,000).[60] If the two groups of arrondissements were sharply demarcated by their respective wealth, so too, and even more strikingly, did they separate with respect to the survival of their residents when struck by cholera.

In his 1834 essay Villermé did not bother to test, and reject, alternative explanations for the observed differences; this had already been done for the city as a whole in the commission's report published in the same year. Only one factor was truly in question, and its powerful effect was now again made patent. The poor and destitute—those who by definition were in a weakened condition, who occupied crowded and ill-provided lodgings, who were constantly exposed to filth of every nature and lacked the means either to seek aid or escape their quarters—were more commonly struck by cholera than were wealthier compatriots, and they died, in the arrondissements sampled, five times more frequently than did their fellow Parisians.

This was not, of course, a new conclusion. It simply reaffirmed, as it was intended to do, the tendency of Villermé's total experience with the numerical analysis of differential mortality of rich and poor that he had begun early in the 1820s. Cholera, to be sure, provided a decisive measure. Here was a disease that, while not ignoring prosperous persons and their families, seemed positively to seek out the poor.[61] Far more than total but undifferentiated mortality, cholera pointed to the deep divisions that rent the social fabric, divisions now being referred to as classes and defined in economic terms.

Phenomena observed transformed the observer. Villermé had begun with the suspicion that death fell unequally upon the diverse members of the population of Paris. Closer inspection of the issue, made possible only by the appearance of unique numerical documentation of the life of the city, changed that suspicion into a conviction, a conviction that in turn received repeated demonstration and public exhibition. Villermé's endeavor was essentially that of discovering how social realities expressed themselves in biological terms or, to give a more exact rendering of his own growing awareness of the close interaction of the medical and social

60. Ibid., pp. 404–5.
61. Despite their own anxiety and well-justified fear of the disease, the middle and upper classes viewed cholera as having a special predilection for the filthy, hungry, and intemperate poor. In Britain, too, sparse figures suggest that the poor died disproportionately often. See Morris, *Cholera, 1832*, pp. 79–94.

domains, how a biological event, death, was found to be a reliable and profoundly disturbing index of social condition.

From the outset Villermé employed, in addition to occasional use of other words, the language of social class. Class, a term then new to social discourse, was appropriate because it expressed social position in strictly economic terms. "It is almost always individuals of the same classes," he wrote, "individuals in, so to speak, analogous occupations and in the same state of wealth, ease, or destitution, who replace one another in [each] of the diverse quarters" of the city.[62] Such language and, more importantly, the mode of analysis that lay behind it and the conclusions that it expressed were in perfect accord with the new social realities under scrutiny. The Revolution and Empire had dramatically shaken the orderly hierarchical social structure characteristic of the Old Regime and had given free reign to individual talent and ambition. Villermé's generation witnessed the consequences of this liberating of the economic forces of the nation, one of whose first, least attractive, and most intractable effects was the creation of an even more radical division between wealth and poverty.

These changes were reflected in Villermé's etiological thinking. In this series of statistical analyses of mortality, he did not engage in discussion with then prevailing views regarding the spread of communicable diseases (which, it may be presumed, accounted for the great preponderance of mortality during the period). The contending advantages and liabilities of anticontagionism, with its miasmatic component, and contagionism found no place in this discussion. To Villermé at this juncture these causes of disease, and indeed all causes of disease, could be comprehended by the all-embracing formula of poverty. Poverty meant risk, undue exposure to all the hazards of life; and the poor thus exposed succumbed. Society itself, its economic organization, had become an etiological agent. Whether the immediate cause of death was malnutrition, excessive exposure to the elements, occupational dangers, overcrowding, or noxious if unspecified contagion, it was evident that the wealthy more frequently avoided contact with such causes and thereby outlived by a significant margin their lesser brethren. Life for the poor is, Villermé concluded, "much more precarious, much more uncertain than for the others, and they lose it much more quickly [than the rich] and so much the more

62. Villermé, "Rapport . . . sur une série de tableaux," p. 217. Political language was evolving rapidly in the early nineteenth century: see A. E. Bestor, Jr., "The Evolution of the Socialist Vocabulary," *Journal of the History of Ideas* 9 (1948): 259–302; Asa Briggs, "The Language of 'Class' in Early-Nineteenth-Century England," in *Essays in Labour History*, ed. Asa Briggs and John Saville (London: Macmillan, 1960), pp. 43–73.

rapidly the poorer they are."[63] Improving this situation would not only benefit directly those who suffered this undeserved burden but would be a sign, as Fourier had indicated, that civilization had indeed advanced and had rendered public prosperity more genuine because more widely enjoyed by the nation.

63. Villermé, "Sur la mortalité en France," p. 80.

Chapter 7

Patterns of Life and Death

Man is born, grows up and dies, according to certain laws which have never been properly investigated, either as a whole or in the mode of their mutual reactions. . . . the laws which relate to the social body are not essentially invariable; they change with the nature of the causes producing them. The progress of civilization, for example, has changed the laws respecting mortality, and must have exercised an influence over the physical and moral condition of man.

Adolfe Quetelet, [1835]

The limited vital statistics of the early nineteenth century inevitably turned the observer's attention towards mortality. Death effected a final division not only from life but between the social classes, and for this reason above all became the favored measure used in sociomedical investigation. In Villermé's hands the death rate pointed to the medical importance of social differences and appeared to indicate that death and disease were due to one or a small set of distinctively social causes.

His arguments in this regard were, however, carefully modulated. On no occasion was social, or economic, condition advanced as the exclusive cause of death or disease. Villermé's focus was always directed towards the chances of life and death among large masses of individuals. It is a striking feature of Villermé's publications, and one to be noted again at the end of this chapter, that disease in general and etiology in particular command there so minor a place.

Villermé clearly understood that to claim that death was socially induced meant that such mortality was due largely to prior deprivation as well as to current inadequacies of food, shelter, and labor. Precisely how, in concrete physiological and pathological terms, these social causes were translated into the loss of one or a host of human beings was a matter in regard to which, surely, he was not indifferent. It was not, however, a subject that received express consideration. Death, simply put, was the

EPIGRAPH: Adolfe Quetelet, *A Treatise on Man and the Development of His Faculties*, trans. anon. (Edinburgh: William and Robert Chambers, 1842; reprinted 1973), pp. 5, 7.

summary statement of an infinitely varied set of previous biological experiences, and the latter—this was too obvious to require formal statement—was held to be a function of individual or familial economic condition.

These considerations reemphasize an essential methodological procedure of early sociomedical investigation, namely, the pursuit of correlations and, commonly, reluctance dogmatically to ascribe a single cause. Much of Villermé's career was devoted to seeking these correlations, of which the most prominent offers the guiding theme of this book, the connection established between poverty and mortality. Other correlations nonetheless were sought, and although in virtually all cases they return one to the dominant motif, they also provide a broader perspective on the scope of the inquiry, the character of the method employed, and the serious limitations of the data available. Like Quetelet, Villermé was convinced that life and death, being phenomena of large numbers, present characteristic patterns. The task at hand, and one pursued simultaneously by both individuals, was to discover these patterns and to ask questions about them. Quetelet, enamored of number and the properties of large numbers, soon came upon the generality of the normal curve and thereupon erected the notion of the average man. Villermé, by contrast, viewed numbers as tools; they gave access to sociomedical phenomena and connections otherwise undemonstrable and perhaps even unsuspected.

It is important, therefore, to examine briefly his dealings with a further and disparate array of vital and social facts. He demonstrated, for example, that body size as well as mortality is correlated with social condition, a study that launched Quetelet in turn on a similar course of inquiry. Analysis of mortality in marsh districts revealed dramatically and unexpectedly the extreme precariousness there of the life of very young children. A study, particularly informative because of its author's insistent inclusiveness, was made of frequency of conception by month of the year. In these studies, each based upon a quite different source of data, connections were revealed and demonstrated or denied by number. Moreover, these studies no less than his others manifested Villermé's keen sense for practical matters. Investigations were conducted not only for their own sake but because they might contribute to the reform of various public and private practices that influenced the health and welfare of a population.

Body Size and Military Conscription

Imperial prefects, always obsessed with problems of military recruitment, had gathered and sent to Paris during the difficult years 1812–13 a vast fund of data pertaining to the physical condition of the inductees and

of those granted deferments. Height; age at reaching full growth; the proportion deferred for reasons of deformity, disability, and sickness; and local conditions, including occupations, were all recorded. Villermé was
among the earliest to exploit this treasure of unpublished statistical
information.

Antoine-Audet Hargenvilliers, Villermé reported, had provided a first
hint of the meaning of these numbers.[1] Comparing two Imperial departments, he had observed that in the first, Bouches-de-la-Meuse (Belgium),
a prosperous land in which children were well-fed and not unduly worked,
average body height was greater (1.677 m) and deferments fewer than in
a much poorer department, Apennins (Italy), whose children (with an average body height of 1.560 m) ate less and labored constantly. Draftees
were taken from the 18–19-year-old age group. A minimum height and
freedom from deformity and serious illness were required. The number of
deferments granted for the two permissible causes varied directly with
these contrasting socioeconomic circumstances. In the relatively poor
Apennins, 204 of every 1,000 draftees failed to attain the minimum height
(1.544 m), and 96 were rejected for deformity or illness; in the wealthy
Bouches-de-la-Meuse, centered on Antwerp, shortness caused rejection of
only 24 per 1,000 and the other causes, 42 per 1,000.[2]

Villermé simply extended Hargenvilliers' mode of analysis. He sought
to avoid, however, the patent hazard of comparing areas long populated
by different ethnic stocks (*races*) by drawing comparisons so far as possible only between local communities, preferably subdivisions of a single
department. Moreover, while he accepted average body height as a general
measure of local well-being, he gave greater emphasis to the proportion
of deferments granted for deformity and illness and the relation of this
proportion to average body height.

Conscription in one department in particular superbly exhibited the correlations desired. Average body height and frequency of deformity and
illness in three arrondissements of the Landes, the great forested, sandy
waste sweeping south from Bordeaux, followed directly relative wealth.[3]
The majority of the communes in the arrondissement of Mont-de-Marsan
were extremely poor. Peasants shared their chimneyless straw huts with

1. L. R. Villermé, "Mémoire sur la taille de l'homme en France," *Annales d'hygiène
publique et de médecine légale* 1 (1829): 351–[99]. See Antoine-Audet Hargenvilliers, *Re-
cherches et considérations sur la formation et le recrutement de l'armée française* (Paris:
Firmin-Didot, 1817); also Gustave Vallée, *Compte général de la conscription de A.-A.
Hargenvilliers, publié d'après le manuscrit originel avec une introduction et des notes*
(Paris: Sirey, 1937).

2. Villermé, "Taille de l'homme," pp. 353–54.

3. Ibid., pp. 365–67.

chickens and the family pig; the principal food was boiled millet. The region was low and marshy, and fevers were endemic. Labor was heavy and unceasing. Average body height in Mont-de-Marsan was 1.584 m. Of every 1,000 draftees 362 were rejected, 216 for height and 146 for deformity or disease. The greatest part of the arrondissement of Saint-Sever was better situated. Labor was less difficult; and rye, wheat, maize, and fruit entered the diet. Here body height attained 1.634 m. Deferments ran 342 per 1,000, with 216 being a result of short stature and 131 for reasons of deformity and sickness. Lastly, the arrondissement of Dax, while presenting great variation in its conditions, nonetheless evidenced the greatest wealth in the department. Even in the marshy areas near the sea, the inhabitants were more prosperous than in the bleak reaches of the true Landes. Average body height reached 1.660 m, and deferments dropped to 309 per 1,000 (182 for height, 127 for deformity and sickness).

There was revealed here a double set of correlations. The number of deferments for deformity and sickness clearly declined as average body height increased. Average body height was, in turn, closely connected to local socioeconomic conditions. No other examples cited by Villermé so completely and regularly demonstrated these correlations. The general tendency of all the cases explored seemed, nonetheless, to confirm the major proposition, namely, average body height at age 18–19 indicated the overall salubrity or insalubrity of a given region. With typical candor Villermé discussed cases that were either ambiguous (Haute-Loire) or appeared to contradict his central contention (Gard).[4] In the latter it appeared that the presence of marshes disjoined the connection of the shortest population (here found in a mountainous area) and the greatest amount of sickness (encountered in the wet lowlands).

Paris and the department of the Seine claimed, as always, special attention. Average body size within the city exceeded that of the population in the rural arrondissements of the department, and average size varied, with some exceptions, with the relative wealth of the urban arrondissements. Tallest were young men in the first, second, and third arrondissements; and shortest, exceptionally, were those in the sixth and eleventh.[5] For Paris Villermé was using an altogether new set of data, namely, conscription reports for the post-Imperial era (1816–23). Because of conscription laws had once again been changed, raising the age of induction to 20–21, direct comparison of the new data with those gathered earlier was disallowed. Comparison of the new induction experience among the urban ar-

4. Ibid., pp. 363–65, 355–56.
5. Ibid. p. 370. Relative wealth was established using the *contribution personnelle* taken from the *Recherches statistiques sur la ville de Paris.*

rondissements was, however, entirely legitimate, and because these comparisons were so consistent with previous analysis, Villermé believed his memoir on average body size stood in closest association with his simultaneous publication regarding differential mortality in the capital.[6] When the twelve arrondissements were once again ranked by wealth (now using a combination of taxes, the *contribution personnelle* and the *patente*), the familiar grouping of the three wealthiest (first, second, third) and three poorest (eighth, ninth, twelfth) arrondissements reappeared. A new correlation with these groupings now became possible. The department as a whole was required to send to the army 5,825 new men during the eight-year period in question. In order to raise this contingent, the department had to examine 11,730 men of age 20–21.[7] There were 5,905 (50.3 percent) found unfit for service. Of these only 25 percent had less than the required stature, the others (an alarming 37.7 percent of the total number examined) being rejected for deformity and illness. Villermé then pursued his inquiry on the local level. On average, the three wealthy arrondissements provided each 375 inductees and 308 deferments (54.9 percent and 45.1 percent, respectively, of each arrondissement's contribution), a record some 5 percent better than that of the department. The three poor arrondissements fared worse than the department as a whole. For every 894 examined, they offered on average 447 inductees (50 percent), while another 447 were rejected. Cause of rejection (shortness of stature, deformity, or illness) was, unfortunately, not stated.

From such figures Villermé drew conclusions important to the administration and anticipated yield of the recruitment process.[8] Whether the example was taken from the Landes or from the Seine, it seemed a demonstrated fact that the number of deferments granted for deformity or serious disease declined as average body height increased. Large average stature at any given age of a population appeared to be a sound index of the relative well-being of that population. To seek, therefore, to increase the number of inductees by reducing the height requirement was vain; at a given age, as height declined, the number of deformities or persistent illnesses increased sharply. In the last years of the Empire, when first height and then even age were increasingly ignored by the recruiting officers, the quality of the French troops fell rapidly. Villermé the military surgeon had himself been witness to this deadly practice.

His observations also had a bearing on statecraft and national ambition. To the long-standing debate on the importance of population size to na-

6. Villermé, "Taille de l'homme," p. 395.
7. Ibid., pp. 372–73. The percentages that follow have been calculated.
8. Ibid., pp. 377–78.

tional strength Villermé contributed strong evidence for the view that such strength is not a function of population size alone. The quality of the population, of which health as well as economic condition is an essential measure, must command equal attention. Countries or regions may have populations equal in size, but they will not be military equals unless those populations possess, as was usually not the case, equal biological strength.

Such reflections, whatever their slight novelty or practical merits, were of course but a prelude to consideration of the underlying cause of this state of affairs. Recruitment data indicated that men reached a greater average height, attained their full development at an earlier age, and manifested demonstrably less deformity and chronic debilitation in precisely those parts of the nation that displayed relative wealth. Here was a biological measure other than mortality that revealed that economic condition is the principal determinant of the physical well-being of the human frame.[9] A social origin for retarded development and disease had once again been identified.

Ease or destitution made their effects felt through housing, diet, clothing, and conditions of labor. Villermé's study was confined exclusively to young men, persons who might be expected to be in peak physical condition. Many, however, fell far short of such condition. The author realized, although he allowed this important point but the briefest passing comment, that the strength and weakness, height and shortness, of the recruits was not the consequence of a recent or transient cause.[10] The body's condition in each of these recruits was the ultimate product of years of favorable or harsh experience. Measurement of height and the recognition of deformity or disease were made in the present, but they were measures that necessarily took into account the total biological experience of the organism. A difficult childhood and youth, one in which food and shelter had been inadequate, disease chronic, and strenuous labor all too common, left an unmistakable mark on the physical appearance of the nation or, more precisely, upon the least privileged members of the nation.

Yet, while that mark was unmistakable, it was not, at least to persons of generous disposition, inevitable. Climate, to be sure, left its own mark on men, and the stock from which one sprang certainly conditioned body size and perhaps even health. But Villermé was determined to show that man was not made by biology alone.[11] The human body, its size, and well-

9. Ibid., p. 388.
10. Ibid., pp. 370, 386.
11. Ibid., p. 393. Quetelet's anonymous translator, in his notes to the *Treatise on Man*, pp. 58–63, insistently ignored Villermé's, and Quetelet's, caution. Body size and its relation to lineage and environment was a matter of active zoological and physiological interest

being were also subject to socioeconomic influence, to social control. There were grounds, therefore, for hoping to improve the biological condition of the poor.

Recruitment data taken from the department of the Seine had made evident a further interesting fact. Since the raising of the contingents of 1816–17 the proportion of recruits of the same age in the taller categories (over 1.651 m) had increased steadily, being 45 per 1,000 in 1816–17 and 50 per 1,000 in 1820.[12] It thereafter had remained close to the higher frequency. Villermé viewed this increase in body height as the consequence of the restoration of peace, the return of civil harmony, and economic expansion. Civilization, the omnibus term for these events, was working here its beneficent influence; the proof was in the numbers. A government, especially one devoted to improving the well-being of the nation, could act at will to increase (within limits) the average body height of its citizens. Peace and prosperity paid genuine biological dividends. No longer need one cower before the powerful command of climate or capitulate to the fatalism of strict hereditarianism.

The Human Cost of Marshes

Since classical antiquity medical writers had viewed the marsh as a major threat to health. Low areas, those subject to seasonal flooding, and regions lying downwind from extensive marshes, particularly if near salt water, were all understood to be particularly hazardous. In such areas the people seemed often emaciated and lacking in energy. Fevers were endemic, and mortality was relatively high. The fevers, or diseases, encountered in these regions represented, no doubt, a medley of different clinical entities. When, however, a definite and periodic recurrence of fever was observed, presumably malaria was present in that locality as a major and occasionally perhaps exclusive component of the overall disease situation.

Marsh fevers were widespread in nineteenth-century Europe. They offered, in fact, a continuing problem that was much discussed by the medical profession.[13] That discussion, unfortunately, seldom led to new con-

---

in the early nineteenth century; see Louis Agassiz, *An Essay on Classification* (London: Longman, Brown, Green, Longmans and Roberts, 1859), pp. 73–75, and William Coleman, "Bergmann's Rule: Animal Heat as a Biological Phenomenon," *Studies in History of Biology* 3 (1979): 67–88.

12. Villermé, "Taille de l'homme," pp. 388–89.

13. See Ambroise Tardieu, "Marais," in *Dictionnaire d'hygiène publique et de salubrité ou répertoire de toutes les questions relatives à la santé publique*, 2nd ed., 4 vols. (Paris: J. B. Baillière, 1862), 2:635–55; J. C. M. Boudin, *Traité des fièvres intermittentes, rémittentes, et continues des pays chauds, et des contrées marécageuses, suivi de recherches sur l'emploi thérapeutique des préparations arsenicales* (Paris: J. B. Baillière,

clusions or preventive measures. Removal from the threatening area or utter abolition of the marsh by means of drainage appeared to be the only truly efficacious means of escaping disease or at least of reducing the incidence of fever. These solutions, like the problem itself, were also of ancient standing.

The topography of France is splendidly varied and throughout its occupation by human society has presented numerous opportunities for the formation and persistence of marshes. Certain regions, although long settled and actively exploited, still included vast reaches of swamp. Salt marshes dominated the lower Atlantic shore and major portions of the broad coastal arc reaching from Perpignan to Nice. The Sologne, lying below the northern bend of the river Loire, was a particularly humid interior region, as were the Dombes and Bresse, lying north of the city of Lyons. All of these and similar areas were notoriously unhealthy, and Villermé only repeated common knowledge in calling attention to the fact. His purpose was not to cover old ground but to accumulate sufficient evidence to reveal the character of the excessive mortality experienced in marshy areas.

It seems clear, however, that conflicting ambitions disrupted this study. In 1834 Villermé had two major projects underway. On the one hand, he was just beginning an investigation of the condition of factory labor requested by the Academy of Moral and Political Sciences (see Chapter 8). On the other hand, he had just completed a major statistical analysis of mortality in the marsh district. This study was never published. Not only is this a remarkable fact in its own right—the author had devoted great effort to the undertaking and expressed no reservations regarding it in the published abstract—but it surely represents a singular loss to epidemiological literature. Never had Villermé been more assiduous in gathering and ranging his data. He reported possessing data for 1,800,000 deaths in the marsh districts; of these 660,000 were said to be age-specific.[14] Perhaps never before had such a prodigious fund of statistical material been focused on a public health problem.

Only the author's anticipated and soon quite real burdens of factory inspection appear sufficient to explain his withholding this major study from publication. What was offered to the public was but a brief abstract, together with an even briefer supplementary report.[15] These nonetheless

---

1842); L. G. Wilson, "Fevers and Science in Early-Nineteenth-Century Medicine," *Journal of the History of Medicine* 33 (1978): 386–407.

14. Villermé, "De l'influence des marais sur la vie," *Annales d'hygiène publique et de médecine légale* 11 (1834); 343.

15. Ibid., pp. 342–62, and "Influence des marais sur la vie des enfans," *Annales d'hygiène publique et de médecine légale* 12 (1834): 31–37.

are adequate to convey a clear notion of the author's principal conclusion and its implications. Two questions had guided the study. In marshy areas, Villermé asked, what is the age-specific mortality directly attributable to distinct local conditions? And what, in fact, are the conditions that render a marsh insalubrious? Of course, numbers would be brought to bear on these questions. In response to the second question, however, Villermé in reality accepted conventional explanations and thus, in this case at least, showed himself an unqualified spokesman for an anticontagionist, specifically the miasmatic, theory of disease.

To the physician a marsh was a very special place. "Medically speaking," Villermé noted, "marshes are places in which each year the soil or a portion thereof is submerged or at least made wet and which soil then more or less thoroughly dries out. These areas are unhealthy at the time of drying."[16] While extremes of heat seemed often to be associated with the ills generated by marshes, Villermé tended to regard temperature as only an indirect source of disease. Heat was the crucial determinant of local dryness and thus of the extent of the marshes. Annual movement of the sun probably accounted for the seasonal pattern of mortality in the marsh districts. In the healthy departments of France mortality peaked in winter and early spring; it was at its lowest during the summer and early autumn. In the marsh districts the difference between these extremes was much reduced, and the normal pattern occasionally reversed. In the Midi summer was usually the season of greatest mortality.[17]

These conclusions were based upon data not presented in the abstract. Villermé's aim was to create a correlation uniting the periodicity of seasonal intensity of mortality with that of the presumed solar influence on the drying of the marshes. The larger goal, of course, was to merge this correlation with another, namely, age-specific mortality in the marsh districts. Only a mere *précis* of the latter correlation was provided, yet it contained what to Villermé was the novelty and much the most important conclusion of his entire investigation.

Common opinion, he noted, placed greatest mortality in the marsh districts in the 35–50 age group. The data (not presented) revealed, however, that this was not so. By far the greatest toll of life taken by the marshes fell upon children aged 1–4. The youngest children (0–1) seemed somewhat less affected. Mortality after age 10 was reduced, but rose again between ages 35 and 55 (but did not even then approximate that of children aged 1–4). Older persons were least affected by the diseases of the marsh districts.[18]

16. Villermé, "De l'influence des marais," p. 344.
17. Ibid., pp. 344–45.
18. Ibid., pp. 345–46.

The seasonal eruption of peak mortality in the 1–4 age group appeared
to allow a separation of the specific influence of the marshes from the
totality of causes of death active in a particular region. Thus, while maximum death in the over-4 age group continued to occur during the winter
months, that of young children had shifted to summer and autumn. Moreover, comparing the death rate of children aged 1–4 in "healthy districts"
across France with that for the same group in eight insalubrious departments of the Midi, the remarkable fact emerged that the death rate of the
latter was half again that of the former (1.546 to 1).[19] In all of this Villermé was persuaded not only that death took young children in superabundance but that its triumph was intimately related to local marshy conditions. He quickly reconfirmed his views by analysis of the published
data from the census of 1831 in Great Britain. The death rate for those
under 10 years of age was markedly higher in the Isle of Ely, surrounded
by the vast fens of East Anglia, than for all agricultural districts combined,
for industrial regions, or for counties of mixed economy. This difference
was much less significant for the 10–40 age group (here, in fact, the
industrial regions proved marginally more deadly than Ely).[20]

Villermé's discussion had led him to consider local ecological conditions as the necessary and probably sufficient cause of marsh diseases. His
stand now was consistently miasmatic. From the insalubrious seasons of
the year and the diseases that result therefrom one can usually, he reasoned, distinguish those effects pertaining to life and death that depend
upon the proximity of marshes from those that do not. But what are the
characteristic diseases of the marshlands? And how are these related to the
noxious emanations or simple humidity of a swamp? Villermé offered primarily questions, not answers. Intermittent and remittent fevers were
surely involved. But why was there so marked a difference in susceptibil-
ity in different age groups? Was the lower death rate of the 0–1 age group,
when compared with that of children aged 1–4, due to some "kind of
immunity," or was it only due to the fact that infants were generally kept
indoors?[21]

Villermé himself felt that a major portion and perhaps even most of
these children were being carried off by an acute disease characterized by
diarrhea and particularly manifest during periods when fevers were preva-
lent. Intestinal irritation was present; recovery, if it came, was prompt and
complete.[22] As a military surgeon Villermé had much earlier observed the
outbreak and effects of such diarrheal disease(s) in the Imperial camps

19. Ibid., p. 346.
20. Villermé, "Influence des marais sur la vie des enfans," p. 33.
21. Villermé, "De l'influence des marais," pp. 353–54.
22. Ibid., pp. 354–55.

along the English Channel and in Spain and was well aware of the catastrophic nature of such an epidemic. Its effect, moreover, seemed always
devastating to those without previous exposure to the disease, namely,
young children. It is obviously impossible today to specify what disease
or diseases he was referring to; he himself applied no names in this context. Certainly, residents of the marshlands—malnourished, surrounded
by mud and animals and the characteristic filth produced by the union of
the two, as well as exposed to unending dampness and a perpetually
fouled water supply—experienced at the very least constant attacks of
typhoid fever and bacillary dysentery. Both are autumnal diseases, and
both have a high mortality rate if the victims remain untreated; both are
common in childhood.

In addition to our inference of the endemicity of these diseases, Villermé himself expressly pointed out that children exposed to "marshy
emanations" were also subject to intermittent and remittent fevers; malaria
was thereby probably indicated. Yellow fever was claimed to be a familiar
visitor in the marsh districts, but it seemed to spare the children.[23] Villermé's study of the medical consequences of living in the marshlands had
neither nosological nor diagnostic intentions. It was obvious to him, as it
is to us, that local conditions provided an excellent setting for what was
probably a diverse set of diseases. These might break out simultaneously
or independently and more than likely manifested themselves in increased
mortality if the season was appropriate, against a similar increase brought
on by endemic malaria. It was not indifference that led Villermé to ex-
claim, "however it may be," with regard to the issue of the cause(s) of the
principal diseases of the marsh districts; he realized that a shortage of
lethal agencies was not at all in question.[24] His words served only to return
the reader's attention to the matter of paramount concern, child mortality.

Here was an anticipation of the grand theme of Villermé's later career.
Most exposed to risk and least fit to cope with the dangers presented by
the marsh and (he would soon discover) the factory and industrial town
were young children. Life in the marshlands was uncommonly perilous,
and young children, it seemed evident, bore much the greatest burden of
sickness and death. But why had this important fact remained heretofore
unknown? The answer was simply that, in a phrase that reflects imme-
morial indifference, no one "pays any attention to the death of the children
of the poor."[25] The marsh districts were inhabited predominantly by the
very poor. They were accustomed to watching their children die and found

23. Ibid., pp. 355, 352.
24. Ibid., p. 355.
25. Ibid., p. 357.

it normal. The few wealthy families in these regions took cognizance of the risk and either removed their children during the worst seasons or took other precautions. Old habits obviously faded but slowly: registration by the parish curate of death of the newborn and the very young was commonly ignored. Those who failed to reach their first communion often simply disappeared from or, more precisely, never made an appearance in the parish record of vital statistics. Given the marked insalubrity of the marshlands and the generally depressed standard of living in such areas, it appeared to Villermé that this vice would here be uncommonly pronounced. (This set of problems—numerous children, high mortality, general neglect, and inadequate records—was to reappear in a radically different setting, namely, the expanding industrial sectors of town and city.)

Some authors might have viewed the desperate condition of life in the marsh districts as promising grounds for easy moralization regarding the sad but inescapable turn of fate that joined poverty and mortality, or for fierce condemnation of the evils of contemporary economic organization that permitted such suffering to occur. These thoughts, notably the latter, did not come to Villermé until the 1840s. His goal in 1834 was amelioration, insofar as this was possible, of perceived social and hygienic shortcomings. One could not, obviously, expect all children of the poor to leave the dangerous area during the season of greatest risk. These children, it was silently implied, were destined to cope with their lot as they found it. Little if anything could be done for them, with the important exception of attempting to improve their economic and hence overall physical condition. It was, however, possible to avoid compounding the problem. Paris often sent her nurslings, legitimate as well as illegitimate, for care in the country; the Sologne was a preferred destination. Lyons sent her young children into the Bresse and Dombes. This was an unnecessary and murderous practice. It could easily be halted and a great many lives preserved.[26] It was equally important to keep a sharp watch on the widespread practice of drainage of the marshes. Drainage had been a cherished scheme of agricultural improvers since the mid-eighteenth century and became a favorite occupation of developers and speculators during the constitutional monarchy. Villermé feared, and experience since the Revolution had confirmed this fear, that drainage would often be improperly conducted or executed in the wrong locality. Instead of creating dry, tillable land, one often created perfect conditions for the formation of seasonal marshes, the most deadly of all; and so-called improvement thus literally brought into being new and serious public health hazards. Villermé hoped that his study of mortality in the marshlands would induce restraint or at

26. Ibid., pp. 355–56.

least provide sound medical guidance for the ongoing process of drainage.

The memoir on the influence of marshes on mortality was one among several that Villermé wrote during this period dedicated to assaying the diverse patterns of human life and death. Its force of argument, notable even among Villermé's many such efforts, derives both from the simplicity of the conclusion reached and from the fund and conspicuous tendency of the evidence employed. Although mortality in the marshlands was shown to be intimately tied to the peculiar physical or climatic factors characterizing such districts, Villermé did not fail to recognize that here, too, there was a prominent social component contributing to differential mortality. The population at risk was in general anything but a prosperous one. Its biological conditions of existence were unfavorable; shelter and clothing were inadequate; life too often rose little above a subsistence level. Hence, bodily dilapidation, often eventuating in outright disability, had combined with utterly impropitious climatic circumstances to create a population whose medical experience was somber indeed. Lurking throughout the entire analysis was Villermé's fundamental persuasion that widespread incidence of disease was as much a matter of social and economic concern as it was the foremost problem of the physician.

Month of Conception: Unclear Patterns

Villermé's assessment of the distribution of body size and of differential mortality in the marshlands was part of a large and very ambitious program of investigation. The focal point of the program was a major essay published in 1831 dealing with yet another vital phenomenon, the periodicity of conception.[27] As its ample title indicates, this essay constituted an attempt at establishing multiple correlations with a given vital event. It may have been that such an approach was envisaged at the outset by its author. It seems far more likely, however, that the multiplicity of factors considered resulted from the fact that each, treated in turn, failed to assure a satisfying correlation. As has been noted, Villermé did not seek to determine the exclusive causal factors of disease, death, or other vital events. Nonetheless, he usually tried to establish what appeared to be the predominant cause in a given situation. The facts regarding the monthly pattern of maximal and minimal conception were readily established, yet other facts that might then have established a correlation between that

---

27. L. R. Villermé, "De la distribution par mois des conceptions et des naissances de l'homme, considérée dans ses rapports avec les saisons, avec les climats, avec le retour périodique annuel des époques de travail et de repos, d'abondance et de rareté des vivres, et avec quelques institutions et coutumes sociales," *Annales d'hygiène publique et de médecine légale* 5 (1831): 55–155.

pattern and one or another putative cause instead made apparent only inconclusive relationships and contradictions.

Birth, because of its obvious relevance to population increase and hence to a populationist program, had long been a favored event in demographic thinking. Correlation of the birth rate with population size, with the death rate, and with the number of marriages had all been explored. So, too, had been the striking regularity of the ratio between the number of male and female births.[28] Villermé, however, claimed to be breaking fresh ground in assaying the parameters bearing upon the annual periodicity of conception. Conception, the critical biological event upon which birth must depend, seemed to transport the observer to the most important moment of the reproductive process. Time of conception was measured, however, in the simplest possible manner, namely, by shifting data regarding births to a period nine months earlier. The potential errors in this procedure were either unperceived or passed over without comment, probably the former. Because of the many hazards of pregnancy and the loss between conception and parturition of numerous fetuses, the rate of conception was probably seriously but perhaps uniformly underestimated.

It was essential first to establish the basic datum, the monthly distribution of conception. Against this pattern could then be compared suspected determining influences, both climatic and institutional. Villermé's first tableau represents a prodigious assemblage of scattered statistical material, offering the monthly number of births in Saint Petersburg and Ostende, Copenhagen and Buenos Aires, Sweden and Italy, and many other localities.[29] France, not unexpectedly, received special attention. For the period 1818–25 the number of births in France peaked, in decreasing order, in February, March, January, and April; months of maximum conception were thus, in the same order, May, June, April, and July. Minimal conception occurred in the autumn, October being the lowest month.[30] Although this exact pattern by no means applied to nations other than France and was, in fact, violated by various regions within France, it did seem to present a general order of wide applicability. Conceptions rose to a peak as spring turned to summer and diminished again as the warm season came to an end. Such a pattern all too obviously pointed to a close relationship between climate and time of conception.

In the Midi, Villermé decided, more conceptions occurred in the winter months, that is, from December through late spring, than in the north, where the peak period shifted to spring through early summer. Already it

28. Contemporary discussion of these issues is summarized by Quetelet, *Treatise on Man*, pp. 10–26.

29. Villermé, "Mois des conceptions," pp. 124–37.

30. Ibid., pp. 59–60.

was clear that the connection between conception and season was not a direct one; conceptions were on the rise before the warmth of spring returned and had reached a low in early autumn, when cold weather had not yet arrived. The north-south pattern appeared nonetheless to be valid for most of Europe: conception was generally earlier in the south. This fact suggested that man, too, in his present "state of civilization," to some degree still felt the "periodic influences" that governed the life of all plants and animals.[31]

Autumn, however, presented an anomaly that demanded an explanation. Its warmth seemed more than adequate to maintain fecundity, and yet the number of conceptions plunged at this time of the year to its lowest point. Perhaps, Villermé reflected, other causes were acting. One such was unmistakable. Autumn in certain regions was the period of greatest morbidity and even mortality. This was particularly true in areas containing extensive marshes. Examining this possibility in the light of mortality in these districts, Villermé saw in the striking "coincidence" of the two periodicities involved (diminishing fecundity and increasing mortality) an unmistakable indication of the "*principal* cause" in operation.[32] This cause was the "insalubrity of marshes," and its action was most probably related to season of the year. The latter, characterized by varying temperatures, controlled the former only indirectly, that is, the beneficial or pernicious effect of a given season was the consequence of the filling or drying out of the marshes. Not only, it appeared, had an explanation of autumnal diminution of conception been discovered, but it had also been shown that the marsh works in at least two ways to reduce the numbers of mankind, attacking at both the moment of conception and with particular vehemence in the decade after birth.

The insalubrious marsh proved, however, a factor of only limited applicability. Other, indeed most, areas reached their lowest rate of conception in these same months. Yet these areas—Paris and parts of Normandy were cited—were troubled only slightly if at all by the effluvia of marshes. Villermé was baffled by the problem and admitted it. "There is something here," he noted, "of which we are ignorant."[33] While this skein of possible causes was developed no further, the form of argument here employed deserves additional notice. Using numbers, Villermé had reached an empirically well-grounded generalization, a simple rule stating that, broadly speaking, conception follows the seasons. An exception was then observed (conception was lowest in the still warm autumn months) and an

31. Ibid., p. 75.
32. Ibid., pp. 76–80.
33. Ibid., p. 80.

explanation introduced to account for it (marshes exert a negative influence on the rate of conception). But that explanation embraced what was obviously a minority of pertinent instances. It was, in short, no general explanation. Also obvious was the fact that other climatic factors were at work and those, unfortunately, remained unknown.

The periodicity of conception might, however, be viewed from a different perspective. Human fecundity might be governed not by the influence(s) of climate but by that of man's own institutions. At the very least, climate and institutions would exert mutual action upon conception. The seemingly most decisive institutional factor proved nonetheless to exert no consistent influence. It stood to reason that, in an era in which deliberate fertility control was still a minority practice, the frequency of conception should follow closely the rate of marriages.[34] The facts proved otherwise. Just as the number of conceptions varied by time and place, creating a characteristic pattern for a given locality, so too did the number of marriages. But the two series could not be harmonized. Months of peak marriage and peak conception differed, and these differences in turn varied according to the locality examined. Conception commonly did not take place on or near the marriage day but required a period of weeks or months, the period in question again varying with locality. "Everywhere and at all times," Villermé concluded, the periodicity of conception was roughly the same; yet the marriage rate varied enormously in diverse localities. Here obviously no correlation was possible. Marriage, surely the human institution which at first glance would seem most directly tied to frequency of conception, was at best "only weakly linked" to conception.[35]

Villermé had found that the number of births, and therefore conceptions, was more evenly distributed over the months of the year in the city than in the country. In the country, there were 29 percent more conceptions in the maximum month than in the minimum month; in the city, that difference declined to 11 percent.[36] Agricultural labor was generally held to be physically more demanding than that involved in the urban trades. Perhaps this fact explained the more uneven pattern of rural conceptions. Regrettably, available data pointed to no such conclusion. Comparison of predominantly agricultural departments with industrial departments indicated no significant seasonal differences in frequency of conceptions. Villermé was aware that the problem might well be in the data themselves.

34. Ibid., pp. 95. See Philippe Ariès, "On the Origins of Contraception in France" and "An Interpretation to Be Used for a History of Mentalities," in *Popular Attitudes towards Birth Control in Pre-Industrial France and England*, ed. Orest Ranum and Patricia Ranum (New York: Harper and Row, 1972), pp. 10–20, 100–125.

35. Villermé, "Mois des conceptions," p. 92.

36. Ibid., p. 82.

Working France as a whole was still overwhelmingly devoted to agricultural pursuits, and major industry, although increasingly important, was confined to small localities. To test the hypothesis properly would require data regarding month of conception (birth) from lesser administrative units, notably the communes, and this was simply not available. Seasons of heavy labor, an "institution" inseparable from the human condition, thus also failed to correlate with the periodicity of conception.[37]

The converse of heavy and constant labor appeared to be a more promising factor, however. The trend towards increasing number of conceptions began to emerge in December and rose over the spring towards a maximum reached in early summer. In normal years, the months of winter were the season not only of greatest repose and socializing but of most abundant nutrition. The harvest was in, labor in the fields reduced or finished, and the new crop available for consumption. Social contact increased and with it, no doubt, sexual activity.[38]

The real measure of this claim was given by the consequences of those years in which there was a sharp reduction in foodstuffs consumed. The crop failure of 1816 was followed by a precipitous fall in the number of conceptions in the seriously affected regions. The north and east of France and the Low Countries suffered most. The assembled data disclosed vividly the course of the period of virtual famine.[39] The normal slowing of the birth rate in late spring was followed by a prolonged period in which not only were previous highs unattained but new lows reached. This depression reached well into the year 1818, thus following the drop in the rate of conception which was, in turn, tied directly to the dearth that had lasted from late 1816 into early summer 1817.

These events merely confirmed the familiar observation that, with man as with animals, "famine induces sterility."[40] A similar effect was also to be sought from causes other than those directly affecting man's food supply. Villermé sought valiantly to demonstrate that fasting before Easter also markedly reduced the frequency of conception.[41] Available data for this purpose were unsure, observation of the obligations of religion had noticeably slackened over the past fifty years, and variations by confession proved most difficult to isolate. Nonetheless, he was confident that in Roman Catholic lands—above all, France and Italy—and particularly during earlier years when traditional practice was closely followed, Lenten fasting had indeed reduced conception. Whether this effect was due to an

37. Ibid., pp. 95–97.
38. Ibid., pp. 98–101.
39. Ibid., pp. 103–94, and pp. 154–55, table 8.
40. Ibid., p. 104.
41. Ibid., pp. 105–11.

insufficiency of food or to a change in the nature of the foodstuffs consumed was a matter left unresolved.

The "Month of Conception" was a long and exceedingly diffuse memoir. As such, it contrasted sharply with the conciseness and clarity of purpose that were usual in Villermé's publications. The fundamental problem in the study was, of course, that the author's ambitions far exceeded both the data available and the capacities of his craft. My researches, he himself observed, demonstrate that "one of the most complex problems [facing sociomedical investigation] is that of the causes that exert an influence upon our fecundity."[42] Use of the plural was especially appropriate here. Any number of causes had been proposed by those who attempted correlations of this kind, and all too often a single cause—climate, altitude, diet, temperature, exposure to the sun, and the like—had been identified as possessing unique force. If, however, Villermé observed, such inquirers "had taken the trouble to extend, collect, and compare observations made in diverse localities, they would have learned that in regions that are, with respect to any of these particulars, similar, the [monthly] distribution of births often varies greatly from one place to another . . . and that, taking into consideration data presented by two localities in any one category, one can at the same time both support and undermine the very same contention."[43]

The methodological problem thus posed proved insurmountable. The role of distinct and perhaps autonomous influences could not be precisely established. Worse yet, since in all probability no single cause controlled fecundity, the relative importance of several cooperating factors had to be determined, and this could not be done. Villermé appreciated the dilemma. "Given the fact that I find it impossible to establish separately the role of each [cause] in this matter of month of conception and the [equal impossibility] of submitting the simultaneous and quite complex circumstances that I have just presented to some kind of analysis," I shall, he wrote, simply assign dual causation (season and institution) to the phenomenon.[44]

Such a conclusion, however, meant retreat from the purpose that had animated the inquiry. Villermé was convinced that the application of reason to number would bring forth novel and important social and medical truths. In many cases his faith was amply justified. With regard to the factors governing fecundity, however, no such assurance was forthcoming. The basic fact had been easily established: there is a recognizable

42. Ibid., p. 115.
43. Ibid., p. 116.
44. Ibid., p. 98.

periodicity to conception. But as the quest for the cause(s) of this periodicity advanced, it became increasingly evident that many, indeed too
many, causes were operating. Without conceptual means to handle this
problem, Villermé could offer only a nonnumerical and verbal conclusion.
The tendency of the facts themselves was beyond question. The annual
pattern of conceptions—that is, births—was a demonstrated reality, and it
was the "resultant of the oscillations of the happenstance of place, time,
and circumstance." Sensing the impreciseness of this conclusion, one that
rendered pointless the elaborate analysis that had been carried out, Villermé ventured a bolder claim. Behind all such random events stood, "de-
finitively put, one cause that dominates and so to speak obscures all the
others." This cause was the annual variation of temperature, in turn due to
the relative position of the sun.[45]

And yet this was not and could not be the definitive cause. In the following paragraph the author, scrupulously honest as always, recalled the
disturbing fact that the season of greatest heat and light was also one of
sharply declining frequency of conception. In amusing desperation Villermé introduced the possibility of a moral cause (the stimulus to human
reproduction was the general reawakening of springtime) and ventured
assorted and familiar fancies regarding the proclivity towards *amour* in
the Mediterranean lands and its rejection by the Lapp. There followed
observations on the seasonal periodicity of sexual activity in animals, with
an eye cast on man as well. These inconclusive conclusions finally wan-
dered to an end with the reiterated conviction that only a "small number
of circumstances" control the periodicity of human reproduction.[46] While
the general trend of the unsure arguments presented in this memoir was to
assign causal priority to climatic factors, the important role of institutional—that is, social—influences in determining fecundity remained central to the argument.

The Biology within Political Arithmetic

The memoir on month of conception was envisaged by its author as the
lead essay in an extensive series dealing with "general mortality, mortality
at each age, and morbidity."[47] The study of body size was a forerunner to
this program, and that devoted to mortality in the marshlands provided an
additional specimen of the kind of analysis projected. The series itself was
to become a major work that would lay bare the relations, numerically

45. Ibid., p. 119.
46. Ibid , pp. 119–21.
47. Ibid., p. 123n.

expressed, between man and the social and biological conditions of his existence. This work was never completed. The larger conception as well as the lesser elements disappeared as Villermé moved increasingly into his factory studies of the 1830s.

What had been envisaged was a study in the grand tradition of political arithmetic. Villermé no less than his predecessors was impressed by the unexpected regularities in social life and biological existence that the numerical approach first and best revealed. These regularities of birth, marriage, death, and other important vital events in human existence demanded an explanation. In the eighteenth century, authors such as William Derham and J. P. Süssmilch detected in these regularities evidence of the divine order that governed the creation. By 1830 their providential argument was yielding to scientific curiosity and criticism and also to apparent social need.[48] With Villermé and Benoiston de Châteauneuf, and to a lesser degree Quetelet, interest in these numbers now shifted to the urgent problem of the connection between a given vital event and its presumed natural cause. To the Parisian sociomedical investigator the important correlation was always that which joined concrete biological fact—above all, mortality—to equally tangible social reality, namely, economic condition. His emphasis was always empirical and his arithmetic no less emphatically political.

The expression *biological fact* requires further consideration. To Villermé and to other hygienists the principal meaning of the term *biological* was that exemplified in the above discussion, namely, the sum total of bodily experience whose net effect might be health, or disease, debilitation, and death. Although most sociomedical observers were physicians who occasionally practiced the medical art and were thoroughly cognizant of the increasing definition of disease entities and conflicting etiological doctrines that informed French medical thought and practice, on the whole they did not explore these issues in their hygienic writings. As has been noted frequently above, their chosen perspective was relentlessly social.

The distinction between their mode of inquiry and the rise of explicit epidemiological analysis after about 1840 should therefore be emphasized. Modern epidemiology takes as its primary subject the interaction of (disease) agent, host, and the environment.[49] With regard to what was

48. See F. N. Egerton, "Changing Concepts of the Balance of Nature," *Quarterly Review of Biology* 48 (1973): 322–50; Franz Weiling, "Die 'Göttliche Ordnung' J. P. Süssmilchs als Erstlingswerk statistischer und biometrischer Arbeitsweise," *Forschung und Fortschritte* 41 (1967): 296–300; Harald Westergaard, *Contributions to the History of Statistics* (London: P. S. King, 1932), pp. 70–78.

49. See A. M. Lilienfeld, *Foundations of Epidemiology* (New York: Oxford University Press, 1976), pp. 9–13.

long the paramount epidemiological problem, namely, infectious disease, this modern view could take definitive form only after the statement and demonstration of the germ theory of disease, an accomplishment of the 1870s and 1880s. Earlier epidemiologists—such as John Snow, William Budd, and Peter Panum, whose inquiries began in the 1830s and 1840s— paid particular attention not only to the characteristic movement of particular diseases through defined populations but also to the biological (or chemical) character and presumed causes of the various diseases in question (cholera, typhoid fever, measles).[50] Villermé, Parent-Duchâtelet, and other hygienists, remarkably enough, paid little or no attention to the then furiously disputed etiology of communicable disease. Theirs was the generation that saw the rise and decline of P. J. Broussais's all-encompassing physiological system; they ignored it.[51] Theirs was also the generation that witnessed the celebrated quarrels over contagionism and anticontagionism, focused primarily on the presumed etiology of cholera and yellow fever; these disputes had little resonance in French sociomedical literature.

Knud Faber provides a suggestive explanation of why this should have been so. The numerical method tended to emphasize discrete instances of the diseased condition, notably physical lesions and the clinical definition of the disease entity with which these lesions were presumably associated. Such instances, of course, provide raw material for enumeration and subsequent analysis. But the numerical method had little interest in the disease process *per se*. P.C.A. Louis, Faber observed, "introduced the statistical, numerical method into clinical research, but in a certain degree this occurred at the cost of direct biological observation."[52] Louis—and his name may be taken here to represent the general tendency of the numerical school in both its clinical and hygienic manifestations—thus diverted attention from the biological (physiological-pathological) events that constitute the disease process. These developments represented, to be sure, only one aspect of the multifaceted program of French medicine. While the numerical school in the hygienists' and in Louis's hands increasingly viewed disease as a discrete social or pathological event, thus making it peculiarly apt for tidy numerical manipulation, the clinical tradition represented by, for example, R.T.H. Laënnec and, above all, P. F. Bretonneau insisted on the importance of the whole course of a particular affliction. Not just the lesion and not just the cataloging of another case of a

50. See C.-E.A. Winslow, *The Conquest of Epidemic Disease: A Chapter in the History of Ideas* (Princeton: Princeton University Press, 1943), pp. 267–90.

51. See E. H. Ackerknecht, "Broussais; or, A Forgotten Medical Revolution," *Bulletin of the History of Medicine* 27 (1953): 320–43.

52. Knud Faber, *Nosography in Modern Internal Medicine* (New York: Paul B. Hoeber, 1923), p. 43.

given disease caught their interest; they sought to provide a complete characterization of specific diseases, a characterization useful to understanding these diseases and, hopefully, also pertinent to effective medical practice. This fact led Bretonneau, more than others, to consider the overall parameters of the specificity of each (infectious) disease, a procedure that in turn led him to stimulating speculation on the character of a supposed causal agent of such diseases.

The interaction of agent, host, and environment were joined in the disease theory of the Bretonneau tradition; they were largely disjoined by the numerical school.[53] When reading Villermé or the work of other Paris hygienists, one is often disconcerted by the absence of consideration of etiological alternatives and of extended discussion or even mention of particular diseases and their immediate bodily consequences. We may well be deceived, however, by our false or limited expectations. The celebrity of Paris medicine has long and properly been due to the diagnostic skills of French physicians after 1800. Necessarily, their regard fell upon the diseased individual, upon the onset, development, and outcome of what came to be recognized as a definite sequence of pathological changes. Yet we may, I suggest, inappropriately be tempted to expect this concern for the disease process to inform most or even all aspects of early-nineteenth-century French medicine. As noted, hygienists were not uninformed regarding disease theory; their concern simply was directed to other matters, matters that were "biological" in a different and, if the expression be permitted, more expansive sense. The hygienist attended to the essential conditions of existence—food; supply and purity of water; presence and absence of human, animal, and other wastes; the conditions of bodily and mental activity, including above all work, shelter, or protection from the elements—and realized that all of these possessed an underlying economic character; the environment was thereby rendered social in nature. The hygienist also realized that this socioeconomic dimension touched directly upon disease sensu strictu.

Margaret Pelling has justly emphasized that etiological questions during the middle third of the nineteenth century rarely received a single or monolithic answer. "Complexity and a sense of compromise," she notes, better characterize the etiological thought of the period; moreover, etiology was by no means "a constant or dominant preoccupation" of the med-

53. Ibid., pp. 43–46. See also P. F. Bretonneau, "Traité de la specificité" [1828], in *Traités de la dothinentérie et de la spécificité*, ed. Louis Dubreuil-Chambardel (Paris: Vigot Frères, 1922), pp. 277–352, and esp. Armande Trousseau, "Spécificité," in *Clinique médicale de l'Hôtel-Dieu de Paris* [1861–62], ed. A. Vanotti et al., 2 vols. (Geneva, Paris, and Brussels: Alliance culturelle du livre, 1963), 1:339–67.

ical profession.[54] English sanitarians with a strong environmental bias (for example, Southwood Smith and Edwin Chadwick) obviously favored the anticontagionist position; very gradually William Farr's views evolved from a chemical zymotic theory of disease transmission to acceptance in the 1870s of the nascent germ theory of disease and thus organismic transmission.[55] The contagionist-anticontagionist struggle, among others, had a long life in Britain, and it must also remain, despite Pelling's sharp criticism, a central theme in our consideration of nineteenth-century French analysis of a number of significant infectious diseases.[56] In spite of these celebrated disputes, French sociomedical investigators commonly followed another path. Etiology, whether chemical, miasmatic, or organismic (the latter being constantly implied by members of the school of Bretonneau), was indeed to them not a "constant or dominant preoccupation," but etiology with its parameters now expressed in the economic conditions of existence was precisely their paramount concern. Before the event, they attended closely to the details of the "biology of man in history," a matter exceeding but also embracing the limits of the medical art and one whose perspective has in recent years generated much original scholarly inquiry.[57]

By means of number Villermé had discovered important sociomedical truths, and numerical argument and a quest for patterns held to be inherent in the cycle of human existence never disappeared from his sphere of attention. They did, however, come to play a less dominant role. Between 1820 and 1834 he had explored in depth a wide range of quantitative materials. Using only the most elementary numerical techniques he had been able to extract from these materials a number of generalizations concerning the intimate relationship between the biological condition of important elements of the nation's population and the socioeconomic and physical factors that most directly influenced their condition. But neither these materials nor, more importantly, available methods could carry Villermé or contemporaries much beyond simple and untested correlations.

54. Margaret Pelling, *Cholera, Fever, and English Medicine, 1825–1865* (Oxford: Oxford University Press, 1978), pp. 303, 301.

55. On the sanitarians, see ibid., pp. 1–33; on Farr, see John M. Eyler, *Victorian Social Medicine: The Ideas and Methods of William Farr* (Baltimore: Johns Hopkins University Press, 1979), pp. 97–122.

56. In this regard, Pelling, *Cholera, Fever, and English Medicine*, pp. 295–310, should be compared with E. H. Ackerknecht, "Anticontagionism between 1821 and 1867," *Bulletin of the History of Medicine* 22 (1948): 562–93.

57. See the introduction and several essays in *Biology of Man in History: Selections from the Annales. Economies-Sociétés-Civilisations*, ed. Robert Forster and Orest Ranum, trans. Elborg Forster and P. M. Ranum (Baltimore: Johns Hopkins University Press, 1975).

Moreover, the nature of the new world that Villermé entered in the middle 1830s, that of the factory and industrial town, also indicated a diminished role for strictly numerical argumentation. Hazardous conditions were obvious even to the most unsophisticated eye and mind. Vital and economic statistics, when available, continued to be utilized, but now Villermé's concern was to convey by precise and abundant verbal description a comprehensive view of the condition of labor both within and without workplace and factory. He thus returned to the procedure he had followed when examining the prisons of Paris and of France. The *Tableau de l'état physique et moral des ouvriers* was above all a descriptive work wherein the verbal regained parity with the numerical.

Chapter 8

Inequality before Death: The Worker

Why is it that a vast amount of illness originates in the very society that men of old inaugurated in order to enjoy a safer life . . . ?

J. P. Frank, 1790

Johann Peter Frank answered his own question. The people's misery was the source not only of frequent sickness but of excess mortality as well. Frank's answer was new neither to European social reality nor to scientific perception. But how the sociomedical relationship was perceived, the methods by which this perception was gained and communicated, and the medical and social purposes that it was to serve had shifted radically between 1790 and 1840. Common to Frank's celebrated discourse of 1790 and Villermé's *Tableau de l'état physique et moral des ouvriers* of 1840 was the people's misery. Distinguishing these works, however, was an altogether new perception: the origin of the people's misery had moved in fifty years from country to city, from agriculture to industry and perhaps the factory.

The *Tableau* is the earliest of three famous texts whose publication marked the culmination of the early public health movement. It was quickly followed by Edwin Chadwick's independent and influential *Report on the Sanitary Condition of the Labouring Population of Great Britain* (1842), and the decade closed with the appearance of the *Report of the Sanitary Commission of Massachusetts* (1850), the creation principally of Lemuel Shattuck. These several reports present many points of similarity but also numerous and significant differences. Spurred by the vagaries of the legislative process Chadwick hastily had to prepare a summary statement of the many investigations then being conducted by his Poor Law Union medical officers. To these he added various other observations, including many made personally. The Chadwick *Report* as submitted to the Home Office was a persuasive document and an extremely effective propa-

EPIGRAPH: J. P. Frank, "The People's Misery: Mother of Diseases," trans. H. E. Sigerist, *Bulletin of the History of Medicine* 9 (1941): 88–89.

ganda instrument.[1] Its argument was multifaceted, not to say often discon-
nected, and its power derived less from organic structure than from repeated exemplification of the dire condition of the British working classes
and from Chadwick's own argumentative fervor. Numerical material was
frequently if not consistently employed, and startling cases of misery, destitution, and death were cited with notable effect. Throughout the *Report*
were evident Chadwick's twin obsessions: disease and premature death
are due above all to filth, and filth is a remediable condition. The remedy
was one that required scientific investigation and then widespread application by duly constituted public authorities of the principles thus discerned to correct social problems. To this supreme bureaucrat public
health was a matter that demanded forceful state intervention.

Shattuck thought highly of Chadwick's work. A publisher by profession
and a statistician by avocation, Shattuck had been instrumental in persuad-
ing the Massachusetts legislature to introduce the systematic recording of
vital statistics in the state. A few years later (1849) he induced the same
body to appoint three commissioners to conduct a sanitary survey of the
Commonwealth. Their report was soon ready.[2] It consisted of a large and
varied set of appendices, recommendations for legislative action on fifty
quite specific measures, and a general consideration of the "sanitary
movement" abroad and at home. The latter contained Shattuck's most direct assessment of the sanitary condition of the people of Massachusetts.
His analysis was predominantly statistical and made dramatically evident
the differential mortality that demarcated subgroups living in the Boston
area and elsewhere in Massachusetts and New England. Shattuck and his
fellow commissioners did not carry out, as Chadwick to a degree had
done, regular and direct inspection of the living and working conditions
of those persons, principally members of the working classes, whose
health and life were most at risk. But comment by others on these matters
was solicited, and evidence cited in sanitary publications was exploited
with great profit.

In sharp contrast to these two great contributions, Villermé's *Tableau*

---

1. See Edwin Chadwick, *Report on the Sanitary Condition of the Labouring Population
of Gt. Britain* [1842], ed. M. W. Flinn (Edinburgh: University Press, 1965). Also S. E.
Finer, *The Life and Times of Sir Edwin Chadwick* (London: Methuen, 1952), pp. 154–242;
R. A. Lewis, *Edwin Chadwick and the Public Health Movement, 1832–1854* (London:
Longmans Green, 1952), pp. 29–123.

2. *Report of a General Plan for the Promotion of Public and Personal Health, Devised,
Prepared and Recommended by the Commissioners Appointed under a Resolve of the Legislature of Massachusetts, Relating to a Sanitary Survey of the State* (Boston: Dutton and
Wentworth, 1850). See B. G. Rosenkrantz, *Public Health and the State: Changing Views
in Massachusetts, 1842–1936* (Cambridge: Harvard University Press, 1972), pp. 8–36.

was a highly personal creation. Charged by the Académie des sciences morales et politiques to conduct "in the departments of France studies in political economy and statistics whose aim is to *establish as precisely as possible the physical and moral condition of the working classes,*" Villermé and his fellow investigator, François Benoiston de Châteauneuf, realized that only direct, on-site investigation of the life and labor of the worker and working family would satisfy this demand.[3] The *Tableau* contains considerable numerical material, some of it derived from published sources and some, including the important mortality tables from Mulhouse, abstracted from registration reports at Villermé's request. But the greater part of the work is devoted to verbal description of what had been seen and heard in the world of textile manufacture, to extended reasoning on the available numerical data, and to sustained and well-focused consideration of the medical and social meaning of this vast fund of information. There is a coherence to this work that is lacking in Chadwick's *Report* and a close union of personal observation and numerical analysis that is not encountered in the Shattuck *Report*.

Chadwick, Shattuck, and Villermé shared the conviction that the indispensable preliminary to social amelioration—specifically, the improvement of the lot of the working poor and the diminution of preventable sickness and death—was the collection of abundant and authoritative information regarding the true medical and social condition of these persons. Science must precede action. Shattuck followed Chadwick in seeking the creation of broadly conceived and administratively powerful public agencies by which needed changes could be introduced and officially asserted demands enforced. Villermé, however, lacked the bureaucratic instinct and, more importantly, conceived the problem always in the context of the principles of political economy. Social amelioration would best be advanced by means of gradual and carefully designed reform. Broad administrative competence always threatened to impose too great a restraint upon individual liberty, including entrepreneurial freedom. At most, therefore, he supported publicly enacted remedies only for quite specific socioeconomic vices, of which child labor was not only the most prominent but virtually the only significant example. But whatever the specific hygienic proposals of these authors for alleviating the misery of the urban and working poor, they each agreed that a principal cause of excessive illness and mortality was social. In the *Tableau*, moreover, Villermé developed the claim that the new system of manufacture was only indirectly the source of this unparalleled suffering. Between life in the factory and ex-

3. L. R. Villermé, *Tableau de l'état physique et moral des ouvriers employés dans les manufactures de coton, de laine et de soie*, 2 vols. (Paris: Jules Renouard, 1840), 1:v.

cessive sickness and death intervened a complex set of social and economic factors. These factors not only freed factory and machine from blame but made it inevitable that medicine would command a prominent place in the nascent empirical social sciences.

The Textile Trades

The Academy of Moral and Political Sciences had sought information regarding the "working classes"; Villermé and Benoiston de Châteauneuf replied with an investigation of the condition of labor in the textile trades. That decision was inevitable, for in contemporary France it was the production of thread and fabric that was most subject to revolutionary technical and organizational change. It was here above all that the factory system took root and here also that the first signs of uncontrolled industrial urbanization became evident.

By the 1840s linen was a stagnant industry. Traditionally closely tied to the land—flax being a major crop in northern France—the manufacture of linen long remained a cottage industry. But mechanical spinning of linen thread had been perfected in England by 1830, and English production soon began to compete on the international market. Mechanized spinning of flax began in France during the crisis of 1837. It soon proved preferable, however, to utilize the coarser but cheaper imported flax from the Baltic lands. The market for the French crop was thus eroded at the same time that employment in domestic spinning was destroyed. Worst of all, the accustomed market for all but the highest quality linens was being steadily reduced by a new competitor, cotton. Cotton was cheaper than linen and was more easily worked. More than linen, whose weaving was a delicate affair and was little done by power looms before 1850, cotton lent itself easily to both mass production and mass consumption.[4]

The second ancient French fabric, wool, prospered during these years. The industry expanded and, more importantly, diversified and modernized. Mechanical spinning was introduced *circa* 1810, and carding and combing operations were mechanized within the following two decades. (Power-loom weaving, however, although ventured had made no significant inroads on hand weaving before 1850.) Both of these operations and the market compelled readjustment of the sources of raw wool. Indigenous supply was inadequate in quantity and in character. Fine merino wool and the long-fibered product of English animals were in great demand. Both were more suited to machine operations, but more importantly, they pro-

4. A. L. Dunham, *The Industrial Revolution in France* (New York: Exposition, 1955), pp. 158–64, 292–306.

vided thread for producing fabrics that satisfied new tastes in woolen goods. The constant trend in the trade, a reflection of consumer demand, was to enlarge production of the middle range of woolens. Lighter fabrics were produced, decoration increased, and styles enormously varied. Flexibility of production marked the successful entrepreneurs who exploited this new market.

The production of woolens tended towards regional specialization. The Norman woolen towns Louviers, an old center of high quality goods, and Elboeuf began to develop fabrics for the middle market. Rheims, also a long-standing center of the trade, sought to produce a full range of woolens. Sedan continued to manufacture the conservative heavy black fabric. Paris was a design center but placed its production in rural areas of northern France. Of all woolen towns, however, none was more singular or prosperous than Roubaix. In fact, Roubaix was less a woolen town than a general textile center, and therein lay its opportunities and strength. The manufacturers of Roubaix used all available raw materials and perfected especially the production and marketing of mixed goods, composed of varying proportions of two or more fibers. Roubaix also specialized in short runs and in quick production of goods on order. The city became the great imitator in textile production.

By the 1840s French industry was producing a vast variety of woolen goods. Intense internal competition had developed. Novelty and a low price, usually at the expense of quality, were essential to success. As production rose, costs declined and prices followed. In the larger market, the middle range of woolens became successful competitors with the established linens and new cottons.[5]

The most singular member of the French textile trade was silk. Weaving with silk thread was begun on twenty looms in Lyons in 1536 and developed over the succeeding three centuries into a large and prosperous industry.[6] The Lyons *fabrique*, as the complex organization of merchants and workers was known, and its *canuts* (weavers) have long commanded attention. Twice, in 1831 and 1834, the canuts, whose suffering during the commercial crisis of 1826–32 and its aftermath was profound, had joined in bloody combat with public authorities. Their grievances focused on the character of industrial organization, and their action has customarily been seen as the first concerted expression of the workers' interest against the demands and practices of the new capitalist order.

5. Ibid., pp. 151–58, 274–91.

6. See Robert J. Bezucha, *The Lyon Uprising of 1834: Social and Political Conflict in the Early July Monarchy* (Cambridge: Harvard University Press, 1974), pp. 1–47; also Villermé, *Tableau*, 1:352–99.

The organization of the Lyons fabrique was not innovative. Silk was an expensive and delicate raw material; silk thread did not easily lend itself to power-loom weaving. Of greater importance, however, were the firmly established economic and social relationships that defined the nature of the fabrique. Production was in the hands of a large number of skilled weavers and their assistants. The weavers, who owned their own looms, including the expensive Jacquard loom, were concentrated in Lyons but had also spread through the nearer reaches of surrounding departments. Their activity was nonetheless controlled by the direct purchaser of their cloth, namely, the powerful merchant class of Lyons and St. Etienne. Despite its extreme concentration of workers and their looms, the Lyons fabrique was not a factory or set of factories on the modern order but held closely instead to the traditional domestic system. Competition between weavers for work was often extreme; the fabrique in general had not been rationalized with maximum production and minimum expense as its guiding themes; systematic mechanization had not been pursued. The operation of the whole was dependent upon a relation of trust between merchant and weaver; when that trust dissolved, as it did in the early 1830s, serious trouble ensued.

Despite these disturbances, silk manufacture maintained a high level of prosperity into the 1850s. Silk cloth, however, was a luxury item and was purchased by a wealthy yet limited clientele. Of all French textiles, silk alone regularly succeeded on the international market, and high-volume production for home consumption by the less affluent emerged only late in the century. The entire fabrique functioned as an assemblage of small manufacturers whose principal members, the canuts, lived relatively well in all but times of severe depression. In terms of organization of production and prospective markets the silk industry was unlike the other textile trades. Yet concentration of the industry in Lyons produced problems not dissimilar to those manifested in other industrial areas. Villermé, who visited the fabrique in 1835 and 1836, nonetheless found the condition of the workers there more attractive than that of most others in France.

Through feast and famine—and both were common enough—the cotton industry continued its expansion.[7] In the more advanced factories major operations were almost entirely mechanized. Beating and carding machines that took the cotton from the bale and prepared it for spinning were utilized in the 1820s. The spinning jenny was in widespread use by 1790 and the water frame or throstle by 1800; the mule was dominant by 1815. Hand spinning had virtually disappeared in France by this time. Self-acting spinning machines—expensive, efficient, and the source of much un-

7. See Dunham, *Industrial Revolution in France*, pp. 164–67, 257–74.

employment—were introduced only in the 1840s. Power-loom weaving, which had triumphed in the English cotton industry during the quarter century when its neighbor had been preoccupied with revolution and war, was introduced into France towards 1820 but began to spread only with the crisis of 1837. Power weaving answered the need to reduce costs of production in the face of depressed prices.

Compared with cotton manufacture in England, that in France was a markedly lesser undertaking. No direct measure of production is available, but the import of raw cotton by France and other nations, stated as a percentage of the raw cotton imported by Britain, is given in Table 8.1. The quantity of raw cotton imported into France rose from 33,623 metric tons in 1832 to 63,903 metric tons in 1849; by comparison, British imports in the same period moved from 125,634 to 286,335 metric tons. Although proportionately less active than their British colleagues, French manufacturers nonetheless managed to increase their production by 90 percent between 1832 and 1849. Since access to foreign markets was virtually closed by British competition, the French product was consumed within the nation, where purchase of cotton goods far outpaced growth of population, largely because of price reductions and because cotton replaced linen as the mass consumer's fabric of common use.

Table 8.1. Cotton consumption: percentage of raw cotton imports relative to Britain

Year	France	Belgium	Zollverein
1832	27	2	2
1836	28	4	5
1843	25	3	7
1849	22	4	7

SOURCE: D. S. Landes, *The Unbound Prometheus: Technological Change and Industrial Development in Western Europe from 1750 to the Present* (Cambridge: Cambridge University Press, 1969), p. 165. Calculated from tonnage figures presented by Landes.

By 1850 sectors of the French cotton industry had been vertically integrated. This was particularly true of the major Alsatian producers.[8] Having begun in the 1740s as cotton printers, the Alsatians, seeking to assure an adequate supply of quality unfinished fabric, had moved into the organization of domestic weaving. For this work, thread was needed, and they thus added spinning to their other endeavors. From the outset Alsace was an industry leader in the coordination of operations, large capitalization,

8. See Claude Fohlen, *L'industrie textile au temps du Second Empire* (Paris: Plon, 1956), pp. 205–7; Paul Leuillot, *L'Alsace au début du XIXe siècle: Essais d'histoire politique, économique, et religieuse (1815–1830)*, 3 vols. (Paris: S.E.V.P.E.N., 1959), 2: 353–460.

and technical innovation. The Alsatian cotton industry is a classic example of an implanted industry, one that owes its origin and prosperity only marginally to the historical, economic, and geographical character of its locale. Although water power was abundantly available and quickly utilized, Alsace, of course, was not a cotton-growing region and was located far from the principal ports receiving cotton. Since bulk transport was very expensive, Alsace, which by French law and custom had to be supplied by overland transport, might appear to have been placed in an impossible position regarding large-scale industrial development.

Yet Alsace prospered, and it did so largely for human reasons, namely, bold and sustained entrepreneurial initiative and an abundant supply of work-hungry and cheap labor. The latter came predominantly from adjacent Swiss cantons and from Baden and elsewhere in south Germany. These areas had been integrated into the French Empire but, following the Congress of Vienna, had reverted to previous political authorities. Their populations were growing, and their economic development was slow at best. The expansion of the Alsatian mills exerted a profound attraction upon their landless and underemployed citizenry. The appearance of the Swiss and Germans in the great Alsatian cotton towns created a new group of workers, one not recruited from surrounding farms but a true proletariat, uprooted and without support save for that provided by their wages and the charity of their employers.

The employers responded to the need and thereby gained renown as the most philanthropic of all French manufacturers. The paternalism of the Alsatian *patronat* was both extensive, ranging from enforced thrift to the construction of *cités ouvrières*, and unrelenting. Great effort was made, consistent with long-term return, to secure and hold an industrious, healthy, and loyal working population. On the whole the effort was successful. To some, and not least to Villermé, the labor practices of the manufacturers of Mulhouse were to be taken as a model for the proper conduct of employer-employee relations. Industrial progress and the physical well-being of labor need not, it appeared, be inconsistent; the better-conducted establishments of Alsace seemed to confirm this fundamental conviction and sincere expectation.

Other cotton regions presented a different aspect. Normandy possessed the greatest concentration of spinners, bobbins, and hand-loom weavers in France. In 1860, of a population of 800,000 in the department of Seine-Inférieure, 200,000 were associated with cotton manufacture or related undertakings (chemicals, mechanical engineering). The Normal product was usually an ordinary and cheap fabric, destined for mass consumption. Weakness in the market was easily felt, and crises struck hard in the area. Ample water power and easy access via Le Havre to raw material and to the British example had been instrumental in establishing the industry. It was sustained largely by merchant support and speculative capital.[9]

Cotton production in the Nord was marked by the entrepreneurial style.[10] Water power was unavailable, and it was here especially that steam, belatedly but steadily, became the foundation for expansion of textile production in the factory setting. Ample labor for these developments was available across the nearby Belgian frontier. Here again was a large and underemployed population, eager to work and not demanding as to its terms. Cotton manufacture expanded rapidly until the early 1830s, and then, as linen and wool reasserted themselves, the Nord was transformed into a powerful multiproduct area. Specialization became evident. The weaving of cotton and manufacture of woolens prevailed at Roubaix, and cotton spinning and linen weaving at Lille. Tourcoing engaged in mixed production and diverse commercial activities. Paternalism was not strong in the Nord, and abrupt discharge of foreign workers was easy and without political peril. Although various towns and establishments in Normandy no doubt presented equally dismal conditions, the Nord soon became synonymous with the worst social and health consequences of the factory system.[11]

The textile industry, and especially cotton manufacture, was dominated by closely held companies. Most were family concerns, and the affairs of the enterprise constituted an extension of those of the entrepreneur and his family. In the Nord and Alsace these entrepreneurs followed a policy of business initiative and fiscal caution. Profits could be enormous but, instead of being diverted to personal expenditure or outside investment, were usually returned to the enterprise itself. Self-financing proved extremely important in the development of the industry and in maintenance of control by the original parties. Capital growth provides an excellent index of the high return possible in such undertakings. The Lille manufacturer Le Blau, a partnership, began in 1820 with a capitalization of 12,000 francs.[12] Despite the shattering depression of 1826–32, capital had grown to 74,000 francs by 1837, a gain of 517 percent, or approximately 30 percent per annum. Profits, however, were neither consistent nor assured. Le Blau in the bad years 1832–33 suffered a loss of 35,000 francs on a

9. Fohlen, *Industrie textile*, pp. 193–205.

10. Ibid., pp. 223–49.

11. See E. Beaujot, "Le département du Nord sous la Restauration: Rapport du préfet de Villeneuve-Bargemont en 1828," *Revue du Nord* 25 (1939–42): 243–77; 26 (1943): 21–45. Also Alban, vicomte de Villeneuve-Bargemont, *Economie politique chrétienne; ou, Recherches sur la nature et les causes du paupérisme en France et en Europe, et sur les moyens de le soulager et de le prévenir*, 3 vols. (Paris: Paulin, 1834).

12. Fohlen, *Industrie textile*, p. 109.

capitalization of 25,000 francs. Recovery was equally dramatic: in the following year (1834) Le Blau earned 53,000 francs on capital of 12,000 (a gain of 441 percent). As capitalization was restored, the rate of return diminished.

These figures provide a rare detailed view of the rapid and extraordinary pecuniary return made possible by the new industrial order. If the entrepreneur took great risks, he did so knowing that great benefits would accompany his success. His profits depended, of course, upon intense exploitation of his factory and effective utilization of available labor. Labor's share of gross income was paid in wages, not in capital gains or profits, and the worker's subsistence or well-being was dependent upon both the shifting relation between wage level and cost of living and the always uncertain prospect of daily employment. Wages and cost of living have long been a central theme in the discussion of the human consequences of the industrial revolution. In question is whether industrialization led to an improvement or diminution of the standard of living, and for whom. The issue was already joined in the 1830s—it received extended discussion by Villermé in the *Tableau* and elsewhere and is discussed below—and has yet to be resolved.

Nevertheless, the effects of a downturn in the economy were perfectly obvious to contemporaries and to all subsequent observers. If the entrepreneur was forced to watch the erosion of his capital, perhaps to the point of ruin, the worker faced ruin the very moment he was discharged. In an era in which unemployment insurance was nonexistent and personal savings virtually impossible, short-term loss of work meant serious difficulty, and prolonged unemployment brought destitution. Shifts in employment level during a period of economic depression were rapid and could affect many workers. A remarkable example of collapsing production and employment is provided by cotton spinning in Roubaix.[13] Growth—in number of spindles, thread produced, spinners employed—was steady and exhibited only minor fluctuations between 1815 and 1826. In the latter year 93,000 spindles were active, 943,000 kg of thread were manufactured, and 430 spinners were employed. The collapse began early in 1827, and its effects were felt immediately: spindles active in 1827 had dropped to 47 percent of the preceding year, production to 22 percent, employment to 51 percent. The depression continued, and the condition of the economic indicators deteriorated. The number of spindles active in 1831 was but 30 percent of those working in 1826; production was but 6 percent of that of 1826; employment stood at 42 percent of the previous level. Michel

13. Michel Raman, "Mesure de la croissance d'un centre textile: Roubaix de 1789 à 1913," *Revue d'histoire économique et sociale* 51 (1973): 470–501.

Raman has noted that the manufacturers appear to have tried to retain, despite the lamentable business climate, a solid core of workers in their mills. Nonetheless, the Roubaix experience reveals how sizeable was the expendable portion of the working population. The first-year cut was from 430 to 220 (1826–27: 49 percent); by 1831 another 40 workers had been discharged (1827–31: 22 percent). The rate of discharge had been reduced although business conditions continued depressed. Unfortunately, place of origin of the retained and discharged workers is not provided. The Roubaix manufacturers could well have been exporting local problems by returning workers to their Belgian homeland.

It was this world of textile factories and rapid changes in production and in the condition of labor, all best exemplified by the situation in the Nord, that caused anxiety amongst manufacturers, administrative personnel, and social observers. The Academy of Moral and Political Sciences gave semiofficial recognition to these developments when it asked two of its members to conduct a survey of the condition of industrial labor in France. To Villermé fell responsibility for scrutiny of the textile industries, particularly those of the north and east, and also the south; Benoiston de Châteauneuf studied conditions in central and western France.[14] The precariousness of public authority was the foremost lesson of recent French history. No government, whatever its real convictions, dared ignore the ever-present threat to its continuity in power posed by the desperation of the unemployed and the miserable. It was in the state's interest to maintain employment and, no less, to possess at all times such information as might be conducive to more effective support and control of industrial activity. Even under the July Monarchy, a regime noted for its scorn for state intervention, the collection of vital and economic statistics by public officials served this function, and semiofficial inquiries, such as those of Villermé and Benoiston de Châteauneuf, were encouraged.

More importantly, despite the juridical changes effected by the Revolution, the feudal conception of the respective rights and responsibilities of master and man was not forgotten. Paternalism was a hallmark of many in the new entrepreneurial class. Theirs was both a genuine and interested benevolence. It was genuine in that they accepted the literal truth of paternal obligation, and interested in their recognition that the most prosperous

14. The academy published only a single joint report by Benoiston de Châteauneuf and Villermé, "Rapport d'un voyage fait dans les cinq départements de la Bretagne, pendant les années 1840 et 1841, d'après les ordres de l'Académie des sciences morales et politiques," *Mémoires de l'Académie des sciences morales et politiques* 4 (1844): 635–734; and two notes by Benoiston de Châteauneuf, "Communication sur l'industrie en Bretagne," *Seánces et travaux de l'Académie des sciences morales et politiques* 2 (1842): 77–85, 189–99, which concluded that Brittany simply had no modern industry.

enterprise was the one that retained diligent, healthy, and trusting workers. It was surely this mood of benevolent paternalism that moved many manufacturers—as a group the most secretive of men—to cooperate freely with an outsider as he explored in depth the condition of labor in their factories. They found in Villermé a shared set of values, at the outset realizing no more than did their visitor that his report, the *Tableau*, could be read and was read more as an indictment than as a neutral description or justification of their endeavors. Faced with a new world, that of factory labor and industrial town, and acutely sensitive to the new problems these presented, Villermé began his inquiries with optimism and ended them with pessimism. He had expected and thought he had found only transitory difficulties of industrialization. His studies intimated, however, that such such solace was too easily taken; and February of 1848 convinced him that prior certainties, including his own, had lost their standing. His career had effectively run its course when the industrial development of France entered a truly revolutionary phase under the Second Empire.

The Structure and Strategy of the *Tableau*

Villermé's purpose was to explore as closely as possible the totality of conditions affecting labor in the textile trades. His inquiry thus embraced inspection of working conditions, housing, and diet; the relation of income to expenditure; relations between master and man, woman, and child; and all matters pertaining to the physical and moral well-being or corruption of the workers. His endeavor was both an industrial inquest and a study in public health conditions.

The *Tableau* consists of two largely independent volumes.[15] The first presents in a systematic manner Villermé's observations on the conduct of the manufacturing processes in the major textile trades and on the condition of the workers in each separate trade and locale. These splendidly detailed descriptions are followed by a volume of general considerations in which the worker's condition is portrayed, the reasons for his or her difficulties are exposed, and modest remedies are put forward. Volume 1 represents the inquiry itself; volume 2 is in effect a treatise that ties politi-

---

15. The only extensive discussion of this work is provided by Hilde Rigaudias-Weiss, *Les enquêtes ouvrières en France entre 1830 et 1848* (Paris: P.U.F., 1936). Yves Tyl provides a brief description in his introduction to the much abridged reimpression of the *Tableau* published in the series "10-18" (Paris: Union générale d'éditions, 1971). Volume 2 of the *Tableau* was first published as "Rapport à l'Académie des sciences morales et politiques sur l'état physique et moral des ouvriers employés dans les fabriques de soie, de coton et de laine," *Mémoires de l'Académie des sciences morales et politiques* 2 (1839): 329–594.

cal economy to concrete social and, in this case, industrial foundations.

Following a regular format Villermé discussed in order the conditions of labor in each of the major textile manufacturing centers of eastern and northern France and parts of the Midi. A model for this discussion was given at the outset. Upper Alsace, embracing the industrial towns of Mulhouse, Sainte-Marie-aux-Mines, Guebwiller, Thann, Colmar, and their environs, was always his favored locale. The condition of its workers he held to be representative of the general condition, but, more importantly, Alsace offered solid indications of the improvements in that condition made possible by the intervention of concerned masters. The size of the working population was first ascertained and, if possible, its proportion to total population determined. The distribution of workers by industry, age, and place of origin was also established as far as was possible. Hours of labor were recorded with particular care, for Villermé thought that excessive work, coupled with inadequate wages, was an important source of the rampant disease and debilitation among the working population.

Lodgings were inspected with care.[16] Villermé noted available furnishings (usually meager and in dilapidated and filthy condition), adequacy of heat and ventilation (both usually deficient), and distance from place of work. The latter, he observed, was a matter of considerable significance. Given the long hours at work—usually fourteen to sixteen hours per day, six days a week—it was a great advantage to live within a short walking distance of the factory. Yet such housing was in short supply, was usually of very inferior quality, and had the highest rents, as landlords and speculators took advantage of a choice situation. To obtain somewhat more adequate lodgings at a more reasonable rate the worker had to move to the fringes of the town or into the country. What he gained in lower rent he lost in time and, no less importantly, in frequent and inescapable exposure to the elements. Villermé often remarked the absence of umbrellas on the streets and at the entrance to the factory: innumerable workers simply could not afford even the most elementary protection against inclement weather.

A reiterated theme was the relation between average individual and family income and the necessary expenses of the working group. In good times, with regular employment, and without illness a worker and his family could make ends meet. A family's position was nevertheless extraordinarily precarious. The slightest interruption of work, of husband, wife, or children and for any reason, could easily plunge the entire family into destitution. Savings on the whole were nonexistent. Given the seemingly inevitable recurrence of crises in the new industrial system, Villermé

---

16. The following several paragraphs are based on volume 1 of Villermé's *Tableau*.

realized that inadequate income more often than not was the root cause of a vast host of misfortunes, including illness and early death, that befell the working classes.

Conditions within the factory were also examined with care. These included the presumed risks of the production processes themselves and, more disturbing still, the moral corruption the new factory system seemed to encourage. Close and unsupervised proximity of the sexes, often at a young age, merely ensured an unparalleled promiscuity within and probably without the factory. Illegitimacy was high in the larger and most rapidly growing industrial towns; the recruiting network for Parisian prostitutes appeared to find abundant candidates in these same towns.

On his travels Villermé repeatedly noted these and related problems in each of the major textile regions. Cotton, the most highly mechanized of the textile industries and hence the leader in factory organization and large-scale enterprise, was also the leader in degradation of its workers. If conditions were bad in Alsace, where the masters at least exercised some benevolence, and always precarious in the Rouen fabrique, they were plainly catastrophic for the lower levels of cotton worker in Lille. Villermé's vivid portrayal of the degradation, drunkenness, and transcience of life of the poor *lillois* cotton worker has come to symbolize the worst aspects of the entire process of industrialization in France.

The woolen industry fared somewhat better. In 1840 domestic weaving was still widespread and made a useful contribution to the income of predominantly agricultural workers. Where the factory had been introduced or where the various manufacturing processes as well as labor had been concentrated, conditions tended to degenerate. Rheims, an ancient woolen center, suffered in this respect. One of its chief products, besides woolen goods, appeared to be an undue proportion of the prostitutes entering the Paris trade. On the other hand, the woolen industry provided Villermé with his chief example of how industrial affairs should be conducted so as to assure the health and good conduct of the worker and the profit of the entrepreneur. The manufacturers of Sedan, who specialized in the production of heavy woolens, were collectively active in repressing the worker's cardinal vice, alcoholism, and in assuring an elementary education to young children. Their vigorous paternalism Villermé praised highly.[17]

Generally speaking, Villermé found conditions in the Lyons fabrique to be favorable. The industry was largely devoted, however, to production of luxury goods and also faced strained relations between its entrepreneurs and producers. As a consequence its affairs fluctuated widely. Tensions were high, and social protest was not infrequent and occasionally violent.

17. Ibid., 1: 258–60.

Besides offering a detailed description of the fabrique, Villermé's primary concern appears to have been to persuade his middle- and upper-class readers that the canuts were not by nature violent men and women and that now the industrial situation in this singular city was again orderly and no longer a cause for anxiety (his visits followed the riots of the early 1830s).

The *Tableau* explored more broadly than perhaps its author intended or realized. On the one hand, Villermé cried out against the excesses and abuses of the new factory system and gave unprecedented force to his warning by reciting the appalling conditions into which a large and increasing portion of the working class had fallen. On the other hand, his indictment was greatly tempered by a general approval of the factory system and by keen enthusiasm for the vast productive potential of mechanization. It was not, he held, the factory system itself but abuses within it, brought on by greed, neglect, or simple ignorance, that was condemned.

But whatever the tensions and contradictions in the author's analysis, matters to be explored more fully below, he had no doubt at all that a high price was being paid for industrial progress and that the costs fell disproportionately upon the worker and his family. Since 1820 Villermé and his associates had been tracing the differential mortality that characterized the rich and the poor. That analysis, heretofore indirect and largely at the mercy of whatever data was available, was now applied directly to the working population of the factory and of the domestic system. The methods employed remained the same: visual inspection, oral interrogation, and use of the numerical method. The results obtained, however, possessed a comprehensiveness and a decisiveness that quite transcended all that had gone before. These results, moreover, were no longer confined to the pages of the medical press but were broadcast in a separate volume designed to reach a wide audience. Not least, Villermé's new study was published under the auspices of the Academy of Moral and Political Sciences, thereby receiving the implicit approval of a public body whose members were generally favorable to industrialization and many of whom were active in the direction of affairs of state, including those pertaining to economic development. The *Tableau* gave voice to a physician and political economist within an intellectual and social community whose values and ambitions he largely shared.

Health; or, the Life and Death of the Worker

"I have heard much," Villermé wrote, " . . . of the insalubrity of factories, particularly of the cotton mills. Let us examine the charges thus lev-

elled against them."[18] With these calm words began one of the most singular chapters in the *Tableau*. Villermé here laid bare the essential public
health aspects of an investigation whose purpose was to reconcile humanitarian concern for the worker with defense of the economic interests
of the entrepreneur. Intrinsic to Villermé's objective was an effort to redi-
rect attention from the hazards of the factory to those of society at large.

The major presumed perils of cotton manufacture were four: a vitiated
or inadequate supply of air; dust; noxious chemicals; and excessive heat
and moisture. The threat posed by poor ventilation was deceptive. Villermé claimed that, despite appearances, air within the mill was constantly
renewed. It was in no way comparable to the stagnant atmosphere that
accumulated in winter in the foul *caves* of spinners and weavers working
on the domestic system. In this respect at least, as well as in the fact that
the mill was regularly heated (albeit usually excessively so), work in the
cotton factory could be regarded as a positive contribution to health.[19]

The cotton mill offered, moreover, an abundance of air to its workers.
Since the eighteenth century, bemused by the discovery of the singular
importance of pure air to all vital processes, persons charged with construction and management had become obsessed with aeration and ventilation in structures which were to hold large numbers of persons within a
confined space. The problem was particularly explored with regard to naval construction and theater, prison, and hospital design.[20] Standards,
often arbitrary, were devised and used as a guide for both construction and
comparison. In French military hospitals of the 1830s the wards were to
offer each sick or wounded inmate a minimum of 20 m^3 of air; this suf-
ficed, Villermé noted, for persons who must pass a full 24 hours per day
in that space. Now, the volume of air available in the cotton mills, he
observed, drawing often on his own measurements, usually exceeded this.
That available in the spinning halls (supposedly the least healthful area of
the factory) ranged from 20 m^3 to 68 m^3 per worker and in most cases
exceeded 40 m^3. In the mechanical weaving rooms this figure varied between 17 m^3 and 26 m^3; in the printing shops 16–30m^3 of air were available for each worker. In addition, Villermé did not fail to note that factories, unlike hospitals, were usually occupied only 15–16 hours per day.[21]
The individual hand weaver, confined to his own cramped quarters, might

18. Ibid., 2: 203.

19. Ibid., pp. 203–5.

20. See A. E. Clark-Kennedy, *Stephen Hales, D.D., F.R.S.: An Eighteenth-Century Biography* (Cambridge: Cambridge University Press, 1929), pp. 151–69, 189–207; Christo-
pher Lloyd and Jack L. S. Coulter, *Medicine and the Navy, 1200–1900*, vol. 3, *1714–1815*
(Edinburgh and London: Livingstone, 1961), pp. 72–77.

21. Villermé, *Tableau*, 2: 205–7.

enjoy 12–15 m³ of air, or considerably less if his room were small or others were working with him.

The charge of inadequate aeration was thus easily dismissed, at least with regard to a vast majority of factory hands. The threat of chemical substances was put aside even more readily. Neither the grease and oil employed on the machines and from them dripping onto and spreading into the factory structure nor the various glues applied to the threads by the weavers nor even the mordants and dyes used in the print works caused any apparent disturbance. Villermé's words regarding this problem are especially revealing of contemporary etiological thinking:

> It is claimed that these odors and the substance from which they ema-
> nate exert a harmful influence upon persons who breathe them in. But
> if you look at these men and women, put questions to them and to
> physicians and others who keep an eye on the workers, you will soon
> be convinced that they are never inconvenienced by these substances.
> It is rare, in fact, that they are even aware of those odors that are so
> striking to newcomers [to the factory]; they would, instead, notice
> much more their absence if, by some impossibility, these smells could
> be stopped immediately.[22]

In keeping with miasmatic doctrine, odor was either a poisonous influence or, more likely, a sign of the presence of some pernicious substance. Chadwick's was largely an etiology of the nose: smell to him was *ipso facto* evidence of filth, and in filth lay the source of disease and sanitary mayhem. His view was a common one in the period before 1860. As has been noted above, Villermé accepted but did not insist upon the miasmatic theory. The present case is important in this regard. Although definite miasmatic elements seemed present within the workplace, Villermé would not attribute deterioration of health to them. Not only was the miasmatic theory here seemingly irrelevant, but an assumed peril of cotton manufacture was rendered unimportant. The poor physical condition of the worker must have other causes.

Two conditions of cotton manufacture were deemed serious threats to health. For one thing, the excessive moisture and heat necessary for certain manufacturing operations—notably, the spinning of finer threads, printing, and various finishing operations—created exceedingly insalubrious working conditions. In the printing, sizing, and finishing rooms temperatures ranged from 75° F to over 100° F; spinning was conducted at temperatures between 60° and 80° F.[23] Steam was the common means of heating and was also used to maintain the exceptionally high humidity that

22. Ibid., p. 208.
23. Ibid., pp. 216–18.

production required. Workers labored in various stages of undress (a point that received appropriate moral comment) and were constantly drenched with sweat. Their shock was great when they returned to less elevated temperatures, particularly in winter. Such workers had a high rate of colds and chest complaints. Older persons were rarely found in these occupations: they could not stand the conditions imposed. In mechanical spinning the need for great physical strength was greatly reduced, and this operation thus became predominantly the preserve of women and children. It was also generally the lowest-paid occupation in cotton manufacture. Such workers were thus doubly at risk, and not unexpectedly their mortality was the highest among the occupations for which Villermé collected data in the great fabrique of Mulhouse.

Also dangerous was the initial preparation of the cotton fibers. These operations involved much handling and beating of the raw cotton and generated a voluminous and unceasing cloud of dust and fluff. Without qualification Villermé considered this atmosphere a very deadly one. The dust and fluff were inhaled, and a cough developed. Unless the victim quickly and permanently left the occupation, a "pthisis," or *pneumonie cotoneuse*, usually appeared and death followed. Both master and workers were well aware of the peril. The former occasionally paid a premium for this work, and the latter arranged among themselves to rotate labor in the beating halls. With the introduction of carding and beating machinery, two changes occurred: women and children began to dominate the operation, and the utterly foul conditions that surrounded hand preparation were diminished. To Villermé the event was indeed a celebration of the benefits of mechanization and its necessary role in the advance of civilization. "The invention of these machines and their application in the woolen and cotton industries, particularly the latter, has been," he happily declared, "of great benefit to the workers and a great economy in the manufacturing process, for in most spinning mills they have allowed the elimination of the hand-pickers, who were very numerous, and diminished in significant degree the numbers of workers employed in beating."[24] The entrepreneur reduced his costs, the worker's life was preserved, and industry prospered. All of this was made possible by a machine, a prime agent not only of profit but also of public health. This advantage was gained primarily by placing distance between a large number of workers, previously employed

---

24. Ibid., p. 213. Dust long remained a serious problem in the manufacture of cotton goods; see James Wheatley, "Manufacture of Cotton," in *The Dangerous Trades: The Historical, Social, and Legal Aspects of Industrial Occupations as Affecting Health, by a Number of Experts*, ed. Thomas Oliver (New York: Dutton, 1902), pp. 702–23. Villermé also felt the replacement of hand weaving by machine weaving of cotton and linen to be a great contribution to improved public health (*Tableau*, 2:238–43).

in preparation of the raw cotton, and a dangerous industrial procedure. The argument was never translated to the level of the individual worker. Those who continued in such employment obviously also continued to be exposed to risk. But their numbers were fewer, and the overall vice was diminished.

Health conditions in the woolen industry appeared to be even more favorable. This trade, particularly in the form it preserved from the period before extensive mechanization, was charged with exposing various of its workers to filthy and thus unhealthy conditions. Initial sorting and washing of the raw wool seemed particularly hazardous. Villermé once again reviewed the charges, finding, not unexpectedly, that the hazards had been exaggerated and that the woolen industry was a relatively healthy one.[25]

Beating of unwashed or dyed woolstuffs did raise dust and thus contribute to the indisposition of the workers. Wool pickers often worked in water or in very humid areas; rheumatisms were their common fate. Virtually all other specialties, however, posed few threats. The production process did not require high temperatures or humidity. Aeration in the factories was at least as good as that in cotton (domestic workers, again, were at the mercy of conditions in their own home or workplace, commonly one and the same building or room).

Salaries in the woolen industry seemed somewhat higher than those in cotton. Women were widely employed, often in the most menial tasks; but in general, children entering the works were some two to three years older than children entering the cotton industry. This to Villermé signified an important advance in civilization. Such children were stronger and more alert; their chances of survival were consequently better, and they promised to be more effective hands in the factory. While admitting, therefore, that certain of the manufacturing processes in woolen production were hazardous, Villermé portrayed an industry that caused very little direct harm to most of its employees. Woolen workers suffered, to be sure, but this was due, not to conditions within the factory, but to hard external economic and social realities which governed the manufacture and marketing of all goods, including woolens.

The same conclusion applied to the silk industry.[26] Except for the preparation of the raw silk drawn from the cocoon, the entire industry seemed not less and perhaps somewhat more salubrious than other branches of textile manufacture. Silk preparation was a particularly foul affair. The work was hot, wet, and filthy; and those employed at the task, mostly older women, were in markedly bad health. The dust that arose from the

25. Villermé, *Tableau*, 2:223–32.
26. Ibid., pp. 233–38.

dried cocoons, a dust uncontrolled in the workplace, was recognized by all as being uncommonly deadly, leading often to chest irritations, serious illness, and death. But with this exception duly noted, the primary threat faced by men and women in the manufacture of silk seemed largely external to the productive operations themselves.

This entire preliminary discussion of the presumed perils of manufacture was conducted in qualitative, not numerical, terms and no doubt for good reason. Accurate numerical data pertaining to the morbidity and mortality of the factory worker had yet to be collected. Indeed, clear methodological principles and appropriate convictions also had yet to be created. Public inquiry into the private affairs of the entrepreneur was, despite the ever imperious claims of the central administration in France, usually impossible. Furthermore, entrepreneurial records might define the economic condition of a particular undertaking but surely would offer little information—and probably no information at all—regarding the physical condition of those employed therein. Public records bearing on matters of health were collected only after the fact, since it was death that was recorded; and their original purpose had more to do with problems of national strength as measured by population than with matters of public health. These records, whether parochial, municipal, or departmental, noted death, marriage, and, when properly kept, birth. There was no continuing public record of sickness. Using such limited materials Villermé nonetheless attempted to bolster his argument by introducing numerical consideration of the risks to life of employment in the factory. His discussion of differential mortality in the cotton fabrique of Mulhouse is by far the most familiar single inquiry he conducted.

The first task was to assemble the needed data. Upon request, he obtained an abstract of the bills of mortality of Mulhouse for the years 1823– 34 inclusive.[27] Villermé was confident, although no tests were conducted, that the bills had been accurately kept throughout the period in question and that they could be used for analytic purposes with real confidence. The bills listed decedents in Mulhouse by name, age, sex, and profession. For deceased married women the profession of the husband was given; for children or unmarried persons the profession of the parent(s) was recorded. The task once again was to explore health by means of death— the data permitted no other course.

The numerical problems thus presented were formidable. Only death was recorded. No census had been conducted in Mulhouse for some 40 years. Not only was the overall population unknown, but the size of spe-

27. The assembled data are presented ibid., pp. 375–86, and discussed ibid., pp. 247– 57.

cific populations at risk in the various professions was altogether beyond knowing. The age structure of the population was also unavailable. Perhaps worst of all, Mulhouse industry fed on foreign workers pouring in from Germany and Switzerland, and there existed no indications whatso-ever of the size of these migrations. Villermé, as he well recognized, was thus prohibited from utilizing death rates. In their place he offered a comparison of average age at death for the community at large and for each of the recorded professions. As this figure was determined for a given locality (whose population admittedly was constantly renewed from outside) and for a common period of 12 years, the ensuing results could at the very least be suggestive of the relative mortality among the diverse professions of Mulhouse. As always, greatest force and perhaps greatest truth would be derived from the extreme cases. Comparison with other communities and other times was not, wisely, attempted.

The extremes thus recorded were truly startling. At birth "life expectancy" (*vie probable approximative*) of cotton spinners was but 1¼ years; children of the entrepreneurial class and of commercial leaders could expect to attain, on average, 28 years of age (see Table 8.2).[28] Even after the dangers of infancy and childhood had passed, children of spinners and weavers died on average at a far younger age than did children of the more prosperous segments of society. At age 4, life expectancies of the two groups were separated by some 20 years (28 years in the case of the spinners alone). Even in full maturity this great disproportion continued: the life expectancy of spinners at age 20 was less than half that of the upper economic levels of Mulhouse society. Because the number of deaths re-

---

28. This table provides a summary of data presented in much greater detail in "Supplément I," ibid., pp. 375–86. The remarkably low "life expectancy"—an expression not to be equated with modern use of that term—of children of cotton spinners was based upon 140 live births reported between 1823 and 1834 (presumably there were more, perhaps many more, births than those reported), of whom but 61 survived at age 2 (ibid., p. 386); for children of manufacturers, managers, and merchants, of 295 live births reported for the same period 204 were alive at age 2 (ibid., p. 377). The table was prepared by a M. Demonferrand of Mulhouse. Population figures for each profession were not stated, and age distribution within each age group remained unspecified. William Farr devoted much effort to exhibiting the shortcomings of these procedures as practiced by early English statisticians and to constructing reliable life tables. See John M. Eyler, *Victorian Social Medicine: The Ideas and Methods of William Farr* (Baltimore: Johns Hopkins University Press, 1979), pp. 66–96, esp. pp. 70–71, 74, 81. Demonferrand's table surely overdramatizes child mortality among the lower orders; no doubt that mortality was disproportionately high but so, too, was the number of children in these groups. Without knowledge of the age structure of the various populations at risk, no firm conclusions can be drawn regarding differential morality. In the text, my task is to portray Villermé's numerical but especially sociomedical uses of available data; I do not propose to correct his reasoning (or reject it because beyond correction).

corded was both small and enormously varied, Villermé himself cautioned
against using the figures given in this table or in the full presentation of
the data from which it was abstracted for purposes of more precise comparison of mortality in the different social orders.

Certain general facts were nonetheless obvious. The "life expectancy"
of the spinner and the weaver was short not only in comparison with persons in more favored economic stations but with that of the municipality
at large. At birth this difference was just over 6 years (see Table 8.2). At
age 10 it was 21 years for spinners and 12 years for weavers; at age 30 the
situation had scarcely improved, the spread now being more than 13 years
for spinners and 10 years for weavers. Worse yet was the comparison
between "life expectancy" at given ages in the entire department (Haut-
Rhin) and in these fatal professions. At birth the children of spinners could
expect a life only one-eleventh as long as that of the average child in the
department; at age 10 "life expectancy" among the latter was still almost
three times that of the former (see Table 8.2). These figures also demon-

Table 8.2. "Life expectancy" (*vie probable approximative*), by age and profession in
Mulhouse and the department of Haut-Rhin, 1814–1823

Profession	Additional years expected to live at					
	birth	age 1	age 4	age 10	age 20	age 30
Manufacturers, managers, merchants	28	43	46	42	34	30
Domestics (N = 93)	21	37	35	32	23	18
Factory workers (trade						
not specified)	18	20	21	28	33	30
Bakers and millers	12	39	43	40	34	26
Tailors	12	36	39	40	32	28
Printers of "indian" cottons	10	40	47	45	38	31
Day-laborers	9	20	33	34	32	26
Masons	4	29	37	35	29	22
Carpenters	4	28	24	30	24	25
Shoemakers	3	31	40	38	31	24
Engravers	3	28	39	35	27	21
Cabinetmakers	3	20	39	38	29	25
Factory foremen (N = 80)	2½	27	35	36	28	23
Locksmiths/ironworkers	1¾	14	23	22	17	13
Weavers	1½	19	28	26	20	17
Factory spinners	1¼	11	18	17	15	13
All professions						
In the town	7½	30	40	38	32	26½
In the department (1814–33)	13½	39	46½	45½	38	31

SOURCE: L. R. Villermé, *Tableau de l'état physique et moral des ouvriers employés dans
les manufactures de coton, de laine et de soie*, 2 vols. (Paris: Jules Renouard, 1840), 2:251.

	A LA NAISSANCE.	A 1 AN.	A 4 ANS.	A 10 ANS.	A 20 ANS.	A 30 ANS.
Dans la classe des manufacturiers, fabricans, directeurs d'usine, négocians, drapiers, etc.	ans. 28	ans. 43	ans. 46	ans. 42	ans. 34	ans. 30
— domestiques (93 observat.).	21	37	35	32	23	18
— ouv. de fabriques, sans indication du métier........	18	20	21	28	33	30
— boulangers et meuniers....	12	39	43	40	34	26
— tailleurs d'habits.........	12	36	39	40	32	28
— simples imprim. d'indiennes.	10	40	47	45	38	31
— journaliers et manœuvres...	9	20	33	34	32	26
— maçons	4	29	37	35	29	22
— charpentiers	4	28	24	30	24	25
— cordonniers.............	3	31	40	38	31	24
— graveurs.................	3	28	39	35	27	21
— menuisiers...............	3	20	39	38	29	25
— contre-maîtres de manufact. (80 observat. seulement)..	2 1/2	27	35	36	28	23
— serruriers................	1 3/4	14	23	22	17	13
— simples tisserands	1 1/2	19	28	26	20	17
— simples ouvriers des filatures.	1 1/4	11	18	17	15	13

Lorsque c'est pour :

	A LA NAISSANCE.	A 1 AN.	A 4 ANS.	A 10 ANS.	A 20 ANS.	A 30 ANS.
La population générale de la ville.	7 1/2	30	40	38	32	26 1/2
Et le département entier (1814-1833)...............	13 1/2	39	46 1/2	45 1/2	38	31

Original presentation of Table 8.2

strated once again what Villermé and a host of others had long claimed. The manufacturing town or city exerted a profound and negative influence upon population, an influence that was most strongly felt in the younger years.

Lastly, it is evident from Table 8.2 that if "life expectancy" at birth was indeed lowest for children of cotton weavers and spinners, their condition was by no means unique. While children of workers in other trades exhibited better life expectancies, the differences between them were not great. Assuming the validity of the general tendency, if not individual accuracy, of these figures, a notable conclusion emerged. Life among the new factory workers was difficult indeed, and children in particular paid the highest price. But workers in other professions also lost their children in superabundance. It seemed evident that conditions within the factory were not the crucial determinant of this mortality. Misery was a mighty company, and the children of workers in trades as yet remote from the new industrial organization (carpentry, masonry, metal work, common labor, tanning, and lead manufacture) also suffered severely. Here, as before, all signs pointed to socioeconomic causes of excessive mortality.

Was all of this analysis—none of it new in kind—merely a continued polemic whose purpose was the exoneration of a vastly augmented system of production? Villermé thought not. He was indeed fortunate in finding a vociferous antagonist to the right. Andrew Ure, Britain's impassioned philosopher of manufacture, had no use for critics of the factory system. In its defense he ventured certain audacious claims that won from the usually generous Villermé a uniquely sarcastic review. Ure asserted that factories, far from harming their inmates, preserved health. They offered warmth and shelter in the cold season. He thought it obvious, moreoever, that health was usually better in the towns than in the country. Admittedly, children of the factory worker might lack the rosy glow of those raised in the country, but unlike the latter, Ure claimed, they experienced less sickness.

Ure was engaged in a furious debate concerning the condition of factory labor in Britain.[29] Medical opinion was cited by some to justify the new system and was used by others against it. Villermé regretted not having visited Britain, since he could not speak from firsthand observation regarding the contested issues. But, when opinion reigned, he knew that it was better "to seek truth from another source," namely, numerical evidence.[30] Exploiting the published abstracts of the English census of 1831 he once again set forth a comparison of mortality in the agricultural and industrial regions of Britain; these data had previously served to estimate mortality in the marshlands (see above, Chapter 7).

Listing the English counties by proportion of deaths at a given age to total deaths, Villermé pointed out that for the years 1813–30 inclusive, death came earlier and in greatest number in the industrial districts.[31] In agricultural Hereford, for example, of 10,000 deaths, 2,801 occurred through age 10 and 4,826 through age 40. In industrial Lancaster, these

29. Andrew Ure, *The Philosophy of Manufactures; or, An Exposition of the Scientific, Moral, and Commercial Economy of the Factory System* (London: Charles Knight, 1835; reprinted, New York, 1967), pp. 374–403. See E. P. Thompson, *The Making of the English Working Class* (New York: Random House, 1966), pp. 189–212, 314–49.

30. Villermé, *Tableau*, 2:265.

31. The following figures are cited from a list ibid., pp. 267–68.

rates were vastly increased: of 10,000 deaths, 4,852 occurred before age 11 and 6,963 before age 41. The county of York presented equally startling contrasts. In the north, of 10,000 deaths, 2,847 occurred through age 10 and 5,044 through age 40; in the west the figures were 4,381 and 6,459. Now, as John Rickman had observed with regard to "difference[s] that divide the two parts [north and west] of the county of York," they are neighboring areas and everything is "similar between them—climate, diet, clothing, housing and so on—except this: in the one there is a great amount of manufacture and in the other none at all."[32] Whence it ensued that "life expectancy" at birth in the industrialized West Riding of Yorkshire was 19 years, whereas in the rural north it was 39. Lifespan in the English towns showed equal differences, although, whatever the character of the town, it was on the average shorter than in the country. "Life expectancy" in mercantile Bristol, a healthy community, was 29 years; in Norwich, a major market town, it was 21; in Birmingham, a growing city of mixed manufacturing character, it had fallen to 15. But in the great textile towns, life expectancy plunged, reaching a low of 7 in both Nottingham and Leeds.

Now then, Villermé inquired, "what are we to believe of the assertions of M. Ure" when we have cast our eyes on these figures?[33] Certainly the Englishmen's claim that the factory system had brought about an unqualified improvement in the health and longevity of the industrial worker stood refuted. The most elementary numerical analysis—and Villermé's analysis offered nothing more than that, in addition to the fallacious notion of "life expectancy" that was employed—demonstrated a regular conjunction of place and elevated mortality. The "place" consistently in question was that of the major manufacturing districts, not least those whose enterprises had adopted comprehensive mechanization and the factory system. Nothing seemed more absurd or vicious to Villermé than Ure's contention. How dared one speak of a salubrious Leeds when "life expectancy" there was as low as or worse than that displayed by Mulhouse?

For Villermé the important point was what may be called the epidemiological conclusion. Contrary to Ure's assertions and consistent with his own data from Alsace and with that provided by the English census, excessive mortality was found to be characteristic of the manufacturing regions. Moreover, that mortality generally reached its peak in districts where the factory system for textile production had made greatest progress. Why then, it was inevitably asked, did this conjunction of locality and mortality exist? Throughout his entire scientific career Villermé had

32. Quoted by Villermé, ibid., p. 269.
33. Ibid., p. 268.

dealt in one form or another with this problem. Advancing now in the *Tableau* to a definitive assessment and resolution of the question, he was brought to make a decisive choice between explanatory, indeed, etiological alternatives. Whether the cause was the factory and the conditions prevailing therein or the miserable lodgings and diet which uncertain and inadequate wages guaranteed, sickness, disability, and death ensued and all too frequently. The suffering worker and his family would probably not have appreciated the distinction but Villermé did. He was obliged to defend his conclusion in explicit and forceful manner. While factory conditions themselves were not entirely exonerated, economic and social practices characteristic of the manufacturing sector were identified as being the principal offender, and the persons responsible for these conditions, whether master and worker, were also identified and condemned. The purpose of the argument was to indicate that the sociomedical peril was not intrinsic to the productive process but was a human creation and presumably remediable.

The Socioeconomic Origin of Death and Disease

Inadequate income, not insalubrious working conditions, was the heart of the problem. "I shall insist no more," Villermé promised (it was an unkept promise), "on proving that the workplace is not exposed to these presumed causes of insalubrity. One is singularly mistaken in attributing to the workplace the diseases that are principally produced by forced labor, lack of rest, carelessness, inadequate food of poor quality, and habits of improvidence, drunkenness, and debauchery; to put it all in a single phrase, by salaries below the real needs [of life]."[34] Thus it was that the various professions were understood to act only in an "indirect [and] mediate" manner on the health of the worker and his or her family.[35]

The matter was best discussed in terms of the then still rudimentary notion of the standard of living. By 1840 three generations of French social observers had focused their attention upon the general issue of the conditions of existence. Montesquieu had sought to determine the nature of the state and the conditions that assured its prosperity and security. He was led to look closely at population and the physical conditions of its existence. Such knowledge, he held, was essential to the legislator who wished to determine which laws were most appropriate to a given time, place, and nation. Genuine harmony and happiness might thereby be assured. The generation of the Revolution, committed to more active me-

34. Ibid., p. 209.
35. Ibid., p. 258.

liorism, was persuaded that man was indefinitely malleable and that correct understanding and intelligent manipulation of the physical and moral conditions of his existence necessarily led to social, even economic, justice and greater happiness. Villermé's perspective was similar because of shared premises, but his outlook was less sanguine. The issue created by the factory system and manufacturing town was no longer the revolutionary regeneration of the citizen but simply the rescue and restoration of a degraded and rapidly increasing segment of the population.

The situation was not promising. Under the most favorable conditions a working family might hope to make ends meet and perhaps discover at week's end a small surplus. Unhappily, such favorable cases were all too rare, and a family's situation often moved swiftly from very modest comfort through bare subsistence to outright destitution. Wages varied with the age, sex, and profession of the worker and were also subject to sharp fluctuations due to disturbances in the marketplace. Prices also varied, often dramatically. The not infrequent conjunction of rising prices—above all, that of bread—and diminished wages or reduced employment (and often both) was the source of much suffering amongst the working population and of long-standing dread to the government.

Villermé, as might be expected, elected to discuss the matter in numerical terms. The diversity of wages and temporal and regional variations in the cost of living made the analysis particularly difficult. Moreover, since systematic collection of authentic economic statistics was the exception and not the rule, each investigator needed to start anew and for the most part to collect his own data. Much of the descriptive first volume of the *Tableau* was devoted to reporting comparative wages and estimates of family expenditures throughout the various textile trades; a résumé of this data and an appreciation of its meaning introduced the argument of the second volume.

From the detailed account prepared by a M.C.★★★, Villermé prepared the abstract shown in Table 8.3 of principal daily expenditures by various workers in the cotton industries in Rouen. The figures indicate that daily expenditure for necessities by the average male worker was minimally 90 centimes and ranged up to 1 franc 4 centimes; for a working woman comparable figures were 86 centimes and 1 franc 7 centimes; for a working child aged 6, the minimum was 84 centimes and the maximum 90 centimes; and for the young worker between ages 12 and 16, 92 centimes. Such spending was restricted to the absolute necessities of life. It left no margin for diversion, savings, luxuries, or debauchery, the latter being in Villermé's mind always the most terrible threat to a balanced family budget. It should be compared, therefore, with the estimated average income of each category of worker in the Rouen fabrique. This information is

presented in Table 8.4. These figures represent full employment and reflect only the upper echelon of the work force. Spinners and day laborers,
both "so poorly paid," were excluded from the table. Their average daily
income in 1833 and 1834 was as follows: male, 1 franc 25 centimes to 2
franc; female, 75 centimes to 1 france 50 centimes; children (undifferentiated by age), 50 centimes to 1 franc.[36]

Table 8.3. Average daily expenditures of workers in the cotton fabrique of Rouen
(in centimes)

Worker	Food	Clothing	Laundry	Housing	Total min.	max.
Man	.70–.75	.09–.15	.03–.04	.08–.10	.90–1.04	
Woman	.65–.69	.07–.17	.05–.11	.09–.10	.86–1.07	
Child of 6	.69–.72	.10–.11	.05–.07	—	.84– .90	
Young worker (12 to 16)	.78	.09	.05	—	.92	

SOURCE: Villermé, *Tableau*, 2:22, n.1.

Table 8.4. Average daily income of workers in the cotton fabrique of Rouen

Adult male	2 francs
Adult female	1 franc
Child, age 8–12	45 centimes
Child, age 13–16	75 centimes

SOURCE: Villermé, *Tableau*, 2:11.

Given this information it is little wonder that Villermé and contemporaries were anxious regarding the continued well-being of the honest and
diligent worker. Expenses continued whatever the economic climate. Income, however, fluctuated with the changing state of the economy. The
figures cited above represent the best possible situation: no sickness, no
reduced hours or unemployment, no diminution of hourly wages, no debauchery. Even so, it was not a happy situation. In general, Villermé observed, "A single man earned enough that he might make some savings,
but it is rare if a single woman earns a bare sufficiency or a child under
twelve earns enough even for his food."[37] A family with working children
fared somewhat better, but only because of the extra margin provided by
a regularly and fully employed father. Minimum daily expenditure by a
family of four (composed of members as listed in Table 8.3) was 3 francs
43 centimes; average daily income, 3 franc 75 centimes. If the second

36. Ibid., 1:144.
37. Ibid., 2:13.

child were a few years older and earning a wage, average family income would increase to 4 francs 20 centimes while expenditures rose only modestly if at all.

Children of working age were thus a major family asset; infants, a great and often catastrophic liability. As Villermé recognized, not all opposition to his campaign for the diminution of child labor in the factories came from employers desirous of numerous hands receiving the lowest possible wages. Work in the mills by all family members, however young, was commonly essential to family survival. Economic realities permitted no other course.

Comparisons of the kind that Villermé made were difficult to draw and were, especially when stated in such specific terms, quite rare in contemporary medical, economic, and statistical literature. Recently, there have been a number of studies of the standard of living during this period, particularly with regard to the evolving economic condition of the English working class. In dispute is whether or not the standard of living of the new factory worker in England was rising or falling in the century of rapid industrialization after 1750. A consensus has yet to be reached on this matter, and, it appears, even agreement on essential criteria for reaching such a conclusion still lies in the future.[38] Historians have scarcely begun analysis of the changing condition of the French worker.

The lived reality of the working family in the factories of England and of France was not, surely, markedly different. Periods of steady and full employment produced a modest family surplus; business depression transformed this quickly into a deficit. As savings were uncommon or inadequate, or both, a continued deficit easily reduced the family to utter destitution. Villermé's data for Rouen are further illuminated and his conclusions reaffirmed by comparable figures of the same period reported for cotton workers in Manchester. William Neild, mayor of Manchester, and an associate collected data regarding income and expenditure from 19 working-class families employed in the cotton mills of that city and nearby Dukinfield.[39] Their information regarding expenditure was highly detailed and probably unique for the period. Its import, however, was anything but unique. During the prosperous year 1836 all families but one enjoyed an income in excess of expenditure; in 1841, with industry in a depressed condition, 10 of the 19 families were "going back in the world." The cost

38. See Harold Perkin, *The Origins of Modern English Society* (London: Routledge and Kegan Paul, 1969), pp. 134–49; A. J. Taylor, "Introduction," in *The Standard of Living in Britain in the Industrial Revolution*, ed. A. J. Taylor (London: Methuen, 1975), pp. xi–lv.

39. William Neild, "Comparative Statement of the Income and Expenditure of Certain Families of the Working Classes in Manchester and Dukinfield, in the Years 1836 and 1841," *Journal of the Statistical Society* 4 (1841): 320–34.

of food in Manchester had risen sharply since 1836 (the price of flour was up 27 percent), and thus weekly expenditures for this necessity could only be increased. Yet family income had fallen sharply. Of course, those employed in the least remunerative manufacturing operations suffered most. Even in prosperous 1836 they had possessed little discretionary income (nicely denominated by Neild as funds "Left for instruction and the purchase of Manufactured Articles"). In 1841 in the seven families from Dukinfield each member was compelled to spend 88.5 percent of his income on food and cooking materials alone, a rise from 46.1 percent in 1836.[40] Neild offered little comment on these depressing figures.

Villermé indicated no knowledge of this description of labor in Lancaster, but he realized very well the implications of comparable if less comprehensive figures collected in France. It was not simply the poor but the poorest worker and his family who suffered first and most. Economic observers recognized that a

> commercial and industrial crisis . . . entails a lowering of wages; this is a well-known fact. But what is less well-known is this. The salary of the most poorly paid workers ordinarily scarcely drops at all if one looks only to the nominal sum paid for a day's work. In reality, however, it drops proportionately as much as that of the others and even more than that if one bears in mind the cost of necessities. The truth is that dismissals usually begin with the poorest workers. They are now employed only three or four days per week instead of six, or six to eight hours per day instead of thirteen; they are happy to have found work at all. Because these unfortunates in periods of industrial prosperity earn scarcely more than is rigorously necessary for their subsistence, the slightest reduction in wages reduces them to extreme indigence.[41]

The social level of persons affected by an economic crisis depended only on the intensity and duration of the business depression.

There was another reason for insufficient income. The worker might indeed be regularly and fully employed and even receive a generous wage, yet this was no assurance that his or her earnings would be directed to their proper purposes. Excessive labor and low wages were but the first part of the industrial problem; loose living was the other.

Alcoholism and prostitution took, of course, a direct and great toll of life.[42] But as part of his repeated insistence upon the corruption of *moeurs*

40. Calculated from data in Table 4, ibid., p. 333.
41. Villermé, *Tableau*, 2:18–19.
42. Ibid., pp. 34–54.

resulting from ill-regulated industrial development, Villermé also vigorously emphasized the fact that this corruption had the indirect but equally deadly effect of reducing family income. The young male worker gave little thought to the future and came to marriage penniless; the single woman, whose income was at best barely sufficient for her needs, foolishly wasted even that small sum on fashion. Once married, the husband, however moderate his drinking habits, soon began to pass too much time and spend far too much money at the cabaret, an institution whose mere mention usually left Villermé in a state of shocked breathlessness. In such situations, the only force giving coherence and hope to the working family was the mother. But when her children were infants they earned nothing and cost much; once they entered the factory close maternal supervision was lost and they contracted evil habits in the mills.

The moral condition of many, but by no means all, in the working class was thus abominable. It was due in part to their own inclination and opportunities. What was spent on alcohol and fancy dress (the worker dressed so well on Sundays, Villermé stated with real annoyance, that often the observer could not distinguish him and especially her from his or her social betters) could not be used to procure life's necessities.[43] A worker's income simply offered no margin for this irresponsible foolishness. But the fault did not lie entirely with the worker. Villermé placed a large, perhaps even the largest, share of the blame on the master. Sexual promiscuity began in the mill and did so because conditions favored it there. What did most manufacturers do to prevent it? Nothing: they failed to take even the first, simple, and inexpensive step of separating the sexes within the factory.[44] Moreover, most manufacturers made no effort to provide positive and negative checks to alcoholism. The latter Villermé viewed as a vice of the idle. It was important, therefore, that idle hands be either supervised or suppressed. During the week the remedy was work, always more work. Empty Sunday, however, was the day of greatest danger; religion had little if any dominion over this unruly horde. It was up to the masters themselves to create programs of instruction and diversion to fill the day.

The woolen manufacturers of Sedan had for a period introduced a definitive check on the problem of alcoholism. Acting collectively, they simply banished drunken workers from the mills; the latter either learned abstinence or remained without employment and income. Even more rigorous control, it was reported, was exercised by the masters of the new

43. Ibid., 1:363.
44. Ibid., 2: 51–53.

cotton works at Lowell, Massachusetts. Villermé admired certain of their provisions.[45] By far the most important feature at Lowell was the watchfulness maintained over the young female hands. Company housing was provided; strict rules of conduct were enforced; savings were encouraged. Not only could poor young women thus protect their honor and earn an industrial wage; they provided for their future by creating their own dowry. Villermé knew of all this only at secondhand and was careful to note that available descriptions might have exaggerated the benefits of the Lowell system. More depressing, however, was the strong possibility that such a plan was utterly inapplicable to the European situation. In Europe not only the masters but the workers competed fiercely with one another, the one for markets and the other for employment itself. In America, it appeared, there was a desperate shortage of hands: the golden west always beckoned to the dissatisfied, and the threat of destitution was not a part of one's daily experience. The nature of unemployment in America seemed incommensurate with the industrial and demographic situation of France and Europe.

It was Villermé's intention throughout his discussion to portray in vivid yet exact terms the miserable and often desperate condition of many workers in the textile trades. Only thus could the manufacturer and entrepreneur be jarred free from their blindness and unconcern. Increased awareness on the part of the master of the reality of the workers' condition was deemed an essential preliminary step to the amelioration of that condition. But Villermé by no means wanted to overstate his case. The lot of today's working man or woman was, he admitted, difficult, but it nonetheless represented a real and probably great improvement upon what had gone before.

"The suffering of the French people must have been dreadful one hundred and forty years ago," Villermé stated at the beginning of the second volume of the *Tableau*.[46] Despite low and uncertain wages, despite wretched housing and an inadequate diet, despite high mortality and moral degradation, the situation of the French working population was vastly better than it had been before the Revolution. Disproportionate "wealth and its privileges," he announced, were much reduced today. Anyone and everyone could now pretend to advance in the world. That very fact, itself the decisive sign of the tangible rewards of liberty, caused the poor who had yet to benefit from the new economic order to feel themselves "more wretched than ever although their condition has in reality improved."[47]

45. Ibid., pp. 76–82.
46. Ibid., p. 1.
47. Ibid., p. 5.

Their perception was false and it was pernicious. After all, to call into question such evident progress was to suggest that the economic system upon which it depended was also injurious. Villermé's analysis was guided in no small part by the desire to defend key features of this new economic system, above all its expanded productive capacity based upon the factory system.

The argument of the *Tableau* thus offered an uneasy juxtaposition of the author's confidence and despair. The working class had indeed been exposed to great risks, but society in general and surely also many components of the working class had benefited by the introduction of machine and factory. Undoubtedly, the increased and often extraordinarily elevated mortality of the working population was an unmistakable indication of the deleterious influence of the new manufacturing system. This surplus mortality was not, however, due to specific conditions within the factory, to the manufacturing processes themselves, the very basis of modern productivity, but to unanticipated economic and other influences that accompanied the rise of the factory system. The latter belonged in the social domain. Modern industry and its rewards could be preserved, but reform was in order if the entire system were to be rendered more humane. Effecting these reforms was an important goal to Villermé. "Reform" meant the elimination of certain vices and the moderation of others; that word was understood literally. Reform, if it did entail social change, was not to alter social structure or shift control of economic power to new hands.

Again, Bold Diagnosis and Conservative Therapy

Villermé was a physician, at first of the individual and then of society at large. The latter role increased steadily until by 1840 it had become his predominant interest. In examining the prison, differential mortality, and various patterns of life and death he had been concerned to seize, using both direct observation and the numerical method, such facts as would permit sound reasoning upon the multiple afflictions that disrupted the harmony and development of contemporary social life. These efforts constituted a diagnosis of the social problem. In gathering his facts he was one with his peers in the Paris clinical school. Like the clinicians, too, he realized that facts alone were mute. They required marshalling, rearrangement, even testing by repeated observation. If properly conducted, these operations should lead to general propositions, to secure prognosis, and perhaps, earnest hope, to a remedy or remedies.

Already by 1840 the clinicians' dream of finding new and effective means of treatment by means of the discoveries made in the hospital or dissection hall was proving premature. Eager expectation changed first to caution and then to despair; an era of therapeutic scepticism and even nihilism began in the European medical community. For those in France captured by the reformer's zeal and dedicated to consideration of how social or economic measures might improve the physical and moral condition of the laboring poor, a comparable moment of rupture came only with the events of 1848. To spokesmen of gradual reform—to be effected, of course, always within the framework of the triumphant liberal economic system—the spring revolution of 1848 and the bold social plans of the Second Republic were unmitigated disasters. Benevolence, paternalism, and the humanitarian instinct, a legacy of the Enlightenment transmitted across the contending claims of the great Revolution, seemed to have lost their focus: he who was to be helped now dared assert his own authority. The worker seemed prepared to assume responsibility for his own condition and for that of society, too; the role of the philanthropist seemed threatened with extinction. The violence and radical republicanism of 1848 quickly passed, but the shock and fright delivered to constituted authority and liberal entrepreneur did not.

France under Louis Napoleon soon launched on a period of unprecedented economic expansion. What Villermé had observed in Mulhouse and Lille proved to be but premonitory signs of what was to follow. Yet after 1848 the workers ever more distinctly did articulate for themselves their own purposes and set in motion means of organization to attain their ends. Villermé's diagnosis of social ills had lost little of its validity, but his few and moderate remedies (see Chapter 9) were ill-matched indeed to a society that had suddenly discovered the depths of its divisions. Moderation and reform were characteristic of an earlier period, one in which it appeared even to critical observers that unregulated industrial capitalism would surely confer its benefits upon all levels of society. This earlier period had formed Villermé's social and political allegiances and had also placed its distinctive mark upon the expectations and behavior of the first generation of French hygienic reformers. A man and a generation, both of liberal persuasion, were now caught up in a maelstrom of social and economic change, and one in which their familiar remedies proved inadequate and seemed unwelcome. While social diagnosis had been pursued with clarity and determination, effective therapy for society's ills remained out of reach.

Part III

Ideology and Inquiry

Chapter 9

Villermé Economist

All persons in France are . . . subject to the same law. But it is only in this respect that there is and can be an equality amongst them. From all other points of view nature has created them unequal.

Louis René Villermé, 1849

Political economy provided not only a coherent view of man and society but also defined the limits within which social improvement might be undertaken. Unlike many other economists and entrepreneurs Villermé both recognized and deplored the deleterious human consequences of urbanization and industrialization. But the discovery and portrayal of these somber consequences provoked in him an ambivalent response. His deep-rooted charitable instinct was checked by appreciation of the serious constraints that human nature appeared to impose on charity's intended recipients, and the prospect of state intervention was tempered by that indispensable condition of industrial progress, economic liberty. These were matters of intrinsic concern to public health, for in Villermé's view, "public hygiene . . . was itself only a branch of social economy."[1]

Villermé's roster of remedies for the social ills of his age reduces ultimately to a single pair of agencies, the exercise of individual initiative and the assumption of individual responsibility. The prudent laborer must of and for himself take steps that will lead to economic security and to its concomitants, better health and longer life. In pursuing his task he requires and must receive the enthusiastic support of his master. The interaction between industrial paternalism and individual initiative promised to create a loyal and assiduous working population, the essential foundation of both social harmony and economic progress. The irresponsible master and the improvident or dissolute worker were equally at fault, and both

EPIGRAPH: L. R. Villermé, *Des associations ouvrières* (Paris: Pagnerre, 1849), pp. 3–4.

1. Villermé, "Rapport verbal de M. Villermé sur un mémoire de M. Marc Espine, intitulé: *Influence de l'aisance et de la misère sur la mortalité*," *Séances et travaux de l'Académie des sciences morales et politiques* 12 (1847): 242. Espine's memoir was published in *Annales d'hygiène publique et de médecine légale* 37 (1847): 323–57, and ibid. 38 (1847): 5–32.

were condemned, the former to moral obloquy and perhaps also economic ruin and the latter no less surely to destitution and quite possibly early death. For those as yet unable to take responsibility for their condition, namely, laboring children, legislative intervention seemed essential; Villermé's part in the campaign for child labor legislation was a major one.

Villermé and other economists categorically rejected one measure for assuring social improvement. This was the collective action of labor, the assumption of social responsibility by the lower classes themselves. Able-bodied men and women were to find their salvation in work, not in association with one another for economic advantage. Association of numerous workers for economic purposes reduced the freedom of others and denied the moral component of the argument based on radical individualism; it posed a no less serious threat to property and social stability.

Villermé also directed much attention to certain important questions often debated by the economists and their critics. Did the economic merits of machine manufacture and the factory outweigh their purported social and individual liabilities? To this question as to so many others, Villermé made at best an equivocal response. The human costs he admitted; the economic advantages he celebrated. He found no coherent solution to the problem. The question itself was often cast in other forms. How do we assess the rival cultural values represented by agriculture and by industry? Which form of society is to be preferred, the rural or the urban? Villermé's reply to these questions showed, not ambivalence, but genuine compromise; small-scale manufacture, family cohesiveness, and the retention of a rural plot approximated his conception of an ideal social organization. He realized, nonetheless, that this solution was wholly inappropriate for members of the urban proletariat and as a result returned over and over again to the moral solution to socioeconomic distress.

Social Remedies

In July of the turbulent year 1848, General Louis Eugène Cavaignac, whose forces a few days earlier had suppressed the Paris insurrection with much bloodshed and who now served France as dictator *pro tempore*, issued an urgent call to the Academy of Moral and Political Sciences. He begged the academicians to contribute with their pens to the reassertion of public authority and the restoration of social tranquility. Their response was enthusiastic. They soon produced the famed *Petits traités*, a large collection of short tracts devoted to a spirited defense of moderate republicanism and the propagation of liberal economic principles. Villermé's most important statement of the liberal ideology, *Des associations ouvrières*, appeared in this series in the year of his presidency of the academy

(1849).[2] Cavaignac, he observed elsewhere in the same year, had understood that "physical suppression of the revolt was insufficient and that there remained a further task [for us] to complete: [we must] reestablish moral order and protect society and civilization."[3] Towards this goal the academy launched its "civilizing propaganda," aiming it particularly at the "people in the factories," whose moral regeneration was the principal end in view.[4]

History, Villermé reported in his own *Petit traité*, is the record of the progress of human labor. From the slave came the serf, and from the freeman came the wage earner. From the ranks of the wage earners were recruited the merchants, industrialists, artists, priests, savants, and smallholders. This reassuring and familiar if fictive evolution identified mobility of the social orders as the central feature of social change. More precisely, the mobility in question was not that of social classes but of individuals or families, whose fortunes rose or fell over the years. All social lines were, in Villermé's opinion, crossable; the social order was not fixed for-eternity. A family whose success was today assured would no doubt be reduced to impotence or penury in some future period.

2. Other titles in the series include Adolfe Blanqui, *Des classes ouvrières en France pendant l'année 1848* (1849); Auguste Mignet, *Vie de Franklin à l'usage de tout le monde* (1848); Victor Cousin, *Justice et charité* (1848); Hippolyte Passy, *Des causes de l'inégalité des richesses* (1848): Charles Dupin, *Bien-être et concorde des classes du peuple français* (1848); and Adolfe Thiers, *Du droit de propriété* (1848).

3. Villermé, "Discours prononcé à la séance publique annuelle par M. Villermé, Président de l'Académie," *Séances et travaux de l'Académie des sciences morales et politiques* 16 (1849); 353.

4. Ibid., p. 354. But the author's expectations were anything but hopeful. To his friend Adolfe Quetelet he wrote: "Enfin, en style de cuisinière, *j'étais dans mon coup de fer.* C'est à dire que j'achevrais d'écrire et que j'allais commencer l'impression d'un petit volume que vous recevrez d'ici à 4 ou 5 jours. . . . Ce travail, dont le sujet est tout-à-fait à l'ordre du jour, fait partie d'une collection de petits traités publiés par mon Académie, qui est aussi la vôtre. La compagnie est excellente: elle se compose jusqu'ici de MM. Cousin, Troplong, Passy, Charles Dupin, Mignet, Barthélemy St. Hilaire, Thiers et votre serviteur. Le président de la cour de cassation, M. Portalis, viendra ensuite. En commençant la publication de ces petits traités, nous aurions voulu les écrire pour les classes ouvrières. Mais nous ne nous sommes fait d'illusion; et d'ailleurs j'affirme que si nous nous en étions fait, nous serions bien loin d'atteindre notre but. Des statisticiens, qui ne marchent qu'accompagnés de leurs armées de chiffres; des économistes, qui étudient les faits sociaux; des historiens, qui s'occupent de l'histoire au point de vue le plus instructif, l'enchainement des faits qu'elle rassemble; des juriconsultes, versés dans la science du droit et des lois; des philosophes, enfoncés dans leurs abstractions et les profondeurs de la métaphysique, ne sont pas des Franklin, et toute leur science n'approchera jamais, pour éclairir le peuple, de la science du bonhomme Richard" (Villermé to Quetelet, 26 January 184[9], Correspondence of Adolfe Quetelet, no. 2561, Bibliothèque royale de Belgique). Also see E. H. Ackerknecht, "Villermé and Quetelet," *Bulletin of the History of Medicine* 26 (1952): 317–29.

The real significance of this (supposed) fact of social life became manifest, Villermé reported, only with the events of the Revolution and in the legislation then adopted. The new reign of liberty dissolved previous economic constraints. With the *corporations* dissolved and liberty of work assured, the working man was freed from the artificial obstacles that previously had narrowed his choices and limited his initiative. He was now free to define his own course in life, to act as he saw fit to attain his objectives—in short, to pursue and find worldly success. He was also free, Villermé well understood, to fail miserably and without appeal, thereby destroying himself and all who had come to depend upon him.

What, then, determined individual success or failure? In response to this question Villermé saw fit to read a stern lesson to the feverish revolutionaries of 1848. The occasion was dramatic, but the arguments were familiar to all who had studied his earlier writings, particularly the *Tableau de l'état physique et moral des ouvriers*. The fatal dictate of nature, he declared, has assigned each of us our lot in life. The capacities given us at birth determine our role in social and economic progress. The law of man assures us of opportunity, but our biological constitution—above all, our inborn moral proclivities—sets our course in life. Education, of course, can perfect our moral capacity, but it cannot bring it into being. To be sure, we remain always subject to personal mishap and to disruptive social events such as economic crisis and war. But what we can gain from instruction and how well we are able to cope with unforeseen hazards are founded in our individual character.

The argument from the nature of things, that hard rock foundation upon which Jean Baptiste Say and the economists based their science, exhibited its power most compellingly when applied to the principal actor on the economic stage, man himself. As human nature, it allowed no dispute as to its social meaning. "To one individual, nature has granted the most precious qualities; to another, she has refused all. These talents," Villermé continued, "give an immense advantage to the former, whereas the latter, lacking them, is fated for a dependent position" in all the affairs of life.[5] Biological necessity would always defeat the good intentions of legislator, social reformer, or even revolutionary. The steady eye of the philosopher simply had to accept this discouraging fact as part of the natural order. Human nature thus stands supreme in the following passage, a résumé of Villermé's conception of the relationship between individual and melioristic social action.

> No doubt we can regret that men are not equal in all regards and that
> each person does not have the same value. Superfluous regrets! He who

5. See Villermé, *Associations ouvrières*, p. 4.

is born sickly and weak; the infirm, the ignorant, and the lazy; the improvident and the debauched—none of them can compete with a man who is intelligent, robust, well-informed, industrious, economical, and of *bonnes moeurs*. Do they, the one and the other, equally succeed in life? No, not at all; a thousand times no. . . . We are dealing here with differences that result from the [biological] organization of each person, from an individual's capacity to persevere and from innumerable accidental causes, and against which the written laws contained in our codes can effect absolutely nothing.[6]

Only the unspecified "accidental causes" suggest the possibility of a non-biological and perhaps social origin of individual economic failure. Individual improvement was in fact possible, but it was not assured. It was possible only because some persons at least could be brought to recognize and to pursue their real interests. The pessimistic tone of Villermé's later essays reveals, however, that his expectation that such cultivation would lead to widespread moral improvement had greatly declined since the hopeful writings of the 1820s. In 1848–49 Villermé tended more to accept than to combat the misery of the industrial proletariat.

Thus the solution to the great social problem of France, if indeed there was a solution, was confined to the moral domain. The reign of liberty and the triumph of individual interest allowed no other course. The vicomte Alban de Villeneuve-Bargemont more than any other person had insisted upon this moral solution to the dilemma of the laboring population.[7] But his remedies looked to the past, to the agrarian and aristocratic ideals of the Old Regime and to the universal social and moral message of the Roman Catholic Church. He aimed to resolve contemporary social problems by denying modern—that is, industrial—society. Some economists may have been moved by the passion of Villeneuve-Bargemont's appeal, yet they scarcely contemplated a solution so inappropriate to their broader ambitions. Villermé, whose social and moral sensibilities yielded nothing to those of Villeneuve-Bargemont, was determined to frame a response that preserved both labor and the new economic order.

His solution was only too familiar, offering only work and insistent moral example as the double key to social regeneration and security. The redemptive value of labor was a central theme in the bourgeois world-view, whether in Protestant or Catholic lands, and was, of course, an es-

6. Ibid., pp. 4–5.
7. Alban, vicomte de Villeneuve-Bargemont, *Economie politique chrétienne; ou, Recherches sur la nature et les causes du paupérisme en France et en Europe, et sur les moyens de le soulager et de le prévenir,* 3 vols. (Paris: Paulin, 1834). See the works by Octave Festy and Jean Baptiste Duroselle cited above, Chapter 3, note 44.

sential motif in the doctrines of political economy.[8] The individual at work was not only making a direct contribution to his own economic well-being and progress but was also, by virtue of that labor and of the time consumed in its exercise, removed from the temptations of unregulated social intercourse. To be sure, idleness was sinful, but it was principally as a social threat that the economists aimed to counter it. Some manufacturers, Villermé observed, dealt with absenteeism by imposing fines; others, by depriving the worker of a day's work and thus his wages. The latter was dangerous. "This approach is not sound. It leads to a day of rest, and a day of rest for many workers is only a day of disorderly behavior."[9] Constant labor was economically, socially, and morally desirable, since it sustained industrial output and inculcated or reinforced discipline amongst the workers.

Not only Monday, a dull day after Sunday's usual drunkenness, but the Sabbath itself was full of risk. Labor deserved a day of rest; both biological necessity and religious practice demanded it. But idle hours were also dissolute hours. Sunday occupations must be provided. Mere diversions had no real effect, and the worker always found an opportunity to slip into the cabaret. Useful instruction, tuition that would "perfect the worker's skills and give him moral and intellectual instruction within a framework of the ideas of order, economy, and religious sentiment," was a noble objective but one rarely attained.[10] In the final analysis, it was religion that would inform labor of its due place in society and, more importantly, reconcile the worker to his social condition and thus preclude his worldly questioning and demands. Rarely perhaps was religion as the opiate of the masses more forcefully enunciated than by this hygienic investigator and economist. When, Villermé observed,

> labor's religious preceptors have seized hold of instruction in sincere and affectionate devotion to the cause of the worker, they can, as M. Guizot states, *devote themselves to divorcing his thoughts from affairs of this world and to turning his desires and hopes towards things on high in order to keep control of such aspirations and to maintain calm here below.* For it is a fact that the greatest consolation of the people, the greatest restraint upon the people, is the belief in a life to come with its own rewards and punishments. It requires only the slightest

8. See Bernard Groethuysen, *The Bourgeois: Catholicism vs. Capitalism in Eighteenth-Century France*, trans. Mary Ilford (London: Barrie and Rockliff, 1968); André Cochot, "Morale (Accorde de l'économie et de la)," *Dictionnaire de l'économie politique*, ed. Charles Coquelin and G.-U. Guillaumin, 2 vols. (Paris: Guillaumin, 1852–53), 2: 239–42; Gustav de Molinari, "Travail," ibid., pp. 761–64.

9. Villermé *Tableau de l'état physique et moral des ouvriers employés dans les manufactures de coton, de laine et de soie*, 2 vols. (Paris: Jules Renouard, 1840), 1: 291, n. 1.

10. Ibid., 2: 68.

suspicion that there is nothing after death to render the worker immoral, to excuse in his eyes the most egotistical passions, the coarsest—if I may use that expression—passions and those most injurious to the social order.[11]

Just as the farmer prepares his fields, so must the priest prepare the worker. This appreciation of the moral and social authority of Christian religion was quite free of sectarian vexations. To Villermé, who accepted Protestant Mulhouse and Catholic Lille with equal ease, it was less theological nicety and doctrinal preference that was in question than the more general and more important matter, religion as the ultimate weapon of social control over a restive and increasingly numerous laboring population. These reflections ensured that responsibility for the moral condition of that population had to be shared. If the worker had need to learn the virtues of regularity, diligence, and sobriety, it was the master's obligation to provide without remiss the control, example, and instruction by which the lesson could be imparted. Paternalism to Villermé was overwhelmingly a matter of moral action. Good habits must be created and bad ones suppressed, for truly, the "habits of the people constitute their moral code."[12] Here spoke the true idéologue, faced with an unthinking mass deemed incapable of rational conduct of its own behavior.

To the master, therefore, fell primary responsibility for the moral condition of factory labor. Certain masters had seized their opportunity and thereby created model industrial communities. Here again the woolen masters at Sedan set the example. At Sedan salaries were high, and most workers retained or had acquired a small freehold.[13] Drunkenness was ruthlessly suppressed. Children younger than 10 to 12 years of age were not hired, a striking exception to practice elsewhere in France, and serious efforts were made to assure them the basic elements of literacy. Major vice was thus avoided and a stronger and more skillful working population created. Only sexual promiscuity escaped control, the seduction of virginal operatives being a major preoccupation of the men in the sexually unsegregated factories. These many advantages and no less this last great flaw were due to the concern, or negligence, of enlightened and determined masters.

Such action required the concerted effort of virtually all entrepreneurs in a given fabrique. Failing this, the nature of competition was such that unscrupulous masters exploited the opportunities created by the restraint of the more humanitarian members of their group. Here, in Villermé's

11. Ibid., p. 69.
12. Ibid., p. 48.
13. Ibid., 1: 253–79.

eyes, was a major and abiding difficulty in finding a generally acceptable solution to flagrant abuses of the factory system, above all, the employment of young children. The Alsation cotton entrepreneurs faced this problem in acute form. Unlike the long-established and stable factory system at Sedan, the cotton mills of Mulhouse underwent rapid expansion during this period. New, untried, and ambitious masters took charge of new and inexperienced factory hands, and the human damage was often great. While the Alsatian fabrique thus lacked the consistency of approach adopted at Sedan, the efforts of its larger and more secure members, those whose interests were given focus by the Société industrielle de Mulhouse, nonetheless provided evidence of sincere concern and sound humanitarian practice.[14] Mulhouse far more than Sedan represented the new and expanding industrial reality, and its problems were precisely those that were becoming general as the factory system advanced across the nation. The social efforts of responsible Alsatian entrepreneurs consequently received Villermé's special emphasis.

Their efforts stressed collective arrangements for assuring individual security and prosperity. Lacking familial and agricultural roots in the area, the Alsatian worker had need of other resources when hard times or personal misfortune struck. The masters supported compulsory savings, used during periods of sickness to provide for the physician's visit and for drugs.[15] Friendly societies and contributory income assurance plans were also vigorously encouraged. Cooperative buying and baking establishments were founded. Modest housing projects were erected by certain masters for their employees and access to these governed by rules estimated to assure sound moral conduct. Some entrepreneurs sought to assure at least minimal educational opportunities for the children of their employees or for children working in the mills. In addition, serious and continued agitation in France for reduction of the hours of child labor began in the late 1820s among certain of the major Mulhouse manufacturers.

Of course, Villermé agreed, the master alone could not accomplish a moral revolution. Yet the master's was the stronger and, more significantly, the knowing hand. Moreover, unless utterly blinded by greed or ambition, he must realize that his economic prosperity and social position depended upon the relative tranquility of the industrial classes. The *Tableau* was addressed to the master, and its author's foremost concern was to impress upon him the importance of active intervention in the affairs of labor. Only thus would his moral influence have a real effect. If the master

14. See Michel Valentin, *Travail des hommes et savants oubliés: Histoire de la médecine du travail, de la securité et de l'ergonomie* (Paris: Docis, 1978), pp. 227–32.

15. Villermé, *Tableau*, 1: 56–61.

had well-founded complaints against labor (the worker's thievery and hatred for his superior were duly noted), the master, and not labor, was probably responsible for these unhappy eventualities. The master who avoided all intercourse with his workers, who refused them encouragement in good times and tangible support when business conditions or a personal situation turned bad—such a master merely reaped a poor harvest of his own making.[16]

In his folly he lost the opportunity to exercise the paramount instrument of social control and, ostensibly, amelioration. His neglect of his men and women constituted a breach in surveillance, an intolerable lapse of control. Such seemed to have been the origin of the Lyons riots of the 1830s. The virtually total divorce that had arisen between *marchand-fabricant* and the silk-weavers, the *canuts*, broke a long-standing personal relationship, the bond necessary for assuring social harmony.[17] The situation of the canuts perplexed Villermé and led him into an altogether expected contradiction. He recognized that the canuts were an energetic, thoughtful, clever, and sober people. They were accustomed to a good income and spent it often on apparent luxuries. Their health was good, mutual aid schemes were common in the fabrique, and they practiced moral restraint: they did not let procreation outrun their income. All of these qualities allowed the canut to live better, often much better, than his fellow textile workers. His independence was striking and, to Villermé, distinctly upsetting.

On the one hand the canut manifested precisely those qualities that a vigorous and productive working class must possess. On the other hand, his very success tended to liberate him from the direct surveillance and direction of a master. The canut, in fact, became his own master. While Villermé admitted and even publicized the fact that the natural inequality of mankind has as its consequence that individual men and women will in time rise or fall in the socioeconomic hierarchy, he was unhappy with this conclusion when he saw its effects among the canuts. Their independence was an excess and a danger. Self-sufficiency he could accept; public expression by the worker of his prosperity and its basic implication—the equality of men—he bluntly rejected. The canuts in their fancy dress were guilty of no crime worse than *lèse-bourgeoisie*, but that crime was sufficiently serious to merit specific notice and warning. The warning was addressed, however, not to the canut but to the master or marchand-fabricant who had allowed this situation to develop. The master who failed to exercise a necessary paternal role could thus hinder economic progress

16. Ibid., 2: 57–63.
17. Ibid., 1: 355–56.

and disturb social harmony either by neglecting his workers and thus assuring their debilitation or ruin, or by ignoring his more assiduous and assertive hands, thereby allowing them to escape from a relation of dependence.

Crudely put, dependence was befitting the vast majority of mankind. Those few whose initiative and capacity allowed them to rise in the social scale, and whose ascent was *ipso facto* witness to the beneficence of the new era of liberty, had but exercised their inborn talents. Their rise was an individual affair and did little if anything to disturb existing class relationships. Worldly success and thus independence was reserved for the minority; those who rose left the working class and joined the domain of master and bourgeois. Others who showed signs of independence or of living in a manner ill-befitting their social standing were simply condemned as being misguided or prey to false and potentially dangerous social philosophies. The growing threat of association gave ample cause for consideration of the latter possibility. But if the source of difficulty was either ignorance or misdirection on the part of labor, responsibility therefor necessarily fell heavily upon the *patronat*. The master who neglected his social responsibilities was quite likely the first to suffer the consequences. The uninstructed worker was a slow and unproductive worker and reduced both output and profits. Labor, when reduced to destitution, finding itself without either employment or the most elementary means of support, threatened to call into question the very social order itself. The entrepreneur, who by definition was a person who applied reason and determination to the productive process, was untrue to himself if he neglected these essential aspects of his endeavor.

This emphasis upon individualized secular salvation implied that parties other than the good master who maintained proper conditions for individual development had no part, or at most a quite minor part, to play with regard to the social problem. With one prominent exception Villermé supported this conclusion: to him as to most other economists neither the state nor any organized charitable institution should intervene on behalf of labor or, in fact, for the benefit of any social group. The single exception, however, was crucial, for upon it depended the future strength and prosperity of the nation.

Child Labor

Throughout his life Villermé exhibited uncommon concern for the welfare of children. His own family life was close and happy, and he saw in the family at large both the basic social group and the single most effective agency for moral instruction. He realized, moreover, and gained fame for publicly insisting upon that recognition, that modern industrial society was taking an especial and quite enormous toll of the children of the laboring classes. The protection of children was a noble cause indeed. In this cause Villermé joined sincere humanitarian concern with full awareness of the consequences for manufacture of the unprecedented destruction of potential hands. As noted above, this was a problem that defied ameliorative action by one or a few entrepreneurs alone. A concerted effort was required, one that extended throughout the nation and allowed no entrepreneur to seize individual advantage from the well-meaning efforts of more benevolent masters.

Let the hesitant or the avaricious beware: "those children who die very young or before they have produced anything, far from being able to contribute in any way whatsoever to the prosperity of a state, are in fact a cause of its enfeeblement and ruin. Others have said it before me: the death of these children is a bankruptcy, a shipwreck, that causes their families and society to lose all that these children have cost."[18] Such children, whom, no doubt, parents loved, had also a market value, and society, by ignoring or rejecting appropriate and feasible hygienic and economic measures, was simply consuming or casting aside its most important capital asset.

What could and what should be done? Some followed the celebrated tradition of John Locke and Etienne Bonnot de Condillac and argued that primary education would allow these children better to cope with the new society. From elementary instruction in reading, writing, and arithmetic children would gain skills of immediate economic value and would also, in a general manner, become more responsible in their behavior and more obedient in social relations. Here was the liberal dream: an educative process that formed independent and morally sound individuals. Villermé, himself of independent mind, would have none of it. Moral statistics, then still a novelty but one nonetheless based on number and not on mere repeated opinion, seemed to demonstrate that primary education did not reduce serious crime.[19] It failed its most important responsibility, moral

18. Villermé, "Sur l'institution, par le gouvernement belge, d'une commission centrale de statistique, et observations sur les statistiques officielles publiées en France par les divers ministères," *Journal des économistes* 13 (1845): 135. One who had spoken earlier was the physician J. B. Bousquet, who remarked of the child who dies young that "all that has been invested in him is lost without return or compensation. Misfortune to that nation whose population is ceaselessly renewed!—it is the poorest of all." (*Traité de la vaccine et des éruptions varioleuses ou varioliformes: Ouvrage rédigé sur la demande du gouvernement* [Paris: Baillière, 1833], p. 358).

19. This was the conclusion of A. M. Guerry, *Essai sur la statistique morale de la France* (Paris: Crochard, 1833). Villermé reasserted Guerry's opinion in his essay review of the principal publication by P.M.S. Bigot, baron de Morogues, *Recherches des causes*

formation. Adolfe Quetelet, the statistician, and Charles Dupin, economist as well as engineer and statesman, wholly agreed with this conclusion.[20] Consequently, Villermé and a small handful of other economists
broke sharply with liberal orthodoxy on this point and tended to view
schooling not as the indispensable instrument of social progress but as a
very uncertain undertaking. If it did not tempt the lower orders to crime
(it did not, Villermé asserted), it nevertheless conveyed to them ideas that
were inappropriate, because unsettling, to their social standing.

   A far more direct measure for alleviating the lot of working children
was called for. The social remedy *par excellence*, the power of the state,
was now invoked. Here Villermé's contribution was important but by no
means predominant. Agitation for passage of a law or laws regulating
child labor had begun among the more prosperous Protestant entrepreneurs of Mulhouse in 1827. Acting through the Société industrielle de
Mulhouse and led by J. J. Bourcart, the Mulhousians conducted factory
investigation, drew up model legislation, waged a propaganda campaign
and petitioned the national assemblies.[21] The problem itself stood revealed
before their eyes. The preferred solution they borrowed from English child
labor legislation, particularly that which began in 1802 and culminated in
the great Factory Act of 1833. Their campaign waxed and waned for ten
years until finally the central government, in the person of the minister of
commerce, decided to launch its own inquiry. Despite a mixed response
(among the cotton fabriques, employers of the great majority of children,
Alsace and Normandy generally favored child labor legislation, while
Lille and the Nord as well as the Midi fiercely opposed it), the government
and the assemblies, led by Dupin sitting in the Chamber of Peers, persisted in pursuing the project. These efforts finally proved successful, cul-

---

de la richesse et de la misère des peuples civilisés . . . (1834), in *Bulletin de la Société des
établissements charitables* 3 (1833): 222–61, esp. pp. 253–57; see also his *Tableau*, 2:
153–58.

   20. Quetelet concluded that elementary schooling without simultaneous moral instruction was the probable source of much crime (*A Treatise on Man and the Development of
His Faculties*, trans. anon. [Edinburgh: William and Robert Chambers, 1842], p. 88). See
Michelle Perrot, "Premières mesures des faits sociaux: Les débuts de la statistique crimi-
nelle en France (1780–1830)," in François Bédarida et al., *Pour une histoire de la statistique*, vol. 1, *Contributions* (Paris: I.N.S.E.S., n.d.), pp. 125–35.

   21. The following discussion is based on Louis Guéneau, "La législation restrictive du
travail des enfants: La loi française du 22 Mars 1841," *Revue d'histoire économique et
sociale* 15 (1927): 420–503. See also André-Jean Tudesq, *Les grandes notables en France
(1840–1849): Etude historique d'une psychologie sociale*, 2 vols. (Paris: P.U.F., 1964), 2:
581–98. Bourcart's proposal appeared as "Proposition de M. Jean-Jacques Bourcart, de
Guebwiller, sur la nécessité de fixer l'âge et de réduire les heures de travail des ouvriers
des filatures . . . ," *Bulletin de la Société industrielle de Mulhausen* 1 (1826–28): 373–88.

minating in the promulgation of the law of 22 March 1841, the first major and for long years the only piece of French labor legislation.[22]

The law itself was weak, and that, no doubt, was an important element in its legislative success. Age limits were lower than those set in England. The inspectorate to whom enforcement was attributed was rendered virtually impotent: it could report abuses and initiate minor police action but could not take serious measures. Small fines were provided for, but, unlike the English law, prison terms were excluded.[23] Worst of all, the inspectorate was recruited largely from former members of the entrepreneurial class. Like the other advocates of the law, Villermé was distressed and disgusted by these developments. He soon had to admit that the law was a failure, that it was not a serious check to the abuses it was meant to correct.[24]

The part of public health inspection in the formulation and passage of this law was indirect. Villermé, of course, was the central representative of hygiene in the agitation for the bill. In the critical year 1837 he presented a first report to his sponsor, the Academy of Moral and Political Sciences, regarding the problem. This document, as well as subsequent publications dealing with the employment of children by the textile industry, was clear and forceful but in large part unoriginal. It was dependent upon previous reports and personal communications prepared by and received from members of the Société industrielle de Mulhouse. The academy had, in fact, only translated to the national level the pointed investigations whose design and execution had already been tested by the physician Achille Penot and others at Mulhouse.[25] Yet, because the acad-

22. The text of the law of 22 March 1841 is given in *Annales d'hygiène publique et de médecine légale* 26 (1841): 242–44. See also Georges Bourgin, "Législation et organisation administrative du travail sous la Restauration," *Revue politique et parlementaire* 66 (1910): 116–52; Paul Leuillot, *L'Alsace au début de XIXe siècle: Essais d'histoire politique, économique et religieuse (1815–1830)*, 3 vols. (Paris: S.E.V.P.E.N., 1959–60), 2: 494–99.

23. Guéneau, "Législation restrictive du travail des enfants," p. 502. The English Factory Act of 1833, its implementation and the opposition it provoked, offered a far more ambiguous model than Villermé and his associates cared to recognize: see Ivy Pinchbeck and Margaret Hewitt, *Children in English Society*, 2 vols. (London: Routledge and Kegan Paul, 1969–73), 2: 387–413, and E. P. Thompson, *The Making of the English Working Class* (New York: Random House, 1966), pp. 331–49.

24. Brief comment on nonenforcement in Paris, attributed to conflicting bureaucratic interests, is made in Villermé, "Sur l'institution . . . d'une commission centrale de statistique," p. 133, n. 1. To Penot in Mulhouse the French legislation was just "another law not put into effect" (quoted in Valentin, *Travail des hommes*, p. 230).

25. Penot's published inquiries began with *Discours sur quelques recherches de statistique comparée faites sur la ville de Mulhouse, lu à la société industrielle, lu dans la séance du 26 septembre 1826* (Mulhouse: the author, 1828); this publication became an important source for Villermé's analysis of many aspects of the Alsatian cotton fabrique. Penot's

emy did represent semiofficial governmental interests and because many among its members were also members of the Chamber of Peers, the legislative leader in the passage of the law, the academy's investigator obviously spoke to the truly important audience and no doubt contributed significantly to opinion favoring the bill.

With regard to the more general question of the connection between political economy and public health the circumstances leading to passage of the law of 22 March 1841 are especially important. They offer an indication of what were held to be the permissible limits to an infringement of the well-nigh absolute principle of liberty, even for this the most humanitarian of objectives. If individual entrepreneurial action could have led to the desired improvement in the condition of young factory laborers, that action would surely have been the preferable course. Yet, in the nature of things, the fact of competition meant that all isolated efforts would be vain. The benevolent entrepreneur would be ruined. The children, too, would be ruined. Pressed by their needy parents, they would have to find a place with another master whose scruples were less demanding. In short, Villermé's analysis, although he himself never dreamed of formulating the matter in this manner, led necessarily to the conclusion that freedom to compete inevitably led to exploitation and that the only feasible solution to the problem was to remove the potential victims from the competitive arena. Competition itself must not be legislatively regulated. Removal of small children from the factory was, of course, only a temporary measure and one that to modern eyes seems to have provided them no protection whatsoever. That judgment, however, is moot, since the law was hardly enforced at all.

The specific terms of Villermé's demand for legislation deserve emphasis. They were at once economic, humanitarian, and hygienic. Children as human beings had unmeasurable intrinsic value. Himself a father whose attachment to his children knew no limits, Villermé eagerly accorded this sentiment to all men and women, whatever their social standing. As one moves, however, from the individual child to children in large numbers they are easily depersonalized, and their aggregate economic advantage can be seen more clearly. This step was often taken by the social observer of the 1820s and 1830s. Did not the masses, after all, reproduce with obvious abandon, surrounding themselves with numerous offspring regarding whose fate they paid little heed? The incipient statistical viewpoint, necessarily dealing with men, women, and children in the mass,

---

reformist hopes were stated in "Rapport de la commission chargée d'examiner la question relative à l'emploi des enfans dans les filatures de coton . . . ," *Bulletin de la Société industrielle de Mulhouse* 10 (1837): 481–501. By this time Villermé himself was a corresponding member of the Société industrielle.

would not, surely, oppose this stress on the collectivity. Nonetheless—and this is an essential qualification—Villermé's perspective was neither fatalistic nor single-minded. He appreciated very well the exploitative nature of the industrial employment of young children. He realized no less, as Sismondi had been the first to emphasize, how essential a child's earnings were to overall family survival. Thoughtful working parents faced an awesome and awful choice. The income of a working child made an indispensable contribution to family income, without which the entire family might slip into destitution or worse; yet putting that young child in the factory exposed it to risks of debilitation, moral degradation, and death far in excess of those of children who were similarly exposed but were of greater age and development. The hygienic solution (that expression here is singularly appropriate) proved to be one consistent with perceived economic necessity. Solicitous regard for the welfare of the worker's young child aimed to preserve that child by keeping him or her out of the factory. This concern created a legislatively imposed sanitary cordon that protected the young. But only for a short period: soon the child must enter the labor market. Yet the marvel of this solution was that the older child entering the labor force had not only survived but possessed the greater common sense, vigor, and stamina of added years. Life had been preserved; a better worker had also been produced. Economic benefits appeared to pour on all parties concerned. Hence, in this domain and in this domain alone, liberty was to be limited; an exception had to be made that could assure the long-term interests of society at large. The child, still unable to formulate and defend its own interests, required protection. Unhappily, reason and benevolence did not triumph; the child in France remained the tempting object of those given over to haste and cupidity.

The Supremacy of Moral Responsibility

Children probably neither knew nor cared that certain among their betters had determined to ease their misery while cultivating their economic potential. At some point they would leave childhood and enter the adult world, there to cope as best they could. Villermé and his associates saw no grounds for legislatively or administratively sanctioned protection of adult workers.[26] The state in this domain had no other role than to assure that liberty, however modulated by class, remained the law of the land.

26. Very late in his career Villermé came to appreciate hazards previously discounted. See his report "Des accidents produits dans les ateliers industriels par les appareils mécaniques," *Journal des économistes* 27 (1850): 215–22. This work is described by Michel Oger, *A propos d'une étude oubliée de Villermé: Le rapport de 1850 sur les accidents du travail* (thèse de médecine, Paris, 1962).

And far worse in the eyes of the economists was another remedy, one that defied common sense, moral authority, and social order. Workers had thought to attempt their own solution to the many industrial and social problems that harassed their working and domestic lives, problems which, hygienists knew better than they, connected the economic realities of the day with labor's excessive sickness and mortality.

These several issues came to a head in the spring of 1848. The factory system and industrialization had by this time created a sizeable urban proletariat whose only resource was uninterrupted work. The migration of workers had swelled the population of the industrial towns and cities. Many workers had severed all connection with their agricultural origins. The functioning of the nation's economic engine found itself at the mercy of a host of influences neither labor nor management could control or even comprehend. The collapse began following the harvest failure of 1846 and by the winter of 1847–48 had spread misery far and wide across France.

Paris, of course, experienced this faltering of the economy with exceptional severity, a function in large part of the disproportionate size and long-standing political activity of its working class. The February revolution called forth a provisional government drawn, however, not from labor but from the frightened bourgeoisie. The Provisional Government little hesitated in promising to satisfy labor's demands. Foremost among the public promises made at this time was the solemn assurance that all able-bodied laborers who sought work would find it, now and in the future. The Provisional Government, spurred on by Louis Blanc, whose *Organisation du travail* (1840) had been raised confidently upon the great principles of 1789—liberty, equality, and fraternity—and whose name now rallied voices claiming yet another right, the right to work, reluctantly began to create a comprehensive program for mass public employment. Thus arose, largely under Blanc's leadership, the famed National Workshops, the hope and often the only resource of the worker but an utter abomination in the eyes of many a sober bourgeois who cherished liberty above all else.[27]

Villermé belonged to this latter group. His *Associations ouvrières* delivered an occasionally cynical, usually ill-humored, and always vigorous attack upon the very notion that labor could solve its own problems, even with public assistance, and upon "the man" (Blanc's name was left unstated) who had conceived so misbegotten an institution. In *Associations*, discussion of public health simply disappeared. The urgent contemporary need had become defense of society itself, defense, that is, of the new

27. See D. C. McKay, *The National Workshops: A Study in the French Revolution of 1848* (Cambridge: Harvard University Press, 1933).

industrial order that had been created during the years of the constitutional monarchy.

An association, Villermé noted accurately, was an arrangement devised for the purpose of manufacture and sale of products in which the state provided shop space, raw materials, and tools, the whole of which was then utilized to provide employment and income for workers who chose to join the undertaking.[28] A number of these associations were created between February and June 1848, most notable of which was perhaps Blanc's own association of tailors; and others appeared in July, when the government, seeking calm after the June uprising, provided new funds for continuing the project.

That the state would engage itself as entrepreneur or at least as banker to a band of petty entrepreneurs struck Villermé as bizarre, if not quite contradictory of sound, that is, private, entrepreneurial activity. Worse yet, an association was only a means to an end, but the end in question was one that had been and would always remain beyond human grasp. Labor demanded guaranteed employment and a regular income, protection from what all observers admitted was the worst feature of the industrial system, namely, the insecurity of a living wage in an era of repeated glut, crisis, and unemployment. But no institution, Villermé observed—neither the corporation under the old regime, nor the association of 1848, nor even competition itself—could offer such a guarantee. To pretend otherwise was to sacrifice our "most sacred and natural right, that of applying [our] labor and [our] industry wherever we believe them to be most profitable."[29] The very notion of association denied that of liberty and thus constituted an officially sanctioned threat to the most cherished of economic principles. In short, as Adolfe Thiers exclaimed, association, by denying the principles of "property, freedom of labor, emulation, or competition," merely gives us "communism," and that means sloth and slavery, industrial anarchy, monopoly, debased currency and perhaps much that was even worse, including the right to work.[30]

But to Villermé the truly critical weakness of the idea of association was human, not political. The masses were simply incapable of guiding their own affairs. To be sure, he admitted, labor had organized one or another autonomous unit of production, but of these only one (jewelers), and this for special reasons, had been successful. All others had failed and would continue to fail. Although admitting that the heart of labor's demand for

28. Villermé, *Associations ouvrières*, pp. 18–19. The "utopia of association" is examined by H. B. Moss in *The Origins of the French Labor Movement: The Socialism of Skilled Workers* (Berkeley: University of California Press, 1976), pp. 31–70.

29. Villermé, *Associations ouvrières*, p. 11.

30. Ibid., p. 21.

association was not wealth or social domination but simply a desperate desire to escape misery, he insisted over and again that the promoters of association had yet to agree that all participants in any enterprise, and not the master alone, must bear the losses as well as share the gains. The *associationistes* pointedly overlooked this matter. They brought no capital to the enterprise. In those associations in which a master also participated, labor's risks were expected to be covered by his contribution, while all would share in the profits. To Villermé and no doubt to all who shared his view this was cloud-cuckoo land, for no capable capitalist, one who by definition knew how to calculate his interest, would participate in such an all-risk undertaking.

It was obvious to Villermé that economic enterprise was a complex and difficult affair, one calling for boldness, calculation, and sustained exercise of will. Just here the very idea of genuine association collapsed, for it was simply a fact of life that men and women did not all possess these qualities. Indeed, very few individuals possessed them; and those persons who did were destined, by virtue of exercising their inborn talents, always to take precedence over others. Inevitably, success in economic or other affairs came only to groups which may have begun with *associationiste* intentions but in which leadership was exercised by one man or a very small handful of men.[31] This fact destroyed the core of labor's program. At the same time it reasserted the conditions that liberal economists sought to preserve unfettered, namely, opportunity for the expression of individual initiative and a situation of dependence for the men and women who would not or could not guide their own destinies. To Villermé, association presented an unwelcome challenge to the idea of an orderly society based upon the reciprocal obligations of master and man. Although truly alarmed by the popularity of the new idea amongst the laboring masses, he realized that the threat was probably not serious in the economic domain. The inherent incapacity of the many to govern their affairs insured that the competent few would soon rise to an appropriate level of entrepreneurial dominance. The possible anger of the radical republican, egalitarian, or socialist reader of these truths was countered with the following sharp declaration, a statement of the faith that had informed some thirty years of hygienic and social experience: "Men are indignant at the inequality of condition that everywhere characterizes mankind. Like you, I

31. Villermé, ibid., pp. 23–30, cites to this effect one of the few published reports of the aborted investigation of the condition of labor called for by the National Assembly in the spring of 1848; the opinions expressed were those of leading Alsatian manufacturers. See also Hilde Rigaudias-Weiss, *Les enquêtes ouvrières en France entre 1830 et 1848* (Paris: P.U.F., 1936), pp. 171–233.

too would prefer that the condition of all men were more prosperous. Nonetheless, you might as well direct your indignation at Providence, whose eternal decrees have established and now maintain this inequality of size, strength, health, intelligence, general competence, and morality and of which inequality of [socioeconomic] condition is merely the consequence or necessary effect."[32] Human nature thus prohibited men and women, notably those less gifted persons who constitute the vast preponderance of society, from seeking by their own efforts to ameliorate their lot in life and to assure themselves a secure economic situation.

This was a hard lesson but also a consoling one—how much easier it is to adjust to hardship, however extreme, when one accepts its inevitability. Nonetheless, certain persons refused to learn the lesson. They dared to expand the meaning of association, to make it an instrument of social change, a means for political action that would obtain for the dispossessed their rightful place in society. Villermé could not overlook this claim. Needless to say, he found in it a real threat and held its proponents for the most part to be men of crude ambition, evil intent, and violent tendencies. Even those of "good will," those who had called for the National Workshops, had failed to see that these *ateliers* would "destroy public confidence," create "unemployment," generate "false ideas, illusory hopes, and sad deception," and subject the nation to an "outbreak of passions, insurrection, and a horrible civil war." In fact, "in this the most civilized of nations," they would bring on "a genuine retreat of civilization." Imagine, then, what men of ill will might accomplish.[33]

Men of ill will did, in fact, exist. Villermé found them especially in associations that were more *fraternelles* than *industrielles*. These troublemakers attended meetings at the Luxembourg Palace, the continuing focus for left-wing agitation and Blanc's principal basis of political support, and went so far as to say "citoyen" to one another, a nice reminder to Villermé's readers (as a group the major beneficiaries of the great Revolution) of the seriousness of the threat posed by others who wished to share their good fortune. These revolutionaries, although stopped in their tracks by Cavaignac's ruthless application of martial law, arrest, and deportation, posed a "sword of Damocles" over the head of the government. They had in mind the creation of a "political army" rather than an "industrial army of genuine and solid workers." Villermé was a fear monger, noting that "he had reason to believe" that all of this agitation was a plot laid by "only two or three men" who aimed to gain control of the wildest members of

32. Villermé, *Associations ouvrières*, p. 21.
33. Ibid., pp. 16–17.

the working class, men of "blind and frenzied passions, always ready for revolt."[34] The return of a better economic climate and Cavaignac's determination soon laid these extreme fears to rest.

The tempestuous social situation of the later 1840s prompted Villermé to speak more openly on the matter of the class structure of society. His ideas in this regard were probably well formed by the early 1830s, at the time when his thoughts began to shift from numerical analysis of mortality to more direct social investigation. The influence of fellow members of the Academy of Moral and Political Sciences and the inquiry conducted at the academy's behest brought these notions to maturity. The economic distress of the 1840s and the violence and audacity of labor in 1848 compelled a more pointed statement of first principles. This, however, only reiterated a familiar message. Without well-defined authority and a hierarchical arrangement of the social classes, society dissolves into anarchy, and its institutions cease to function. The most important of these institutions, that which was, in fact, virtually coextensive with society, was the complex of economic relations by which the nation's business was conducted. The conduct of economic affairs provided a model for the organization and operation of society itself. Authority should be exercised benevolently but never divided. In the factory the power of the master has been and must remain supreme. The master alone can suppress "the anarchy of will and egoism" which others, if given freedom, would inevitably generate, and he can guide his men and women toward virtue and greater productivity.[35] The egoism of the master, a notorious feature of life under the July Monarchy, was good because his will was informed and directed towards socially valuable goals; the egoism of subordinates was evil because these persons were incapable of intelligent and sustained decision and action.

Of the major options available for alleviating the condition of the laboring poor, the economists flatly rejected direct state assistance and dealt even more harshly with the notion that labor as a collectivity could find a remedy for its difficulties. Both alternatives violated liberty and the rights of property and were based upon an erroneous and pernicious conception of human nature. The reformers consistently ignored the fact that Providence, not man, set the conditions of our biological and social existence. Some men have been endowed by nature with the capacity to prosper; they rise in the social scale. Others possess sufficient talent and have acquired suitable moral strength to establish for themselves a secure if modest station in life. Others still either lack genuine capacity or, more com-

34. Ibid., pp. 79, 83.
35. Ibid., p. 92.

monly, are deficient in sound moral principles. These persons, the social residuum, lead either a marginal and unhappy existence or perish.

Unscrupulous men, cognizant of these facts, might decide that systematic exploitation of the socially impotent offered the quickest route to economic success. For such thoughts and the exploitative practices that all too commonly did in fact follow, Villermé had utmost contempt. Social inequality, he held, gave no grounds for the inhumane treatment of any man or woman. Just the opposite was true: economic success entailed heavy social responsibilities. These responsibilities required careful definition, however, for they had to be circumscribed within a sphere of reasonable and desirable possibilities as laid down by the principles of political economy.

Villermé's social program was defined by a simple humanitarian impulse. The master was obliged to create opportunities for his employees, encouraging their thrift, spurring their ambition, and assuring them a just reward for their labor. Implicit in all of this was the fundamental notion of moral improvement. The master might create opportunities and bring them to the attention of his worker, but only the worker could respond to the call. That response, if it came, contained the entire ameliorative act. The worker alone possessed the key to his economic and social salvation. The master only encouraged him and removed artificial obstacles to his progress. He did not attempt to change the man himself. The wise master knew, and labor had to learn, that one cannot "remake what has never been and never will be remade: the heart, the passions, and the mind of man."[36]

Villermé's conclusion continued, with crucial modification, the humanitarian tradition of the Enlightenment. The idéologues proclaimed that men and women, when they had fully realized their potential, behaved as rational beings. They derived knowledge of the world through the senses and guided their actions by reasoned and generalized use of their sensations. The rational individual pursued his own interest, learning too that an element in one's success was due concern for the well-being of those with whom one entered into social intercourse.

The French humanitarian of the years after 1815 emphasized the motif of individual self-help. Such was the orientation of the duc de La Rochefoucauld-Liancourt, of the Société philanthropique de Paris, of the concerned masters of Mulhouse and Sedan, and of the growing group of hygienic and social investigators, among whom Villermé stood foremost. They condemned traditional charitable practices, especially institutionalized charity. Organized charity did create, of course, a relation of depen-

36. Ibid., p. 15.

dence but it was of altogether the wrong kind. Regular alms or shelter invited workers—even the able-bodied and those whose initiative could yet be stirred by regular experience of that most effective stimulus, need— to take refuge under the care of benevolent but socially misguided individuals. Instead of compelling the expression of individual initiative, charity blunted it and thus denied society the services of men and women who might well be rendered productive. Religious charity suffered from these same vices. Moreover, its resources were inadequate to the great burden created by industrial society, and its leaders, both the clergy and their financial supporters, represented old France, not the new society dedicated to economic progress.

Worst of all was that special horror, the unreformed English Poor Law. Villermé, anything but alone in his opinion, regarded this ancient legislation as simply the granting of "a legal premium to improvidence or sloth." The poor rate was "an exorbitant [and] disastrous tax" that "deprived benevolence of its principal merit." Poor relief was merely a "palliative for social ills, not a cure."[37] A cure could result only from an inner moral strength developed by the suffering individual. While short-term relief might occasionally be needed, the English example proved that long-sustained support only debased those whom it was intended to serve.

The Academy of Moral and Political Sciences often discussed this issue. A full session was devoted to it in 1860, one of the last sessions that Villermé was able to attend. A memoir by P. A. Dufau critical of the economists' distrust of charity gave the defenders of individual initiative an opportunity to mount a defense.[38] Lavergne repeated the canard that the best charity is also the least. The philosopher and statesman Victor Cousin stressed that misfortune and improvidence are ills that neither man nor society can cure. The incorrigible Charles Dunoyer, whose defense of

37. Villermé, "Quelques reflexions sur les établissements de charité publique, à l'occasion d'un ouvrage de M. David Johnston," *Annales d'hygiène publique et de médecine légale* 3 (1830): 92–93, 99. Johnston's volume (*A General, Medical, and Statistical History of the Present Condition of Public Charity in France . . .* [Edinburgh, 1829]) provided a comprehensive description of Parisian hospitals and charitable services; this work had also given rise to one of Edwin Chadwick's first public discussions of the related problems of poverty, sickness, and charity: see his ["Public Charities in France"] *London review* 1 (1830): 536–65. On the reform of the English Poor Law, its aftermath, and contemporary charitable concerns, see S. E. Finer, *The Life and Times of Edwin Chadwick* (London: Methuen, 1952), pp. 39–49, 69–95; Derek Fraser, ed., *The New Poor Law in the Nineteenth Century* (London: Macmillan, 1976): David Owen, *English Philanthropy, 1660–1960* (Cambridge: Harvard University Press, 1964), pp. 97–181.

38. P. A. Dufau, "Mémoire sur la conciliation de l'économie politique et de l'économie charitable ou assistance," *Séances et travaux de l'Académie des sciences morales et politiques* 51 (1860): 89–107. The remarks cited appear in the "Discussion," ibid., pp. 107–17.

liberty was absolute, praised the now reformed English Poor Law (1834).[39] If we must have public assistance, he observed, citing English experience, then we must make its delivery as "painful and humiliating as possible," thus discouraging a good number of those who might seek aid. Here, indeed, was an honest disciple of Jeremy Bentham, author of the principle of least eligibility, and Edwin Chadwick, his advocate. The old Saint-Simonian and indefatigable economist Michel Chevalier held that economic science meant above all else the creation among men of a strong sense of "personal responsibility." State support always posed a serious menace. In this company, the aged Villermé was tame indeed, confining himself to admonishing his doctrinaire associates that one should closely observe the destitute before boldly discussing destitution. Observation revealed that the *misérables* were a various lot and that perhaps not all deserved the fate reserved for the morally weak or irresponsible. He remarked, lastly and justly, that "a word [here is] necessary to express the regret that Sismondi's name has not been cited in this discussion. He it was who gave the first cry of alarm" regarding the terrible fate of factory labor in our new society.[40]

The spokesmen of political economy were, in their own understanding of the word, meanly realistic. They were often inflexible and presented to the world an insufferable rectitude. But probably they were neither knowingly brutal nor devoid of all sense of the unhappy and often desperate condition of those whose welfare they claimed to advance. Happily for them, their science made very evident what should not be done and, as its positive program, simply shifted responsibility to the affected party himself, namely, the worker. Responsibility was made an individual moral affair.

The economists were well aware of this, in their eyes, necessary limitation. A. E. Cherbuliez, writing in the *Dictionnaire de l'économie politique*, was explicit: "With regard to the question of pauperism, political economy really provides only negative advice. It repulses state intervention as being always impotent and often dangerous. No less does it reject every system of social organization based upon the denial of [the rights of] property or of the family or based upon the right to work; all of these solutions can lead only to universal suffering and the dissolution of society."[41] To this conclusion Villermé could fully subscribe. Furthermore, because his every investigation had demonstrated that security in one's economic and social existence was the necessary prerequisite to a long

39. See Edgard Allix, "La déformation de l'économie politique libérale après J.-B. Say: Charles Dunoyer," *Revue d'histoire économique et sociale* 4 (1911): 115–47.
40. Villermé "Discussion," following Dufau, "Mémoire," pp. 114–15.
41. A. E. Cherbuliez, "Paupérisme, " *Dictionnaire de l'économie politique*, 2: 338.

and healthful life, the essential prelude to all considerations of public health was a sound understanding of political economy. Economic science defined the limits of humanitarian social action. It promised logical rigor and a scientific and unsentimental view of difficult problems and hard choices. It provided an escape from the vagaries of opinion of mere social philosophers and the dangerous passions of social reformers and revolutionaries. Political economy dealt instead with facts, with concrete social realities—or so it was claimed. Said Léon Faucher of the new faith: "Political economy is a science of observation or it is nothing. The principles that it proclaims it deduces from facts, and these principles [in turn] provide the most general expression of or, to put it most succinctly, the very law that governs these facts."[42] Empirical social science, of which hygienic investigation was an early and essential constituent, originated in this milieu dedicated to the supremacy of the irreducible fact and to the advance of civilization by means of industrial and mercantile expansion.

Factory and Farm

Villermé never resolved his discordant views of the benefits and liabilities of modern machine manufacture. Moreover, while recognizing the human threat seemingly inherent in the new system of manufacture, he refused to contemplate a purely agrarian solution to the social problem. The social setting of agriculture doubtlessly exercised a positive moral influence on labor, yet to attempt to return society to its earlier economic basis was impossible and, more importantly, would have to be effected at the expense of manufacture. The latter, however, represented progress. It was vastly more productive of wealth than agriculture had ever been, and it was the accomplishment of a new and praiseworthy social class whose rights, only recently given liberty of expression, had now to be fully secured. In the face of such conflicting demands it is not surprising that Villermé praised both large-scale manufacture and the independent farmer, all the while realizing that the former often degraded man and the latter seemed inconsistent with economic progress.

Villermé's essay the "Influence of Modern Machines and the Present Organization of Industry on the Condition of Labor" (published as chapter 10 of the second volume of *Tableau*) provides a concise statement of his philosophy of manufacture.[43] An ideal industrial order is here portrayed;

42. "Observations sur la doctrine de Malthus relative à la population, par MM. Passy, Dunoyer, Lord Brougham, Villermé, Guizot et Faucher," *Séances et travaux de l'Académie des sciences morales et politiques* 24 (1853): 457.

43. Villermé, "Influence des machines modernes et de l'organisation actuelle de l'industrie sur le sort des ouvriers," *Tableau*, 2: 295–326. On the philosophy of manufacture

the reader will also encounter the inconsistency of the author's program. The factory's presumed advantages for the laborer were easily listed; its contribution to the entrepreneur required no discussion. The factory in question was that which systematically employed prime movers, especially steam power, and which had means for conveying the power thus produced to machines variously located within the mill. In such a factory capital costs were high, division of labor well advanced, and strict internal discipline an economic necessity.

In Villermé's view, the new system of manufacture placed a much reduced physical burden upon the worker. No longer need human muscular effort be used to drive machinery, as it still was in certain French prison shops. Numerous repetitive and filthy operations, notably those involved in the preparation of raw fibers for spinning, were now performed by machines. Although extensive mechanization established a novel and rigorous regimen within and even without the factory, Villermé remained confident that the worker enjoyed a sufficient amount of leisure time. Only young children suffered in this regard, and their problem was really a working day that was too long and not tasks that were too burdensome. Neither in the *Tableau* nor elsewhere in his writings did he recognize the threat to the physical and moral well-being of the worker that was posed by the rapid pace and dulling routine necessitated by the factory system.

The single greatest benefit of modern manufacture was an indirect one. The factory hand earned a relatively high if occasionally uncertain wage at the same time that the new system was driving down the price of manufactured articles. Because of steam power, machine manufacture, and rationalization, the worker had become a consumer.[44] His needs, stimulated by new experience and opportunity, could now be satisfied and, better yet, constantly increased. Almost literally the idéologue philosophy, incarnate in Say's faith that products will always find their market, was translated into radical consumerism. Labor's satisfaction meant, of course, that the entrepreneur was well-rewarded for his risks and would thus be emboldened to invest in further expansion of his enterprise. If so, employment increased, more goods were produced, probably at a lower price, and the circle of mutual contentment was both sustained and enlarged.

There seemed to be, however, a natural and recurrent check to this cycle. Villermé and his generation were astonished and dismayed by the occasional breakdown of commercial exchange and the productive pro-

---

in Britain see the invaluable study by Maxine Berg, *The Machinery Question and the Making of Political Economy, 1815–1848* (Cambridge: University Press, 1980); there is no comparable work dealing with French industrial thought.

44. Villermé, *Tableau*, 2: 306.

cess. Business crises were perhaps the principal hazard created by large-scale manufacture. "If industry," he observed, "organized as it is today, presents one of society's [most] admirable spectacles, as soon as there is a crisis that same industry becomes one of [its] most dreadful" experiences.[45] Yet crises were simply an inherent "condition" of large-scale manufacture. It was, moreover, easier to accept their periodic manifestation when one realized that crises are, at worst, confined to certain times and places. Overproduction on a truly global scale Villermé appeared to consider an impossibility, thus following Say and rejecting Sismondi. Within narrower, for example, national, limits it had nonetheless become an all too familiar and frightening reality. The bust that followed the boom (the latter fueled by great expectations, increased employment, new needs, and new habits) could thus be viewed as a peril, albeit a temporary one, directly attributable to modern methods of manufacture.

Another apparently serious problem created by industry was reported. Workers engaged in artisanal manufacture were sure to be displaced by machine manufacture. Indeed, as machines were perfected, even some factory workers found themselves unemployed. But this too was a transient problem. Expanded manufacture reduced the price of finished goods, thereby engendering greater demand, which in turn forced manufacturers to recall discharged workers and even take on new hands. Economic law made the system self-correcting and showed it to be genuinely progressive.

All of these problems were either resolved by the system itself or were simply insoluble. Society had to accept them as an inescapable cost of industrialization. Other difficulties, however, translated the observer to a more homely level. Here Villermé's doubts regarding the unqualified benefits of large-scale manufacture became more prominent. The central issue was moral and has been remarked on several occasions above. The large factory sinned by both commission and omission. Regarding the latter, scale alone had caused the divorce of master and man. No longer directly involved in the production process and perhaps not even present in the factory at all, the master had abdicated his moral role. The worker, dispossessed of property, to Villermé always a lesser problem, now also had to make do without sound and repeated moral example. He was left either to his own devices, to the supervision of uncaring foremen, or, catastrophe itself, to the evil influence of his fellows in the factory. The philanthropic entrepreneurs of Mulhouse had asked after the character of these coworkers and had received a discouraging reply. The factory, they learned, had attracted from the calm life of the farm a horde of humanity

45. Ibid., p. 310.

that was "almost always . . . *defective, a kind of social scum.*"[46] Alas, no mutual guidance in healthy moral or social instincts could be expected from such a lot.

Add now to this uncertain beginning, continued Villermé, who felt he knew the type very well, the foul and crowded housing that these men and women were forced to occupy and the sexual license they displayed in the workplace. The sure result was moral and physical ruin, not only of adult workers but also of the children from whose numbers the unthinking master had to select his future hands. Housing was a matter that often could be controlled, even improved, by the attentive master. Separation of the sexes within the factory was a matter wholly within his power. Only reluctantly and because he recognized the futility of the effort did Villermé stop short of demanding a law that would compel strict segregation of male and female employees.[47]

This qualified indictment of modern manufacture was especially directed at the large factory utilizing steam and employing dozens, even hundreds, of workers. Villermé fully appreciated the rewards of this large-scale enterprise, but he also recognized its human costs. The factory promised increased production, cheaper goods, greater employment, and enhanced profits. Nonetheless, those profits were not only unequally shared—an altogether satisfactory arrangement to any sound economist,—but they were created in large part through the suffering of labor. Villermé was profoundly disturbed by this realization, but, convinced that the difficulty was at worst a transient one, he sought no solution to the problem. The difficulty was largely inherent in the nature of things; it was simply a constituent element of the economic process.

One solution, in addition to the modest effort at legislative action represented by the law of 22 March 1841, nonetheless did win favor. Even here, however, Villermé found it necessary to qualify the ideal by noting the imperious demands of the new industrial order. For security of employment, the cultivation of moral probity, and the assurance of social tranquility no form of economic activity exceeded agriculture. Between 1815 and 1848 the rural population had steadily increased and had created an even greater disproportion between available land and willing agricultural labor. The factory tended to draw off the surplus rural population, but in so doing, it had created another problem, namely the mass of undisciplined, debased, and socially dangerous workers that inhabited the new industrial town.

46. Ibid., p. 324.
47. Ibid., pp. 355–56.

How might this rural population be controlled, or more importantly, how might the creation and perpetuation of an urban proletariat be prevented? One solution, enthusiastically endorsed and occasionally attempted during the 1820s and 1830s, was the creation of agricultural colonies within France. Leadership in this movement was assumed by charitable members of the landed aristocracy, anxious to reestablish the healthy moral principles of Christianity.[48] Acting through the Société de morale chrétienne and especially the revived Société royale d'agriculture, the spokesmen of the movement—Villeneuve-Bargemont, Bigot de Morogues, the baron d'Haussez, Huerne de Pommeuse, and others—sought to interest the government in formally sponsoring their projects. Communal or as yet unoccupied land would be made available to men and women who agreed to occupy it and develop its agricultural potential. Each colony was to be limited in size, thus ensuring the economic and moral advantages of an intimate and functionally integrated community. In this setting, self-respect and self-sufficiency would develop alongside one another, vagabondage would be reduced, and destitution eliminated. The primary impulse driving labor to the factories was thus to be checked, and, a further and most important advantage, an institutional basis would be created for reasserting the traditional values of rural France.

Villermé looked closely at these proposals and found them wanting.[49] Their advocates' intentions he admired; their impracticality he regretted. He also very much disliked the sharp break with industrialization that agricultural colonization entailed. Reviewing at length Morogues' programmatic volume, Villermé stressed certain factors that made the success of these colonies very uncertain. To succeed in agricultural exploitation, one needed good soil, a relatively stable climate, and men and women of sound character. De Morogues had hoped to collect his colonists from among the urban *misérables*. To Villermé this seemed a most unpromising source of men and women for a risky pioneering endeavor. Communal lands, furthermore, could be allocated only once, and all presently untilled land was by no means suitable for exploitation. The formation of new agricultural colonies would surely come to a halt after one or perhaps two generations. It offered, therefore, no enduring solution to the problem it was meant to resolve.

But worst of all, urban workers had already expressed their view of the plan. During an earlier period of great distress, a charitable landowner of

48. Georges Cahen, "L'économie sociale chrétienne et la colonisation agricole sous la Restauration et la Monarchie de Juillet," *Revue d'économie politique* 17 (1903): 511–546.

49. Villermé, review of Morogues, *Recherches des causes de la richesse et de la misère*, pp. 242–53.

Amiens had offered to provide generous assistance to those workers who would return to the cultivation of land that he would make freely available. Not one family accepted the offer. The fact is, Villermé observed, that every day workers "pour into the city from the country," but they rarely move in the opposite direction. Furthermore, those families that "know only the industrial way of life . . . never or almost never desire to embrace an agricultural life; when reduced to indigence, they beg, they die in destitution, they launch upon a career in crime," but they do not return to the land.[50] Morogues and his associates had overlooked this crucial fact of industrial life: no matter how dreadful its conditions, labor no longer wanted to leave the city. Lastly, the agricultural colonies were to be closely regulated communities. In the name of collective endeavor and mutual responsibility they threatened to infringe upon a primary value of the economist, the independence of the individual. Here was another reason to discard the proposal.

Villermé's own remedy for the dilemma of factory labor stopped far short of this radical solution. He dreamed of saving at one and the same time the nuclear family, the security and presumed moral stimulus of simple rural life, and the availability of a numerous, eager, and skilled labor force for industry. His solution was utterly unoriginal, being familiar almost to the point of banality. The factory system must be limited to a small and thus human scale and the agricultural connection of labor maintained. Some mill towns, notably Roubaix and Tourcoing, had already shown how a just proportion between mechanized industry and limited agricultural activity could be assured. In contrast to crowded and hideous Lille, many workers in Roubaix and Tourcoing possessed a hut and a field on the edge of town. They walked to work and returned to their own homes at night.[51] There were fewer taverns here, debauchery was far less than in the vast mill town immediately to the south, and the general health of the working population was notably better. Villermé made similar observations regarding the balanced industrial-agricultural economy at Tarare, Sedan, and especially Zurich.[52]

Such examples and the conventional comparison with the condition of labor in the expansive mill towns pointed to a general and important conclusion regarding the relative merits of factory and farm, of city and country.[53] Economically, the city represented industry and progress; its devel-

50. Ibid., p. 250.

51. Villermé, *Tableau*, 1: 107–15.

52. Ibid., pp. 194–97 (Tarare), 253–79 (Sedan), 418–36 (Zurich).

53. See C. E. Schorske, "The Idea of the City in European Thought: Voltaire to Spengler," in *The Historian and the City*, ed. Oscar Handlin and John Burchard (Cambridge: M.I.T. Press, 1963), pp. 95–114; S. L. Thrupp, "The City as the Idea of Social Order,"

opment was thus applauded. Socially and morally, the city threatened all who entered it and thus had to be approached with extreme caution. Economically, agriculture provided security but little opportunity for expansion; it thus offered no measure of man's real productive capacities. Socially and morally, the farm and family preserved the most sacred of human values; their influence had therefore to be maintained in the face of the corrupting materialism rapidly becoming the philosophy of industrialism.

Villermé aimed to combine familial security, individual self-sufficiency, and factory-based manufacture. As always, the condition of labor provided his essential guide.

> The worker who lives in the city exists solely by means of his wages. The worker who resides in the country has a happier situation. Often he owns the house that he occupies. He even has a garden and sometimes a small field where he raises potatoes. Besides, many among them have rights to the pasture and woodlot of their local commune, and every year a large number of the weavers' families raise a few pigs whose flesh and lard are a great resource to them, especially in the winter. Some also possess one or two goats.
>
> In general, they all support their family without difficulty and raise their children in a sound manner; and many, particularly those who live in the villages, make small savings. Nowhere, in fact, have I met so many workers who told me that they were pleased [with their condition]. They believe that among their number those who work in the factories [pour les fabricans] are generally better off than those who work in their own homes.[54]

Labor's best social condition, as seen from Villermé's perspective, was consequently neither that of the factory laborer without other resources, nor the situation of the worker in the domestic system, nor even that of the self-sufficient small farmer. The owner of a freehold enjoyed the security afforded by such property, but he could move ahead in the world only by receiving the wages that factory manufacture alone offered. Such a worker, furthermore, was not withdrawn from the urban labor market as he would be if he resided in an agricultural colony, and he was not cast loose unrestrained as he would be had he simply moved into the city and abandoned all connection with rural life.

Villermé's remedy was but a dream and he knew it. Whatever we may conclude, he declared, regarding the advantages or inconveniences of the

---

ibid., pp. 121–32; Lewis Mumford, *The City in History: Its Origins, Its Transformations, and Its Prospects* (New York: Harcourt Brace, 1961), pp. 410–81.

54. Villermé, *Tableau*, 1: 267.

"introduction of machines into industry," we must concede that this process is "today stronger than anything we can do to stop it. We must, therefore submit to this fact and admit that nothing is to be gained by fighting
it."[55] A vast revolution has begun, he continued, and it has not yet run its
course. Workers who once divided their time between farm and factory
were now employed only by the latter. "In a great number of cities they
form a large proletariat which is usually dissatisfied with its lot and which
tends to increase remarkably in numbers." These changes, Villermé simply noted, "are precursors of others which are already in preparation and
must inevitably take place." We know not where our "revolution" is leading us; industry is still subject to all manner of perfection, and we cannot
anticipate the pace of development. But this we do know: "Industry today
is essentially progressive."[56] In that knowledge alone there was consola-
tion enough.

With these remarks Villermé settled firmly if somewhat uncomfortably
into the legions of industry. By sentiment attached to agriculture, especially to the amiable combination of cottage gardening and employment in
small-scale manufacture, he faced the new industrial world and found that
it was good, despite its several and notorious flaws. More importantly, the
factory system could not be refused. At best the rapid influx of labor into
the industrial towns could be slowed (but surely not stopped) and thus an
excessive number of recruits denied the industrial army. This would be the
hygienic solution, placing prevention before cure.[57] But the impractical
schemes of agricultural colonists could not be realized, and the happy
semi-independence of the workers of Roubaix or Zurich could not easily,
if at all, be duplicated or perhaps even continued. What remained was a
present reality frantically reproducing itself into the future, and both present and future were economically and socially controlled by large-scale
mechanized industry.

Villermé's Endeavor

Throughout Villermé's long career one feature remained constant: the
priority accorded at all times to direct experience of social conditions.
"The best and most lasting praise we can offer [him]," Alfred Legoyt,
director of the Statistique générale de France, declared, "is that it was he

55. Ibid., 2: 307.

56. Ibid., p. 326.

57. In Villermé's own words: "One understands, moreover, that if curing a disease is a
good deed, an altogether greater service is preventing it; and the best means of relieving
destitution is to put a halt to reducing men and women to poverty" (review of Morogues,
Recherches des causes de la richesse et de la misère, pp. 259–60).

who in France gave the first and most powerful stimulus to the creation of social statistics."[58] From the unprecedented horrors of the Peninsular Campaign under the First Empire to the quickening urbanization of the prosperous years of the July Monarchy, from the unreformed prisons of the Restoration era to the first manifestations of the factory system in France, and in Paris, microcosm of virtually all social transformations, Villermé had accumulated unparalleled experience with destitution and human suffering and with their influence upon the physical and moral well-being of the nation. His experience was not incidental but increasingly the result of systematic investigation. It was just this systematic character of public health inquiry that made this endeavor the most significant element in the early years of empirical social investigation. Villermé's own career exemplifies this activity.

His pursuit of a comprehensive view of society and its problems was informed by a small set of unshakable moral and economic convictions and guided by maturing methodological concerns and practices. Between his convictions and practices there was closest harmony. The science of society to whose early articulation he contributed was coextensive with an equally important science of man. In Villermé's endeavor is encountered the realization, albeit imperfect and much transmuted, of Cabanis's and the idéologues' ambition to create a new science of man and society.

Man himself was the center of this new discourse. Human nature provided the foundation upon which individual behavior depended and social intercourse was transacted. Villermé appears to have begun with the generous conviction of the more enthusiastic reformers of the Revolutionary era, who had argued that wisely reconstructed institutions would not only regenerate but truly reconstruct man. Years of experience with incessant social turmoil and with mankind at its worst as well as at its best and a new appreciation for the threat that this radical meliorism appeared to hold for the economic and social prerogatives of the newly ascendant bourgeois proprietor and industrial entrepreneur tempered this expectation. Human nature no longer was to be remade but was now simply to be given, in each individual case, fair opportunity to attain its fullest expression. Being biologically diverse, men and women possessed variable social potential. All persons of good will surely would want to assist each man and woman to realize his or her potential. Social improvement depended, therefore, upon individual improvement. The latter, in turn, depended upon moral instruction and example. An informed and model segment of the citizenry,

58. A.L. [Alfred Legoyt], "L. R. Villermé," *Journal de la Société statistique de Paris* 5 (1864): 47.

persons of property and probity, must mold the character of the remaining masses. From the latter there arose the occasional individual, and family, who in due course took his or her place among the economically privileged and socially powerful. Most individuals, however, did not rise. Their improvement consisted principally in instruction in the basics of economic security (diligence, frugality, sobriety) and in the reasoned portrayal of the sheer inevitability of the system in which they were caught up.

A new science, political economy, gave expression to the principles and consequences of this system. As with number, so with science: one argued with the conclusions of neither. Villermé accepted the central doctrines of political economy and, as has been seen, applied those doctrines to matters of public health. He was not and never pretended to be a theoretician of or the public spokesman for political economy. In this he was typical of other hygienists enamored of the science. All realized that inquiry regarding bodily or mental well-being could not ignore the great importance of the socioeconomic framework within which man lived. To these *hygiénistes-économistes*, however, realization meant acceptance and, ultimately, also justification. From this fact arose the singular nature of their activity as well as the painful contradiction constantly before them: empirical investigation revealed little but the suffering of the working population, while science continued to preach progress and hope.

Villermé did precisely as he claimed to do. He gathered social facts, and he reasoned earnestly and imaginatively upon those facts. He did not perceive, however, how often his reasoning anticipated his evidence, and he overlooked numerous instances in which the evidence simply failed to support his contentions. He was persuaded, nonetheless, that his manner of social analysis was greatly preferable to that of contemporary social philosophers, men of the mind alone and not the senses and socially a dangerous group indeed. No doubt their criticism was sincere, and they did not err in emphasizing the many and profound difficulties that troubled industrial society. They did err, however, by failing to investigate at first hand and in various settings over long periods of years the facts of the matter. Theirs might be nominally the philosophical approach to society, but it was not the scientific approach.

Villermé occasionally verged upon arguing that, even if the conclusions stated in a given case were proved erroneous, the truth of the facts that had been gathered remained inviolate and their value undiminished. Thus, with regard to the first among methodological tools for social analysis, he declared that "statistics is the science of agreed upon and numerically expressed facts" and its aim is "to discover and present these facts, without

granting or applying any theory or opinion whatsoever to them."[59] Facts
so securely established and so modestly exhibited would seem to constitute the utterly neutral data of social science. Such had been Faucher's
claim for political economy. Perhaps, against all probability, such a claim
is true. Villermé himself wisely qualified his own assertion:

> All that the statistician need do after he has established his facts is to
> assemble the data and to bring together those that are analogous or of
> the same kind and to present them, naked, counted, measured. Then
> [he has] to compare them with facts of another kind, to determine the
> frequency relationships of the former with the latter and *to point out* as
> far as possible the laws that bind these sets of data together. [He will
> also have to] relate this immense quantity of facts or individual phe-
> nomena to a small number of phenomena or general facts that express
> all of them, that are, if you will, their principles. In a word, [he will
> need to] present his facts in such a manner that the greatest number of
> conclusions ensues therefrom, particularly such conclusions as are of
> greatest importance to man and society.[60]

Emphatically, Villermé did not view sociomedical investigation as mere
data-gathering. His major investigations were conducted with a particular
goal or goals in mind, and each inquiry was designed to elicit information,
social "facts," that bore directly upon the problem at hand. Over and again
his purpose was to offer a demonstration—whether of the differential mortality by economic status in the quarters of Paris or of the varied condition
of workers in the different textile fabriques—and not simply to record
observations. And over and again his demonstration was one that stressed
the hygienic implications of important socioeconomic distinctions. The
latter, although usually expressed in economic terms, were generally held
to be due to moral differences between the populations in question. In
such a context, the very notion of gathering statistical or any other socially
relevant data without, as was suggested, "applying any theory or opinion
whatsoever to them" was patently untenable, and Villermé never made the
attempt. To reason on number was a different endeavor, one peculiarly
fitted to socioeconomic investigation, and to this Villermé was wholly
given. The principles for such reasoning were provided, of course, not by
number or social fact but by political economy.

Jean Baptiste Say had given much thought to these ideas. Unthinking
men, he observed, wanted only "*facts and figures*," little realizing that
"facts and figures have meaning only insofar as they prove something, and

---

59. Villermé, "Recensement de la population sarde pour l'année 1838: Rapport verbal,"
Annales d'hygiène publique et de médecine légale 24 (1840): 248–49.
60. Ibid., pp. 249–50.

this they can do only when aided by reason."[61] Because of the growing complexity of society, encouraged by the rapid and beneficent progress of the division of labor, Say determined to consider society a living organism. The study of its structure and function was, he concluded, a veritable "physiology." Hence, all social phenomena without exception are intimately related to all others. The study of society is the general science and economics only its most important and suggestive subdiscipline. For this reason Say contemplated the idea of a science called *économie sociale*. He wrote: "The study that has been made of the nature and functions of the different parts of the social body has itself created a set of ideas, a science, to which has been given the name *political economy* and which might perhaps better have been called social economy."[62] Social economy was to be the study of the totality of the ongoing process of society, *économie* itself referring to the "inner laws governing organisms, communities, and nations."

Unlike many contemporary physicians and economists, Villermé avoided explicit use of the long-familiar metaphor of the social organism.[63] Nevertheless, he fully appreciated the supposed phenomenal bases for its new popularity. Sociomedical investigation had laid bare many and often unsuspected interconnections between seemingly independent social, environmental, and moral phenomena. The numerical method had proved especially useful in identifying these interconnections.[64] From one perspective, therefore, sociomedical investigation of the period 1815–48 may be viewed as the earliest systematic effort to seize the complex interrelations governing social structure and change. It was also an effort to create a science of society, a science which, when brought to maturity, seemed certain to replace the long reign of mere opinion, party interest,

61. J. B. Say, *Cours complet d'économie politique pratique*, 2nd ed., 2 vols (Paris: Guillaumin, 1840), 1: 15.

62. Ibid., p. 1: 2: 237. The economists were obsessed with precise denomination of their science; see Joseph Garnier, "De l'origine et de la filiation du mot *Economie politique* et des divers autres noms donnés à la science économique," *Journal des économistes* 32 (1852): 300–316; 33 (1852): 11–23.

63. Usage of the metaphor returned with great force in nineteenth-century biology, medicine, and political and social theory in general. See F. W. Coker, *Organismic Theories of the State: Nineteenth-Century Interpretations of the State as Organism and as Person* (New York: Columbia University Press, 1910); Owsei Temkin, "Metaphors of Human Biology," in *Science and Civilization*, ed. R. C. Stauffer (Madison: University of Wisconsin Press, 1949), pp. 167–94; Gunther Mann, "Medizinisch-biologische Ideen und Modelle in der Gesellschaftslehre des 19. Jahrhunderts," *Medizinhistorisches Journal* 4 (1969): 1–23. Say's views are expressed in his *Cours complet*, 1: 1–2, also 2: 507–40.

64. It may be noted that Say, given to the Cartesian manner of reasoning and suspicious of the notion of probability, discounted statistics and the numerical method; see his *Cours complet*, 2: 483–507.

and political confusion with a secure core of well-established social facts and rigorously deduced truths.

Say certainly promulgated this sad self-deception, but Villermé never entertained it. He knew full well that his inquiry had uncovered terrible abuses in the new economic system. Yet he also insisted that, despite these abuses and the suffering they caused, the dominion of capitalist industry was both desirable and unstoppable. It was the finest expression of individual initiative. Furthermore, industry, like economic progress in general, was the best index of the moral strength of the nation. If some economists, notably those of the severe English classical school, had deceived themselves into thinking that they had discovered truly "amoral laws of wealth," their laws were, insofar "as regards poverty, moral in import. And in fact they served to prove one basic proposition: individual regeneration was the only hope of the poor."[65] This proposition guided the constructive thought of the French economist, too, and in the hands of certain authors, notably Charles Dunoyer and Frédéric Bastiat, was offered in justification of the virtual abandonment of public responsibility for society's unfortunates. Sociomedical observers, with Villermé in the lead, accepted the dogmas of political economy but rejected the abstractness of that so-called science. Long nurtured on direct experience of society's worst problems, exposed on a daily basis to the actual living, and dying, conditions of those persons whose apparently inadequate moral strength had failed to bring them prosperity or even minimal economic security, these observers faced an especially difficult problem. They had to reconcile the conflicting claims of a suffering multitude with the enhanced productivity and progressive character of large-scale mechanized manufacture and its economic consequences. Villermé's intellectual career was largely devoted to establishing and defending this reconciliation. Nevertheless he was not alone in his efforts, for in this same period a small but voluble party of physicians eagerly shared the task of melding political economy and public health. Their efforts, and the emerging socialist opposition, are described in the concluding chapter.

---

65. Calvin Woodward, "Reality and Social Reform: The Transition from Laissez-Faire to the Welfare State," *Yale Law Journal* 72 (1962): 316. See, in addition to Woodward's essential essay, Jacob Viner, "The Intellectual History of Laissez Faire," *Journal of Law and Economics* 3 (1960): 45–69. Adolfe Quetelet pursued an identical train of thought: he observed that "one of the general principles that must never be lost from view is that society must avoid allowing itself to substitute for [the actions of] individuals in all matters of [economic] foresight" (quoted in John Bartier, "Quetelet politique," in *Adolfe Quetelet, 1796–1874: Contributions en hommage à son rôle de sociologue*, Mémorial Adolfe Quetelet publié à l'occasion du centième anniversaire de sa mort, no. 4 [Brussels: Académie royale de Belgique, 1977], p. 30).

Chapter 10

Public Health and Political Economy

A social body cannot be constructed like a machine, on abstract principles which merely include physical motions, and their numerical results in the production of wealth. The mutual relation of men is not merely dynamical, nor can the composition of their forces be subjected to a purely mathematical calculation. Political economy, though its object be to ascertain the means of increasing the wealth of nations, cannot accomplish its design, without at the same time regarding their happiness, and as its largest ingredient the cultivation of religion and morality.

James Phillips Kay, 1832

The tension inherent in the outlook of the French hygienists during the 1830s and 1840s was caused by the discord between their ready perception of the seriousness of the social problem and their failure to seek more than symptomatic relief of its consequences. Political economy the science lay at the root of their dilemma. The hygienists sought knowledge of society but refused to contemplate significant social reform based upon their new insight. They thought they knew the world, but as economists, they had no intention of changing it.

Critics of the economists insisted upon this fatal shortcoming. Eugène Buret, author of the prize-winning essay *De la misère des classes laborieuses en Angleterre et en France*, an important source for the emerging socialist critique of classical political economy, identified the problem with precision and rhetorical flourish. Political economy, he noted,

is not responsible for the existence of industrial anarchy but only for having regarded it as an [unqualified] boon to mankind. The historian is not the cause of the wars and scourges of which he writes and yet, unhappily, political economy has sought to make itself an historical discipline, an effort in erudition rather than an active, practical science, one that can destroy what is harmful and that can do good [for man-

EPIGRAPH: J. P. Kay, *The Moral and Physical Condition of the Working Classes Employed in the Cotton Manufacture in Manchester* (London: James Ridgeway, 1832; reprinted, Shannon, 1971), p. 39.

kind]. This science, which should have become social medicine, has timidly halted at anatomy and physiology; it has lacked the courage to grapple with the difficulties and perils of therapeutics. Yet society has need not only of knowledge about itself; it also demands the means to cure [its problems]! It no longer suffices to know *how things are constituted*; we need to seek how things should be constituted so that this world of ours may present less suffering and destitution. Now, to reach this goal, we must not simply relate a story but judge its meaning.[1]

Villermé, who by the 1840s was widely recognized as the foremost spokesman of the hygienists, exhibited in particularly striking manner this dualistic social perspective—and also the impossibility of adhering strictly to it. Buret fully appreciated his contemporary's unsatisfactory situation: "M. Villermé . . . drifts indecisively between optimism and the ideas that have inspired our own work," these being pessimism regarding social peace and progress unless major reforms were quickly inaugurated. "An optimist in his principles and intentions," Buret continued, "he cannot refrain, when faced by the dreadful facts that [modern] industry puts before us, from blaming the economic system that has produced this situation."[2] But, as has been repeatedly observed above, to blame meant at most to assign responsibility and not, save in special instances, to seek a remedy via legislation or social change. To the hygienist-economist, the suffering of the laboring classes was real but only temporary, and its alleviation was to be sought by means of individual moral improvement and economic expansion, not public intervention.

No group of social observers before 1848 had contributed more broadly or more pointedly to popular recognition of the disproportionate risks and inordinate suffering faced by the worker and his family than the first generation of French sociomedical investigators. They made differential mortality the critical index of social malaise and well-being. They rendered social fact in numerical form and because of this laid claims to scientific, hence authoritative, status for their endeavor. At the outset of scientific social analysis *misère* was medically defined. Yet its elimination was seen to transcend the medical domain. If action were to be taken, such action would necessarily have political dimensions. The economists denied such

1. Eugène Buret, *De la misère des classes laborieuses en Angleterre et en France; de la nature de misère, de son existence, de ses effets, de ses causes et de l'insuffisance des remèdes qu'on lui a opposés jusqui'ici; avec l'indication des moyens propres à en affranchir les sociétés*, 2 vols. (Paris: Paulin, 1840), 2: 124–25. Buret's outlook and language, strikingly similar to Marx's view of political economy, are analyzed and compared with the usages of the German philosopher by Hilde Riguadias-Weiss, *Les enquêtes ouvrières en France entre 1830 et 1848* (Paris: P.U.F., 1936), pp. 134–57.

2. Buret, *De la misère*, 2: 199.

a need. They thus again gave witness to their central conviction: under a regime of liberty, the individual is alone the master of his fate.

But a new solution to social injustice and destitution was then in creation. The sharpening socialist voice demanded systematic social reform, even total social reconstruction. Whereas political economy preached patience to the *misérables* and counted on growth and moral improvement to correct flaws in social organization, and while advocates of vigorous charitable assistance in general sought the restoration of traditional hierarchical social organization and a renewal of the authority of crown and church, the socialists saw no need either to re-create the past or preserve the present. Before 1848 socialism remained inchoate and was still largely utopian. The economists, as men of science, regarded their new rivals with scorn—but also with growing apprehension. The socialist challenge requires therefore brief consideration in this assessment of the connection between public health and political economy.

The economists' case against socialism and, indeed, against all alternative social remedies was grounded in their optimistic persuasion. With the advance of civilization, of the new bourgeois order rising upon expanded commerce and industrialization, they concluded that wealth sufficient to alleviate the condition of all morally deserving men and women was becoming available. If sickness and death had social origins—a major conclusion of sociomedical investigation—so too did they have social remedies, but not those created by the imaginings of men, medical, political, or otherwise. Instead, the solution was to be found in the nature of things, in respect for those natural and hence inevitable processes by which society itself had slowly progressed from savagery and barbarism to its present promising condition. In the second section of this chapter I review the arguments regarding the sociomedical meaning of *civilisation* and its untoward or fortunate contributions to human well-being.

The events of 1848 in France brought social conflict dramatically into the open. Nonetheless, the Revolution of 1830 had awakened the political nation—the electors and contending bourgeois improvers—to the existence of a depressing and dangerous social problem. Sociomedical observers had taken the lead in this process of national self-enlightenment, even before the July Revolution directing attention to concrete vital differentiae and pointing out the basis therefor in relative wealth and poverty. Villermé, of course, provided sustained initiative for this enterprise, and his long career spanned the entire course of the French public health movement. I have chosen to relate the principal features of the central ideology of the movement in terms of that career. But Villermé was not merely a leader; he was also a member of a larger group, a *parti d'hygiène publique*. In my concluding section I deal with other members of this party.

In the writings of Louis François Benoiston de Châteauneuf, François Mélier, Jean Baptiste Parent-Duchâtelet, and others are discovered further dimensions of early French sociomedical investigation. The widespread appeal of liberal ideology also will become evident, an appeal that points again to the connection between the world of the economist and that of sociomedical investigation.

The Socialist Challenge

Socialism in France arose from the expectations left unresolved by the Revolution and from the social disharmonies created by industrialization.[3] The Revolution had destroyed the old social order, but no plan amongst the many proposed for construction of a new order had gained wide acceptance. The economists provided theoretical justification for the activities of one of the greatest beneficiaries of the Revolution, the commercial and industrial class, and largely left other members of society to find a place befitting their individual initiative or moral strength. The difficulties of the expanding urban proletariat in gaining a secure social position gave principal stimulus to the search for a truly new and more just organization of industrial society.

Early socialist thought is immensely varied, its advocates comprising a host of headstrong, imaginative, and often colorful figures. Despite sharp doctrinal differences, they shared important beliefs and exhibited a common character. To the economist as to the later so-called scientific socialist of Marxian persuasion, the French socialists were hopelessly utopian. They indulged their reason, translated their dreams into definite plans for a new social order, and on celebrated occasions, such as the Saint-Simonians' retreat at Ménilmontant and the various phalansteries founded in the name of Charles Fourier, attempted to give tangible form to their inventions. To Karl Marx these efforts stood condemned at the outset because they failed to issue from social transformations founded upon a radical reordering of economic relations, changes to be introduced not by reason and benevolent meddling but by conscious action, probably revolutionary, on the part of the proletariat itself.

The economists, too, disdained their fellow social philosophers but for other reasons. Louis Reybaud, for example, writing in the *Dictionnaire de l'économie politique*, made no pretense of treating these "utopias" with sympathy.[4] Their fantastic quality he well appreciated and attempted to

3. See George Lichtheim, *The Origins of Socialism* (New York: Praeger, 1969). Also Frank E. Manuel, *The Prophets of Paris* (Cambridge: Harvard University Press, 1962).

4. Louis Reybaud, "Socialistes," *Dictionnaire de l'économie politique*, ed. Charles Coquelin and G.-U. Guillaumin, 2 vols. (Paris: Guillaumin, 1852–53), 2: 629–41.

convey to his reader. But it was more important to indicate what was, in the eyes of political economists, their decisive shortcoming, a flaw that had obvious bearing on the possibility or desirability of social intervention by public authorities with regard to matters of health.

Socialism—an expression which, from its introduction in 1832 until the late 1840s referred to one or another speculative scheme, each lacking serious working-class support—demanded the creation of genuine community, a community in which the harmonious interaction of men and women and the assurance of overall well-being were made supreme goals. Social order and human dignity, lost in the whirlwinds of Revolution and industrialization, would be recaptured by means of association. Men and women might combine in egalitarian communities, the Fourierist vision, or in a religio-technocratic state, with its hierarchies based on expertise, as envisaged by Saint-Simon and his disciple Prosper Enfantin. The Saint-Simonians welcomed industrialization and its prodigious augmentation of human productivity; the Fourierists sought instead the self-sufficiency of the autonomous and small community and were repelled by the scale and consequences of mass commercial and industrial society. Both, however, anticipated that French society could heal its wounds and return to a harmonious existence only by reestablishing in the very structure of society itself an intimate association among men. On a more limited but more practical level this was the ambition, too, of Louis Blanc and others whose aim was to assure, again by deliberate social reorganization, the availability of work to all who desired it.

The economists countered, as expected, by reviling association, denouncing the presumed moral laxity of communitarian experiments, and reasserting the fundamental creed of individualism. To resolve the common problems, namely, social order and economic security, political economy offered the assurance that unfettered exercise of individual initiative led inevitably to an increase in collective wealth and happiness. Perceived social disorder and individual deprivation were not denied but simply held to be transient disturbances in the steady march of economic development. "What anabaptism was to the fifteenth century socialism is to ours," cried Reybaud.[5] Socialism was the formal appeal to indulgence

5. Ibid., p. 637. Reybaud catalogued marvellously the fears of the liberal bourgeoisie: "Le socialisme a eu son jour de vogue; bien des gens sont allés vers lui comme on va vers la nouveauté; puis la foule s'en est mêlée, sans bien comprendre de quoi il s'agissait, mais avec le sentiment confus qu'elle y trouverait son intérêt et qu'á défaut de conviction elle devait y adhérer par calcul. Comment s'en serait-elle défendue? On lui promettait un âge d'or d'où toute souffrance serait bannie, un plus fort salaire en échange d'un moindre travail, des jouissances de toute nature, sans en excepter celles de la vanité, l'aisance, le luxe, les honneurs et jusqu'à l'empire. Aux uns on montrait la spoliation en perspective; aux

of the senses, to compensation without proportionate labor, and an artificial construction raised in defiance of the laws of nature. The socialist dream thus was destroyed by the fundamental truth in the economists' armamentarium, human nature. Each man or woman prospered only by cultivation and exercise of his or her unique abilities. Social organization was important only in assuring that such exercise was not hindered by artificial and thus false constraints.

The anxiety of the economists rose to its peak as the decade of the 1840s closed. Doctrines that sound science, namely political economy, had rejected as contrary to reason and even to common sense the worker now found increasingly attractive. Many workers in the Lyons fabrique, Villermé anxiously observed, "are adopting with enthusiasm the ideas of Fourier, Louis Blanc, and others, and [they] dream only of association [or] phalanstery, or self-styled organization of work and community of property. These illusions are themselves sources of error and have already become dangerous . . . because by the inevitable march of logic they can give rise, as occasion presents, to deplorable actions." Today in Lyons, he continued, the thought of "revolution" was in the air, social ambitions were excited, and a "vast association," cleverly divided into cells to evade police surveillance, had been formed.[6]

Villermé's concern was not misplaced. It was in the 1840s that radical republicanism and socialism were joined by the first manifestations of the French working-class movement. The socialist alternative when proposed by Saint-Simonian or Fourierist enthusiast or even by the unfortunate Louis Blanc might be ridiculed and easily refuted and the economist, now become the protective apologist of a new industrial society, still rest easy. But the revolutionary element in French socialism, implanted there by the Babeuf conspiracy of 1795–96, had never been lost. Its aim was to seize political power, by violence if necessary, and that aim seemed to many to be dangerously near realization in 1848. To ardent republican and socialist alike the promise of *blanquisme*, social change by means of insurrection and fierce egalitarian reorganization, appeared about to be fulfilled. But labor, like the socialist, did in fact lose its revolution in 1848. Yet liberal republicanism, whose principles had since the Charter of 1814 constituted

---

autres, le relâchement du frein social; à ceux-ci, l'humiliation des classes élevées; à ceux-là, le nivellement des conditions. Tous les mauvais instincts étaient sollicités et conviés à un immense déchaînement. Faut-il s'étonner qu'un semblable vertige ait été contagieux et qu'un instant il ait pu prendre un caractère aussi alarmant?"

6. Villermé, "Notes sur quelques monopoles usurpés par les ouvriers de certaines industries, suivie de quelques observations sur la situation actuelle des ouvriers dans les bassins houillers de la Loire et du Centre," *Journal des économistes* 17 (1847): 167. The author offered no evidence to support these inflammatory claims.

the ideal of economist and hygienist, lost even more. Liberalism during these years of turmoil simply gave up all credibility. Saved by the army, then captured by *bonapartisme*, the leaders of the constitutional monarchy had been unable and, in truth, unwilling to offer even symptomatic relief to the laboring masses upon whom the nation's new industrial wealth was critically dependent.

With some exceptions, the utopian socialists appear not to have devoted particular attention to problems of public health or individual medical care.[7] Fourier evaded the central issue, the condition of the industrial town, by seeking salvation in the self-contained, essentially agricultural phalanstery. The Saint-Simonians and Louis Blanc embraced the industrial order, the former admiring its power and rationality, the latter seeking to bend it to better serve the interests of its primary servants, factory labor. Their concerns focused on property relations, increased production, or the assurance of work, all matters of paramount importance because they were the economic preconditions for a healthful existence. Their argument was phrased, however, in essentially political terms, terms that gave expression to bold conceptions of social reorganization, and not in the language of the hygienist.

The socialist challenge twice missed the hygienic mark. Its proponents aimed at global social reconstruction and thus attended little to the specifically hygienic problems of urban and industrial France. More importantly, hygienic expertise, one of the great social acquisitions of the pre-1848 era, was largely in the hands of persons either unsympathetic or wholly hostile to the ambitions of socialism. To association these hygienists opposed individualism; to public responsibility for the nation's hygienic welfare they opposed the necessity of individual self-sufficiency. As a consequence comprehensive knowledge of the true dimensions and implications of the sanitary condition of the French nation and especially of the proletariat belonged to men who put the public as a collectivity foremost in matters of public health only with greatest reluctance, if at all. Knowledge did not, because it could not, entail action. Buret's charge was valid: Villermé and the *parti d'hygiène* were seized by indecision, their optimism being constantly denied by present realities. Yet it was the hy-

7. This appearance may well be false; no comprehensive study of the medical and hygienic views of the French utopians is available. But see the suggestive essay by Herman Hausheer, "Icarian Medicine: Etienne Cabet's Utopia and Its French Medical Background," *Bulletin of the History of Medicine* 9 (1941); 294–310, 401–35, 517–29. Also see Dora B. Weiner, *Raspail, Scientist and Reformer* (New York: Columbia University Press, 1968), esp. pp. 135–63, 268–88; François André Isambert, *De la Charbonnerie au Saint-Simonisme: Etude sur la jeunesse de Buchez* (Paris: Editions de Minuit, 1966); idem, *Politique, religion et science de l'homme chez Philippe Buchez (1796–1865))* (Paris: Cujas, 1967).

gienists who had created genuine public awareness of specific health consequences of industrialization and urbanization, and not those who had
first raised the socialist challenge.

Civilization

Shibboleth of the economists, *civilisation* assembled in a single word
all previous social progress and offered promise of a still better world to
come. The voices of *civilisation* celebrated the arrival of the new industrial
order and the ascendancy of the class that had assured that order's creation, the bourgeoisie. Civilization made known the economic and moral
advances that had severed modern man once and for all from his savage
predecessors and marked off nineteenth-century European society from
the numerous still barbarous peoples occupying less privileged regions of
the globe. Other social observers might be given to anger or to gloom, but
optimism reigned in the camp of the economists; civilization was their
supreme witness.

The medical issue regarding civilization had been polemically formulated by Jean Jacques Rousseau in his celebrated discourse on the origin
of inequality among men (1755). Praising (a hypothetical) man as he existed in a (hypothetical) state of nature, Rousseau condemned the artifi-
ciality and hence the vice of man's rise to civilization. The life of reason,
the cultivation of the arts and sciences, the false usages of polite society—
all divorced man from his natural condition. They rendered him unfit for
genuine, that is, harmonious, social existence, and they seriously weakened his very biological being. If, Rousseau declaimed, nature has indeed
"destined us to be healthy," a proposition the author accepted as an article
of faith, "I daresay that the act of reasoning [*état de reflexion*] puts us in
a condition *contra Nature* and that the man who meditates is a depraved
animal. Savages, who are not given to reflection, suffer almost no afflictions save wounds and age. Without hesitation we draw the conclusion
that we can easily re-create the history of human disease by writing that
of civil society."[8]

---

8. J. J. Rousseau, *Discours sur l'origine, et les fondemens de l'inégalité parmi les
hommes*, ed. Jean Starobinski, in *Oeuvres complètes*, ed. Bernard Gagnebin and Marcel
Raymond, 4 vols. to date (Paris: Gallimard, 1968–), 3: 138; Starobinski's notes are particularly valuable. Rousseau's reflections offer a curious and willful redirection of the ancient
medical doctrine of the "nonnaturals": see William Coleman, "Health and Hygiene in the
Encyclopédie: A Medical Doctrine for the Bourgeoisie," *Journal of the History of Medicine*
29 (1974): 399–421. The argument regarding a connection between civilization and disease
antedates Rousseau; see Carl Haffter, "Die Entstehung des Begriffs der Zivilisationskrank-
heiten," *Gesnerus* 36 (1979): 228–37.

Rousseau's extravagant challenge lived on well into the nineteenth century. It became a topic for repeated consideration by members of the medical profession and gave obvious provocation to physicians who sought to defend, whether on hygienic or other grounds, the contrary position, namely, that modern society, far from being a detriment to the welfare of mankind, was in fact the essential precondition and accompaniment of human improvement. The economists and their friends never tired of congratulating Europe on its new-found good fortune. The historian and statesman François Guizot, having equated civilization with progress, sought terms to measure the latter:

> Take all the facts of which the history of a nation is composed, all the facts which we are accustomed to consider as the elements of its existence—take its institutions, its commerce, its industry, its wars, the various details of its government; and if you would form some idea of them as a whole, if you would see their various bearings on each other, if you would appreciate their value, if you would pass a judgment upon them, what is it you desire to know? Why, what part they have done to forward the progress of civilization—what part they have acted in the great drama, —what influence they have exercised in aiding its advance. . . . Civilization is, as it were, the grand emporium of a people, in which all its wealth—all the elements of its life—all the powers of its existence are stored up.[9]

Guizot's histories focused, however, upon progress as measured by political forms (the emergence of the constitutional state) and by Western man's spiritual liberation (in which the Reformation played a decisive part). Economic expansion and, above all, industrialization remained minor actors on his stage. To many contemporaries, also staunch partisans of progress, this shortcoming demanded a remedy, one provided by the doctrinaire economist Gustav de Molinari with uncommon gusto.

Molinari explained the coming of civilization in the language of the idéologues.[10] Man's needs drive him to action and repeated activity ultimately brings satisfaction; the pursuit of gain is covered by this formula. At some point or points along the route to satisfaction, frustration and even suffering is sure to be encountered. This difficulty faces the individual and no doubt also society at large. Yet the problem remains always a temporary one and in the end is probably always transcended. Thus, knowledge does in fact increase with time, and material wealth is also augmented. It is that peculiar condition called liberty which, by allowing

9. F.P.G. Guizot, *General History of Civilization in Europe*, ed. G. W. Knight (New York: Appleton, 1892). p. 6.

10. Gustav de Molinari "Civilisation," *Dictionnaire de l'économie politique*, 1: 370–77.

us maximum free exercise of our mind and will, guarantees the progressive development of civilization. We gain additional satisfaction from the assurance inherent in the rights of property that our exertions have not been and will not be in vain.

Morality does not, as the popular view of Rousseau proclaimed, decline with an advance in material prosperity. In uncertain proof of this contention Molinari cited the triumph of Christianity over paganism and, more pointedly, the replacement of the activity of Saint Dominic and Torquemada by contemporary Christian society. Molinari regarded the advance of civilization as being well-nigh inevitable. Its fullest expression was given by the degree of "development of man's power over nature," a measure tied directly to the increasing pace of trade and industrialization.[11] The ancients, Molinari noted, had entertained a notion of progress in the artistic domain, but they had failed—as Guizot, too, was seen to fail—to realize that it was also the nature of man to explore and then exploit his physical environment. Progress, hence civilization, was manifest in the economic and technical sphere as much as and perhaps much more than in either the aesthetic or political domains. The factory and its product offered visible proof of the prowess and superiority of modern European society.

As an explicit medical theme the issue of civilization and disease had also gained a wide hearing by 1830. The great hygienist Jean Noël Hallé still doubted the beneficence of the urban industrial order, but members of the younger generation rose strongly in its defense. Sociomedical investigation using the numerical method appeared to offer decisive proof that civilization reduced the incidence of disease and death and contributed directly to improved physical well-being. Many authors discussed this theme (see below), but few addressed it so directly or with such a fund of curious evidence as did Villermé. The blessings of civilization had provided, of course, the continuing argument of his statistical inquiries, especially those dealing with the vital condition of the population of Paris. He also made the theme the centerpiece of the remarkable essay that he entered in support of his candidacy for a chair at the Academy of Moral and Political Sciences.[12] Here civilization rose truly triumphant, hygiene

11. Ibid., pp. 376–77. The economists gave particularly bold expression to the long-standing notion in Western thought that mankind was created to exercise dominion over this world and its many creatures; for the background to this argument see the works cited in William Coleman, "Providence, Capitalism, and Environmental Degradation: English Apologetics in an Era of Economic Revolution," *Journal of the History of Ideas* 37 (1976): 27–44.

12. Villermé, "Des épidémies sous les rapports de l'hygiène publique, de la statistique médicale et de l'économie politique," *Annales d'hygiène publique et de médecine légale* 9

and statistics uniting to form one authoritative statement of the principles essential to the science of political economy.

In all nations, nothing so captures public attention and evokes popular concern as the incursion of epidemic disease. Although Europe had had long experience with major epidemics, the cholera outbreak of 1832 proved uncommonly disturbing. For several generations France had not faced a comparable medical calamity. There had been ample warning and preventive measures had been taken, yet the spread of cholera proved sudden and devastating. Was the cholera, were other epidemics, an indication that the accomplishments of civilization were in fact inadequate for the protection of society? Were the civilized Europeans condemned to suffer disease just like the heathen in India or the barbarians on the steppes of Asia? Did the attainment of civilization offer man no assurance, either today or in the future, that his basic biological interest had been and would be protected? With such questions in mind Villermé mounted a medical defense of civilization.

Varied evidence suggested that the severity of epidemic outbreaks in Europe had diminished since the early eighteenth century. Except for cholera, France had experienced no widespread and deadly epidemic since the famine and disease of 1709–10 (plague, however, was locally severe in Marseilles in 1720–21). Paradoxically, cholera itself offered melancholy witness to the benefits of the civilized condition. At the time of writing evidence was becoming available that seemed to prove beyond any doubt that this was a disease that chose its victims primarily from among the poor. Those who participated least in the benefits of industry, whose incomes were lowest and least secure, provided the preponderance of cholera deaths. Cholera, of course, offered only a special case of the general proposition that "epidemics everywhere . . . strike the destitute or miserable classes much more than they do persons of quality."[13] Since the level of civilization that a society or social class had attained was ultimately to be measured by its respective economic condition, by, to use an expression not yet coined, its standard of living, this conclusion reaffirmed that the severity of an epidemic was relative but measurable, not just in epidemiological terms but in degree of civilization attained.

Joseph Fourier, moreover, had discovered that annual variations in mortality in Paris since the eighteenth century had shown a progressive diminution. Whereas in an earlier period this variation on occasion reached a

(1833): 5–58. This essay is drawn largely from an earlier publication, "Epidémies, épidémiques (maladies)," *Dictionnaire de médecine; ou, Répertoire général des sciences médicales sous le rapport théorique et pratique*, ed. N. P. Adelon et al., 2nd ed., 30 vols. (Paris: Bechet, 1832–45), 12: 130–72.

13. Villermé, "Des épidémies," p. 14.

level equal to one-quarter, even one-half of that of a normal year, contemporary Paris saw this figure drop to one-fifteenth or even less. The achievement was due, in Fourier's opinion, to a "more enlightened and humane attitude towards public assistance" and "to a general [and improved] disposition of mind, to experience, and to the progress of industry." Indeed, he noted, epidemic mortality has diminished in proportion to the spread of "useful knowledge" among men, that is, "to the degree that civilization has progressed or become more diffused in society."[14]

Figures collected by Thomas Short, an English physician especially concerned with the pattern of mortality in London, although surely exaggerating evident differences, purported to prove that epidemics "ordinarily" were less severe in the city than in the country. This, Villermé thought, was due to the "difference of civilization" that separated these two social worlds. Civilization, again, explained the disappearance of fever in Viareggio, a coastal town near Lucca. The installation of floodgates in 1741 had led to obliteration of the local marshes. Mortality and sickness declined dramatically. A "climate" had been changed and great medical benefit gained. The important matter at Viareggio was that man, not nature, had accomplished the change. The triumph of rational hygienic intervention—"this miracle," Villermé exclaimed—was one wholly "effected by civilization."[15]

There was a stated double reference in Villermé's use of the term *epidemic*.[16] On the one hand *epidemic* referred to the relatively rare outbreak of an uncommon disease (plague) or even a hitherto unknown disease (cholera). Such events usually brought with them exceptionally high mortality and could lead to serious social dislocation. On the other hand, and this was Villermé's usual application, *epidemic* referred to a season or seasons of unduly high mortality or morbidity brought on by familiar disease(s), especially smallpox and any of a host of fevers. Doubtless most persons remarked the former phenomenon, but far fewer observers detected and appreciated the social as well as the medical significance of the latter.

It was this second usage that informed Villermé's argument that the frequency no less than the severity of epidemics had diminished under the influence of civilization. Number appeared to grant authority to his argument. An "epidemic year" was defined as a year exhibiting mortality at least 10 percent higher than either the preceding or following year. The epidemic experience of Paris since the seventeenth century was then tabu-

14. Joseph Fourier in vol. 2 (1823) of the *Recherches statistiques sur la ville de Paris*, quoted in Villermé, "Des épidémies," p. 12.
15. Villermé, "Des épidémies," pp. 9–11.
16. Ibid., p. 8.

lated by decade (see Table 10.1).[17] A similar computation of epidemic mortality for all France seemed to disclose that epidemic years had declined from five in the period 1771–83 to none between 1817 and 1829. Villermé realized full well that certain regions of the nation, just as particular sections of a city, could be and usually were subject to regular or intermittent outbreaks of epidemic disease. Nonetheless, these events occurred *ipso facto* on a lesser scale and would not seriously disturb the much larger numbers that measured national mortality or mortality in so vast an urban agglomeration as the department of the Seine. Villermé's data appeared to indicate, therefore, that France, like Paris, had over a period of approximately a century and a half largely freed itself from constant and heavy epidemic mortality.

Table 10.1. Diminution in frequency of epidemics in Paris

Decade	Number of epidemic years
13 years in 17th century	6
1709–20 (12 years)	5
1721–30	4
1731–40	5
1741–50	4
1751–60	4
1761–70	4
1771–80	4
1781–90	4
1791–1800	5
1801–10	3
1811–20	3
1821–30	2

SOURCE: L. R. Villermé. "Des épidémies sous les rapports de l'hygiène publique, de la statistique médicale et de l'économie politique." *Annales d'hygiène publique et de médecine légale* 9 (1833): 17. Years in the seventeenth century are unspecified.

The purpose of this well-known essay was to demonstrate that civilization, by reducing the severity and frequency of epidemics, had made a direct contribution to mankind's physical well-being. Civilization meant to Villermé and to other sociomedical observers precisely what it had meant to Molinari, namely, improvement in the abundance and diversity of foodstuffs, better internal and external communications, more comfortable and salubrious housing, cheaper clothing, sounder public administration, and industrial development. All of these factors, whose net effect was to render "*aisance* more common than it had heretofore been" and to

17. Ibid., p. 16.

diminish the frequency of dearth and famine, were ultimately a function of man's free exercise of his reason. Reason, liberty, and industry spelled progress and revealed themselves as Europe's greatest glory, her civilization. "Quite definitely," Villermé announced, "we owe to the advance of civilization the fact that today we encounter in our nations lower mortality than in previous ages. We observe everywhere that epidemics diminish in frequency and intensity as barbarism retreats, that is, as [our useful] arts and [social] institutions evolve and attain perfection and come to affect or to serve an ever greater number of persons."[18]

Other evidence tended to confirm this conclusion. The fact that the sharply marked seasonal periodicity of maximum number of conceptions characteristic of old France had tended to decrease in recent years suggested to Villermé that man as a biological being was growing increasingly independent of the constraints imposed by his physical environment.[19] By means of civilization man was now more than ever before creating his own world. The converse of the happy results obtained at Viareggio had also to be considered. Swamp drainage was commonly salubrious and profitable, yet it could also prove hazardous to health and entail great financial loss. One had to know what one was doing; mindless action had rarely brought benefit to mankind and was quite unlikely to further the progress of civilization. It was civilization, furthermore—that is, a better and more secure diet, coupled with a diminution of disease—that no doubt accounted for the increase in body height and strength recently found to be characteristic of conscripts in post-Imperial France. Lastly, the sustained theme of the author's *Tableau de l'état moral et physique des ouvriers* was civilization, its conditions and its consequences. Some persons had not shared its benefits; this fact was admitted and deplored, but also assigned to individual moral inadequacies. Other workers, notably those in Sedan, had found a position of modest comfort and reasonable security, proof that industrial society conferred very real benefits on mankind. All such blessings were, in fact, the gift of civilization, and most remarkable of all, civilization was itself of man's own making.

These medical reflections were offered as a pointed rejection of Rousseau's claims. To the economist as to the hygienist it was imperative to demonstrate that the natural condition of man was social and industrial, not solitary and agrarian. "The true state of nature for all creatures," Jean Baptiste Say insisted, "is that in which each attains the greatest development of which it is capable." Man, by definition a rational being, thus reaches his maximum development in society, by means of constant inter-

18. Ibid., p. 7.
19. This and the following arguments are discussed above, Chapters 7 and 8.

action with his fellows and careful calculation and pursuit of his individual interest. "Civilization . . . multiplies our needs but at the same time provides means for satisfying them." This stimulus, a fundamental premise of idéologue, economist, and hygienist, virtually guaranteed the progress of civilization and thus man's steady departure, wherever he was free, from barbarism. Say admitted that civilization cannot "preserve us from all the afflictions that befall humankind" but contentedly also noted that it does "protect us from at least some among them and offers us compensation for the others."[20]

Economic development, for which a new science of wealth had been created, demanded much of human nature. Man was a sensate animal who responded to both imperceptible and recognized needs. His responses were diverse but also cumulative, and the activity they reflected was the dynamic by which civilization had been brought into being and would be continued into the future. Rousseau seemed to deny the very possibility of this progress and, more significantly, declared that if realized, it would be morally reprehensible. The economist could cite hard fact to counter the first proposition; in answering Rousseau's second claim, however, he had to admit the very real threat that urban life and contemporary industrialization posed to human dignity and physical well-being. Irresponsible commentators and pessimistic observers simply ignored the condition of labor or eased their consciences by admitting that the poor got only what they deserved. Optimists like Say and the early Villermé conceded the difficulty, granting both its extent and seriousness, but cherished the belief that the peril was only a transient one. Labor's dilemma reflected a stage, unfortunate to be sure but nonetheless inevitable, in the development of civilization, and that fact alone offered justification for the admitted social and economic upheaval.

Just as the progress of civilization was neither halted nor truly tarnished by occasional economic uncertainty or crisis, so that progress was no longer hindered by events of a medical character. Like destitution itself, the epidemic seemed to be but an interlude in a larger process of cumulative advance. That interlude might prove alarming and adversely affect numerous persons. Yet all evidence indicated that such moments were becoming rarer and their effects less damaging. The apparent decline of epidemic disease in contemporary Europe could be received, on the one hand, as a consequence of the multiple parameters of the complex phe-

---

20. J. B. Say, *Cours complet d'économie politique pratique: Ouvrage destiné à mettre sous les yeux des hommes d'état, des propriétaires fonciers et des capitalistes, des savans, des agriculteurs, des manufacturiers, des négoçians, et en général tous les citoyens, l'économie des sociétés*, 2nd ed., 2 vols. (Paris: Guillaumin, 1840), 1: 53, 23, 511.

nomenon called civilization; on the other hand, it could itself be properly numbered among those parameters. But in either case, it was in the civilized condition, humanity's natural place, and not in Rousseau's state of nature, that epidemic disease had begun to recede.

Le Parti d'Hygiène

The intimate connection between public health and the interests of political economy was first identified by Erwin Ackerknecht. Drawing attention to the dual problem of quarantine and contending theories about the cause of communicable disease, Ackerknecht related how the ascendancy of anticontagionist etiology after 1830 entailed destruction of long-standing procedures for the sanitary control of a nation's frontiers.[21] Anticontagionism denied the transmission of disease by personal contact or by means of fomites. It also assumed a political stance, providing medical and scientific justification, Ackerknecht argued, for freeing commerce and its manufacturing base from the yoke of quarantine. The abolition of quarantine was held to constitute an important step in the direction of free trade and to be, in consequence, a major event in the advance of liberty, progress, and civilization.

Ackerknecht's argument reaches well beyond the doctrinal issues that surrounded the French physicians' campaign against quarantine and the presumed triumph of the anticontagionist over the contagionist theory of disease causation.[22] These disputes were special elements in a larger debate whose principal theme was the relationship between modern civilization and the medical condition, broadly construed, of the population. The health of the nation seemed to give decisive testimony in favor of progress. The physical well-being of men and women was the direct beneficiary of the advance of the arts and sciences, particularly of the useful arts and the new industries designed to exploit them. Members of the *parti d'hygiène*, a group I so designate for convenience of reference and also to emphasize its central concern—man's recently acquired and still evolving mastery of his social and physical condition—gave sustained consideration to these questions.

The hygienic party noted especially the general consonance in a population between degree of civilization and its health condition and agreed that when hygienic problems on a large scale did arise they were funda-

21. E. H. Ackerknecht, "Anticontagionism between 1821 and 1867," *Bulletin of the History of Medicine* 22 (1948): 562–92.

22. The contagionist position remained in Britain, and no doubt also in France, a vigorous rival to anticontagionism. See Margaret Pelling, *Cholera, Fever, and English Medicine, 1825–1855* (Oxford: Oxford University Press, 1978).

mentally social in origin and were remediable. This perspective was, in Ackerknecht's words, "a fundamental, internal necessity for those who started an epoch of sanitary reforms in a growing industrial society."[23] The hygienic party was a party of reform, its optimistic voice being heard most clearly during the decade 1825–35, the years in which liberal interests gained firm control over French public policy. Hygienic problems whose source was society itself could be alleviated by social action. Similar problems whose origin lay in human nature or individual moral inadequacy— and these problems were numerous—were recognized and analyzed, but they could not easily be corrected, if in fact correction was possible at all. The hygienic party tended not to join or sustain the contagionist-anticontagionist dispute as so formulated. Their attention turned instead to a further option, social etiology.

The parti d'hygiène was numerous and its membership diverse in both opinion and ambition. I have followed the articulation of this opinion through the sociomedical investigations of Villermé and have sought to portray the melioristic intention of his endeavor and define the ideology underlying its conduct. I now recall these themes in far more concise manner, allowing the views of Frédéric Joseph Bérard, Jean Baptiste Parent-Duchâtelet, Jean Baptiste Bousquet, Louis François Benoiston de Châteauneuf, and François Mélier to speak for the French hygienists.

Bérard (1789–1828), editor of and commentator on Cabanis and professor of hygiene at Montpellier, launched a vigorous medical defense of civilization. The enemy, of course, was Rousseau and those who either wittingly or blindly followed his lead. Rousseau's notion that man was a "depraved animal" was to Bérard merely an "absurdity" not worthy of its author.[24] The truth of the matter was that man was born for the social condition, a fact revealed by his physical and moral traits. Consequently the social condition improves as man advances in the cultivation of his talents; such cultivation is nothing other than the progress of civilization. Civilization alone permits full development of the human intellect and assures its application to useful undertakings.

It seemed to be the peculiarity of the improvements brought by civilization that they affected ever larger numbers of persons. That civilization was good for all members of society was proved by the fact that mecha-

23. E. H. Ackerknecht, "Hygiene in France, 1815–1848," *Bulletin of the History of Medicine* 22 (1948): 141. Later English concern with the issue is described by L. G. Stevenson, "Science down the Drain: On the Hostility of Certain Sanitarians to Animal Experimentation, Bacteriology, and Immunology," *Bulletin of the History of Medicine* 29 (1955): 1–26.

24. F. J. Bérard, *Discours sur les améliorations progressives de la santé publique par l'influence de la civilisation* (Montpellier and Paris: Gabon, 1826), pp. 36–37.

nization of production had introduced an era of ever lower prices and therefore broader social access to consumer goods. Bérard here touched on the most sensitive point in the hygienic appreciation of civilization, the unmistakable fact that industrialization did not benefit all men equally. To the claim that civilization does, in general, reduce distinctions of wealth he appended the necessary observation that, in contrary instances, those in which some and perhaps many members of society drew little or no such benefit, the growing inequity between men did nonetheless serve an important social purpose, namely, it acted "to the advantage of industry and public prosperity."[25] Civilization was self-justifying, the good of the whole and of the most civilized classes outweighing the possible loss of the poor, the feckless, or the simply unfortunate.

Diverse evidence proved to Bérard that civilization as an accomplished condition—such seemed the condition of contemporary Europe—is beneficial to public hygiene. Drawing upon the early publications of Villermé and Benoiston de Châteauneuf, he argued that the incidence of death declines and life expectancy increases with the advance of civilization.[26] The short lives of the urban poor merely showed that the poor are less civilized than the rich. The city, moreover, although still often insalubrious, was daily being improved and was, furthermore, quite indispensable for progress, since urban life was deemed the basis of all true civilization. In flat contradiction of Rousseau, Bérard announced that contagious diseases originate among savages and disappear with civilization; civilization was marked by chronic diseases, themselves testimony to civilized man's humanitarian care for and preservation of the weak, the sick, and the aged.[27]

Such fact and argument, Bérard concluded, demonstrated that "with regard to public health, man gains much more than he loses by the influence of civilization; there has been a vast improvement between barbarous times and our own day." Mankind was invited to put away its "gloomy prejudices and melancholic declamations," these being the substance of Rousseau's view of things, and learn to appreciate the fact, newly revealed, that our "greatest physical or moral well-being is joined to the

---

25. Ibid., p. 45. This easy confidence was not shared by all hygienists. François Emanuel Fodéré of Strasbourg deplored the failure of economists to attend to matters of distributive justice; see his *Essai historique et moral sur la pauvreté des nations: La population, la mendicité, les hôpitaux et les enfants trouvés* (Paris: Huzard, 1825), pp. 270–92.

26. Bérard, *Discours*, pp. 48–74.

27. Ibid., pp. 113–15. The shift described by Bérard's polemical and unexpected statement has become a mass reality in Western nations of the twentieth century, producing there profound medical and social changes. See Thomas McKeown, *The Role of Medicine: Dream, Mirage, or Nemesis?* (Princeton: Princeton University Press, 1979); also Macfarlane Burnet and David O. White, *Natural History of Infectious Disease*, 4th Ed. (Cambridge: Cambridge University Press, 1972).

utmost development of all the faculties" that we have received from the creator.[28] The potential for progress having been implanted in human nature, civilized nations became the tangible realization of that potential. Civilization, industry, and urbanization—all were progressive, and all acted beneficially upon public health.

Bérard's *discours* offered a notable, enthusiastic celebration of the hygienic blessings of civilization. Decidedly more muted were the views of Parent-Duchâtelet (1790–1836). Contemporaries regarded Parent-Duchâtelet as Villermé's equal in many areas of hygienic inquiry and his superior in still others.[29] No other individual knew the physical infrastructure of Paris so thoroughly, and few had conducted such exacting inquiries into the hygienic circumstances surrounding a diversity of manufacturing processes. By seeming predilection Parent-Duchâtelet came to scrutinize every species of filth known to the metropolis. His examination of the capital's sewers, latrines, cesspools, and horse-rendering establishments have become classics in the literature of public health. With regard to what he considered to be but another, more extensive study of filth, "a sewer of another kind," he wrote, "only one more foul than all the others," Parent-Duchâtelet produced what long remained the definitive study of the recruitment and physical condition of the Parisian prostitutes.[30] Other trades posing other hazards received comparable attention.

Yet Parent-Duchâtelet's announced religion was fact and the implications of fact. He largely avoided general considerations, and he made no programmatic declarations of the kind delivered by his close friend Villermé or by Bérard. This exemplary empirical investigator left no considered statement of his view of the relationship, benign or otherwise, between civilization and disease, just as he offered no public reflections on the intimate connection between political economy and public health. Regarding such matters his outlook must be inferred from incidental comment and from the overall orientation of his work.

Parent-Duchâtelet's scientific career was fundamentally a reaction to the problems created by the rapid and enormous expansion of the population of Paris. Population growth had created social needs of unprecedented

28. Bérard, *Discours*, pp. 118, 120.
29. See A. F. La Berge, "A.J.B. Parent-Duchâtelet: Hygienist of Paris, 1821–1836," *Clio medica* 12 (1977): 279–301.
30. Parent-Duchâtelet, *De la prostitution dans la ville de Paris, considerée sous le rapport de l'hygiène publique, de la morale et de l'administration: Ouvrage appuyé de documents statistiques puisés dans les archives de la Préfecture de Police*, 3rd ed., 2 vols. (Paris: J. B. Baillière, 1857), 2: 6. This work, plus the posthumous *Hygiène publique: ou, Mémoires sur les questions les plus importantes de l'hygiène appliquée aux professions et aux travaux d'utilité publique*, ed. François Leuret, 2 vols. (Paris: J. B. Baillière, 1836), contains virtually the entirety of Parent-Duchâtelet's publications.

proportions. Parent-Duchâtelet analyzed these needs, determined their nature, and sought means for satisfying them. He assayed existing but imperfect institutions, practices, and municipal facilities with the aim of instituting changes that would reform while preserving, improve but not transform. What is most remarkable in his studies of, for example, the storm sewers of Paris, the horse-rendering installation at Montfaucon, or tobacco manufacture is the apparent demonstration, against all expectation, that these structures or enterprises were generally innocuous. In many cases they posed few if any serious threats to health, and often their improvement or removal was required only for aesthetic or economic reasons or was not required at all.

Sewers, like factories, were social artifacts. They had been created for useful purposes, and these they in fact served unless vitiated by neglect or misdirection. When they fell into disarray, improvement always seemed possible, the most remarkable example of such an accomplishment being the thorough cleansing, under Parent-Duchâtelet's direct supervision, of the Amelot sewer beginning in 1826. Similar action, if properly conceived and conducted, might eliminate the filthy condition of the river Bièvre and the center of *équarrissage* at Montfaucon, render tobacco manufacture still more salubrious, and assure the close sanitary supervision if not elimination of prostitution in Paris.[31]

An enthusiastic agent of the Health Council of the Seine Parent-Duchâtelet welcomed industrialization. He also appreciated its hazards but held these to be in the main either avoidable or remediable. He was not an outspoken apologist for the new economic order and as a member of the Health Council was prepared to refuse as well as approve plans submitted for the installation of new factories. All depended on the nature of the proposal and the special conditions of the desired locality. Industrialization was thus encouraged, but it was to be pursued in an orderly and what was believed to be a healthful manner.

Parent-Duchâtelet was a hygienist of immense stature in the period 1815–36, and his reputation scarcely diminished after his death. His opinion was esteemed by his associates and relied upon by public authorities.

---

31. See Parent-Duchâtelet's own monographic description: "Rapport sur le curage des égouts Amelot, de la Roquette, Saint-Martin et autres" (1829), in *Hygiène publique*, 1: 308–437. François Mélier (see below) appreciated his esteemed colleague's benevolent view of the manufacturing process and wrote: "That excellent man, [Parent-Duchâtelet], so justly loved and now regretted, was always so preoccupied with the honorable fear of attributing to an industry certain hazards [*inconvénients*] which in reality might not have existed, thus bearing harm to that industry, that he ended by deceiving himself regarding those that did indeed exist" ("De la santé des ouvriers employés dans les manufactures de tabac," *Mémoires de l'Académie royale de médecine* 12 [1846]: 639).

(Given its sources in the archives of the Prefecture of Police, his *Prostitution dans la ville de Paris* was virtually an official report.) If the relatively abstract relationship between civilization and disease did not attract his attention, the many tangible products of contemporary civilization most definitely did. Some seemed and were proved to be hazardous; these were to be either eliminated or their character changed. Others seemed hazardous but in reality were only marginally so; reform was again in order, here a relatively easy task. Others posed no threat at all; now anxieties might be put to rest and need not rise again. He who best knew their dangers wholly accepted both urbanization and industrialization.

The career of Benoiston de Châteauneuf showed many parallels to that of his friend and occasional working associate Villermé. A Parisian like Villermé and Parent-Duchâtelet, Benoiston de Châteauneuf (1776–1856) received his medical training at the Ecole de médecine and the military hospital of Val-de-Grâce.[32] He then served for several years as field surgeon in the Imperial armies. Upon returning to Paris in 1810, he entered the state financial administration, remaining there until a legacy from his father gave him complete independence. His concerns were fundamentally economic, but they held profound implications for public health.

Using the numerical method Benoiston de Châteauneuf sought especially to gain a secure measure of social differences as expressed in vital statistics. After completion of an innovative study of the consumption of foodstuffs and other necessities in the city of Paris, he turned to a varied set of hygienic issues ranging from the number and condition of foundling children in Europe to differential mortality in the army and the incidence of phthisis in various trades.[33] These several studies gave support to his election to the Academy of Moral and Political Sciences. Among his inquiries, that concerning the relative length of life of the rich and the poor best exhibits its author's concern for the critical link joining problems of public health and the doctrines of political economy.

Villermé having already exhibited the difference in mortality between rich and poor, Benoiston de Châteauneuf approached that same social distinction with a new measure, average duration of life. Comparing age at death for two series of figures, the first reflecting a sample of approximately 1,600 wealthy persons and the second, some 2,000 members of

---

32. M. Prévost, "Benoiston de Châteauneuf, Louis-François," *Dictionnaire de biographie française* (Paris: Letouzey and Ané, 1933–).

33. Benoiston de Châteauneuf, *Recherches sur les consommations de tout genre de la ville de Paris en 1817, comparées à ce qu'elles étaient en 1789* (Paris: the author, 1820); idem, "Essai sur la mortalité dans l'infantérie française," *Annales d'hygiène publique et de médecine légale* 10 (1833); 289–316; idem, *Considérations sur les enfants trouvés dans les principaux états de l'Europe* (Paris: Martinet, 1824).

Table 10.2. Age-specific death rates among the rich and poor

Age (years)	Number of deaths per 100 persons	
	Rich	Poor
30–39	1.08	1.57
40–49	1.17	2.13
50–59	1.99	3.59
60–69	3.60	7.50
70–79	8.04	14.36
80–89	13.22	100.00

SOURCE: Louis François Benoiston de Châteauneuf, "De la durée de la vie chez le riche et chez le pauvre," *Annales d'hygiène publique et de médecine légale* 3 (1830): 12. Data for the wealthy are taken from the years 1821–29; for the poor Benoiston de Châteauneuf only reports collecting figures "for several years," presumably during the 1820s.

that other class, the one "devoted to struggle and labor, one that lives in need and dies in the hospital," Benoiston de Châteauneuf demonstrated once again that mortality varies directly with poverty (see Table 10.2).[34] Villermé had been quite right, Benoiston de Châteauneuf observed, in noting that death spared the rich more than the poor at all stages of life but especially in the younger and the more advanced years. But it need not always be so: "to die at age twenty for want of a bit of money" was not in the nature of things.[35]

The problem was a social one, created by the improper functioning of society and the economy. It was, consequently, open to correction. Sociomedical investigation revealed the nature of the difficulty; an enlightened and determined administration might take steps to alleviate its consequences. Such an administration was not unaware, the author-administrator assured his reader, that "by favoring instruction, work, and liberty by means of wise laws and protective institutions, industry, wealth, and sound behavior are encouraged and, like a second providence come to this world, an [able] administration at its pleasure creates virtue, happiness, and men themselves."[36] To Benoiston de Châteauneuf as to other members of the hygienic party, the demands of industry were to be respected, and absolute liberty was to be preserved. Industry and liberty were the expressions of civilization. If they caused distress, as occasionally they did, their benefits far outweighed their liabilities. Moreover, the problems they presented were, within the limits imposed by human nature and individual initiative, remediable. Social problems had social solutions.

34. Benoiston de Châteauneuf, "De la durée de la vie chez le riche et chez le pauvre," *Annales d'hygiène publique et de médecine légale* 3 (1830): 12.
35. Ibid.
36. Ibid.

Common to Bérard, Parent-Duchâtelet, Benoiston de Châteauneuf, Villermé, and other hygienists was the conviction that the size and strength of a given population was influenced by economic development. Population size and individual well-being were subject also to medical influence, yet the latter, it appeared, played only a secondary role. It was because of this persuasion, of course, that political economy came to assume so central a role in the hygienists' analysis of the social problem and its possible solution. Perhaps no one developed this argument more pointedly than Bousquet. Medical consultant to the Orléans family and for many years secretary to the administrative council of the Royal Academy of Medicine, in which role he edited the Academy's famed *Bulletin*, Bousquet (1792–1872) was the very model of an official physician.[37] Indeed, Bousquet's wide-ranging analysis of the effectiveness and social importance of vaccination was published, as the title page itself announced, "upon the request of the government."[38] In the concluding chapter of this work, a hygienic and economic *tour de force*, Bousquet demonstrated that a healthy nation must be built first of all upon vigorous economic activity and only secondarily upon preventive measures available to the physician, of which vaccination was at that time the only truly effective example. Most certainly, Bousquet did not seek to denigrate the medical art, but he felt compelled to demonstrate that satisfying man's biological conditions of existence was more important to the statesman than assuring widespread vaccination.

Assuming, as the economists commonly did, that a large and growing population provided the best indication of a strong and prosperous state, Bousquet rendered that assumption the conclusion itself. A population was large and continued to expand only when economic activity was vigorous, in fact, only *because* the economy was expansive. Well-constituted agricultural societies soon reached a limit to population growth. Their productive potential could not be expanded; their population remained stable; vaccination could help them little if at all. But industrial society seemed to Bousquet to offer unlimited productive potential. Here, new lives might find a useful place and contribute to national wealth. In this case vaccination, by preventing death in younger years, quite probably did contribute to social well-being and progress. Medicine—that is, vaccination—was thus socially effective only when man's indispensable biological needs had first been met. Economic development and vaccination "are two rival powers which lend one another mutual support. If vaccination res-

37. See A. M. Latour, "Bousquet, Jean Baptiste," *Dictionnaire de biographie française*.
38. Jean Baptiste Bousquet, *Traité de la vaccine et des éruptions varioleuses ou varioliformes: Ouvrage rédigé sur la demande du gouvernement* (Paris: J. B. Baillière, 1833).

cues a [potential] victim from death, one at least need not fear that famine, thirst, cold, and destitution intervene to destroy its work. In every land that produces more than its inhabitants can consume there remains room for others, and in such places medicine can exercise its rights to the utmost extent."[39] Bousquet's argument meant only that before medicine, or vaccination, came economics, or increased production.

Production by men was in fact deemed more important than the propagation of men. Our social purpose, if such an expression be permitted Bousquet, was not that of preserving men until they reached their reproductive years. Vaccination, of course, did just this; yet "its true claim to public recognition was to preserve men less for propagation than for work. This, I say, is how it truly contributes to the growth of population."[40] Bousquet consistently made production—and he meant especially production by modern industrial processes—both the standard by which social progress was to be judged and the goal towards which such progress must always be directed. Obviously, all of these developments as they came to pass were but signs of the advance of civilization. Some men still claim, Bousquet observed, that population size today is less than at the beginning of nations. They ask, is this not the inevitable conclusion to be drawn from the admitted cultural glories of ancient Greece and Rome, of the Florence of the Medicis, of the France of Louis XIV? But however true this be, he sourly noted, it ignored the most important matter: one does not build populous and strong nations on literary or artistic grounds, but only on economic development: "The spirit of letters and the *beaux-arts* is not that of the sciences and of industry. Quite apart from the realm of imagination stands the positive world, and here everything advances slowly and progressively. Just as it would be absurd to claim that civilization had attained greatest perfection at its moment of birth, so it is equally absurd to say that men were more numerous at the beginning of society than they are at present."[41] Bousquet the physician had knowingly given medicine a status subordinate to economics. Medicine, or vaccination, might ease the lot of the individual or perhaps even that of a population and "thus ready the people to create more products" as well as prolong their lives, but it could not without prior assurance of increased and still increasing wealth increase the size of that population.[42] Growth was Bousquet's objective, and as might be expected of one so imbued with the principles of political economy, growth also provided the standard by which the (limited) capacity of the medical art itself was to be measured.

39. Ibid., p. 354.
40. Ibid., p. 359.
41. Ibid., pp. 360–61.
42. Ibid., p. 356.

With the exception of Parent-Duchâtelet members of the hygienic party publicly and repeatedly insisted upon the intimate connection between public health and political economy. The culmination of their argument was reached in an essay by François Mélier, long a leader in the French hygienic movement. Mélier (1798–1866) combined an interest in problems of occupational health with a concern for state surveillance of communicable disease and its control.[43] In 1851 he was appointed general inspector of sanitary services to the central French government and for the remainder of his life was deeply involved in virtually all aspects of sanitary inquiry and action.

Mélier sought to provide a numerical demonstration of the progress of civilization. By correlating price series of wheat and bread with the record of contemporary mortality, he discovered that since the Revolution and especially since 1820, periods of widely varying prices were associated with progressively smaller variations in mortality.[44] This fact appeared to prove that the price of bread, the foodstuff that was the preponderant component in the diet of the great majority of Frenchmen, no longer dictated the mortality of the masses. The French nation seemed finally to have become insulated from the previously catastrophic consequences of an inadequate supply of life's basic necessity. Whether due to harvest failure, faulty internal transport, or financial manipulation, an inordinately high price for bread no longer dramatically elevated the death rate.

Mélier did not investigate the precise reasons for the remarkable advance in national well-being thus disclosed. His principal concern was simply to prove that specific economic conditions had had concrete and equally specific medical or biological consequences. Economic expansion, in Mélier's eyes the essential characteristic of French society since 1815, had brought with it an improvement in the medical condition of the multitude, and that in itself testified to the beneficence of the new economic order. Increased production and better distribution of wheat and bread were surely involved in the perfection of civilization, Mélier agreed, and the introduction and widespread consumption of the potato he viewed as a social triumph of no small proportions. In the decline of mortality Mélier celebrated the progress of agriculture (he was equally the friend of industrial progress) and noted that this decline was due above all else to the advantages that new and more progressive economic legislation had

43. See J. Bergeron, "Eloge de M. Mélier," *Mémoires de l'Académie nationale de médecine* 36 (1888): 1–38; William Coleman, "Medicine against Malthus: François Mélier on the Relation between Subsistence and Mortality (1843)," *Bulletin of the History of Medicine* 54 (1980): 23–42.

44. Mélier, "Etudes sur les subsistances envisagées dans leurs rapports avec les maladies et la mortalité," *Mémoires de l'Académie royale de médecine* 10 (1843): 170–205.

provided. "A people's health," briefly put, "depends as much upon its laws and its government as it does upon the advice given by medicine."[45]

Public Health and Political Economy

Economist and hygienist were dedicated to justifying and extending the development of the new industrial world that sanitary inquiry so clearly and so unsettlingly described. They appreciated James Phillips Kay's injunction that political economy must deal with men and women not merely in terms of mathematical calculation but with a view to increasing the sum of human happiness. It was their conviction, however, that the most suitable and perhaps the unique route to that goal was to guarantee each man and woman complete liberty of action. Liberty once attained and then secured transferred responsibility to the individual. Success and thus happiness now lay within the reach of every person; artificial constraints having been removed, human nature was allowed full and free expression.

But individuals, it was recognized, differed. They were not all equally well endowed with regard to physical strength, moral integrity, or intelligence. Some persons (and the optimistic economist probably saw these individuals as constituting the majority) experienced difficulties in the new society because they failed to cultivate their inborn capacities. Their failure might be due to ignorance or to weakness of will. Both problems, especially the former, were remediable. Patience, sobriety, diligence, basic skills—all could be imparted to the laboring classes. But not all members of society's lower orders heard or responded to the uplifting message. The hygienists were persuaded that it was especially this latter unregenerate group that suffered most from the social dislocations and economic deprivation that was the inescapable though transient consequence of industrialization and rapid urbanization.

It was in itself a sign of progress that many hygienist-economists reached such a conclusion. The pessimists among their ranks understood well the source of the problem but contemplated no escape for the worker whom fate had introduced into factory and city. The optimists, and here stood Villermé until his later years together with many members of the hygienic party, foresaw a gradual improvement in the overall economic and physical condition of the laboring population and hence of the nation itself. The difficulties facing this population were numerous and severe. Hygienists unshirkingly insisted upon these difficulties, yet they also insisted upon the fact that, having been largely generated by flaws in social activity, the social problem was open to correction by concerted investi-

45. Ibid., p. 193.

gation and socially sanctioned ameliorative measures. The problems described were not inherent in industrial society nor, indeed, were they due to irreparable flaws in the nature of man.

These thoughts sustained the confidence of the hygienic party. Beneficiary and ofttimes creator of the new economic order, the hygienist-economist refused absolutely to consider a return to the past. He was, perhaps, still infused with a strong charitable instinct inherited from Christian doctrine and from the institutions of the Old Regime. No individual better represents the continuity of this instinct than the Duc de La Rochefoucauld-Liancourt. His leadership was felt before and during the Revolution and again became manifest under the Restoration, providing then the crucial early stimulus for Villermé's dedication to the cause of sociomedical investigation. The duke's charitable orientation was, however, secular, not ecclesiastical, and so in general was that of those who shared his outlook concerning improvement of the lot of the poor or the unfortunate. The hygienist as man of doctrine did not look to the church and the past for resolution of society's current difficulties. His expectations of public authority, moreover, were few and embraced only such activities as a central government could alone provide. Save for the administration of justice, preservation of public order and national security, and execution of unduly expensive public works, the hygienist made scant appeal to the crown and its agents. Again the past was avoided. Crown and church, especially as both grew increasingly assertive during the 1820s in an attempt to reestablish their interrelated claims, seemed the very contradiction of the reign of liberty that France had bloodily yet justly earned during the Revolution.

If appeal to traditional authority was excluded from the economist's serious consideration, all the more so was the slowly growing number of voices that suggested that the difficult position of labor was really due to an improperly or viciously constituted society. The socialist demanded far-reaching social reconstruction. Redefining the relation between capital and labor, he sought to create a society in which sharp distinctions of wealth would not arise and harmony would prevail, all the while often insisting with a vehemence equal to that of the orthodox economist himself that industrialization and urbanization were indicators of genuine human progress. But socialism to the economist meant the utter denial of individual economic initiative and hence of liberty itself. Under no circumstances was the latter to be sacrificed to such egalitarian and, what was no less damning, impractical dreams. The hygienist-economist found his solace, a word often on his lips, in the unshakable conviction that today's difficulties will be gone tomorrow if only we understand their nature and pursue appropriate action and have patience. There was simply no need to cast down and rebuild society when it was clear that intelligence and energy would overcome such problems as were truly amenable to improvement. For the social residuum nothing could be done by either economist or socialist, the only difference being that the economist realized why this was necessarily so, while the socialist cherished the illusion of transforming human nature.

Separating the wealthy from the improvable poor and the latter from the residuum—this is what the social component of hygienic inquiry was all about. Sociomedical investigation gave positive identification, number serving as its shorthand for fact, of the medical distance that separated the rich and the poor. The poor died at a younger age and suffered more sickness than the wealthy. These differences in vital fact were frequently large. Yet they were also often unnecessary and could be greatly reduced. It was not the economic system that was at fault. Its occasional imperfections were admitted but, from the perspective of public health, were seen to be of lesser importance. "One understands," Villermé observed in his last and most pointed statement of a lifetime's concern, "that . . . mortality cannot be the same in all parts of a large nation, amongst all categories of its inhabitants or in regions that are healthy or insalubrious. One's manner of living, wages, the condition of industry and commerce, public administration, years of abundance and those of famine, in a word, everything that contributes to affluence and civilization, produce great variations in the death rate. In other words, affluence or wealth—that is to say, the conditions of existence that such means provide those who enjoy them—is here in truth the most important of all hygienic factors, namely that which best assures the very preservation of life."[46]

The critical factor was the worker himself. His character determined his capacity to improve himself, to live that settled, sober, and industrious life that protected him from falling over the economic abyss and that might also propel him upwards in the social order. Society, furthermore, especially as represented by its most powerful figure, the benevolent master, could exert paternal influence and discipline over the worker, therby ensuring that his would become an exemplary existence, full of benefit to himself and his family and a model for others.

Woe only to the worker whose character was hopelessly flawed or whose will was without force. He became the residuum and in the eyes of hygienist and economist was altogether lost to society. Of course, such persons were themselves accountable for their own failures. The utopian socialist had at least the satisfaction of his dreams; his new society would not only eliminate this residuum but the very reasons for its existence. The

46. Villermé, "Considérations sur les tables de mortalité," *Mémoires de l'Académie des sciences morales et politiques* 9 (1855): 901.

economist cherished no such illusions. He knew—and sociomedical investigation especially had given him this knowledge—that human frailty was the source of social disorder as well as individual suffering. He knew that both were common and that both might be reduced but surely never altogether eliminated. Progress did not entail perfection, either today or in the near future.

Least of all did the hygienist-economist hide from himself the harsh reality of the daily life of the laboring population. He had no need to do so. That the industrial world was a difficult one he knew well; no one else had so clear a view of the threat to man's biological existence posed by the rapidly growing city. Sociomedical investigation studied these problems, and it succeeded in remarkable manner in conveying to a socially removed and uninformed, not to say hostile, audience a fine sense of the perils that society itself had created for its less fortunate members. The purpose of this knowledge was to provide secure grounds for action. But what action? That was prescribed by political economy. On balance the new industrial world was a good and eminently desirable world. Its flaws, of course, were real and occasionally serious, but they would soon be transcended. Modest hygienic intervention, aided by sociomedical investigation, would surely help them pass all the more quickly. The hygienist adopted at most a program of gradual and piecemeal social reform. Revolution, whether peaceful or violent, he saw as the inevitable consequence of the socialist prescription for social amelioration and wholly unwarranted. Return to traditional Christian charitable practice, especially when guided by established ecclesiastical authorities, he viewed as the repudiation of the greatest acquisition of the Revolution, liberty in all its dimensions. Neither socialist nor traditionalist sufficiently appreciated the true dimensions of human nature. The one saw man as potentially malleable, perhaps infinitely so, and the other continued to emphasize his depraved condition and thus his need for firm guidance with only a narrow measure of freedom. Hygienist and economist emphasized man's autonomy, realizing very well that his powers could lead to violence, suffering, and destitution as well as to the continued progress of a commercial and industrial society. Liberty thus pointed in both directions or, in fact, in no particular direction. To its aid came an inveterate optimism, founded upon and ever pursuing the ideal of civilization. The effort of the French hygienist was simultaneously one of justification and criticism. He accepted and commonly praised the basic principles—liberty, individual initiative, and economic success—that underlay his society but rarely failed also to indicate the individual and social dilemmas that strict adherence to these principles often entailed. With values focused on the individual he nonetheless created a thoroughly social view of the process of industrialization and found, hindsight must judge, no easy or consistent reconciliation between the two perspectives. In the domain of public health the charge that early French sociomedical investigation stressed diagnosis to the exclusion of therapy is just. But it needs be added that this seeming oversight was not such at all; it was intrinsic to the nature of the endeavor. Political economy provided a theoretical context for scientific comprehension of society. It defined the scope of both permissible and desirable public action and thereby set narrow limits to potential ameliorative action. It was within these limits that the hygienic party conducted its inquiries and articulated, at best, an occasional and isolated case for reform.

Bibliography

Index

Bibliography

Works by Villermé

Biographical notices of Villermé are cited in Chapter 1, note 1. Of particular importance is the analytical study by B. P. Lécuyer, "Démographie, statistique et hygiène publique sous la monarchie censitaire," *Annales de démographie*, 1979, pp. 215–45. The principal works by Villermé used for my study include the following (further references are given by Alphonse Guérard, "Notice sur M. Villermé," *Annales d'hygiène publique et de médecine légale* 21 (1864): 173–77):

Sur les fausses membranes. Thèse de médecine, Paris, 1814.

"De la famine et de ses effets sur la santé dans les lieux qui sont le théâtre de la guerre." *Journal général de médecine, de chirurgie, de pharmacie, etc.; ou, Receuil périodique de la Sociéte de médecine de Paris* 65 (1818): 3–24.

"Prison (hygiène publique)." *Dictionnaire des sciences médicales.* 60 vols. Paris: Panckoucke, 1812–22. Vol. 42, pp. 208–63.

Des prisons telles qu'elles sont et telles qu'elles devraient être: Ouvrage dans lequel on les considère par rapport à l'hygiène, à la morale et à l'économie politique. Paris: Méquignon-Marvis, 1820.

"Rapport sur un ouvrage intitulé: *Recherches statistiques sur la ville de Paris et le département de la Seine.*" *Bulletins de la Société médicale d'émulation,* 1822; pp. 1–41.

"Rapport fait par M. Villermé, et lu à l'Académie de médecine, au nom de la Commission de statistique, sur une série de tableaux relatifs au mouvement de la population dans les douze arrondissements municipaux de la ville de Paris pendant les cinq années 1817, 1818, 1819, 1820, et 1821." *Archives générales de médecine* 10 (1826): 216–45, plus two tables.

"Mémoire sur la mortalité en France dans la classe aisée et dans la classe indigente." *Mémoires de l'Académie royale de médecine* 1 (1828): 51–98.

"Mémoire sur la mortalité dans les prisons." *Annales d'hygiène publique et de médecine légale* 1 (1829): 1–100.

"Memoire sur la taille de l'homme en France." Ibid., pp. 351–95, plus three tables.

"Sur la population: Sommaire." *Journal des cours publics de la ville de Paris* 1 (1828): 189–90. "Population-Hygiène: Première Leçon." Ibid., pp. 257–76. "Population-Hygiène: II." Ibid. 2(1829): 24–27. "Population-Hygiène: III." Ibid., pp. 125–28.

"Quelques réflexions sur les établissements de charité publique, à l'occasion d'un ouvrage de David Johnston." *Annales d'hygiène publique et de médecine légale* 3 (1830): 92–111.

"De la mortalité dans les divers quartiers de la ville de Paris, et des causes qui la rendent très différente dans plusieurs d'entre eux, ainsi que dans les divers quartiers de beaucoup de grandes villes." Ibid., pp. 294–339, plus two tables.

"De la distribution par mois des conceptions et des naissances de l'homme, considérée dans ses rapports avec les saisons, avec les climats, avec le retour périodique annuel des époques de travail et de repos, d'abondance et de rareté des vivres, et avec quelques institutions et coutumes sociales." Ibid. 5 (1831): 55–155.

"Des épidémies sous les rapports de l'hygiène publique, de la statistique médicale et d'économie politique." Ibid. 9 (1833): 5–58.

"*Recherches des causes de la richesse et de la misère des peuples civilisés* . . . par le baron de Morogues. Rapport sur cet ouvrage fait à la Société des établissements charitables." *Bulletin de la Société des établissements charitables* 3 (1833): 222–61.

"De l'influence des marais sur la vie." *Annales d'hygiène publique et de médecine légale* 11 (1834): 342–62.

"Notes sur les ravages du choléra-morbus dans les maisons garnies de Paris, depuis le 29 mars jusqu'au 1er août 1832, et sur les causes qui paraissent avoir favorisé le développement de la maladie dans un grand nombre de maisons." Ibid., pp. 385–409, plus two tables.

"Influence des marais sur la vie des enfans." Ibid. 12 (1834): 31–37.

Tableau de l'état physique et moral des ouvriers employés dans les manufactures de coton, de laine et de soie. 2 vols. Paris: Jules Renouard, 1840.

"Rapport fait à l'Académie des sciences morales et politiques sur un ouvrage intitulé: *De la véritable loi de la population (The true law of population)* par M. Thomas Doubleday." *Journal des économistes* 6 (1843): 397–417.

"Rapport verbal de M. Villermé sur un mémoire de M. Marc Espine, intitulé: *Influence de l'aisance et de la misère sur la mortalité.*" *Séances et travaux de l'Académie des sciences morales et politiques* 12 (1847): 242–48.

"Note sur quelques monopoles usurpés par les ouvriers de certaines industries, suivie de quelques observations sur la situation actuelle des ouvriers dans les bassins houillers de la Loire et du Centre." *Journal des économistes* 17 (1847): 157–68.

Des associations ouvrières. Paris: Pagnerre, 1849.

"Discours prononcé à la séance publique annuelle par M. Villermé, Président de l'Académie." *Séances et travaux de l'Académie des sciences morales et politiques* 16 (1849): 353–59.

"Des accidents produits dans les ateliers industriels par les appareils mécaniques." *Journal des économistes* 27 (1850): 215–22.

"Sur les cités ouvrières." *Annales d'hygiène publique et de médecine légale* 43 (1850): 241–61.

"Considérations sur les tables de mortalité." *Mémoires de l'Académie des sciences morales et politiques* 9 (1855): 885–918.

Other Works

I have utilized the work of many contemporary and earlier scholars. Their publications are cited throughout the notes. Listed here are titles which, in addition to the essay by Lécuyer already noted, have proved to be of special assistance in assessing the work of the French sociomedical investigators.

Abrams, Philip. *The Origins of British Sociology; 1834–1914: An Essay with Selected Papers*. Chicago: University of Chicago Press, 1968.

Ackerknecht, E. H. "Beiträge zur Geschichte der Medizinal-Reform von 1848." *Sudhoffs Archiv für Geschichte der Medizin* 25 (1932): 61–183.

Ackerknecht, E. H. "Hygiene in France, 1815–1848." *Bulletin of the History of Medicine* 22 (1948): 117–55.

Ackerknecht, E. H. "Anticontagionism between 1821 and 1867." Ibid., pp. 562–93.

Ackerknecht, E. H. *Medicine at the Paris Hospital, 1794–1848*. Baltimore: Johns Hopkins Press, 1967.

Allix, Edgard. "La méthode et la conception de l'économie politique dans l'oeuvre de J. B. Say." *Revue d'histoire économique* 4 (1911): 321–60.

Baker, K. M. *Condorcet: From Natural Philosophy to Social Mathematics*. Chicago: University of Chicago Press, 1975.

Braudel, Fernand, and Ernest Labrousse, eds. *Histoire économique et sociale de la France*. Vol. 3. Paris: P.U.F., 1976.

Chevalier, Louis. *Laboring Classes and Dangerous Classes in Paris during the First Half of the Nineteenth Century*. Trans. Frank Jellinek. New York: Howard Fertig, 1973.

Cullen, M. J. *The Statistical Movement in Early Victorian Britain: The Foundations of Empirical Social Research*. New York: Barnes and Noble, 1975.

Deane, Phyllis. *The First Industrial Revolution*. Cambridge: Cambridge University Press, 1969.

Eversley, D. E. C. *Social Theories of Fertility and the Malthusian Debate*. Oxford: Clarendon Press, 1959.

Eyler, J. M. *Victorian Social Medicine: The Ideas and Methods of William Farr*. Baltimore: Johns Hopkins University Press, 1979.

Fischer, Alfons. *Geschichte des deutschen Gesundheitswesens*. 2 vols. Berlin: Urban und Schwarzenberg, 1933; reprint, Olms, 1965. See esp. 2: 285–497.

La Berge, A. F. "Public Health in France and the French Public Health Movement, 1815–1848." Ph.D. dissertation, University of Tennessee, 1974.

Lazarsfeld, P. F. "Notes on the History of Quantification in Sociology: Trends, Sources, Problems." *Isis* 52 (1961): 277–333.

Lécuyer, Bernard, and A. P. Oberschall. "The Early History of Social Research." In *International Encyclopedia of the Social Sciences*. Ed. D. L. Sills. 18 vols. New York: Macmillan, Free Press, 1968–79. Vol. 15, pp. 36–53.

Lorimer, Frank. "The Development of Demography." In *The Study of Population: An Inventory and Appraisal*, ed. P. M. Hauser and O. D. Duncan, pp. 124–79. Chicago: University of Chicago Press, 1959.

Manuel, F. E. *The New World of Henri de Saint-Simon*. Cambridge: Harvard University Press, 1956.

Manuel, F. E. *The Prophets of Paris*. Cambridge: Harvard University Press, 1962.

Murphy, T. D. "The French Medical Profession's Perception of Its Social Function between 1776 and 1830." *Medical History* 23 (1979): 259–78.

Myrdal, Gunnar. *The Political Element in the Development of Economic Theory*. New York: Simon and Schuster, 1969.

Parent-Duchâtelet, A.J.B. *De la prostitution dans la ville de Paris, considérée sous le rapport de l'hygiène publique, de morale et de l'administration*. 2 vols. Paris: J. B. Baillière, 1836.

Parent-Duchâtelet, A.J.B. *Hygiène publique; ou, Mémoires sur les questions les plus importantes de l'hygiène appliquée aux professions et aux travaux d'utilité publique*. Ed. François Leuret. 2 vols. Paris: J. B. Baillière, 1836.

Ponteil, Félix. *L'éveil des nationalités et le mouvement libérale (1815–1848)*. New ed. Paris: P.U.F., 1968.

Pouthas, C. H. *La population française pendant la première moitié du XIXe siècle*. I.N.E.D., Travaux et documents, cahier no. 25. Paris: P.U.F., 1956.

Rigaudias-Weiss, Hilde. *Les enquêtes ouvrières en France entre 1830 et 1848*. Paris: P.U.F., 1936.

Rosen, George. "What is social medicine? A genetic analysis of the concept." *Bulletin of the History of Medicine* 21 (1947): 674–733.

Rosen, George. "Problems in the Application of Statistical Analysis to Questions of Health: 1700–1880." Ibid. 29 (1955): 27–45.

Rosen, George. "Hospitals, Medical Care, and Social Policy in the French Revolution." Ibid. 30 (1956): 124–49. Reprinted in Rosen, *From Medical Police to Social Medicine*, pp. 220–45 (see below).

Rosen, George. *A History of Public Health*. New York: MD Publications, 1958.

Rosen, George. *From Medical Police to Social Medicine*. New York: Science History Publications, 1974.

Staum, M. S. *Cabanis: Enlightenment and Medical Philosophy in the French Revolution*. Princeton: Princeton University Press, 1980.

Sussman, G. D. "From Yellow Fever to Cholera: A Study of French Government Policy, Medical Professionalism, and Popular Movements in the Epidemic Crises of the Restoration and July Monarchy." Ph.D. dissertation, Yale University, 1971.

Tulard, Jean. *La Préfecture de Police sous la Monarchie de Juillet, suivi d'un inventaire sommaire et d'extraits des rapports de la Préfecture de Police conservés aux Archives nationales*. Paris: Imprimerie municipale, 1964.

Tudesq, André-Jean. *Les grands notables en France (1840–1849): Etude historique d'une psychologie sociale*, 2 vols. Paris: P.U.F., 1964.

Vaillard. "Rôle de l'Académie de médecine dans l'évolution d'hygiène publique." *Bulletin de l'Académie nationale de médecine* 84 (1920): 401–29.

Valentin, Michel. *Travail des hommes et savants oubliés: Histoire de la médecine du travail, de la securité et de l'ergonomie*. Paris: Docis, 1978.

Vedrenne-Villeneuve, Edmonde. "L'inégalité sociale devant la mort dans la pre-
mière moitié du XIXᵉ siècle." *Population* 16 (1961): 665–98.
Weiner, D. B. *Raspail: Scientist and Reformer*. New York: Columbia University
Press, 1968.
Westergaard, Harald. *Contributions to the History of Statistics*. London: P. S.
King, 1932.
Wrigley, E. S. *Population and History*. New York: McGraw-Hill, 1969.
Zeldin, Theodore. *France, 1848–1945*, 1: 11–282. 2 vols. Oxford: Clarendon
Press, 1973–1977.

Additional Works

The following works were unknown or unavailable to me during preparation of
this volume.

Gillett, M. C. R. "Hospital Reform in the French Revolution." Ph.D. disserta-
tion, American University, 1978.
Head, B. W. "The Origin of 'Idéologue' and 'Idéologie.'" *Studies on Voltaire
and the Eighteenth Century* 183 (1980): 257–64.
Murphy, T. D. "Medical Knowledge and Statistical Methods in Early Nineteenth-
Century France," *Medical History* 25 (1981): 301–19.
Piquemal, Jacques. "Succès et décadence de la méthode numérique en France à
l'époque de Pierre-Charles Louis." *Médecine en France*, no. 250 (1974), pp.
11–24.
Sewell, W. H., Jr. *Work and Revolution in France: The Language of Labor from
the Old Regime to 1848*. Cambridge: Cambridge University Press, 1980.
Villermé, L. R. "Mort." *Encyclopédie méthodique. Médecine*. Par une Société de
médecins (begun by Félix Vicq-d'Azyr). Paris: Panckoucke; Liège: Plomteux,
1787–1830. Vol. 10 (1821), pp. 298–320.
Villermé, L. R. "Mort apparente." Ibid., pp. 320–34.
Villermé, L. R. "Mortalité." Ibid., pp. 334–35.
Villermé, L. R . "Prisons." Ibid., 13, supplement (1830): 651–69.

Index

315

JACKET DESIGNED BY DESIGN FOR PUBLISHING, BOB NANCE
COMPOSED BY GRAPHIC COMPOSITION, INC., ATHENS, GEORGIA
MANUFACTURED BY INTER-COLLEGIATE PRESS, INC., SHAWNEE MISSION, KANSAS
TEXT AND DISPLAY LINES ARE SET IN TIMES ROMAN

Library of Congress Cataloging in Publication Data
Coleman, William, 1934–
Death is a social disease.
Bibliography: pp. 309–313
Includes index.
1. Public health—France—History—19th century.
2. Economics—France—History—19th century.
3. Villermé, Louis René, 1782–1863.   4. France—
Social conditions.   I. Title.   [DNLM: 1. Public
health—History—France.   2. Socioeconomic factors—
History—France.   3. Industry—History—France.
WA 11 GF7 C6d]
RA499.C57   362.1'042   81–69817
ISBN 0–299–08950–9   AACR2